HISTORY OF THE JEWS IN RUSSIA AND POLAND

FROM THE EARLIEST TIMES
UNTIL THE PRESENT DAY

HISTORY OF THE JEWS IN RUSSIA AND POLAND

FROM THE EARLIEST TIMES UNTIL THE PRESENT DAY

BY

S. M. DUBNOW

TRANSLATED FROM THE RUSSIAN BY

I. FRIEDLAENDER

VOLUME III

FROM THE ACCESSION OF NICHOLAS II. UNTIL THE PRESENT DAY WITH BIBLIOGRAPHY AND INDEX

PHILADELPHIA

THE JEWISH PUBLICATION SOCIETY OF AMERICA

1920

COPYRIGHT, 1920, BY
THE JEWISH PUBLICATION SOCIETY OF AMERICA

NOTE

The present volume, which concludes Dubnow's "History of the Jews in Russia-Poland," contains, in addition to the text, an extensive bibliography and an index to the entire work. In the bibliography an enormous amount of material has been collected, and it is arranged in such a way as to enable the reader to ascertain the sources upon which the author drew. It is thus in the nature of notes, and is therefore arranged according to the chapters of the book. The index, which has been prepared with the utmost care by the translator, is really a synopsis of Jewish history in Russia and Poland, and its usefulness cannot be over-rated.

Professor Friedlaender, the translator of this work, who left the United States at the beginning of this year, did not see the proof of the bibliography and index.

The tragic news has just reached this country that Professor Friedlaender was murdered under the most revolting circumstances. An eminent scholar and writer has thus been removed from American Jewry, and the entire house of Israel together with the Jewish Publication Society of America, on whose committee Professor Friedlaender served with conspicuous merit for a number of years, mourns this irreparable loss.

July, 1920.

CONTENTS

CHAPTER		PAGE
XXXI.	THE ACCESSION OF NICHOLAS II.	
	1. Continued Policy of Oppression	7
	2. The Martyrdom of the Moscow Community..	12
	3. Restrictions in the Right of Residence	15
	4. The Economic Collapse of Russian Jewry	22
	5. Professional and Educational Restrictions...	26
	6. Anti-Semitic Propaganda and Pogroms	31
XXXII.	THE NATIONAL AWAKENING.	
	1. The Rise of Political Zionism	40
	2. Spiritual Zionism, or Ahad-Ha'amism	48
	3. Spiritual Nationalism, or National-Cultural Autonomism	51
	4. The Jewish Socialistic Movement	55
	5. The Revival of Jewish Letters	58
XXXIII.	THE KISHINEV MASSACRE.	
	1. Pogroms as a Counter-Revolutionary Measure	66
	2. The Organized Kishinev Butchery	69
	3. Echoes of the Kishinev Tragedy	76
	4. Doctor Herzl's Visit to Russia	82
XXXIV.	CONTINUED POGROMS AND THE RUSSO-JAPANESE WAR.	
	1. The Pogrom at Homel and the Jewish Self-Defence	87
	2. The Kishinev Massacre at the Bar of Russian Justice	90
	3. The Jews in the Russo-Japanese War	94
	4. The "Political Spring"	97
	5. The Homel Pogrom Before the Russian Courts	101
XXXV.	THE REVOLUTION OF 1905 AND THE FIGHT FOR EMANCIPATION.	
	1. The Jews in the Revolutionary Movement...	105
	2. The Struggle for Equal Rights	108
	3. The "Black Hundred" and the "Patriotic" Pogroms	113
	4. The Jewish Franchise	121

CONTENTS

CHAPTER		PAGE
XXXVI.	THE COUNTER-REVOLUTION AND THE OCTOBER MASSACRES.	
	1. The Fiendish Designs of the "Black Hundred"	124
	2. The Russian St. Bartholomew Night	127
	3. The Undaunted Struggle for Equal Rights....	131
	4. The Jewish Question Before the First Duma	135
	5. The Spread of Anarchy and the Second Duma	139
XXXVII.	EXTERNAL OPPRESSION AND INTERNAL CONSOLIDATION.	
	1. The New Alignments Within Russian Jewry..	143
	2. The Triumph of the "Black Hundred"......	149
	3. The Third, or Black, Duma..................	153
	4. New Jewish Disabilities....................	156
	5. The Spiritual Revival of Russian Jewry......	160
	RUSSIAN JEWRY SINCE 1911.....................	164
	BIBLIOGRAPHY	171
	INDEX	205

CHAPTER XXXI

THE ACCESSION OF NICHOLAS II.

1. Continued Policy of Oppression

In the course of the nineteenth century every change of throne in Russia was accompanied by a change of policy. Each new reign formed, at least in its beginning, a contrast to the one which had preceded it. The reigns of Alexander I. and Alexander II. marked a departure in the direction of liberalism; those of Nicholas I. and Alexander III. were a return to the ideas of reaction. In accordance with this historic schedule, Alexander III. should have been followed by a sovereign of liberal tendencies. But in this case the optimistic expectations with which the new ruler was welcomed both by his Russian and his Jewish subjects were doomed to disappointment. The reign of Nicholas II. proved the most gloomy and most reactionary of all. A man of limited intelligence, he attempted to play the rôle of an unlimited autocrat, fighting in blind rage against the cause of liberty.

This reactionary tendency came to light in the very beginning of the new reign. During the first few months after the accession of Nicholas II. to the throne—between November, 1894, and January, 1895—the liberal Zemstvo assemblies of nine governments,' in presenting addresses of loyalty to the new Tzar, were bold enough to voice the hope that he would eventually invite the representatives of these autonomous institutions

[' See on the Zemstvos, vol. II, p. 173, n. 1.]

to participate in the legislative acts of the Government. This first timid request for constitutional rights met with a harsh and clumsy rebuff. In his reply to the deputation representing the nobility, the Zemstvos, and the municipalities, which appeared in the Winter Palace on January 17, 1895, to convey to him the greetings of the Russian people, the Tzar made the following pronouncement:

In several Zemstvo assemblies there have been heard lately the voices of men carried away by preposterous delusions concerning the participation of the representatives of the Zemstvos in the affairs of the inner administration. Let everybody know that I shall guard the principle of autocracy as firmly and uncompromisingly as it was guarded by my never-to-be-forgotten deceased parent.

This veiled threat was enough to intimidate the faint-hearted constitutionalists. It was universally felt that the autocratic régime was still firmly entrenched and that the old constitution of "enforced safety" ^{1}—this charter of privileges bestowed upon the police to the disadvantage of the people—was still unshaken. The hope of seeing Russia transformed from a state based upon brute force into a body politic resting upon law and order was dashed to the ground.

The Jews, too, were quick to realize that the war which had been waged against them by Alexander III. for fourteen long years was far from being at an end. True, the addresses of welcome presented in 1895 by the Jewish communities of Russia to the young Tzar on the occasion of his marriage elicited an official expression of thanks, which was not marred by any rebuke for harboring "preposterous delusions." But this was purely for the reason that these addresses were not tainted by

[^{1} See vol. II, p. 246.]

any allusions to the hopes for emancipation entertained by the Jews. There was nothing, indeed, which might have warranted such hopes. The same dignitaries who, under Alexander III., had stood forth as the champions of savage anti-Semitic policies, remained at the helm of Russian affairs: Pobyedonostzev, the head of the Holy Synod, Durnovo, the Minister of the Interior—towards the end of 1895 he made room for Goremykin, who was not a whit less reactionary—and Witte, the double-faced Minister of Finance, who was anxious at that time to fall in line with the reactionary influences then in vogue. The thoughts which occupied Pobyedonostzev's mind at the beginning of the new reign may be gauged from the report submitted by him to the Tzar in 1895, concerning the state of affairs in the Greek-Orthodox Church. The "Grand Inquisitor" was deeply worried by the alleged fact that the Jews were exercising a dangerous influence over the religious life of their Christian domestics:

The minors, after living among Jews for several years, prove entirely forgetful of the Greek-Orthodox faith. But even the beliefs of the adults are being undermined. The priests who listen to the confessions of the domestics employed in Jewish homes are stricken with horror on learning of the abominable blasphemies uttered by the Jews against Christianity, the Savior, and the Holy Virgin, which, through the domestics, are likely to gain currency among the people.

These charges, which might have been bodily quoted from the sinister writings of the mediæval guardians of the Church, were intended as a means of preparing the young sovereign for a proper understanding of the Jewish problem. They were brought forward by the procurator-in-chief of the Holy Synod, the same ecclesiastical functionary who inflicted severe persecutions on the Russian dissidents and soon afterwards forced the Dukhobortzy, an Evangelistic sect, to leave their native land and to seek refuge in Canada. Having failed to realize his great ambition—to clear Russia of its Jewish population, with the help of Baron Hirsch's millions^1— Pobyedonostzev resumed his professional duties, which were those of a procurator^2 of Jewry on behalf of the Holy Synod, the *sanctum officium* of the militant Greek-Orthodox Church.

Not content with brandishing his rusty ecclesiastical sword, Pobyedonostzev resorted to secular weapons in his fight against the hated tribe. When, in 1898, the Council of the Jewish Colonization Association in Paris sent a delegation to St. Petersburg to apply to the Government for permission to settle Russian Jews as agricultural farmers in Russia itself, Pobyedonostzev replied: "Nos cadres ne sont pas prêts pour vous recevoir,"^{3} and he went out of his way to explain to the delegates that the Jews were a very clever people, intellectually and culturally superior to the Russians, and, therefore, dangerous to them: "The Jews are displacing us, and this does not suit us." When questioned as to the future of Russian Jewry under the system of uninterrupted persecutions, Pobyedonostzev on one occasion made the following candid statement: "One-third will die out, one-third will leave the country, and one-third will be completely dissolved in the surrounding population."

Such being the attitude towards the Jewish problem of the ruling spheres of Russia, any improvement in the situation of

[^{1} See vol. II, p. 421.]
[^{2} The Russian title for a prosecuting attorney.]
[^{3} "Our frame (of society) is not ready to receive you."]

Russian Jewry was manifestly out of the question. Even where such an improvement might have been found to tally with the anti-Semitic policies of the Government, it was ruled out as soon as it bade fair to benefit the Jews. Thus, when in 1895, the governor of Vilna, in his "most humble report" to the Tzar, advocated the desirability of abrogating the Pale of Settlement for the purpose "of weakening the detrimental influence of Jewry," since the latter constituted a majority of the population in the cities of the Western region,' Nicholas II. penned the following resolution:² "I am far from sharing this view of the governor." The leaders of Russian Jewry knew full well that the wind which was blowing from the heights of the Russian throne was unfavorable to them, and their initial hopefulness gave way speedily to a feeling of depression. A memorandum drafted at that time by prominent Jews of St. Petersburg, with the intention of submitting it to one of the highest functionaries at the Russian court, mirrors this pessimistic frame of mind:

The Russian Jews are deprived of that powerful lever for intellectual and moral advancement which is designated as the hope for a better future. They are fully aware of the fact that the highest authority in the land, influenced by the distorted information concerning the Jews, which is systematically presented to it by officials acting from avaricious or other selfish motives, is exceedingly unfavorable to the Jews. They must resign themselves to the fact that there is actually no possibility of directing the attention of the Tzar and Sovereign to the true state of affairs, and that even those dignitaries who themselves act justly and tolerantly towards the Jews are afraid of putting in a good word for them for fear of being charged with favoritism towards them.

[¹ See on this term vol. II, p. 16, n. 1.]
[² See on the meaning of this term, vol. I, p. 25, n. 1:]

2. The Martyrdom of the Moscow Community

The attitude which officials of high rank were prone to adopt towards the Jews was luridly illustrated at that time in Moscow. It will be remembered that the small Jewish colony which had been left in the second Russian capital after the cruel expulsions of 1891 was barred from holding religious services in its large synagogue which had been closed by order of Alexander $III.^1$ In view of the forthcoming festivities in honor of the coronation of Nicholas II., which were to be held in Moscow in the spring of 1896, the representatives of the Jewish community of the second Russian capital petitioned the governor-general of Moscow, Grand Duke Sergius Alexandrovitch, to secure for them the Tzar's permission to have their synagogue open at least during the coronation days, "as a special act of grace, in order that the Jews of Moscow may be given a chance to celebrate the joyful event with due solemnity." But the grand duke, maddened by Jew-hatred, notified the petitioners through the Chief of Police that their petition was "an insolent violation of the imperial will" and could not be considered.

The martyrdom of the Moscow community, the heritage of the past reign, stood out like a black stain even upon the gloomy background of the new era. An imperial ukase issued in 1892 had decreed that the structure of the sealed-up Moscow synagogue should be sold to the highest bidder unless it was converted into a charitable institution.^{2} The community was naturally anxious to prevent the desecration of its sanctuary and to preserve the edifice for better days to come. With this end in view it placed in the synagogue building

[^{1} See vol. II, p. 423.]
[^{2} See vol. II, p. 424.]

the trade school for Jewish children which had been established in memory of Alexander II. The anti-Semitic authorities of Moscow scented in this step a wicked design. The governor-general got into communication with the Ministers of the Interior and of Public Instruction, and, as a result, on May 27, 1896, the executive board of the Moscow community received the following order: To stop the admission of pupils to the trade school and to close the school altogether after the completion of the prescribed course of studies by the present contingent of students. Thereupon the Jews of Moscow made another attempt to save their synagogue by transferring hither their school and asylum for poor and orphaned children, the so-called Talmud Torah. This attempt, too, was frustrated by the Muscovite Hamans. On October 28, 1897, the governor-general announced that, after consultation with the Minister of the Interior, the decision had been reached to close the asylum, which sheltered about one hundred poor children, on the fanciful ground that these children might just as well receive their instruction in Russian educational establishments. The underlying motive of the new order was unmistakably revealed in its latter part: Unless in the course of two months the building of the synagogue will be reconstructed and so altered as to be fitted for a hospital or a similar charitable institution, it will be sold at public auction.

Once more the Jewish community endeavored to save its sanctuary, which its enemies had made up their minds to destroy. The synagogue structure was rebuilt to meet the purposes of a hospital and a shelter. But the commission appointed by the governor-general to examine the alterations found that they were not sufficiently extensive and therefore suggested that the interior of the synagogue should be entirely remodelled so as to exclude the possibility of its ever being used for devotional purposes. The struggle centering around the alterations dragged on for another eight years—until the revolution of 1905 and the assassination of the ferocious governor-general. It was then that the Jews finally succeeded in releasing their sanctuary from the death sentence which had been passed upon it.

The motive which animated the Muscovite Jew-haters was perfectly evident: it was their fervent desire to wipe out the last remnants of the local Jewish community by subjecting the Jews to religious and administrative persecutions and thereby compelling them to flee from the center of Greek Orthodoxy. The growth of the Jewish settlement at Moscow was checked in ruthless fashion. The Jewish artisans had been expelled as far back as 1891, but the Jewish merchants who purchased their right of residence in the second Russian capital at the annual cost of one thousand rubles—the tax levied on first guild members—had been allowed to remain. Moreover, as the largest industrial center of Russia, Moscow naturally attracted a goodly number of Jewish merchants who came there temporarily on business. These "newcomers" were handled more severely than are alien enemies in war-time. Police detectives prowled about on the streets and at the railroad stations, seizing passers-by who happened to exhibit a "Semitic" countenance, and dragging them to the police stations, "with a view to the examination of their right of residence in Moscow." The unfortunate Jews, whose documents did not comply with all the technicalities of the law, were expelled at once. The *Moscow Police News* carried a regular advertisement offering a reward for the capture of "rightless" Jews. In October, 1897, the Moscow Chief of Police announced a premium of equal amount for the capture of one Jew or of two burglars.¹

Finally, the Russian Government took a most effective step towards preventing the increase of the Jewish population of Moscow. On January 22, 1899, an imperial ukase was issued forthwith prohibiting Jewish merchants of the first guild from settling in Moscow, unless they shall have obtained special permission from the Minister of Finance and from the governor-general of Moscow, it being beforehand agreed that no such permission should be granted. The same ukase enacted a number of offensive discriminations against the Jewish merchants already settled in Moscow by depriving them of their vote in the commercial associations, and by other similar devices. On a subsequent occasion the admission was candidly made that all these measures were prompted by the desire "to rid as far as possible the government of Moscow of the Jews already settled there on a legal basis."

3. Restrictions in the Right of Residence

Whereas the régime of Grand Duke Sergius in Moscow represented an acute stage of Judaeophobia, manifesting itself in cruelties of an exceptional character, the central Government in St. Petersburg exhibited the same disease in a more

¹ These barbarities were suspended only for a few days during that year, while the International Congress of Medicine was holding its sessions in Moscow. The police were ordered to stop these street raids upon the Jews for fear of compromising Russia in the eyes of Western Europe, since it was to be expected that the membership of the Congress would include medical celebrities with "Semitic" features.

"normal" form. Here, the oppression of the Jews was pursued systematically and quietly, and was carried on as one of the most important functions of the public administration. The sacrosanct institution of the Pale of Settlement and the other mainstays of political anti-Semitism were zealously guarded by the faithful watchdogs of Russian reaction—the various Ministers of the Interior who followed one another between the years 1895 and 1904: Durnovo (until the autumn of 1895), Goremykin (1896-1899), Sipyaghin (1899-1902), and Plehve (1902-1904). True, during the régime of the last two Ministers the anti-Semitic temperature rose above normal, but it was only due to the fact that the increased revolutionary propaganda of those days had generally stimulated the powers of reaction to a greater display of energy. Quite aside from these exceptional conditions, the rigid consistency in enforcing the restrictive laws was sufficient to account for many tragedies in the life of the Jews, while the despotism of the provincial authorities aggravated the situation still further and turned the tragedies into catastrophes.

As far as the Pale of Settlement is concerned, the Government continued its old-time policy of cooping up the Jews within the area of the cities and towns by shielding the villages carefully against the influx of Jews. Since the promulgation of the "Temporary Rules" in 1882, the authorities of St. Petersburg had been aiming at the gradual elimination of those rural Jewish "old timers" who had been allowed under those rules to remain in the villages.¹ They had been looking for-

¹ The "Temporary Rules" were not given retroactive force, and those settled in the villages before the promulgation of the law of May 3, 1882, were accordingly permitted to stay there. [See vol. II, p. 311.]

ward to the time when the eyes of the Russian moujik would no more be offended by the sight of a Jew. But this pious wish did not materialize quickly enough. Several governors put forth the simple proposition to expel all Jews from the villages, not excluding those who had been settled there for a long time. This step, however, was deemed too radical. The Minister of Finance, Witte, wished to solve the problem in a different way. He sought to persuade the Tzar that the introduction of the state liquor monopoly would automatically have the effect of forcing the Jews to leave the country-side, inasmuch as the liquor traffic formed the principal occupation of the village Jews.

Witte's conjecture was to a certain degree borne out by the facts. By the end of the nineties the Jewish country population of Russia had been considerably reduced. Nevertheless there was no relief in sight. For the lust of the administration had grown in proportion. The governors and the other gubernatorial authorities resorted to all kinds of cunning devices to force the Jews out of the villages or out of the railroad stations which were situated outside the town limits. The Christian land-owners frequently complained about these deportations, and petitioned the governors to permit the Jewish grain merchants, who were engaged in buying and shipping the grain from the manorial store-houses, to reside at the railroad stations. The Senate was compelled over and over again to pass upon the appeals of illegally deported Jews and to enter into an examination of all kinds of hair-splitting questions involved in the manipulation of the anti-Jewish laws by the lower courts, whether, for instance, an old-time Jewish villager who returns to his home after a brief absence is to be regarded as a new settler who has no right to live in the country, or whether a Jew who lives on an estate which happens to be situated in two contiguous villages is allowed to remove from the one to the other. As a rule the authorities decided these questions against the Jews, though the most revolting decisions of this kind were later reversed by the Senate.

In connection with the prohibition of residence outside the cities, a new problem had arisen in Jewish life—the "summer resort question." The authorities frequently prohibited Jewish families from spending the summer in the outskirts of the cities if a particular resort or cottage was found to be situated outside the city line. Thousands of Jewish families were thus deprived of an opportunity to rest in God's free nature during the summer months, and to breathe the fresh air of the fields and forests, for no other reason than that they were Jews—a new variety of territorially affixed city serfs.

The law was just as merciless in the case of Jews afflicted with disease. The watering-places situated outside the towns were barred to Jewish sufferers who wished to take a cure there. The Crimean watering-place Yalta, in the neighborhood of the imperial summer resort Livadia, was the object of particular vigilance, having been barred to the Jews by order of the dying Alexander III.^{1} The Jewish consumptives who had managed to obtain "illegal" access to this spa were pitilessly expelled. The following incident, which was reported at that time in the Russian press, may serve as an illustration of this ruthless policy:

The wife of a [Jewish] physician had come to Yalta to improve her shattered health. While she was suffering from severe blood-

[^{1} See vol. II, p. 428 *et seq.*]

spitting, a policeman invaded the bedroom of the sick woman, insisting on her giving a written pledge to leave the place within twenty-four hours. The patient was terribly frightened. On the following day the deportation was stopped, in consequence of the testimony of her physician that the slightest motion was fraught with danger to the invalid. But the fright and uncertainty had intensified the cough; the young woman became worse, and soon afterwards died.

As it happened, the action of the police was subsequently found to be entirely unwarranted; for, as the wife of a physician, this victim of bureaucratic heartlessness was, even according to the letter of the law, entitled to the right of residence in Yalta.

A similar case was that of a sick Jewish student who had been sent by his physicians to Yalta to cure his lungs. He was expelled in the dead of winter and deported under a police convoy, together with a batch of prisoners, to Sevastopol, notwithstanding the fact that he was in a feverish condition. The correspondent of a local paper in Sevastopol reported that "along the entire road from the harbor to the prison, which was traversed by the batch, passers-by would stop in their walk, staggered by the extraordinary spectacle." The sufferer appealed to the Senate, but the latter found that the orders of the police "contained nothing contrary to the law." The highest tribunal of the empire went with equanimity on record that a Jewish student was liable to the penalty of being arrested and marched under a police escort, together with criminal offenders, for an attempt to heal his lungs in the warm southern climate.

But no place in the empire could vie as regards hostility to the Jews with the city of Kiev—this inferno of Russian

Israel. Though surrounded on all sides by a string of towns and townlets with a dense Jewish population, the southwestern metropolis was guarded by a host of police watchdogs against the invasion of "aliens." Apart from the "privileged" Jews who formed part of the permanent population, the police were forced to admit into the city Jewish visitors who came to Kiev for a few days to attend to their affairs. Yet, haunted by the fear lest these visitors might stay there too long, the police arranged *oblavas*, or raids, to hunt them down like stray dogs. About once a week, during the night, the police would raid certain hostelries in which the Jews were wont to stop, put those that were caught under arrest, and then expel them from the confines of the city. This additional heavy "night work" called for a larger police staff, and to meet this increased expenditure, an annual sum of 15,000 rubles was appropriated—from the proceeds of the Jewish meat tax. This revenue, collected from the Jews for the purpose of maintaining the charitable and educational institutions of the Jewish communities, was now used to pay the police agents to enable them to hunt down these Jews and expel them in merciless fashion. To put it more plainly, the convict, after being sentenced to be hanged, was forced to buy the rope. The methods of the Russian inquisition gradually reached the top notch of efficiency. Even the "*Kievlanin*" ("The Kievian"), the anti-Semitic official organ of Kiev, was bound to confess on one occasion that "in the course of the month of July (of the year 1901) things have taken place in Kiev which are hardly conceivable."

As far as the general disabilities are concerned, the entire area of the Russian empire outside the Pale of Settlement, though open to foreigners of all nationalities, remained hermetically closed to the Jewish citizens of Russia, and the borders of that prohibited area were guarded even more rigorously than they had been during the previous reign. In the consistent enforcement of this principle the Government did not shrink from the most revolting extremes. A law passed in 1896 interdicted Jewish soldiers from spending outside the Pale of Settlement even the brief leave of absence which they were granted during their term of military service. A Jewish soldier serving in a regiment which was stationed, let us say, in St. Petersburg, Moscow, or even in far-off Siberia, was forced, under this law, to travel hundreds and even thousands of miles to the Pale of Settlement to spend his month of furlough there, being denied the right to remain in the city in which he was discharging his military duty, and it made no difference even if the furlough was granted to him for the purpose of recuperating his health.

In many places of the empire, the whimsicality of the local authorities in construing the law of residence was of a nature to suggest that they had no other end in view except that of making sport of the Jews. The administration of Siberia, for instance, invented the following regulation: a Jewish merchant or artisan who is registered in one of the Siberian cities shall have the right only to live in the particular city of his registration, and in no other. Since very many Jews resided outside the localities of their accidental registration, a transmigration of Siberian Jewry was the result. The Jews registered, *e. g.*, in Tomsk, though they might have lived from the day of their birth in Irkutsk, were deported in batches to Tomsk, meeting on the way parties of exiled Jews from

Tomsk who had the misfortune of having their names entered upon the records of Irkutsk. Human beings were shuffled like a pack of cards. This revolting practice of the Siberian authorities, which had begun at the end of the preceding reign, was sustained by the Senate in a decision handed down in 1897.

4. The Economic Collapse of Russian Jewry

The result of all these persecutions was the complete economic collapse of Russian Jewry. Speaking generally, the economic structure of the Russian Jews experienced violent upheavals during the first years of Nicholas II.'s reign. The range of Jewish economic endeavor, circumscribed though it was, was narrowed more and more. In 1894, the law placing the liquor trade under Government control was put into effect by Witte, the Minister of Finance. Catering to the prejudices of the ruling spheres of Russia, Witte had already endeavored to convince Alexander III. that the liquor state monopoly would have the effect of completely undermining "Jewish exploitation," the latter being primarily bound up with the sale of liquor in the towns and villages. In view of this, the monopoly was introduced with particular zeal in the western governments, where a little later, in the course of 1896-1898, during the reign of Nicholas II., all private pot-houses were replaced by official liquor stores, the so-called "imperial barrooms." In consequence of this reform, tens of thousands of Jewish families who had derived their livelihood either directly from the liquor trade, or indirectly from occupations connected with it, such as the keeping of inns and hostelries, were deprived of their means of subsistence. It goes without saying that, as far as the moral aspect of the problem was concerned, the best elements of Russian Jewry welcomed this reform, which bade fair to wipe out an ugly stain on the escutcheon of the Jewish people—the liquor traffic bequeathed to the Jews by ancient Poland. Known as the most sober people on earth, the Jews had been placed in the tragic position that thousands of them, in their search for a piece of bread, were forced to serve as a medium for promoting the pernicious Russian drunkenness. The memory of the days when the Jewish saloon was the breeding-place of pogroms, in which the Russian peasants and burghers filled themselves with Jewish alcohol to fortify themselves in their infamous work of demolishing the homes of the Jews, was still fresh in their minds. Cheerfully would the Jewish people have yielded its monopoly of the liquor trade to the Russian bar-room keepers and to the Russian Government who seemed genuinely attracted toward it, had it only been allowed to pursue other methods of earning a livelihood. But in closing the avenue of the liquor traffic to two hundred thousand Jews, the Government did not even think of removing the special restrictions which barred their way to other lines of endeavor. Having been robbed of the scanty livelihood they derived from their country inns, thousands of rural victims of the state monopoly flocked into the cities, only to clash with a host of urban victims of the same reform who had also been deprived of their means of sustenance. The growth of the proletariat within the Pale of Settlement, both in business and in the trades, assumed appalling proportions. The observers of economic life in the Pale, such as the well-known Russian economist Subbotin and others, called attention to the frightful increase of pauperism in that region. Between 1894 and 1898 the number of Jewish families in need of assistance increased twenty-seven per cent. as compared with former years. In 1897, the number of Jews without definite occupations amounted in certain cities to fifty per cent and more. The number of destitute Jews applying for help before the Passover festival reached unheard of proportions, amounting in Odessa, Vilna, Minsk, Kovno, and other cities to forty and even fifty per cent of the total Jewish population. The crop failures of 1899 and 1900 in the south of Russia resulted in a terrible famine among the impecunious Jewish masses. Whereas the peasants who suffered from the same calamity received financial assistance from the Government, the Jews had to resort to self-help, to the collection of funds throughout the empire to which only here and there liberal Christians added their mites.

Many of these Jewish proletarians were willing to take up agriculture, but the "Temporary Rules" of 1882 blocked their way to the country-side, and made it impossible for them to buy or even lease a piece of land. Prominent Jews of St. Petersburg, such as Baron Günzburg and others, petitioned the Government to allow the Jews to purchase small parcels of land for personal use, but, after long deliberations, their petition was rejected. Thus, at the end of the nineteenth century, the ruling spheres of the Russian empire proved more anti-Semitic than at the beginning of the same century, when the Government of Alexander I. and even that of Nicholas I. had endeavored to promote agriculture among the Jews and had established the Jewish agricultural colonies in the south of Russia.^{1} The mania of oppression went so far as to prohibit

^{1} According to the statistics of 1898-1901, some 150,000 Jews in Russia engaged in agrarian pursuits. Of these, 51,539 were occupied with raising corn in the colonies, 64,563 engaged in special branches of agrarian economy, 19,930 held land as owners or lessees, and 12,901 were engaged in temporary farm labor.

the Jews from buying or leasing parcels of land which were part of a city, but happened to be situated outside the city line. A rich Jew of Minsk, by the name of Pollak, petitioned, in 1897, the local Town Council to sell him a piece of suburban property for the establishment of a Jewish agricultural farm, but his petition was refused. This refusal was thoroughly consistent. For the fact that the Jews were forbidden to own land made the training of Jews in the art of agriculture entirely superfluous. It may be added that this prohibition of land ownership was upheld by the Government even in the case of the Jewish students who had completed their course in the school of the Jewish Agricultural Farm near Odessa.

Similar methods were employed to check the development of arts and crafts, which were widely represented among the Jews, but stood on a very low technical level. Even the efforts to organize mutual help among the working classes were blocked by the Government in all kinds of ways. The well-known Jewish millionaire, Brodski, of Kiev, wishing to assist the toiling masses without distinction of creed, offered to open a trade bank in that city and to contribute towards that purpose the sum of 120,000 rubles. When, in 1895, he submitted the constitution of the proposed bank to the local authorities for their approval, he was required to insert a clause to the effect that the directors and the chairman of the bank council should always be Christians and that the council itself should not include more than one Jewish member. To this insolent demand Brodski made the only fitting retort: "Being myself a Jew, I cannot possibly agree that the constitution of an establishment which is to be founded with the money contributed by me and which is to bear my name shall contain restrictions affecting my coreligionists." He naturally withdrew his offer, and Kiev was deprived of a trade bank. The fact that the failure of the project also affected the Christian artisans did not disturb the authorities in the least. It was enough of a compensation that the Jews were made to suffer not only materially, but also morally, and the purpose of the highly-placed Jew-baiters was accomplished.

5. Professional and Educational Restrictions

In the domain of those liberal professions to which the Jewish intellectuals, being barred from entering the civil service, were particularly attracted, the law went to almost any length in its endeavor to keep them closed to the Jews. The legal career had been blocked to them ever since the passage of the law of 1889, which made the admission of a properly qualified Jew to the bar dependent upon the granting of a special permission by the Minister of Justice. In the course of a whole decade, the Minister found it possible to grant this permission only to one Jew, who, it may be added, had sat on the bench for twenty-five years—there were two or three such "relics," dating back to the liberal era of Alexander II. In consequence of this provision, the proportion of Jews at the bar, which prior to the enactment of the restriction had reached from fourteen to twenty-two per cent, was reduced to nine per cent. In 1897, a committee appointed by the Government was considering the proposal to place the disability on the statute books and to establish a ten per cent norm for Jewish lawyers. The reasons advanced by the committee for the proposed restriction were of the distinctly mediæval variety:

The conduct of a lawyer is determined by the impulses of his will, of his conscience,—in other words, that sphere of his inner life which finds its manifestation in religion. Now the admission of Jews constitutes a menace, resulting from views peculiar to the Jewish race, which are contrary to Christian morality.

Subsequently, the champions of "Christian morality" on the staff of the Ministry of Justice bethought themselves that it might even be better and nobler to stop the admission of Jews to the bar altogether, and the proposal regarding the percentage norm was tabled. Hundreds upon hundreds of young Jews who had completed their legal education at the universities, or who had acted as assistants to sworn attorneys, saw once more their hopes for the legitimate pursuit of their profession vanish into the air.

Jewish physicians were restricted to private practice and robbed of their right to occupy a Government or public position. Even the autonomous Zemstvo institutions adopted more and more the practice of refusing to appoint Jews, and very frequently the printed advertisements of the Zemstvos offering medical positions contained the stipulation *kromye yevreyev* ("except the Jews").

The scholastic education of the Jewish children was throttled in the same pitiless manner as theretofore. The disgraceful school norm which had been introduced in 1887^1 performed with ever-increasing relentlessness its task of dooming to spiritual death the Jewish youths who were knocking at the doors of the gymnazia and universities. In the beginning of 1898, the post of Minister of Public Instruction, which had been occupied by Dyelanov, was entrusted to Professor Bogolepov of Moscow. While Dyelanov had been occasionally inclined

¹ See vol. II, p. 350.

to soften the rigor of the school norm—it was commonly rumored that this good-natured dignitary could not bear to see a woman cry, and the tearful entreaties of the mothers of the rejected scholars made him sanction the admission of a certain number of Jewish children over and above the established percentage norm—his successor Bogolepov, an academic teacher who had become a gendarme of education, was impervious to any sentiment of pity. In the course of the three years of his administration, he not only refused to admit the slightest departure from the established norm, but attempted to curtail it still further. Thus, orders were issued to calculate the percentage norm of the Jewish applicants for admission to the universities not in its relation to the total number of the annual admissions, but separately for each faculty (1898-1899). This provision was designed to limit the number of Jewish students who flocked to the medical and legal faculties, since, in view of the fact that the Jews were entirely barred from appointments in the general educational institutions, the other faculties did not offer them even a sporting chance of earning a livelihood. The ruthlessness displayed by the Ministry of Public Instruction towards the Jewish youth was officially justified on the ground that certain elements among them were affiliated with the revolutionary movement which, just at that time, had assumed particular intensity in the Russian student body. This sentiment was openly voiced in a circular of the Ministry, issued on May 26, 1901, which makes the following statement: "The disorders which took place at the end of the nineties in the institutions of higher learning testified to the fact that the instigators of these disorders were, to a large extent, persons of non-Russian extraction."

Bogolepov himself, the reactionary Minister of enlightenment, fell a victim of this agitation among the student body. He died from the bullet of a Terrorist who happened to be of unadulterated Russian extraction. His successor, General Vannovski (1901-1902), though endeavoring to assuage the university disorders by a policy of "kindly solicitude," maintained the former uncompromising attitude as far as the Jews were concerned. In view of the fact that, in spite of all restrictions, the ratio of Jewish students at all universities actually exceeded the norm prescribed by law, the new Minister decreed that the percentage of Jewish admissions be temporarily curtailed in the following proportion: Two per cent for the capitals (instead of the former three per cent), three per cent for the universities outside of the Pale of Settlement (instead of five per cent), and seven per cent for the Pale of Settlement (instead of ten per cent).

Even the restrictions placed upon the admission of the Jews to the gymnazia were intensified. In 1901, Jewish children who had graduated from a pro-gymnazium ^{1} were forbidden to continue their education in the advanced classes of a gymnazium unless there was a free Jewish vacancy within the percentage norm—a truly miraculous contingency. The same policy was extended to the commercial schools established with funds which were provided by the merchant class and the bulk of which came from Jews. In the commercial schools maintained by the commercial associations Jewish children were admitted only in proportion to the contributions of the Jewish merchants towards the upkeep of the particular school. In

[^{1} A pro-gymnazium is made up of the six (originally four) lower grades of a gymnazium which embraces eight grades.]

private commercial schools, however, percentages of all kinds, varying from ten to fifty per cent, were fixed in the case of Jewish pupils. This provision had the effect that Jewish parents were vitally interested in securing the entrance of as many Christian children as possible in order to increase thereby the number of Jewish vacancies. Occasionally, a Jewish father, in the hope of creating a vacancy for his son, would induce a Christian to send his boy to a commercial school— though the latter, as a rule, offered little attraction for the Christian population—by undertaking to defray all expenses connected with his education. Yet many Jewish children, though enduring all these humiliations, found themselves outside the doors of the intermediate Russian schools.

It is worthy of note that in this attempt at the spiritual extermination of the Jewish children by barring them from intermediate educational institutions the Russian law followed strictly the ancient rule of the Pharaohs: "If it be a son, then ye shall kill him; but if it be a daughter, then she shall live." The Government schools for girls were opened to the Jewish population without any restriction, and the influx of Jewesses to these gymnazia was only checked unofficially by the anti-Semitic authorities of this or that institution, thereby turning the tide of applicants in the direction of private girls' schools. But as far as the higher schools were concerned, Jewish girls were subjected to the same restrictions as the boys. The Higher Courses for Women and the Pedagogic Courses in St. Petersburg restricted the admission of Jewesses to five per cent. The constitution of the Medical Institute for Women, founded in 1895, provided at first for the entire exclusion of Jewesses. But in 1897, the doors of this institution were opened to the hated tribe—just enough to admit them to the extent of three per cent.

It was scarcely to be expected that the Jewish youths who had been locked out of the Russian school should entertain particularly friendly sentiments towards a régime which wasted their lives, humiliated their dignity, and sullied their souls. The Jewish lad, driven from the doors of the gymnazia, became an embittered "extern," who was forced to study at home and from year to year present himself for examination before the school authorities. An immense host of young men and women who found their way blocked to the higher educational institutions in Russia went abroad, flocking to foreign universities and higher professional schools, where they learned to estimate at its full value a régime which in their own country denied them the advantages granted to them outside of it. A large number of these college youths returned home permeated with revolutionary ideas—living witnesses to the sagacity of a Government which saw its reason for existence in the suppression of all revolutionary strivings.

6. Anti-Semitic Propaganda and Pogroms

The reactionary Russian press, encouraged and stimulated by the official Jew-baiters, engaged in an increasingly ferocious campaign against the Jews. The Russian censorship, known all over for its merciless cruelty, which was throttling the printed word and trembling at the criminal thought of "inciting hatred toward the Government," yet granted untrammeled freedom to those who propagated hatred to Judaism, and thereby committed the equally criminal offence of "inciting one part of the population against the other." The *Novoye*

Vremya, the most wide-spread semi-official press organ, and its satellites in the provincial capitals were permitted to do what they pleased. They were free to slander the Jewish religion, the Jewish people, and the Jewish communities. When the famous Dreyfus affair had started in France, the *Novoye Vremya*, the oracle of Russia's ruling spheres, arrayed itself on the side of the Jew-baiters from among the French general staff, and launched a savage campaign of slander against the Jews of the entire globe. Many an article published in the anti-Semitic press was scarcely distinguishable from the proclamations calling upon the mob to massacre the Jews.

By far the most effective propaganda on behalf of pogroms was carried on, sometimes without a conscious realization of the consequences, by the Government itself: by persisting in its anti-Jewish policy. Observing this uninterrupted maltreatment of the Jews on the part of the Russian legislation and administration, which treated the Jews as if they were criminals, witnessing the expulsions inflicted upon the "illegally residing" Jews and the raids engineered against them, watching the constant mockery at the Jewish children who were driven from the doors of the educational institutions, and seeing the endless multitude of other humiliating disabilities, the unenlightened Russian populace necessarily gained the conviction that the extermination of Jewry was a noble and patriotic duty. Coupled with the usual economic and national conflicts, this trend of mind could not but lead to acts of violence.

At the end of the nineties the Russian horizon was darkened again by the ominous shadow of the beginning of the eighties: pogroms, at first sporadic and within circumscribed limits, broke out again in various parts of the Pale. On February 18 and 19, 1897, an anti-Jewish riot took place in Shpola, a town in the government of Kiev. The following officially inspired account of the excesses, in which the facts were undoubtedly toned down, appeared in the *Novoye Vremya:*

At three o'clock in the afternoon an immense crowd of peasants rushed into our town, and wrecked completely the stores, homes, and warehouses belonging exclusively to the Jews. A large number of rich business places and small stores, as well as hundreds of houses, were demolished by the crowd, which acted, one might say, with elemental passion, dooming to destruction everything that fell into its hands. The town of Shpola, which is celebrated for its flourishing trade and its comparative prosperity, now presents the picture of a city which has been ravaged by a hostile army. Lines of old women and children may be seen moving [into the town] to carry home with them the property of the "Zhyds." Of essential importance is the fact that these disorders were undoubtedly prearranged. The local Jews knew of the impending disaster four days before it took place; they spoke about it to the local police chief, but the latter assured them that "nothing is going to happen."

Two months later, on April 16 and 17, the Christian inhabitants of the town of Kantakuzenka, in the government of Kherson, indulged in a similar "amusement" at the expense of the Jews. To quote the words of a semi-official report:

A cruel pogrom has taken place. Almost the entire town has been destroyed by an infuriated mob. All Jewish stores were wrecked and the goods found there were thrown about. A part of the merchandise was looted by the rabble. The synagogue alone remained unscathed.

Here, too, it was known beforehand that a pogrom was in the course of preparation. The Jews petitioned the authorities to avert the catastrophe, but the local police force was found inadequate to cope with the situation.

In both devastated towns the governors of the respective provinces eventually appeared on the scene with detachments of troops, but in the meantime the revolting performances were over. Many rioters were placed under arrest and put on trial. More than sixty were sentenced by the courts to a term in prison from eight to fourteen months. One of the defendants, a Little-Russian peasant, who had been arrested for having taken part in an anti-Jewish riot, voiced his amazement in these characteristic words: "They told us we had permission to beat the Jews, and now it appears that it is all a lie."

A pogrom on a more comprehensive scale, arranged in honor of the Easter festival, and lasting for three days (April 19-21, 1899), was allowed to take place in the city of Nicholayev, the South-Russian port of entry. Bands of rioters, to the number of several thousand, among them many newly arrived Great-Russian day laborers, and a few "intellectual" ringleaders, fell upon Jewish stores and residences and destroyed or looted their contents, complying faithfully with the established pogrom ritual, while the police and Cossack forces proved "powerless." On the third day, when the news of the freedom accorded to the rioters and robbers at Nicholayev reached the villages in the vicinity, a whole army of peasants, both men and women, numbering some ten thousand, started towards the city on their wagons, with the intention of carrying off the property of the Jews—but they were too late; for in the meantime Cossacks and soldiers had been ordered to stop the pogroms and disperse the rioters. The peasants were driven off and had to return to their villages on their empty wagons. Exasperated by their failure, the peasants vented their fury upon the Jewish cemetery outside the city, demolishing a large number of tombstones, and then, scattering all over the district, made an attack upon the Jewish population in the neighboring settlements and villages. In the Jewish agricultural colony of Nagartava all farm-houses and stores were wrecked and looted, and the agricultural implements demolished. The Russian peasant was unscrupulously ruining and robbing his Jewish fellow-peasant. In the adjacent colonies, the Jews, being of a robust physique, were able to put up an effective defence.

The only protest against this new outbreak of barbarism was voiced by the "Son of the Fatherland" (*Syn Otyechestva*), a liberal Russian press organ:

When at last—questioned the paper—will that terrible relic of the gloomy era of the Middle Ages take an end? When will there be a stop to this breaking of windows, this beating of men and this wrecking of houses and stores?

This time the orders from St. Petersburg were explicit: the local authorities were commanded to prevent the further spread of the pogrom agitation. The reason for this unaccustomed attitude is not difficult to guess. Two weeks after the Nicholayev atrocities, the first International Hague Conference opened its sessions (May 6-18), having been called at the initiative of the Russian emperor to discuss the question of disarmament, and this Conference must have suggested to the Tzar the advisability of first disarming the anti-Jewish rioters in Russia itself. However, he failed to draw the more important conclusion from the Conference called by him: that it was necessary to stop, or at least to reduce, the constant arming of his own Government against the Jews and to discard the mediæval weapons of oppression and persecution which spelled destruction to an entire nation. This alone is enough to expose the hollowness of the spectacle at the Hague, which had been designed by the feeble-minded Nicholas as a sort of diplomatic entertainment.

That the Russian authorities, when so minded, were fully capable of grappling with the pogrom agitation was demonstrated by the rapidity with which, on a later occasion, they suppressed the anti-Jewish excesses in the Polish city of Chenstokhov (August 19, 1902). In this hotbed of dismal Polish clericalism, the goal of thousands of Catholic pilgrims, who arrive there to worship the Holy Virgin on the "Bright Mountain," a street brawl between a Jewish tradesman and a Polish woman grew, owing to the instigations of Catholic priests, into a monstrous assault upon Jewish houses and stores by a crowd of fifteen thousand Poles. Here, too, the customary shouts were heard: "Beat the Jews! Nothing will happen to us." But the Chenstokhov rioters made a grievous error in their calculation. The protection of the Russian authorities did not extend to the Poles who were not considered politically "dependable," and were known to be equally hostile to the Zhyds and the "Moskals."¹ The excesses had started in the morning, and in the evening they were at an end, a volley from the soldiers having put the tremendous crowd to flight. When the case came up before the courts, the public prosecutor pleaded for the severe punishment of the culprits. The guilty Poles were sentenced to penal servitude and to terms

[¹ A contemptuous nickname for Russians customary among the Poles.]

in prison, and in some cases even damages were awarded to the Jewish victims—an extraordinarily rare occurrence in legal proceedings of this kind.

The union of Polish anti-Semitism with Russian Judaeophobia brought again to life the old monstrous accusation against the Jews—the ritual murder libel. A Polish servant girl in the employ of David Blondes, a Jewish barber in Vilna, steeped, as she was, in gross superstition and being a pliant tool in the hands of fanatical priests, ran out one night (March, 1900) into the street, shouting that her master had wounded her and had tried to squeeze blood from her for the Matzah. A crowd of Christians quickly assembled, and seeing the scratches on the neck and hands of the girl, fell upon Blondes and gave him a severe beating. The "criminal" was thrown into prison, and the prosecuting authorities, listening to the "voice of the people," were zealous in their search for the threads of the crime. The anti-Semitic press launched a well-planned campaign against the Jews in the hope of influencing the judicial verdict. The lower court recognized the fact of the assault, but denied the presence of any murderous intent, and, leaving aside the possibility of a ritual motive, sentenced Blondes to imprisonment for four months. The counsel for the defence, the well-known lawyer Gruzenberg, and others, fearing lest this sentence might be construed by the enemies of Judaism as a corroboration of the ritual murder libel, appealed from the verdict of the court, and proved victorious: a decision handed down by the Senate ordered the case to be sent back for a second trial to the District Court of Vilna, and the court of jurymen, after listening to the statements of authoritative experts and the brilliant speeches of the defence, rendered a verdict of not guilty (February 1, 1902). The prisoner was set at liberty, and the nightmare of the "ritual murder Dreyfusiad" was dispelled for the time being.

Even the Russian stage was made subservient to the purposes of Jew-baiting. A converted Jew by the name of Efron-Litvin, who had joined the anti-Semitic business firm of the *Novoye Vremya*, wrote a libelous play under the title "The Sons of Israel," or "The Smugglers," in which Jews and Judaism were made the subject of the most horrible calumnies. The play was first produced at St. Petersburg, in the theatre controlled by Suvorin, the publisher of the *Novoye Vremya*, and in the course of 1901-1902 it made the rounds of the provincial stage. Everywhere, the Russian Jew-haters welcomed this talentless production, which pictured the Jews as rogues and criminals, and represented the Jewish religion and morality as the fountain-head whence the supposed hatred of the Jews against the Christians derived its origin. Naturally enough the Jews and the best elements among the Russian *intelligenzia* looked upon the mere staging of such a play as an incitement to pogroms. They appealed repeatedly to the police, calling upon them to stop the production of a play which was sure to fan national and religious hatred. The police, however, were not guided by the wishes of the Jews, but by those of their enemies. As a result, in a considerable number of cities where the play was presented, such as Smolensk, Oryol, Kishinev, Tiflis, and others, violent demonstrations took place in the theatres. The Jewish spectators and a part of the Russian public, particularly from among the college youth, hissed and hooted, demanding the removal from the stage of this libel on a whole people. The anti-Semites, in turn, shouted: "Down with the Jews!", and started a fight with the demonstrators. The police, of course, sided with the anti-Semites, attacking the demonstrators and dragging them to the police stations. This agitation led to a number of legal proceedings against the Jews who were charged with disturbing the peace. During the trial of one of these cases (in the city of Oryol), the counsel for the defence used the following argument:

The play inflames the national passions, and makes the national traits of a people the object of ridicule and mockery,—of a people, moreover, which is denied equal rights and has no means of voicing its protest. The production of such a play should never have been permitted, the more so as the police were well acquainted with the agitated state of the public mind.

The argument of the defending attorney was scarcely convincing. For the article of the Russian law which forbids the "incitement of one part of the population against the other" loses its validity when the "other part" means the Jews.

CHAPTER XXXII

THE NATIONAL AWAKENING

1. The Rise of Political Zionism

For two decades the sledge hammer of Russian reaction had been descending with crushing force upon the vast community of the six million Russian Jews. Yet in the end it was found that the heavy hammer, to use the well-known simile of Pushkin, instead of shattering the national organism of Jewry, had only helped to steel it and to harden its indestructible spiritual self. The Jewry of Russia showed to the world that it was endowed with an iron constitution, and those that had hoped to crush it by the strokes of their hammer were ultimately forced to admit that they had produced the opposite result. At first it seemed as if the effect of these blows would be to turn Jewry into a shapeless mass. There were moments of despair and complete prostration, when the approaching darkness threatened to obliterate all paths. This stage was followed by a period of mental haziness, marked by dim yearnings for regeneration, which were bound to remain fruitless because unaccompanied by organizing energy.

This transitional state of affairs lasted throughout the eighties and during the first half of the nineties. But by and by, out of the chaos of these nebulous social tendencies, there emerged more and more clearly the outlines of definite politico-national doctrines and organizations, and new paths were blazed which, leading in different directions, converged toward one goal—that of the regeneration of the Jewish people from within, both in its national and social life.

The turning-point of this process is marked by the year 1897. That year, in which the first International Zionist Congress held its sessions, inaugurated not only the political Zionist movement, but also the development of other currents of Jewish national and political thought. The entire gamut of public slogans rang through the air, all bearing testimony to one and the same fact: that the era of national prostration had come to an end, and that the vague longings for liberation and regeneration had assumed the character of a conscious endeavor pursuing a well-defined course. The careful observer could scarcely fail to perceive that beneath the hammer of history the formless mass of Jewry was being forged into a well-shaped instrument of great power. The organization of the Jewish people had made its beginning.

Among the movements which arose at the end of the nineteenth century there were some which came to the surface of Jewish life rather noisily, attracting the attention of the Jewish masses as well as that of the outside world. Others, however, were imbedded more deeply in the consciousness of the educated classes and were productive of a new outlook upon the national Jewish problem. The former were an answer to the question of the "Jewish misery," of the *Judennot*, in its practical aspect. The latter offered a solution of the national-cultural problem of Judaism in its totality. The movements of the first kind are represented by Political Zionism and Territorialism. In the second category stand Spiritual Zionism and National-Cultural Autonomism. On a parallel line with both varieties of the national movement, and frequently intersecting it, went the Jewish socialistic movement, tinged to a lesser or larger degree by nationalistic tendencies.

For fifteen years, the "Lovers of Zion," or the *Hibbat Zion* movement, had been pursuing its course in Russia, without showing marked progress in the direction of that universal Jewish goal which had been formulated by its champions, Lilienblum and Pinsker.^{1} During that period some fifteen Jewish agricultural colonies had sprung up in Palestine. The Jewish population of the Holy Land had been increased by some twenty thousand souls, and an effort had been made to create a national model school and to revive the ancient Hebrew tongue; but needless to say all this was far from solving the burning question of the six million Russian Jews who were clamoring for relief from their intolerable condition. At the slow rate of progress which had hitherto characterized the Jewish endeavors in Palestine any attempt to transfer a considerable portion of the Russian center to the Holy Land was doomed to failure, particularly in view of the hostility of the Turkish Government which was anxious to check even this insignificant growth of Jewish colonization.

At that juncture, the air of Europe resounded with the clarion tones of Theodor Herzl's appeal to the Jews to establish a "Jewish State." The appeal came from Western Europe, from the circles in which the sufferings of their "Eastern brethren" had hitherto been viewed entirely from the philanthropic point of view. It came from a young Viennese journalist who had been aroused by the orgy of anti-Semitism in the capital of Austria (the agitation of Burgomaster Lueger, and others), and by the exciting anti-Jewish scenes enacted in the capital of France, where, as a correspondent of the Viennese daily "*Die Neu Freie Presse*," he followed the Dreyfus affair

^{1} See vol. II, p. 332.

in its first early stages. Herzl became suddenly conscious of the acute pain of the Jewish misery. He saw the anti-Semitism of Western Europe closing ranks with the Judaeophobia of Eastern Europe. He saw the ideal of assimilation crumbling to pieces, and he made up his mind to hoist the flag of Jewish nationalism, scarcely aware of the fact that it had already been hoisted in the East.^{1} His pamphlet ("The Jewish State"), which appeared in the beginning of 1896, was in its fundamental premises a repetition of the old appeal of Pinsker. The author of the new publication was convinced, like his predecessor, that the only relief from the Jewish misery lay in the concentration of the Jewish people upon a separate territory, without determining the question whether that territory should be Palestine or Argentina. But, in contradistinction to Pinsker, Herzl was not satisfied with formulating the problem theoretically; he offered at the same time a plan of political and economic organization by means of which the problem was to be solved: the creation of special representative bodies which were to enter into negotiations with rulers and Governments concerning the cession of an appropriate territory to the Jews under an international protectorate, and were also to obtain huge funds to carry out the transplantation and resettlement of vast Jewish masses. Representing a combination of theoretic enthusiasm and practical Utopias, the "Jewish State" of Herzl revived the nearly smothered political hopes which had been cherished by the *Hobebe Zion* circles in Russia. The Russian Jews, groaning under the yoke of an Egyptian bondage,

^{1} After the publication of his *Judenstaat*, Herzl openly confessed that at the time of writing he did not know of the existence of Pinsker's "Autoemancipation."

flocked to the new Moses who announced the glad tidings of the Exodus, and Herzl, beholding the ready hosts in the shape of the *Hobebe Zion* societies, was quick to adjust his territorialistic scheme to the existing Palestinian movement.

In this wise, the organization of political Zionism sprang into life, using as its medium of expression the international party congresses, most of which convened in Switzerland, in the city of Basle. The first Basle Congress held in August, 1897, was an impressive demonstration of the national awakening of the Jewish people. For the first time, the united representatives of Eastern and Western Jewry proclaimed before the world that the scattered sections of Jewry looked upon themselves as one national organism striving for national regeneration. From the center of Western assimilation, advocating the disappearance of Jewry, came the war-cry, proclaiming the continued existence of the Jewish nation, though that existence was conditioned by the establishment of a separate "publicly and legally assured" territorial center. Of the four articles of the "Basle program," which were adopted by the first Congress, three deal with the fundamental task of the party, the political and financial endeavors looking to the colonization of large Jewish masses in Palestine, and only one voices the need "of strengthening the Jewish national feeling and self-respect."

In the further progress of the Zionist organization, these two principles, the political and the cultural, were constantly struggling for mastery, the Zionists of the West gravitating toward political activities and diplomatic negotiations, while the Zionists of the East laid greater emphasis upon internal cultural work along national lines, looking upon it as an indispensable prerequisite for national rebirth. The struggle between these two principles continued at each succeeding annual Congress (at the second and third held in Basle in 1898 and 1899, at the fourth in London in 1900, and at the fifth in Basle in 1901). On the one hand, the Zionists were feverishly engaged in the external organization of the movement: the consolidation of the Shekel-payer societies, the creation of the Jewish Colonial Trust and the Jewish National Fund, the conduct of diplomatic negotiations with the Turkish Government and with the political representatives of other countries for the purpose of obtaining a guaranteed "charter" for a wholesale colonization in Palestine. On the other hand, endeavors were made to nationalize the Jewish intellectual classes, to promote the Hebrew language, to create a national school, and "to conquer the communities" for Zionism, that is, to strengthen the influence of the party in the administration of the Jewish communities. The Convention of Russian Zionists, held at Minsk in 1902, paid particular attention to the cultural aspirations of the party, and adopted a resolution calling for the appointment of two committees, an orthodox and a progressive, to find ways and means for placing Jewish education on a national basis. The same Convention demonstrated the growth of the movement, for, during the first five years of its existence, the Zionist organization in Russia had succeeded in securing about seventy thousand Shekel-payers who were organized in approximately five hundred societies.

Yet the political and financial achievements of Zionism during that period of bloom—prior to the crisis of 1903—were insignificant. The diplomatic negotiations of the Zionist leader, Dr. Theodor Herzl, with the Sultan of Turkey and his Government, as well as with the German emperor and several other European sovereigns, failed of their purpose—the obtaining of a Turkish charter for the wholesale colonization of Palestine. The financial instrument of the party, the Jewish Colonial Trust, proved as yet too weak to collect the proposed fund of ten million dollars—a modest sum when compared with the purpose for which it was destined. The colonization of Palestine proceeded at a slow pace, and its miniature scale was entirely out of proportion to the grand plan of establishing a national autonomous center in Palestine. Withal, Zionism proved during that brief interval a potent factor in the national awakening of Jewry. The strength of the movement lay, not in the political aims of the organization, which were mostly beyond reach, but in the very fact that tens of thousands of Jews were organized with a national end in view. It lay, moreover, in the current national-cultural activities, in the *Gegenwartsarbeit*, which, yielding to necessity, had been raised from a means to an end. In Western Europe, the principal significance of Zionism lay in its effect as a counterbalance to assimilation, Herzl having declared that "Zionism aims at the establishment of a publicly and legally assured home for those Jews who, in their present places of residence, are not able, or not willing, to assimilate themselves." In Russia, however, where Jewish life was dominated by more powerful nationalizing influences, the chief importance of political Zionism lay in this very propaganda of a national rebirth in the midst of those whom militant Judaeophobia was endeavoring to reduce by intolerable oppression to the level of moral degenerates. The apathy and faint-heartedness which had characterized public Jewish life during the eighties and the first half of the nineties was followed by a period of noisy bustle, of organizing activity, and of great animation. The Pale of Settlement resounded with the din of its hundreds of Zionist societies, with the speeches of Zionist agitators at public meetings and in the synagogues, with the intense agitation preceding the elections for each Zionist congress, with the heated debates about the program between the political and the cultural Zionists, between the Mizrahists (the faction of orthodox Zionists) and the Progressives. The public utterances of the Zionist leaders, Herzl and Nordau, were the subject of interminable discussion and comment. The Russian Jews were particularly stirred by the annual Congress addresses of Nordau on the "General Situation in Jewry," in which the famous writer pictured with characteristic vividness the tragedy of the *Golus*, the boundless extent of Jewish misery, having a material aspect in the lands of oppression and a moral aspect among the emancipated sections of Jewry, and which culminated in the thought that Jewry could not exist without Zion.

Nordau's motto, "Jewry will be Zionistic, or it will not be," was differently interpreted in the different circles of the Russian Jewish *intelligenzia*. Among the Russian leaders of the party only a minority (Dr. Mandelstamm of Kiev, and others) were fully in accord with the extreme political views of the Western leaders. The majority of the former workers in the ranks of the *Hobebe Zion* movement (Ussishkin, Chlenov, and others) sought to harmonize the political functions of Zionism with its cultural aspirations and combine the diplomatic negotiations concerning a charter with the up-keep of the existing colonization work in Palestine, which latter was contemptuously branded by the hide-bound adherents of political Zionism as "infiltration." This Babel of opinions within the ranks of the organization could not fail to weaken its effectiveness as an agency for the attainment of the ultimate Zionist goal. At the same time, it brought life and animation into the movement. The crack of the whip of the Egyptian taskmasters remained unheard amidst the clash of ideas and the proud slogans of national liberation which resounded throughout the Jewish Pale.

2. Spiritual Zionism, or Ahad-Ha'amism

And yet, political Zionism viewed as a theory failed to offer a satisfactory solution of the great Jewish problem in all its historic complexity. Born of the reaction against anti-Semitism, and endeavoring to soothe the pain of the wounded Jewish heart, it was marked by all the merits and demerits of a theory which was substantially Messianic in character and was entirely dependent on subjective forces, on faith and will-power. "If you only will it, then it is no fairy tale"^{1}—in these words the ultimate goal of political Zionism is indicated by its founder, who firmly believed that an extraordinary exertion of the national will would transform the fairy tale of a "Jewish state" into reality. When confronted with the question as to the future of the Jewish nation in case faith and will-power should prove unable to grapple with the conditions over which it had no control, and the "fairy tale" of a united political autonomous center should not be realized, political Zionism either remained silent or indulged in a polemical retort which was

[^{1} The motto prefixed to Herzl's Zionistic novel *Altneuland.*]

in flagrant contradiction to Jewish history: "Without Zion, Judaism is bound to perish." The national conscience, however, could not be reconciled to such an answer. A more or less satisfactory solution of the problem of Judaism could not spring from the external reaction against anti-Semitism, but could only mature as the fruit of profound contemplation of the course of development pursued by the Jewish people in the Diaspora; such a solution could only be found in the endeavor to adapt the new national movement to this historic course. From this point of view political Zionism was rectified by "Spiritual Zionism," the teaching of the publicist and philosopher Ahad Ha'am (U. Ginzberg).

Even before political Zionism, or "Herzlianism," appeared on the scene, Ahad Ha'am had succeeded in substantially modifying the Palestinian idea as formulated by Lilienblum and Pinsker. In the program of the semi-Masonic order *Bne Moshe* ("Sons of Moses"), established by him in Odessa,¹ he laid down the fundamental principle that the preparation of the land for the people must be preceded by the transformation of the people into a firmly-knit national organization: "We must propagate the national idea, and convert it into a lofty moral ideal." Having become associated with the Palestinian colonization in a practical manner, as a leading member of the Odessa Palestine Society, founded in 1890,² Ahad Ha'am indefatigably preached that the significance of this microscopic colonization was not to be sought in its economic results, but in its spiritual and cultural effects, in establishing upon the historic soil of Judaism a nursing-ground for a pure national

¹ It was founded in 1889 and disbanded in 1897.
[² See vol. II, p. 421 *et seq.*]

culture which should be free from foreign admixture, and from the inevitable cultural eclecticism of the Diaspora. After the spectacular appearance of political Zionism on the Jewish stage this fundamental idea of "Neo-Palestinianism" was more fully elaborated by Ahad Ha'am, assuming the shape of a comprehensive doctrine, known as the doctrine of "Spiritual Zionism." When the first Basle Congress was over, Ahad Ha'am declared that the "Jewish State," as formulated by Herzl, was beyond realization, for the reason that, under the prevailing circumstances, it was entirely impossible to transfer to Palestine the whole Diaspora, or even a substantial part of it. Consequently, the Palestinian colonization could not put an end to the material "Jewish misery," whereas a small Jewish center, gradually rising in Palestine, might, with the help of a proper organization, solve the national-spiritual problem of Judaism. The formation of a spiritual center in the historic homeland of the nation, the creation in that center of a Jewish national school, the revival of the Hebrew language as a medium of daily speech, the untrammelled development of a Jewish culture, without the pressure of a foreign environment—such in short he held to be the true goal of the Palestine idea. A "publicly and legally assured home for the Jewish spirit" of this kind would exert an uninterrupted nationalizing influence upon the Diaspora, serving as a living center of attraction for a genuine Jewish culture, and acting like a focus which scatters its rays over a large periphery.

The Zionist doctrine of Ahad Ha'am, as a counterbalance to official Zionism which was hall-marked by the "Basle Program," led to interminable discussions among the partisans of the movement. It did not succeed in creating a separate party or a special public agency for its realization; yet the elements of that doctrine have mingled in a larger or lesser degree with the views of the political Zionists in Russia, and manifested themselves in the protests of the cultural Zionists against the extreme political advocates of the movement at the Zionist Congresses. The Zionist Convention at Minsk, referred to previously, resulted in a partial triumph for the ideas championed by Ahad Ha'am, who submitted a report on the "Spiritual Regeneration of Judaism." ^{1} The Convention adopted a resolution calling for a larger measure of cultural work in the schedule of the party activities, but rejected at the same time the proposal of the referee to create a Jewish world organization for the revival of Jewish culture, on the ground that such an organization might destroy the political equilibrium of Zionism.

3. Spiritual Nationalism, or National-Cultural Autonomism

Both political and spiritual Zionism have their roots in the same common ground, in "the negation of the *Golus*": in the conviction that outside of Palestine—in the lands of the Diaspora—the Jewish people has no possibility of continuing its existence as a normal national entity. Both political and spiritual Zionists have their eyes equally fixed upon Zion as the anchor of safety for Judaism, whether it be in its material

[^{1} Ahad Ha'am's report is embodied in the second volume of his collected essays (Berlin, 1903) under the title *Tehiyyat ha-Ru'ah*, "The Spiritual Revival." An English version of this article is found in Leon Simon's translation of Ahad Ha'am's essays (Jewish Publication Society of America, Philadelphia, 1912), p. 253 *et seq.*]

or in its spiritual aspect. Neither doctrine had formulated a clear idea of the future destinies of the Jewish Diaspora, that is, of the destinies of the entire Jewry of the world, minus the section settled in Palestine. The political Zionists evaded the question as to the fate of the Jewish people in case their aspirations should not materialize, and, faithful to the motto proclaimed by Nordau, were ready, as it were, to sentence the entire Diaspora to death, or to a life worse than death, in the eventuality of the Palestine charter being refused. The cultural Zionists protested against this hypothetical Zionism, insisting that the Diaspora would preserve its national vitality by mere contact with a small cultural center in Palestine. But how the tremendous bulk of the Diaspora Jewry should be organized for a Jewish life on the spot, how it should be enabled to liberate itself from the political and cultural pressure of the environment—that question remained unanswered by both wings of Zionism. An answer to this question could not be found by considering merely the last stage of Jewish history, but by viewing the latter in all its phases, beginning with the ancient Greco-Roman and Eastern Diaspora. Such an answer, based upon the entire Jewish past, was attempted by the doctrine of "Spiritual Nationalism," or, more correctly, "National-Cultural Autonomism." Its fundamental principles have been formulated by the present writer in his "Letters Concerning Ancient and Modern Judaism."^{1}

[^{1} A number of articles under that title appeared originally in the Russian-Jewish monthly *Voskhod*. They were subsequently enlarged and published in book form in 1907. The first two "Letters" were rendered into German by the translator of this volume and published in 1905 by the *Jüdischer Verlag* in Berlin, under the title *Die Grundlagen des Nationaljudentums*.]

The theory of Autonomism takes as its point of departure the historic fact that at all times, with the exception of a few brief and partial deflections, the Jewish Diaspora, taken as a whole, represented a national organism, in which the absence of political or territorial unity was made up by the stronger cohesion of its spiritual and cultural ties and the greater intensity of its social and autonomous life. For many centuries the entire culture of Judaism assumed a religious coloring and its communal autonomy was centered in the synagogue—which circumstance gave the modern champions of assimilation reason for thinking that the Jews were only **a** religious group scattered among various nations. It was **a** fatal error on the part of the Parisian Synhedrion convoked by Napoleon when, in its declaration of 1807, it proclaimed that "Jewry to-day does not constitute a nation," an error which during the nineteenth century became an article of faith with the Jews of Western Europe. The latest development of the national movement has shown that Jewry, though scattered among various political states, is a nation full of vitality, and that the Jewish religion is only one of its functions. The Jewish national idea, secularized to a certain degree, is based on the assumption that all sections of the Jewish people, though divided in their political allegiance, form one spiritual or historico-cultural nation, which, like all national minority groups in countries with a mixed population, are in duty bound to fight in their several lands at one and the same time not only for their civil equality, but also for their national rights—the autonomy of the Jewish community, school, and language. What Jewish orthodoxy has for centuries stood for and still stands for, under the guise of religious

Judaism, progressive Jews should fight for under the banner of a national Jewish culture. The fate of universal Jewry ought not to be bound up with one single center. We should take into account the historic fact of a multiplicity of centers of which those that have the largest numbers and can boast of the most genuine development of a national Jewish life are entitled to the hegemony of the Jewish people. In those lands in which civil emancipation has been achieved the fight must go on for national emancipation, the recognition of the Jews as a nation which is entitled to a comprehensive communal and cultural autonomy. In Russia, the struggle must be carried on simultaneously for civil as well as national rights. Temporary set-backs in this struggle for a national existence ought not to discourage a nation which has endured the most terrible sufferings for centuries and has been able to preserve its spiritual freedom even in the midst of slavery.

A certain measure of relief from these sufferings might be found in the old-time remedy of Jewish history, in the emigration from the lands of bondage to countries enjoying a greater amount of freedom. If in one of the centers the Jews are subject to prolonged persecution, then their gradual transplantation, be it partial or complete, to another center offering more favorable opportunities in the struggle for existence ought to be attempted. Thus, during the last decades, the partial exodus of the Jews from Russia has helped to create an important Jewish center in North America and a smaller, yet spiritually valuable center, in Palestine. The latter may become a medium for the nationalization of the entire Diaspora, but only then when the Diaspora itself will be organized *directly* upon the foundations of a cultural autonomy. Zionism, when reduced to its concrete possibilities, can form only one plank in the universal platform of the Jewish nation. The Palestinian center may strengthen the national development of the Diaspora, but it does not constitute a *conditio sine qua non* for its autonomous existence.

Similar to Spiritual Zionism which had not succeeded in forming a special party, and yet acted as a lever in the general Zionist movement, Autonomism, too, failed to find its embodiment in a party organization, and yet became an integral part of the politico-national movements of Russian Jewry at the beginning of the present century. During the revolutionary struggle in Russia, in 1905 and 1906, the demand for a national-cultural autonomy was embodied in various degrees by nearly all Jewish parties and groups in their platforms, aside from, and in addition to, the demand for civil equality.

4. The Jewish Socialistic Movement

On a parallel line with the nationalistic ideology, which formed a counterbalance to the assimilationist theory of Western Europe, the doctrine of Socialism came gradually to the fore, emphasizing the principle of the class struggle in a more or less intimate connection with the national idea. The Jewish labor movement was born at the end of the eighties in Lithuania—in Vilna, and other cities; its adherents were recruited from among the Jewish workingmen who were mainly engaged in handicrafts. In the nineties, the movement spread to the growing manufacturing centers of Lithuania and Poland— Bialystok, Smorgon, Warsaw, and Lodz. At first, the labor societies were established with a purely economic end in view—

¹ See later, p. 108 *et seq*.

the organization of strikes for fewer working hours, increased wages, and the like. The leaders of these societies who were recruited from among the young Jewish *intelligenzia*, some of whom had received a university education abroad, endeavored to model the movement upon the pattern of the West-European Social-Democracy. The doctrine of Marxian Socialism was applied, sometimes rather hastily, to the primitive stage of capitalistic production in the Pale of Settlement where it was still very difficult to draw a line of demarcation between the poverty-stricken "petty bourgeoisie," forming the bulk of the Jewish population, and the labor proletariat.

In the second half of the nineties, the Jewish Socialistic societies were drawn into the maelstrom of the Russian revolutionary movement. In 1897, all these societies were consolidated in the "League of the Jewish Workingmen of Lithuania, Poland, and Russia," known under its abbreviated name as *Der Bund* ("The League"). The first secret convention of the "League" took place in Vilna in the month of September, just one month after the first Zionist Congress at Basle. Various party centers were organized in Russia—clandestinely, of course; the party organ, published in the language of the Jewish masses, in Yiddish, appeared abroad under the name of *Die Arbeiter Stimme*. It is worthy of note that the formation of the Jewish "Bund" gave a year later the stimulus to the organization of the "Russian Social-Democratic Party," which united the formerly existing Russian labor societies. The "Bund" now joined the ranks of Russian Social Democracy as a separate autonomous group, although a number of Jewish Social Democrats who had adopted the viewpoint of assimilation or cosmopolitanism occupied a conspicuous place in the leadership of the Russian party at large.

At subsequent conventions the "Bund" endeavored to formulate its national program. At first, the tendency prevailed to limit the national element in the party platform to the use of the popular Jewish vernacular as a propaganda medium among the masses. At the third convention of the "Bund," which took place in Kovno in 1899, the proposal to demand national equality for the Jews was voted down on the ground that the attention of the workingmen should be concentrated upon their class interests and ought not to be diverted in the direction of national aspirations. The fourth convention of the party, held in 1901, similarly declared "that it was premature, under the present circumstances, to put forward the demand for a national autonomy for the Jews," although it realized at the same time that "the concept of nationality is also applicable to the Jewish people." Only after prolonged debates in the party press, and after a violent struggle with the centralizing tendencies of the Russian Social-Democratic Party, the convention of the "Bund," held in 1905, adopted a resolution, demanding "national-cultural autonomy" in the domain of popular education as well as public rights for the language spoken by the Jews.

In this wise, the national element gradually permeated even the doctrine of Socialism which, in its essence, had always been opposed to it and had placed in its stead the principle of internationalism and class interests On the other hand, an attempt was made to inject the Socialistic element into Zionism. Beginning with 1901, the *Poale-Zion* ("The Zionist Workingmen") began to organize themselves in separate societies which proclaimed the territorial principle of Zionism as the only means of solving the Jewish social-economic question, proceeding from the assumption that in the lands of the Diaspora the Jewish masses would always be barred from the domain of big industry.

5. The Revival of Jewish Letters

This national revival of Russian Jewry found its expression also in Jewish literature. The periodical press, particularly in the Hebrew language, exhibited new life and vigor, and in other domains of literary productivity various big talents made their appearance. As early as the end of the eighties, the two weekly Hebrew organs, the *ha-Melitz* in St Petersburg, and the *ha-Tzefirah* in Warsaw, were transformed into dailies. The Hebrew annuals pursuing purely literary and scientific aims, such as the *ha-Asif* ("The Harvest"), *Keneset Israel* ("The Community of Israel"), *Pardes* ("The Garden"), and others, made way for the more energetic *ha-Shiloah*, a monthly publication which reacted more rapidly on the questions of the day.^{1} This review, which is the equal of the leading periodicals of Europe, exercised considerable influence upon the views of the nationalist Jewish youth during the period of transition from the nineteenth to the twentieth century.

At one and the same time, considerable headway was made by the periodical press in the popular vernacular, called Jargon, or Yiddish. The *Jüdisches Volksblatt*, a weekly publica-

^{1} The *ha-Shiloah* was edited from 1896 to 1902 by Ahad Ha'am in Odessa, though it was published in Berlin. Beginning with 1903, it was edited by Dr. Joseph Klausner, also in Odessa.

tion, appeared in St. Petersburg from 1881 to 1890. The *Hausfreund*, the *Jüdische Volksbibliothek*, the *Jüdische Bibliothek*, edited by Spektor, Shalom Aleichem, and I. L. Perez, respectively, were published in Warsaw and Kiev between 1888 and 1895. *Der Jud*, a Yiddish weekly, was issued in Warsaw in 1899-1902.

As for the Jewish press in the Russian language, the former mouthpiece of the progressive *intelligenzia*, the *Voskhod*, which appeared at the same time as a weekly and as a monthly publication, leaned more and more towards the national movement. Another Russian-Jewish weekly, *Budushchnost*, "The Future," which appeared in St. Petersburg from 1899 to 1903, was Zionistic in tendency.

In the theoretic branch of publicistic literature the dominant figure during that period was Ahad Ha'am, whose articles endeavored to answer not only the exciting questions of the day, but also the perpetual problems of Judaism. His brief semi-philosophic, semi-publicistic essays, under the general heading *Perurim* ("Titbits"), served as a lode star for those who hoped to find the synthesis of "Jew" and "man" in modern Jewish nationalism. In a series of articles he lashes "slavery in freedom," ^{1} or the assimilation of the emancipated Jews of Western Europe; he criticizes the theory of "Nationalism without Zion," and the manifestations of a Jewish Nietzscheanism with its denial of the Jewish ethical doctrine. Not satisfied with mere criticism, he formulates in these articles the principles of a "spiritual revival" ^{2} in the sense of a

[^{1} *'Abdut be-tok Herut*, the title of one of these articles.]

[^{2} *Tehiyyat ha-Ru'ah*, the title of another article, based upon his report at the Zionist Convention at Minsk. See above, p. 51.]

nationalization of Jewish culture. The essays of Ahad Ha'am, which were subsequently collected under the title '*Al Parashat Derakim*, "At the Parting of the Ways,"' represent a profound and closely reasoned system of thought which is firmly grounded in historico-philosophical premises.

In the forefront of publicists of a less theoretic turn of mind stood the talented Nahum Sokolow, the editor of the *ha-Tzefirah* in Warsaw, who, after some vacillation, joined the ranks of political Zionism. In the border-land between journalism and literary criticism the most conspicuous figures were David Frischman and Micah Joseph Berdychevsky. The former emphasized in his brilliant literary essays the necessity of a "Europeanization" of Judaism, while the latter championed the cause of Nietzcheanism, protesting against the suppression of the "man" in the "Jew," and against the predominance of the spiritual over the material in the doctrine of Judaism. Berdychevsky is also the author of a number of sketches portraying the tragic split in the soul of the Jewish intellectual and the primitive harmoniousness of the old hasidic world.

In the realm of Jewish *belles lettres* S. J. Abramovich, known under his pen-name *Mendele Mokher Sforim*, the writer of the "Era of Reforms," remained as theretofore the acknowledged leader. The creative energy of this author, who mastered with equal skill both the national and the popular language,

¹ The first three volumes appeared in 1895-1904. [The fourth volume appeared in 1913. A German rendering of Ahad Ha'am's selected essays by the translator of the present volume was published in Berlin in 1904; a second enlarged edition appeared in 1913. An English translation by Leon Simon was issued by the Jewish Publication Society of America in 1912.]

attained to even greater heights during the period of the new Jewish martyrdom. His novel *Wünschfingerl*, "The Wishing Ring," which was originally written in Yiddish, and, in its Hebrew version, grew into a large volume, *Be-'Emek ha-Bakha*, "In the Valley of Tears," (1897-1907), constitutes a great epic depicting Jewish life during the gloomy reign of Nicholas I. and the "Era of Enlightenment" under Alexander II. A series of sketches, marked by inimitable humor, portray the disintegration of the old mode of life under the influence of the pogroms of 1881 and the subsequent emigration from Russia (*Bime ha-Ra'ash*, "In Stormy Days," and others). His autobiographical series (*Bayyamim Hahem*, "In Those Days") and his incomplete *Shloime Reb Hayyims* ("Solomon the son of Hayyim") reveal the power of rare psychological analysis.

Abramovich's literary activity, extending over half a century,^{1} earned for him the title of "Grandfather of Neo-Hebrew Literature" (*Der Zeide*).^{2} He was privileged to witness the brilliant successes of his "sons and grandsons" who came gradually to the fore, particularly in Yiddish literature. His younger contemporary, Isaac Leib Perez, wrote, during the first period of his literary endeavors, clever stories, portraying the life of the Jewish masses in Poland and distinguished by a powerful realism, often tinged with satire (his series *Reisebilder*, "Travel Pictures," and other sketches which were written mostly during the nineties). Later on, Perez leaned more and more towards modern literary symbolism, drawing

[^{1} He died, after the completion of the present volume by the author, on December 15, 1917.]

[^{2} The Yiddish equivalent for "Grandfather."]

his inspiration mostly from the mystic legends of the Hasidim (his series *Hasidish*, which was subsequently expanded into two volumes under the title *Volkstümliche Geschichten*, "Popular Stories," 1909).¹

Towards the end of the century, the talent of the great Jewish humorist Shalom Aleichem (S. Rabinovitz) ² attained its full bloom. He was particularly successful in his masterly delineation of the *Luftmensch* type of the Pale of Settlement, who is constantly on the hunt for a piece of bread, who clutches at every possible profession and subsists on illusions (his sketches *Menahem Mendel*). Using the popular vernacular with its characteristic idioms and witticisms as his vehicle of expression, Shalom Aleichem draws the pictures of the "Little People" of the Russian ghetto (his series *Kleine Menshelekh*), describes the joys and sorrows of their children (*Maassios far Jüdishe Kinder*, "Stories for Jewish Children"), and puts into the mouth of the unsophisticated philosopher of the ghetto, "Tevye (Tobias) the Dairyman," the soul-stirring epic of the great upheavals in this secluded little world (the series of sketches under the name *Tevye Der Milchiger*). To these big stars on the sky of Jewish *belles-lettres* may be added the host of lesser luminaries who write in the rejuvenated ancient language of the nation or in the vernacular of the masses, the Yiddish.

The literary revival manifested itself with particular vigor in the domain of poetry. At the beginning of the nineties, the

[¹ A collection of his sketches, translated into English by Helena Frank, was issued by the Jewish Publication Society of America in 1906.]

[² Died in New York on May 13, 1916.]

voice of Judah Leib Gordon, the poet of the "Era of Reforms" ' was silenced (he died in 1892). The singer of the national sorrow, Simon Frug,' who was carried away by the new ideas of Zionism, began to sing his "Zionids" in the Russian language, writing at the same time for the masses sonorous poems in Yiddish, though neither of them reveals the poetic charm of his older national elegies.

New stars now glisten on the horizon. The middle of the nineties saw the ripening of the mighty talent of Hayyim Nahman Bialik, who brought the poetical forms of ancient Hebrew speech to unprecedented perfection. The magnificence of form is matched by the wealth of content. The greatest creative power of Bialik is displayed in his treatment of national *motifs*. Himself the product of the rabbinical Yeshibah and Bet ha-Midrash, he sings of the spiritual beauty hidden behind these ancient and outwardly unattractive walls, in this antiquated citadel of the Jewish spirit, where the cult of intellectual knighthood reigned supreme, where the spiritual shield was forged which preserved a nation of lambs amidst a horde of wolves (his wonderful poems *Im Yesh Et Nafsheka la-Da'at,' ha-Matmid,* "the Diligent Student," and others). The sufferings and humiliations heaped upon his people by its enemies bring the poet to the brink of despair, for he realizes that the old shield has been laid aside, and no new shield has taken its place. He is filled with indignation at the indifference of the Jewish masses to the appeal for

[' See vol II, p. 228 *et seq.*]
[' See vol. II, p. 330, n. 1.]
[' "If thou wishes to know the fountain—whence thy martyred brethren drew their inspiration."]

regeneration sounded by Zionism (*Aken Hatzir ha-'Am*, "Verily, the People are like Grass," and others). At a later stage, beginning with the Kishinev pogrom of 1903, Bialik's lyre becomes more and more pessimistic, adopting the tone of wrathful rebuke and fiery denunciation.

In contra-distinction to this singer of the national soul, another contemporary poet, Saul Chernikhovsky, sounds the keynote of general human experience and the joy of living. He demonstratively prostrates himself before the statue of Apollo (*Lenokah Pesel Apollo*, "Before the Statue of Apollo"), offering to it the repentant prayer of the Jew for having denied the ideal of beauty. He raves about "Hellenism," the cult of joy and light, repudiating the one-sided spirituality and rigorism of old Judaism. Erotic *motifs*, descriptions of nature, ballads, rustic idylls—such are the characteristic features of Chernokhovsky's poetry which forms, as it were, a general human *pendant* to the poetry of Bialik, though yielding to it in the depth of literary conception. Both Bialik and Chernikhovsky fructified the field of Jewish poetry, which in the beginning of the twentieth century found a whole host of more or less talented cultivators, most of them writing in the ancient national language, though in a rejuvenated form.

Less rapid was the progress of Jewish scholarly endeavors. Yet, beginning with the eighties, even this domain is marked by an uninterrupted activity which forms a continuation of the scientific achievements of the West. The nineties inaugurate systematic efforts directed toward the elucidation of the history of the Jews in Russia and Poland. A series of scholarly researches, monographs, and general accounts of Jewish history, written mostly in Russian, make their appearance. Particularly noteworthy are the efforts to blaze new paths of Jewish historiography converging towards the national conception of Judaism. The Jewish historians of the nineteenth century in Western Europe, who were swayed by assimilationist ideas, viewed Jewish history primarily from the theological or spiritualistic point of view. The scholarly endeavors of Russian Jewry constitute an attempt to understand the social development of the Diaspora as a peculiar, internally-autonomous nation which, at all times, has sought to preserve not only its religious treasures, but also the genuine complexion of its diversified national life.

CHAPTER XXXIII

THE KISHINEV MASSACRE

1. Pogroms as a Counter-Revolutionary Measure

The frenzy of political reaction, which raged for two decades, was grist to the mill of the Revolution. Stunned by the blow it had received at the beginning of the eighties, the Russian revolutionary movement came back to consciousness at the beginning of the twentieth century, when the hopes for a change of policy on the part of Nicholas II. had been completely blasted. The agitation among the students and the workingmen, the "disorders" at the universities, the strikes at the factories, the revolutionary propaganda carried on in the underground press at home and in the public press abroad—all these endeavors were gradually co-ordinated within the frame of the two revolutionary organizations, the Social-Democratic and the Social-Revolutionary parties, both of which assumed definite shape between 1898 and 1900. The Social-Revolutionary party favored terrorism as a weapon in its struggle with the Russian Government, which had made use of all the appliances of police terrorism to suppress the faintest stirring for liberty. This official terrorism raged with unrestricted violence. Nocturnal raids, arrests, prisons, and places of deportation or of penal servitude, filled to overflowing with "political criminals," mostly young men and women—such were the agencies by means of which the Government hoped to stamp out the "revolutionary hydra," even when manifesting itself in the form of moderate constitutional demands. The revolutionaries fought terrorism with terrorism, and one of their victims was the reactionary Minister of the Interior, Sipyaghin, who was assassinated in April, 1902. The exasperated Tzar retorted by appointing to the same office von Plehve, one of the most experienced henchmen of the Russian political inquisition, who had long before, in his capacity of Chief of the Political Police, brought its mechanism to the top notch of efficiency.^{1} He was destined to play an ill-fated rôle in the martyrology of Russian Jewry.

It was easily to be foreseen that the Russian revolutionary movement would make a strong appeal to the Russian Jewish youth. Had any other cultured nation been tormented and humiliated as cruelly and as systematically as were the Jews in Russia it would surely have given birth to an immense host of desperate terrorists. True, the Jews supplied the revolutionary army with a larger number of fighters than was warranted by their numerical proportion to the rest of the Russian population. Yet their number was insignificant when compared with the atrocities which were constantly perpetrated against them. As a rule, the Jewish college youth joined the ranks of the Social-Democratic organization, which disapproved of political assassination. There were particularly numerous Marxists among the Jewish young men and women who had been turned away from the Russian institutions of learning and had gone to Western Europe where they imbibed the doctrines and methods of German Social Democracy. There were fewer Jews among the Social Revolutionaries (Gershuni, Gotz, and others), and these, too, did not as a rule take a direct part in the terroristic plots. As a matter of fact, the only terrorist act committed by a Jew was that of the workingman Hirsh Lekkert, in Vilna. Stung by the

[^{1} See vol. II, p. 381.]

barbarous conduct of the governor of Vilna, von Wahl, who had given orders to flog the Jewish workingmen in public for having arranged a demonstration on May 1, 1902, Lekkert fired upon that official. The governor escaped unscathed, and Lekkert paid with his life for the attempt. But on the whole, the revolutionary activity of the Jews was limited to the frequent political demonstrations arranged by the "Bund," and to the organizing endeavors of a certain section of the Jewish intellectuals who had joined the ranks of both Russian Socialistic parties.

Had the Russian Government been guided by a genuine interest in the body politic, the spread of the revolutionary movement among the Jews, which was the child of its own system of oppression, would have inevitably induced it to mitigate a system which was bound to turn millions of people into desperadoes. But the Russian Government was, properly speaking, not a Government. It was a caste of officials who had degraded the administration of the country to the systematic endeavor of saving their own personal careers and class interests, both of which were indissolubly bound up with unlimited autocracy. The Russian bureaucracy regarded the revolution as a personal threat, as a menace to its existence, and looked upon the Jewish participants in the revolution as their own individual enemies whose deeds were to be avenged upon the whole Jewish people. Thus there ripened in the mind of Plehve, the head of the bureaucratic inquisition, a truly devilish plan: to wage war against the Russian revolution by waging war against the Jews, and to divert the attention of the Russian public, which was honeycombed with the revolutionary propaganda, in the direction of the "aliens," thereby stigmatizing the entire emancipatory movement in Russia as "the work of Jewish hands," as an anti-patriotic cause which was foreign to the Russian people. It was part of this plan to engineer somewhere a barbarous anti-Jewish pogrom in order to intimidate the Jewish revolutionaries and to put it forward as a protest of the "Russian people" against the "Jewish revolution." "Drown the revolution in Jewish blood!"—this motto underlay the terrible scheme which, beginning with 1903, was put into execution by the underlings of Nicholas II. at the most crucial moments in the Russian revolutionary movement.

2. The Organized Kishinev Butchery

Needless to say, there was plenty of inflammable material for such an anti-Jewish conflagration. One of the criminal haunts of these incendiaries was situated at that time in Kishinev, the capital of semi-Moldavian Bessarabia. Until the end of the nineteenth century, the fifty thousand Jews of that city had lived in peace and harmony with their Christian neighbors who numbered some sixty thousand. At the beginning of the new century, these friendly relations were severed, owing to the untrammelled anti-Semitic agitation of a local yellow journalist, a petty official by the name of Krushevan. This official had been publishing in Kishinev since 1897 a local sheet under the name of *Bessarabetz* ("The Bessarabian"). Having originally embarked upon a moderately progressive policy, the paper soon sold itself to the local anti-Semitic reactionaries from among the nobility and bureaucracy, and was thenceforth subventioned by the Government. For a number of years Krushevan's paper carried on an unbridled agitation against the Jews. The Jews were accused of every possible crime, of economic "exploitation," of Socialism, of "hatred towards the Christians," of ritual murders, and of fathering the "Godless revolution." Favored by the powers that be, the *Bessarabetz* could do what it pleased. The censorship of the paper lay in the hands of the deputy-governor of Kishinev, Ustrugov, who during his administrative activity had proved himself a past master in the art of persecuting the Jews and curtailing the crumbs of rights that were still left to them. Under the auspices of such a censor, who was in reality a contributor to the paper, the latter was sure of immunity even when it proceeded to print appeals calling on the Christian population to make pogroms upon the Jews.

This agitation was particularly dangerous in view of the fact that the *Bessarabetz* was the only press organ in the province, the Government consistently refusing to license the publication of any other newspaper. As a matter of fact, Krushevan's activity in Bessarabia was so well thought of by Plehve that in 1902 the mercenary journalist received considerable sums from a special slush fund for the publication of a newspaper in St. Petersburg, under the name *Znamya* ("The Banner"), with a similarly reactionary anti-Semitic tendency. However, in the capital, the filthy sheet was unable to find readers. But as far as the *Bessarabetz* was concerned, its influence was clearly felt. Russian public opinion was affected by the poisonous doses administered to it daily. The sinister instincts of the mob became inflamed more and more, and there was the foreboding of a storm in the air.

In the beginning of 1903, Krushevan found an occasion to give a definite turn to his accustomed pogrom propaganda. In the town of Dubossary the mutilated body of a Russian peasant boy, Rybalenko, had been found, who, as was subsequently brought out by the judicial inquiry, had been slain by his uncle in the hope of appropriating his portion of a bequest. The *Bessarabetz* immediately launched a campaign against the Jews, accusing them of ritual murder. "Death to the Jews! Let all Zhyds be massacred!"—such appeals were almost daily repeated in the paper which was read in all the saloons and public-houses of Bessarabia. The unenlightened Russian mob itched for an occasion to lay its hands upon the Jews. An attempt at a pogrom was made at Dubossary, but it was frustrated by the local Jews who were of a sturdy physique.

On the eve of the Easter festival of 1903, mysterious rumors were set afloat in Kishinev itself telling of the murder of a Christian servant girl, whose death was ascribed to the Jews. In reality the girl had taken poison and died, despite the efforts of her Jewish master to save her life. The goings-on in Kishinev on the eve of that Easter bore the earmarks of an energetic activity on the part of some secret organization which was hatching an elaborate fiendish scheme. That criminal organization was centered in the local Russian club which was the rallying-point of the officials of the province. Shortly before the holiday, there suddenly appeared in the city an emissary of the political police, the gendarmerie officer Levendahl, who had been despatched from St. Petersburg; after Easter, when the sanguinary crime had already been committed, the same mysterious envoy vanished just as suddenly.

The triumvirate Krushevan-Ustrugov-Levendahl was evidently the soul of the terrible anti-Semitic conspiracy. Printed hand-bills were scattered about in the city, telling the people that an imperial ukase had been published, granting permission to inflict a "bloody punishment" upon the Jews in the course of the three days of the Christian Passover. The police made no attempt to suppress these circulars, for, as was subsequently brought out, they were in the conspiracy. Several police officials even hinted at the impending events in their talks with Jewish acquaintances. In the saloons and in the tea-houses, the approaching pogrom was the subject of public discussion. The Jews were fully aware of the coming storm, though they scarcely realized that it would take the form not merely of an ordinary pogrom, but of a regular butchery. On the eve of the festival of Passover, the representatives of the Jewish community waited upon the governor and the Chief of Police, praying for protection, and received the cool reply that the necessary instructions had already been given and that the proper measures for their safety had been adopted. The local Greek-Orthodox bishop asked the rabbi, who came to see him on the subject, whether it was true that there was a Jewish sect which used Christian blood for ritual purposes.

The conflagration which was openly prepared by the incendiaries broke out at the moment determined upon. On Sunday, April 6, the first day of the Christian Passover and the seventh day of the Jewish holiday, the church bells began to ring at noontime, and a large crowd of Russian burghers and artisans, acting undoubtedly upon a given signal scattered all over the town, and fell upon the Jewish houses and stores. The bands were preceded by street urchins who were throwing stones at the windows. The rioters, whose number was swelled by these youthful "fighters," seeing that the police made no attempt to interfere, began to break into the houses and stores, and to throw the contents on the street where everything was destroyed or plundered by the festive crowd. But even then the police and soldier detachments who were stationed on the streets remained passive, and made no attempt to arrest the rioters. This attitude served in the eyes of the mob as a final proof that the rumors concerning the permission of the Tzar "to beat the Jews" were correct. An immense riff-raff, in a state of intoxication, crowded the streets, shouting "Death to the Zhyds! Beat the Zhyds!"

In the evening looting gave way to killing. The murderers, armed with clubs and knives, assailed the Jews in the cars, on the streets, and in the houses, wounding them severely, sometimes even fatally. Even then, the police and military remained inactive; only when in one place a group of Jews, armed with sticks, attempted to drive off the murderers, the police stepped in at once and disarmed the defenders.

At ten o'clock in the evening the looting and killing were suddenly stopped. Rumor had it that the general staff of the rioters were holding a meeting concerning the further plan of military operations, and were making arrangements for a systematic butchery. The "army" soon received the necessary orders, and in the course of the entire day of April 7, from daybreak until eight o'clock in the evening, Kishinev was the scene of bestialities such as find few parallels even in the history of the most barbarous ages. Finding themselves defenceless and exposed to the passions of a savage crowd, many Jewish families hid themselves in their cellars, or in their garrets, and sometimes sought safety in the houses of their Christian neighbors, but the murderers succeeded in hunting down their unfortunate victims. The Jews were slain in most barbarous fashion. Many of them were not killed at once, but were left writhing in pre-mortal agonies. Some had nails driven into their heads or had their eyes put out. Little children were thrown from garrets to the pavement, and their brains dashed out upon the stones. Women had their stomachs ripped open or their breasts cut off. Many of them became the victims of rape. One gymnazium pupil who saw his mother attacked by these fiends threw himself single-handed upon them, and saved at the cost of his life his mother's honor; he himself was slain, and his mother's eyes were put out. The drunken hordes broke into the synagogue, and, getting hold of the Torah scrolls, tore them to shreds, defiled them, and trampled upon them. In one synagogue, the old *Shammes* (beadle), arrayed in his prayer-shawl, and shielding with his body the Ark containing the sacred scrolls, was savagely murdered by the desecrators on the threshhold of the sanctuary.

Throughout the entire day, wagons were seen moving in the streets, carrying wounded and slain Jews to the hospitals which had been converted into field-lazarettes.

But even this sight did not induce the police to step in. The Russian population, outside of a few isolated cases, made no attempt to defend the tormented Jews. The so-called "intelligent" public, the officials with their wives and children, the students, the lawyers, the physicians, walked leisurely upon the streets and looked on indifferently, and sometimes even sympathetically, while the terrible "work" was going on. The governor of Bessarabia, von Raaben, who, on the morning of the second day of the pogrom, was waited upon by a Jewish deputation begging for protection, replied that he could do nothing since he had received no instructions from St. Petersburg.

At last at five o'clock in the afternoon, a telegram was received from Plehve, and at six o'clock large detachments of troops, fully armed, appeared on the central streets. No sooner had the crowd noticed that the soldiers were ready to act than it took to its heels, without a single shot being fired. Only in the outskirts of the town, which had not yet been reached by the troops, the plunder and massacre continued until late in the evening.

It is needless to point out that had this readiness of the police and military to attend to their duty been displayed in Kishinev at the inception of the pogrom, not a single Jew would have been murdered nor a single house destroyed. As it was, the murderers and rioters were given a free hand for two days, and the result was that forty-five Jews were slain, eighty-six severely wounded or crippled, five hundred slightly wounded, apart from cases of rape, the number of which could not be determined. Fifteen hundred houses and stores were demolished and looted. The victims were mostly among the lower classes of the Jewish population, since many well-to-do Jewish families were able, by bribing the police heavily, to secure the protection of the latter and to have the rioters turned away from their houses. As against the enormous number of Jewish victims, there were only two fatalities among the intoxicated rioters. The Kishinev Jews seemed unable to resist the murderers and sell their lives dearly.

3. Echoes of the Kishinev Tragedy

A cry of horror rang throughout Russia and the more or less civilized countries of the world when the news of the Kishinev butchery became known. The entire liberal Russian press voiced its indignation against the Kishinev atrocities. The most prominent Russian writers expressed their sympathy with the victims in letters and telegrams. Leo Tolstoi voiced his sentiments in a letter which could not be published on account of the censorship.^{1} The humanitarian writer Korolenko portrayed the horrors of Kishinev in a heart-rending story under the title "House No. 13," in which, on the basis of personal observation, he pictured how the Jewish residents of one house were tortured to death by the rioters. The story was circulated in an illegal edition, its publication having

^{1} The following extract may show that the great writer had a profound insight into the causes of the Kishinev barbarities:

"My opinion concerning the Kishinev crime is the result also of my religious convictions. Upon the receipt of the first news which was published in the papers, not yet knowing all the appalling details which were communicated subsequently, I fully realized the horror of what had taken place, and experienced simultaneously a burning feeling of pity for the innocent victims of the cruelty of the populace, amazement at the bestiality of all these so-called Christians, revulsion at all these so-called cultured people who instigated the mob and sympathized with its actions. But I felt a particular horror for the principal culprit, our Government with its clergy which fosters in the people bestial sentiments and fanaticism, with its horde of murderous officials. The crime committed at Kishinev is nothing but a direct consequence of that propaganda of falsehood and violence which is conducted by the Russian Government with such energy. The attitude adopted by the Russian Government in relation to this question may only serve as a new proof of the class egotism of this Government, which stops at no cruelty whenever it finds it necessary to check movements that are deemed dangerous by it. Like the Turkish Government at the time of the Armenian massacres, it remains entirely indifferent to the most horrible acts of cruelty, as long as these acts do not affect its interests."

been strictly forbidden by the censor. But in Russia itself, the cry was stifled by the heavy hand of Plehve's censorship. and wherever a fraction of the terrible truth managed to slip through the barriers of the censor, Plehve sent out warnings to the papers threatening to discontinue their publication for the "pursuit of an injurious policy." Such a fate actually overtook the Russian-Jewish *Voskhod*, in St. Petersburg, the legal journal *Pravo* ("The Law"), and others. The entire Russian press was forced by the Government to publish the falsified version embodied in its official reports, in which the organized massacre was toned down to a casual brawl, and the inactivity of the troops was explained either by the inadequacy of their numbers—despite the fact that several battalions were stationed in the city—or by the incapacity of the police, while the dead and wounded were referred to in a vague manner so as to suggest that the victims of the "brawl" were to be found on both sides.

But the revelations in the foreign press were of a nature to stagger all Europe and America. The correspondent of the London *Times* published the text of a secret letter addressed by Plehve to the governor of Bessarabia, in which, two weeks before the pogrom, the latter official was told that, in the case of anti-Jewish "disorders," "no recourse shall be taken to armed interference with the urban population, so as not to arouse hostility to the Government in a population which has not yet been affected by the revolutionary propaganda." The authenticity of this letter is not entirely beyond suspicion. But there can be no doubt that instructions to that effect, rather by word of mouth than in writing, probably through the secret agent Levendahl, had been actually transmitted to the authorities in Kishinev.

From the fact that on the second day of the pogrom the governor was still waiting for instructions from St. Petersburg permitting him to discontinue the massacre it is evident that he must have received previous orders to allow it to proceed up to a certain point. The horrors of the Armenian massacres in Turkey, against which even Russian diplomacy had protested more than once, faded into insignificance before the wholesale butchery at Kishinev. Europe and America were deeply agitated. The Jews outside of Russia collected large funds for their unhappy Russian brethren, but their efforts exhausted themselves in sympathy and philanthropy.

The effect of the catastrophe upon Russian Jewry was more lasting. A mixed feeling of wrath and shame seized the Jewish public—wrath against the organizers and abetters of the terrible crime, and shame for the tortured and degraded brethren who, not having a chance to save their lives, had failed to save their honor by offering stout resistance to these beasts in human shape, who were sure of immunity. The poet Frug poured forth his sentiments in a Yiddish poem, voicing his sorrow at the physical helplessness of his nation and confining himself to an appeal to the kind Jewish heart:

Too keen and grievous is our pain, too weak our hand the blow to parry.

Come on, then, tender Jewish heart, and love and comfort to us carry !

Brothers, sisters, pray, have pity; dire and dreadful is our need: Shrouds we want the dead to bury, and bread that the living we may feed.¹

¹ *Schlaff is unser Hand zu streiten, stark un schwer is unser Schmerz,*
Kum-zhe du mit Treist un Liebe, gutes heisses jüdisch Herz!
Brüder, Schwester, hot rachmones: groiss un schrecklich is di Noit,
Giebt di Toite oif Tachrichim, giebt di Lebedige Broit!

A little later, the young poet Bialik gave powerful utterance to his feeling of wrath and shame in his "Burden of Nemirov."¹ He makes God address these words to the martyred nation:

Your dead have died in vain, and neither you nor I
Can say for what they gave their lives, and why . . . .
No tears shall flow for you!—the Lord swears by His Name—
For though the pain be great, great also is the shame,
And which of them the greater, thou, son of man, decide . . . .

In picturing the memorial services held in honor of the Kishinev victims at the synagogues, he angrily exclaims in the name of God:

Lift thine eyes and look how steeped they are in grief.
You hear them cry and sob and mournful prayers read.
You see them beat their breasts and for forgiveness plead . . . .
What are they praying for ? . . . . Tell them to protest!
To shake their fists at Me and justice to demand!
Justice for all they've suffered throughout the generations,
So that My Heaven and Throne shall quake to their foundations !

Neither the pogroms at the beginning of the eighties, nor the Moscow atrocities at the beginning of the nineties can compare, in their soul-stirring effect upon Russian Jewry, with the massacre of Kishinev. It awakened the burning feeling of martyrdom, but with it also the feeling of heroism. All were seized by one and the same impulse—the organization

¹ *Massa Nemirov.* This heading was chosen to appease the censor. As the name Kishinev could not be mentioned, Nemirov was chosen, being the name of the town which yielded the largest number of victims during the Cossack massacres of 1648. [See vol. I, p. 146, *et seq.*—In a later edition the poem was renamed *Be-'Ir ha-Haregah,* "In the city of Slaughter."]

of self-defence, as if to say: "Since the Government fails to defend our life and honor, then we ourselves are bound to defend it." The pogrom panic which spread over the entire South following upon the terrible days of April 6-7 led to the organization of self-defence societies in a number of cities. Plehve knew of these preparations, and found himself in a difficult position. He realized that these endeavors might interfere with the engineering of the pogroms, since the latter would no longer be safe for the murderers and plunderers, and he was, moreover, full of apprehension that these self-defence societies might become hotbeds of a revolutionary propaganda and provide a training ground for political demonstrations. These apprehensions were voiced in a circular issued at the end of April, in which the Minister instructed the governors, first, that "no self-defence societies should be tolerated," and, second, that the authorities should adopt measures for the "prevention of violence" and the "suppression of lawlessness." Subsequent events showed that the latter order was never put into effect. The first instruction, however, was carried out with relentless cruelty, and, during the following pogroms, the troops made it their first business to shoot down the members of the self-defence.

Such being the frame of mind of Russian Jewry, the ukase of May 10, 1903, opening up to the Jews for "free domicile" one hundred and one localities in various governments of the Pale of Settlement, which had hitherto been barred to them under the "Temporary Rules" of 1882, was received with complete indifference. As a matter of fact, many of the rural settlements, included in that ukase, were in reality towns which had been converted into "villages," at the instigation of spiteful officials, for the sole purpose of rendering them inaccessible to the Jews. The stolen property was now returned with a slight surplus. The Danaid gift, which seemed to be offered to the Jews as a compensation for the Kishinev horrors, could not but fill them with disgust. Parenthetically it may be remarked that the Government itself nullified the moral effect of its "act of grace " by issuing on the same day a new repressive law prohibiting the privileged Jews who were entitled to the right of domicile outside the Pale of Settlement from acquiring real property in the villages and hamlets. The knot of rightlessness was loosened by a hair's breadth in one place, and tightened in another.

Grief and shame over " the Kishinev days " armed the hand of Pincus Dashevski, a high-minded Jewish youth, against the most culpable instigator of the massacre—Krushevan. Dashevski, the son of a military surgeon, travelled from Kiev, where he was a student at the Polytechnicum, to St. Petersburg to inflict punishment on the miserable hireling of Judæophobia, who had caused the Kishinev conflagration by his criminal newspaper agitation. On June 4, 1903, he assailed Krushevan in the heart of the capital, on the so-called Nevski Prospect, wounding him in the neck with a knife. The wound proved of no consequence, and the " victim " was able to go home, without accepting the first aid proffered to him in a Jewish drug store nearby. Dashevski was arrested and brought to trial. At the preliminary examination he frankly confessed that he had intended to avenge the Kishinev massacre by killing Krushevan. Krushevan, now more ferocious than ever, demanded in his newspaper *Znamya* that the Jewish avenger be court-martialled and executed, and his demand was echoed by the entire anti-Semitic press. The case was tried in a district court behind closed doors, the Government of Plehve evidently fearing the appearance of the sanguinary ghost of Kishinev in the court-room.

Krushevan was represented by the anti-Semitic lawyer Shmakov, who subsequently figured in the Beilis trial. The counsel for Dashevski (the lawyer Gruzenberg and others) pleaded that his client's act had been inspired by the intention not to kill, but merely to voice his protest against the unbridled criminal activity of Krushevan. Dashevski received the severe sentence of penal military service for five years (August 26). An appeal was taken to the Senate, but the judgment of the lower court was sustained. The youth who, in a fit of righteous indignation, had given vent to the outraged feelings of his martyred nation, was put in chains and sent into the midst of murderers and thieves, while the venal instigator, whose hands were stained with the blood of numerous victims, escaped unscathed, and assisted by public funds, continued his criminal activity of fanning the hatred of the populace against the Jews.

4. Doctor Herzl's Visit to Russia

The alert bureaucratic mind of Plehve was quick to make its deductions from the Dashevski case. He realized that the Kishinev massacre would inflame the national Jewish sentiment and divert the national or Zionist cause into the channel of the revolutionary movement. Accordingly, on June 24, 1903, Plehve issued a circular to the governors, which was marked "strictly confidential," and sent out through the Police Department, ordering the adoption of energetic measures against "the propaganda of the ideas of Zionism," which had departed from its original aim—the transfer of Jews to Palestine—and "had directed its activity towards strengthening the Jewish national idea," preaching "the organization of the Jews in secluded societies in the places of their present domicile." Acting upon these orders, the police began to persecute the Zionists in a number of cities, prohibiting the sale of Jewish Colonial Trust shares, collections for the Jewish National Fund, and meetings and conferences of the Zionist societies.

Shortly thereafter, on July 25, the leader of the Zionists, Dr. Herzl, arrived in St. Petersburg to induce the Russian authorities to discontinue these persecutions. Apart from this immediate object, Herzl had another more important mission in mind. He hoped to obtain a promise from the Russian Government to exert a diplomatic pressure upon Turkey in favor of permitting the settlement of Jews in Palestine on a large scale. During his four interviews with Plehve, the Zionist leader succeeded in convincing the minister that "it was in keeping with the interests of the Russian Government to assist the Zionist movement." Plehve replied—and subsequently confirmed his reply in writing—that the Russian Government was willing to help Zionism so long as its political activity would be directed towards the attainment of its aims outside of Russia, towards the creation of a Jewish center in Palestine and the emigration of the Jews from Russia, but that as soon as the movement would be turned inwards, that is, towards the propaganda of the Jewish national idea and the organization of Jewry in Russia itself, it would not be tolerated, being subversive of the Russian national policies. Herzl assured Plehve that political Zionism *sans phrase* had no other aim in view, except the creation of a center outside of the Diaspora.

Both Plehve and Herzl seemed to be satisfied with the results of their conversation. Herzl saw also the Minister of Finance, Witte, and the Minister of Foreign Affairs, Lamsdorff, and left St. Petersburg in a hopeful mood. On his way to St. Petersburg, particularly during his stay in Vilna, Herzl was the object of stormy ovations by the Zionists. At the same time, he was severely criticized by the representatives of other Jewish political groups who thought that he had lowered the national dignity of the Jewish people by conducting negotiations for the salvation of Jewry with the man on whose forehead was stamped the Cain's mark of Kishinev.

It seems that the severe crisis which had set in for political Zionism, when the hope for obtaining a charter from the Sultan had receded into a distance, had impelled Herzl to catch at a straw, at negotiations with the Russian Government. He was evidently of the opinion that the Russian Pharaohs who had countenanced the methods of reducing the Jewish population in Russia, such as had been practised at Kishinev, might be willing to achieve the same object by rendering its diplomatic assistance to the Zionist plans. A pledge in this direction was actually given to Herzl. But Herzl overestimated the importance of the promises made to him by potentates who merely looked upon him as a noble-minded dreamer.

Two weeks after Herzl's visit to St. Petersburg, the acuteness of the Zionist crisis manifested itself at the sixth Congress at Basle (August 11-16, 1903). On that occasion Herzl announced his new project, the colonization of Uganda, in British East Africa, by virtue of a charter which had been offered to him by the British Government. He pointed out that this project had a definite aim in view—the amelioration of the terrible condition of Russian Jewry, for which purpose Zion at that particular moment was not available. Herzl's pronouncement rent the Congress in twain: one section seized enthusiastically upon the Uganda project, which held out the promise of at least a temporary shelter in Africa, a *Nachtasyl*, for a part of the agonized nation. The other section protested violently against this attempt to create a "Zionism without Zion," against the abandonment of Palestine and the higher aspirations of the movement. After many stormy and soul-stirring scenes, the majority of the Congress adopted a resolution to send an expedition to Uganda to investigate the proffered country from the point of view of its fitness for Jewish colonization. Thereupon, all the opponents of the Uganda project, the so-called *Neinsager* (the "Nay-sayers"), mostly Russian Zionists, left the Congress hall in a body.

The movement was now rent by a severe conflict, the result of the struggle between the two principles which had long been intermingled in the theoretic foundations of Zionism: Palestinianism and Territorialism. This internal conflict culminated in an open split between these two principles. Out of the Zionist movement was born the Territorialist Organization, which proclaimed as its object the creation of a Jewish autonomous center on any available point of the globe. For the blood of Kishinev cried out for an exodus from the new Egypt. The emigration to the United States, where the prisoners of Tzardom had in the course of twenty years, beginning with 1881, succeeded in forming a big Jewish center, had passed the million mark, and was expected to assume larger and larger dimensions. The Jewish public press insisted on the necessity "of regulating the emigration to America not only as a social-economic, but also as a national factor." It was pointed out that a considerable portion of the historic national center in Russia and Poland was, under the pressure of external events, in the process of removing to North America, and that practical Jewish politics had the direct duty of organizing this great rising center of Jewry.

CHAPTER XXXIV

CONTINUED POGROMS AND THE RUSSO-JAPANESE WAR

1. The Pogrom at Homel and the Jewish Self-Defence

No sooner had the Zionist Congress, at which the heated discussions concerning the salvation of Judaism were intermingled with sobs bemoaning the martyrs of Kishinev, concluded its sessions than a new catastrophe broke out in the dominions of the Tzar—the pogrom at Homel, in the Government of Moghilev. In this lively White-Russian town, in which the twenty thousand Jews formed fully one-half of the population, public Jewish life was marked by great vigor. There existed in the city important societies of Zionists and Socialists. Both of these parties had organized several self-defence contingents, and it was to be expected that the disgrace of Kishinev would not be repeated at Homel, and that, in the case of an attack, the Jews would give a good account of themselves.

On August 29, 1903, a fight broke out on the market-place between a crowd of Jews and Christians. The cause of the quarrel was a trivial incident, one peasant trying to carry off from a Jewish store a barrel of herrings at a lower price than the one demanded by the storekeeper. The rowdyish purchaser was pushed out of the store, but the peasants on the marketplace took sides with him, and in the ensuing fight between them and the Jew, one peasant was accidently killed. The peasants were scared and took to their heels, while the police began to make arrests among the Jews. The Jews might have been satisfied with the fact that their energetic attitude had succeeded in preventing a pogrom, did they not anticipate the revenge which was sure to be wreaked upon them.

Two days passed in a state of tense agitation. On the third day, on September 1, a crowd of Russian workingmen, numbering about two hundred, issued forth from the railroad shops, and began to demolish Jewish residences and houses of worship. The rioters were joined by a mob of stone-cutters, daylaborers, and ragamuffins. Here and there the crowd was incited by a few "intellectuals": a merchant, a student, and a teacher. On the Konnaya Square, the mob was checked by a large detachment of the Jewish self-defence, consisting of several hundred men. The rioters were on the point of giving way before the gallant attack of the self-defence; but at that moment the troops appeared on the scene, and fired a volley in the direction of the Jews, resulting in three killed and several wounded. The assistance rendered by the troops filled the rioters with fresh courage, and they continued their work of destruction with renewed vigor. All over the town a chain of soldiers shielded the attacking hordes against the Jewish selfdefence contingents which tried in vain to break through the chain. The defenders were driven off with rifle butts and bayonets, while the rioters were allowed to destroy and murder without let or hindrance. In the evening, the pogrom was stopped; the results were twelve killed or dangerously wounded Jews, eight killed or dangerously wounded Christians, a large number of maltreated and slightly wounded Jews and over two hundred and fifty devastated Jewish residences and stores. Among those arrested by the police was a considerably larger number of self-defending Jews than of attacking Christians.

Two days later, the governor of Moghilev came to Homel, and, having summoned the Jews to the Town Council, treated them to the following harangue:

I am sorry for the unhappy victims, but how could such bitterness have arisen? Religious toleration in Russia is complete. The causes of the latest events lie deeper. The Jews have now become the leaders and instigators in all movements directed against the Government. This entire "Bund" and the Social-Democrats—they are all Jews. You are yourselves to blame for all that has happened. You do not educate your children properly. You have no influence over them. But at least you can surrender them, pointing them out to the Government, whereas you conceal them. You propagate disobedience and opposition to the Government among an uncivilized population. But the Russian populace does not care for it and turns against you.

It would seem as if Plehve himself had spoken through the mouth of the governor. The Russian functionary expressed with naïve and clumsy frankness the hidden thought of the Chief of the Political Inquisition—the idea of punishing the fathers for the revolutionary leanings of their children, who were to be surrendered to the police, and of discrediting the entire Russian liberty movement as a "Jewish cause." In a Government communication which appeared after the pogrom the events at Homel were reported in such a way as to suggest that they were brought about by an attack of the Jews upon Christian residents and upon the troops, in consequence of which the latter had been forced to fire in "self-defence." The final deduction was formulated thus: "The cause of the disorders lies in the extremely hostile and defiant attitude of the local Jews toward the Christians." Thus were the actual facts distorted in an official document, and the tortured were put forward as the torturers.

The Homel pogrom did not attain to the dimensions of the Kishinev massacre, nor was it as painful to the moral consciousness of the Jews. For in Homel the Jews did not allow themselves to be beaten and slaughtered like sheep, but put up a valiant defence. Had the troops not turned against the self-defence, the pogrom would not have taken place, and the cowardly rabble would have taken to flight before the gallant defenders of their national honor. Already in the spring, Plehve had foreseen that the Jews would attempt to organize a self-defence of their own, and he had in his previously mentioned circular declared in advance that this most fundamental right of human beings to defend their lives was "inadmissible." Accordingly, several Jewish heroes paid with their lives for having violated this ministerial circular. Their death was the foreboding of a new Jewish martyrdom. All this had the natural effect of enormously intensifying the revolutionary sentiments of the Jewish youth and of inspiring them with hatred towards a régime which permitted some of its citizens to commit murder and prohibited others to defend their lives.

2. The Kishinev Massacre at the Bar of Russian Justice

In the fall of 1903 the judicial investigation in connection with the spring pogrom in Kishinev was nearing its end. The investigation was conducted with a view to obliterating the traces of the deliberate organization of the pogrom. The representatives of Government authority and of the better classes whose complicity in the Kishinev massacre had been clearly established were carefully eliminated from the trial, and only the hired assassins and plunderers from among the lower classes, numbering about four hundred men, were brought to justice. Prompted by fear lest the terrible truth might leak out in the court, the Ministry of Justice ordered the case to be tried behind closed doors. By this act, the blood-stained Russian Government refused in advance to rehabilitate itself before the civilized world, which looked upon it as the instigator of the catastrophe.

In the court proceedings, the echo of which penetrated beyond the walls of the closed court-room, the counsel for the defence from among the best representatives of the Russian bar (Karabchevski, Sokolov, and others, who were Christians, and the Jews Gruzenberg, Kalmanovich, and others) succeeded in proving that the prisoners at the bar were only blind tools in the commission of the crime, whereas the organizers of the butchery and the ring-leaders of the mob were escaping justice.^{1} They demanded that the case be probed to the bottom. The court refused their demand, whereupon the lawyers, having stated their reasons, withdrew from the court-room one after the other.^{2} The only advocates left were the anti-Semite

^{1} One of the instigators, Pisarevski, a notary public, had blown out his brains before the beginning of the trial. Other instigators from among the Kishinev *intelligenzia* appeared merely as witnesses.

^{2} The speech of Karabchevski justifying his withdrawal was particularly powerful. He openly declared that the pogrom was only "the fulfilment of a criminal order given from above." "The whole of Kishinev," he said, "was converted during the excesses into an immense circus of antiquity, where, before the eyes of curious spectators from among the administration and the army, before a festively attired crowd, a terrible drama was enacted in the depth of the arena. From the one side defenceless victims were driven upon the arena, and from the other maddened beasts were set at them, until the signal to stop was given, and the frightful spectacle was ended at once."

Shmakov and other whole-hearted defenders of the Kishinev massacre, who regarded the latter as a manifestation of the honor and conscience of the Russian people. In the end, the court sentenced a score of murderers and rioters of the first group to hard labor or penal service, dismissing at the same time the civil actions for damages presented by the Jews.

Six months later the Kishinev case came up before the Senate, the Jews appearing as complainants against Governor von Raaben (who had been dismissed after the pogrom), Deputy-Governor Ustrugov, and the Kishinev Chief of Police, upon whom they fastened the responsibility. The bureaucratic defendants cynically declared "that the losses suffered by the Jews have been covered many times over by contributions from Russia, Western Europe, and America." All the eloquence of the well-known lawyer Vinaver and of his associates failed to convince the judges of the Senate, and the petition for damages was dismissed. The Government did not wish to create a precedent for compensating pogrom victims out of public funds, for "this might place the representatives of the administration in an impossible position," as was stated with naïve frankness by von Raaben, since it might become necessary to increase the imperial budget by several million rubles a year.

In the midst of these ghastly proceedings Plehve conceived the plan of "regulating the legislation concerning the Jews." In August, 1903, he sent out a circular to the governors, calling upon them, in view of the extraordinarily complex and tangled condition of the Russian laws affecting the Jews, to point out ways and means "of bringing these legal enactments into proper order and into as harmonious a system as possible."

In reply to this circular, the governor of Vilna, Pahlen, submitted an extensive memorial, in which he pointed out that all the restrictive laws within the boundaries of the Pale of Settlement ought to be repealed on account of their pernicious political influence, since they were driving the Jews into the ranks of the paupers or revolutionaries. At the same time he suggested to retain the repressive measures "against the manifestation of the injurious characteristics of Judaism on the part of certain individuals " and also to exclude the Jewish youth from the Christian schools and establish for them special elementary and intermediate schools under the supervision of Christian teachers. A few other governors, among them the new governor of Bessarabia, Urussov, also expressed themselves in favor of mitigating the repressive policy against the Jews.

In January, 1904, a committee of governors and of several high officials representing the Ministry of the Interior met to consider the Jewish question. From the very beginning the conferees were given to understand that in "the highest spheres" every thought of the slightest mitigation of the condition of Jewry was taboo. The only liberal member of the committee, Governor Urussov, subsequently stated that after the Kishinev pogrom and the agitation raised by it "one could feel quite tangibly the unfriendly attitude of the highest spheres toward the Jews"—in other words, that the hatred toward the Jews was shared personally by the Tzar and by his *camarilla.* The committee therefore applied itself to the task, not of reforming Jewish legislation, but rather of systematizing the anti-Jewish code of laws. Its labors were interrupted by the outbreak of the Russo-Japanese War, on January 27, 1904.

3. The Jews in the Russo-Japanese War

On the day following the declaration of war, the organ of Russian Jewry, the *Voskhod*, wrote as follows:

This is not the time to irritate the old wounds. Let us endeavor, as far as it is in our power, to forget also the recent expulsion from Port Arthur,¹ the pogroms of Kishinev and Homel, and many, many other things. . . . . Let the Jewish parents not think of the bitter fate of their children who had been thrown overboard [by being barred from the educational establishments]. The Jews will go forth into battle as plain soldiers, without any hope of attaining an officer's rank, or shoulder-straps, or distinctions—the blood of our sons will flow as freely as that of the Russians.

The Jews marched to the Far East to assist Russia in making the province of Manchuria part of Siberia in which they were forbidden to reside. The number of Jews at the front was disproportionately large—it amounted to some thirty thousand, owing to the fact that, in accordance with the usual military regulations, the Jewish recruits from the Western governments were generally despatched to Siberia, so that, at the very outset, they were near the theatre of military operations. Disproportionately large was also the number of Jewish physicians in the reserves. They were mobilized at once, evidently for the reason that they lived on their private practice and were not allowed to occupy any state or public office, whereas the Russian physicians were not drawn upon to the same extent, so as not to divert them from their administra-

¹ About two months before the war, the Russian viceroy of the Far East had prohibited the Jews from residing in Port Arthur and upon the Kuantung Peninsula, whence the Russians were expelled by the Japanese a year later.

tive, municipal, or Zemstvo services.^{1} Hundreds of Jewish physicians had to work and to encounter the murderous fire of the Japanese because of the fact that an unjust law deprived them of the right of civil service in time of peace.

While scores of thousands of disfranchised Jews were fighting for the prestige of Russia in the Far East, the whip of rightlessness did not cease to lash their brethren at home. In a number of places the authorities began to expel the families of the soldiers and physicians who had been sent to the war, on the ground that with the departure of the head of the family the wife and children had forfeited the right of residence, the latter being conditioned by the profession of the husband or father. This policy, however, was too monstrous even for St. Petersburg, and Plehve was soon forced to decree that the families of the mobilized Jews should be left in their places of residence, "pending the termination of the war."

Though the Government was compelled to relax for a while its oppression of the Jews, social Judæophobia, fanned by the chauvinism incident to war time, broke out with greater violence than ever. Irritated by the rapid failures of the Russian arms and by the unexpected military superiority of the Japanese, the reactionary press, headed by the *Novoye Vremya*, began to circulate preposterous rumors to the effect that the Jews were secretly helping the Japanese, their "kinsmen by race," in order to wreak their vengeance upon Russia for having perpetrated the Kishinev massacres. The story of the Jewish-Japanese alliance issued from the public press of the capital to

^{1} Out of the thirty physicians who were mobilized in Kiev twenty-six were Jews. In Odessa, the Jews furnished twenty-one physicians out of thirty.

make its rounds through the provinces, and each day gave birth to a rumor more absurd than the other: the Jews are exporting gold abroad, they are purchasing horses for Japan, they are collecting money to build cruisers for the Mikado, they are provoking England and America against Russia, and similar preposterous stories. It was clear that these rumors were the work of a gang of unscrupulous agitators *à la* Krushevan, who were eager to instigate anti-Jewish pogroms on a modern basis—the accusation of "treachery." This assumption is confirmed by the additional fact that these incendiary rumors were particularly circulated in February and March, before the Easter festival, the old-time pogrom season, just as in the preceding year the ritual murder libel of Dubossary had been kept afloat during the same months. "The incendiaries have already set out upon their work"—with these words the Jewish organ *Voskhod* warned its readers in its issue of March 11. A week later, the same paper had occasion to publish accounts of the panic which had spread among the Jewish population, particularly in the South. In Kishinev, a second pogrom was feared, calling forth an intensified emigration to America. In Odessa, the Jews were agitated by sinister rumors, and began to prepare themselves for self-defence. This state of alarm was reflected in the foreign press. It was rumored that the American ambassador at St. Petersburg had received instructions to make representations to the Russian Government—which rumor was subsequently officially denied.

Fortunately the Government itself came to the conclusion that the time of war was not a fit opportunity for arranging pogroms. The governors received orders to adopt energetic measures for the prevention of Passover excesses.

Governor Urussov of Bessarabia and the city-governor of Odessa addressed serious warnings to the Russian population. These steps had the desired effect. As soon as the police and population realized that the pogroms were not desired from above, the agitation collapsed; and in April the papers were able to tell their readers that "Passover has passed quietly everywhere." In his *Memoirs* Urussov tells us that, during the restless day preceding the Easter festival in Kishinev, he had been engaged, together with the Chief of Police, in working out a plan looking to the maintenance of public order in the city; during this conference he noticed that the Chief of Police was rather hesitant and puzzled. This hesitation continued until the governor received from Plehve a telegram in cipher, calling upon him to prevent pogroms. No sooner had Urussov shown the Chief of Police the deciphered telegram than the latter exclaimed: "Don't trouble yourself—now there will be no disorders in Kishinev." Such was the spirit in which the provincial administrators had been trained. Without a special order from St. Petersburg, they did not have the courage to suppress the pogroms.

4. The "Political Spring"

On the morning of July 15, 1904, the square before the Warsaw depôt in St. Petersburg presented a terrible sight. Upon the pavement lay the blood-stained body of Plehve, who had been smitten by the bomb of the Russian terrorist Sazonov while on his way to Peterhof where he was to report to the Tzar. This meant that the revolution had again raised its head. After two years of frenzied police terrorism, and in spite of all attempts to divert the attention of the public from the necessity of reforms, first by pogroms and then by the war against Japan—Plehve had insisted upon the declaration of war, hoping to drown the "seditious" movement in chauvinism—the revolutionary spectre was once more haunting the country. The martyrs of the autocratic inquisition perceived the "finger of God" in the calamities caused by the war and in the miserable end of Plehve. In February, 1904, the Russian censor confiscated an issue of the *Voskhod* in which a young Jewish sibyl, in a poem entitled "To Haman," referring to the biblical *Mene, Mene, Tekel u-Farsin*, predicted a shameful death for the new Haman who was easily identified as the hero of Kishinev. One could feel in the air the coming of a cleansing tempest. Even the reactionary Government was taken aback by the approaching storm. It did not dare to answer the terrorism of the revolution with police terrorism. On the contrary, it made an attempt to moderate the régime of serfdom.

On August 11, on the occasion of the birth of the heir-apparent Alexis, an imperial manifesto was issued, granting "favors" and "privileges" to the population, the most important of which consisted in the abrogation of corporal punishment for peasants and soldiers. On the same day, a ukase was promulgated in which the Tzar "thought it *just* to introduce, pending the general revision of the legislation affecting the Jews, several amendments in the enactments concerning their rights of residence at present in force." The amendments were trifling: the Jews with a higher education were permitted to live in the villages and acquire real property there, as well as to carry on business everywhere. Those who had participated in the Japanese war, and had distinguished themselves or had conducted themselves irreproachably were to be accorded the right of universal domicile. The wives and under-aged children of the Jews with a higher education were granted the right of residence even after the death of their husbands and fathers. These rights were the only ones which the Government thought it "just" to confer upon the Jews, who had sent thirty thousand people into the active army to fight on the fields of Manchuria. The Jewish public received this niggardly gift with chilly indifference, and turned its gaze to wider horizons which were then opening up before Russia. The country was on the eve of a "political spring."

On August 26 the post of Minister of the Interior was entrusted to Svyatopolk-Mirski, who in his previous capacity of governor-general of Vilna had displayed comparative administrative leniency. The new leader of internal Russian politics promised that he would strive for the restoration of "confidence" between the Government and the people by adjusting his actions to the demands of "true progress." The Jewish deputation which waited upon him at Vilna and the representatives of the foreign press were told that as far as the Jewish question was concerned, he would be guided by justice and "kindness." Unfortunately, at the very beginning he showed himself powerless to stem the new tide of pogroms. At the end of August, the Russian South was the scene of several "regular" pogroms, beginning with a quarrel in a Jewish store and ending with the demolition of Jewish stores and houses—as was the case in the town of Smyela, in the government of Kiev, on August 22, or in the city of Rovno, in Volhynia, where a similar attempt was made on the same day.

Soon these "regular" riots gave way to a new variety of pogroms, which were distinguished by a peculiar coloring and might be termed "mobilization pogroms." The mobilized Russian reserve troops, wrought up over their impending departure to the fields of death in Manchuria where the Russian army suffered defeat after defeat, directed their protest along the line of least resistance—against the Jews. The soldiers, fortifying themselves with goodly doses of alcohol, began their "gallant exploits," and, accompanied by the street mobs, engaged in the task of devastating Jewish homes, maltreating their inmates, and looting their property. A sanguinary pogrom took place in Alexandria, in the government of Kherson, on September 6 and 7. On the sacred day of Yom Kippur a horde of intoxicated assassins invaded the synagogue which was crowded with worshippers, and butchered there twenty people in a most barbarous fashion. Among the severely wounded, who soon afterwards died from the wounds, were several gymnazium and university students. The police made no attempt to stop the killing and looting, and only on the second day, when the excesses were renewed, the Cossacks were summoned from an adjacent town, and succeeded in restoring order.

A month later, the mobilized Russian reservists began to perpetrate a series of pogroms in the North, in the region of White Russia. In the city of Moghilev the lawlessness of the soldiers and the local hooligans assumed appalling dimensions (October 10). The poorest quarters of the town suffered most. Among the victims of the riots were also the families of Jewish reservists who had gone to war. From the capital of the government the pogrom epidemic spread all over the region. Everywhere the intoxicated "crusaders," prior to their departure for Manchuria, engaged in destruction, looting, and incendiarism. In some places, as was the case in the government of Vitebsk, the rioters acted with perfect religious toleration, and even attacked the police, although the center of the "stage" was still occupied by the Jews.

The Government was manifestly unwilling to adopt energetic measures against the "defenders of the Fatherland" for fear of irritating them still further and spoiling the progress of mobilization. It was not until the end of October that the mobilization pogroms died out.

5. The Homel Pogrom Before the Russian Courts

In the same month of October, 1904, the case of the Homel pogrom of the previous year came up before the Court of Appeals of the Government of Kiev, which held its sessions at Homel. The department of justice had taken a whole year to prepare the evidence, prompted by the desire not so much to investigate the case as to entangle it and present it in a perverted political interpretation. The investigation which had started in the lifetime of Plehve and proceeded under the pressure of the anti-Semitic reactionary, Minister of Justice Muravyov, resulted in a bill of indictment which was a flagrant example of deliberate misrepresentation. The whole affair was pictured as an anti-Russian pogrom which had been perpetrated by the Jews. According to this version, the Jews of Homel, wishing to avenge the Kishinev massacre, had taken up arms and attacked the Christian population on August 29, thereby calling forth a counter-pogrom on the part of the Russian workingmen on September 1, when again the armed Jewish self-defence had taken an aggressive attitude and thereby forced the soldiers to shoot at them. Sixty people were indicted on this charge, among them thirty-six Jews, representing the part of the population which had been the victims of the pogrom. The Jews who had dared to defend themselves stood at the prisoners' bar side by side with their assailants. Yielding to the pressure of public opinion, the Government decided to have the Homel case tried in open court, but the president of the tribunal was instructed to eliminate from the judicial proceedings all political revelations which might embarrass the Government. The élite of the legal profession, both among Jews and non-Jews (Vinaver, Sliosberg, Kalmanovich, Ratner, Sokolov, Kupernik, Zarudny, and others), assembled at Homel to plead the cause of the indicted Jews and to defend the action for damages brought by the Jewish pogrom victims. The trial was drawn out for nearly three months, reducing itself to a duel between the counsel who endeavored to bring out the facts, and the bench which was anxious to suppress them. The depositions of the witnesses and the cross-examinations of the Jewish lawyers succeeded in demolishing the entire structure of the indictment, but when the case reached the stage which was bound to lead to the detection of the real authors of the pogrom and lay bare the conduct of the authorities, the president stopped the counsel despotically, denying them the floor. The gross partiality manifested by the president of the court had the effect that the counsel for the defence lost their patience, and on December 21, after a violent scene, refused to participate in the trial and demonstratively left the court-room.

This action aroused public opinion throughout Russia to an extraordinary degree; it caused a storm of indignation against this official miscarriage of justice, and the fearless defenders received innumerable expressions of sympathy. The indicted Jews, too, joined in the noble demonstration of their lawyers, which was in itself an eloquent plea for a righteous cause. The trial terminated in January, 1905, and ended in the acquittal of half of the accused Jews and Christians and a verdict of guilty against the other half from among both groups. The guilty were sentenced to comparatively light penalties—to imprisonment for brief terms—and, in addition, the court decided to petition the Tzar for a mitigation even of these penalties.

This verdict displayed the Jesuitic character of Russian politics. The reprobate murderers and plunderers from among the Russian group were either acquitted altogether, or were sentenced to trifling penalties and placed on the same level of culpability with the members of the Jewish self-defence whose only crime was that they had stood up for their life, honor, and property. The Russian law journal *Pravo* ("The Law"), the organ of the progressive Russian *intelligenzia*, published on this occasion a strong article which concluded with the following words:

The truth stands out in bold relief even in this verdict, and it does so against the wish of its authors. If, as is implied in this verdict, both the Jews and Christians are guilty of murder, violence, and plunder to a minimum degree only—for how could otherwise the extraordinary leniency of the verdict be justified?—then everybody is bound to ask himself the question: Who then is the real author of all the horrors that were perpetrated at Homel? Those who have followed the course of the judicial investigation with some degree of attention can only have one answer: Besides the Christians and the Jews, there is still a third culprit, the politically rotten officialdom. This culprit did not stand at the prisoners' bar, but the verdict is against him. . . . The best elements of the Russian public, and the Jews in particular, have been thirsting for justice and for the disclosure of the truth, but it was just that third accomplice who was afraid of justice and has managed to cover it up by a general amnesty.

Such was the end of the two ill-fated years of Russian-Jewish history (1903-1904)—years, marked by the internal war against the Jews and by the external war against Japan, filled with the victories of the reaction at Kishinev and Homel and the defeats of the Russian arms at Port Arthur, Liao-Yang, and Mukden. This ghastly interval of reactionary terrorism, which began to subside only towards the end of 1904, drove from Russia to America more than 125,000 Jewish emigrants who fled for their very lives from the dominions of the Tzar.

However, at the end of the long nightmare, the political horizon began to clear up. The tide of the liberty movement surged forward again and it looked as if the Russian people, and with it tormented Russian Jewry, would soon behold the new dawn. Yet the six million Jews of Russia were destined to pass through two more stormy years, standing between the firing lines of autocratic despotism and the revolutionary movement, and suffering the excruciating agonies of suspense, while hovering between degradation and emancipation.

CHAPTER XXXV

THE REVOLUTION OF 1905 AND THE FIGHT FOR EMANCIPATION

1. The Jews in the Revolutionary Movement

The "political spring," manifesting itself in the attempt of the Government, headed by Svyatopolk-Mirski, to establish friendly relations with the liberal elements of Russia, gave the first impetus to an open movement for political emancipation. The liberal "conspirators," who had hitherto been secretly dreaming of a constitution, gave public utterance to this tabooed aspiration. In November, 1904, the conference of Zemstvo workers, assembled in St. Petersburg, adopted a resolution pointing out "the anomaly of the political order" of Russia which is founded on autocracy and proclaiming the necessity of associating the representatives of the people in the work of legislation. About the same time, a large mass-meeting, which took the form of a public banquet, attended by lawyers and littérateurs, adopted a similar resolution calling for "the repeal of all national and denominational restrictions." Taking advantage of the temporary relaxation of police despotism, the press spoke up more boldly, while the better elements of the population began to organize themselves in all kinds of public bodies.

The Government was slow in making concessions, and harshly condemned the "boisterous assemblages" which called for changes in "the unshakable foundations of our political order." Nevertheless, an imperial ukase, published on December 12, 1904, promised a number of partial reforms—improvement of the legal status of the peasantry, enlargement of the activities of the Zemstvos, the establishment of a state insurance for workingmen, relaxation of the severities of police and censorship, and likewise "a revision of the laws restricting the rights of aliens," with the retention of those provisions only "which are called forth by the genuine interests of the state and the manifest needs of the Russian people." It is almost needless to add that the latter clause held forth no promises to the Jews. For their disfranchisement could always be justified by "the genuine interests of the state"—a state built upon the foundations not of law, but of police force. The carrying into effect of the promised semi-reforms was entrusted to a bureaucratic body, the Committee of Ministers. The services of the popular representatives were repudiated.

The new movement for liberty forced further concessions from Russian officialdom, but these concessions could only be wrested from it in small doses and were granted only after a desperate resistance. The "bloody Sunday" of January 9, 1905, marked the beginning of the open revolution in which social, economic, and political demands were interwoven with one another. The demonstration of the striking workingmen of St. Petersburg, who marched in immense numbers to the Winter Palace to present a petition to the Tzar for economic and political reforms, ended in a tragedy. The petitioners who marched with crosses in their hands, under the leadership of the priest and demagogue Gapon, were received with a shower of bullets, resulting in a large number of victims from among the participants in the demonstration, as well as from among the public. There were also several Jews among them—a first-aid nurse, a dentist, a pharmacy student and a journalist. This scandalous conduct of the Tzar, who replied with bullets to a peaceful appeal for reforms, led to a series of demonstrations, labor strikes, and terrorist acts in the provinces.

In the Western governments and in the Kingdom of Poland the Jews played a conspicuous rôle in the revolutionary movement, counting as they did a large number of organized workingmen. In Odessa, a Jewish workingman by the name of Stillman fired at the Chief of Police and wounded him (January 19). In Moghilev, a Jewish youth made a vain attempt upon the life of the local Chief of Police who was accused of having instigated the pogrom which had taken place there in the fall of 1904. These incidents served in the hands of the reactionary Government—on January 9, Svyatopolk-Mirski had been dismissed for his excessive leaning toward liberalism—as an excuse for continuing its oppression of the Jews as the "ringleaders of the revolution." The president of the Committee of Ministers, Witte, was the only one who advocated a different point of view. At the meeting of the Committee, held on February 11, he contended that "the hostile attitude toward the Government, now noticeable among the Jews, is due to the sad material conditions in which the bulk of Russian Jewry lives, being weighed down by the pressure of restrictive laws." Witte prophesied that the police authorities would be bound "to fight with redoubled zeal against the antigovernmental activity of the Jews, until the amelioration of the condition of the aliens, promised in the ukase of December 12, would be carried into effect."

2. The Struggle for Equal Rights

Notwithstanding these pleas, the Government was slow in realizing even the moderate reforms which had been outlined in the imperial ukase. In the meantime the representatives of Russian Jewry had decided to place before it their own more comprehensive demands. In February, 1905, several mass petitions, demanding equal rights for Jews, were addressed to Witte. A petition signed by thirty-two Jewish communities— St. Petersburg, Vilna, Kovno, Homel, Berdychev, and others— began with these words:

The measures adopted for the last twenty-five years toward the Russian Jews were designed with the deliberate end in view to convert them into a mass of beggars, deprived of all means of sustenance, and of the light of education and human dignity. Consistency and comprehensiveness marked the system of oppression and violence which was skilfully planned and carefully executed . . . . The entire machinery of the state was directed to one end—that of making the life of the Jews in Russia impossible.

The petition repudiates the idea, voiced in the ukase of December 12, 1904, of a gradual amelioration of the position of the Jews, and of a few "mitigations"; for "the insulted dignity of man cannot be reconciled to half measures; it demands the complete removal of rightlessness."

All the Jews of Russia are permeated at the present moment by one thought: that the cruel system of endless restrictions and disabilities undermines the very basis of their existence, that it is impossible to continue such a life . . . . Worn out by all they have had to go through, and filled with grave anxiety about their future destinies, the Jews are waiting at last for their entire enfranchisement; they are waiting for a radical repeal of all restrictive laws, so that, enjoying freedom and equality with all others, they may, shoulder to shoulder with the other citizens of this great country, work for its welfare and prosperity.

A memorandum couched in more resolute terms was sent by twenty-six Jewish communities—Moscow, Odessa, and others—and by the radical groups of the communities which had signed the first petition.

We declare—the memorandum states—that we look upon the attempt to satisfy and appease the Jewish population by any partial measures of improvement as doomed to failure. We expect equal rights, as human beings in whom the feeling of human dignity is alive, as conscious citizens in a modern body politic.

The memorandum of the Vilna community made the following addition to the last clause: "As a cultured nation, we demand the same rights of national-cultural self-determination which ought to be granted to all the nationalities that go to make up the Russian body politic."

Memorials and telegrams, addressed to the president of the Committee of Ministers, with the demand for equal rights, were also sent by many individual Jewish communities.

In the meantime, the general revolutionary movement in Russia proceeded apace. Professional organizations were springing into existence, such as the leagues of railroad workers, engineers, and lawyers. Here and there, huge railroad strikes were called. The college youth were in a state of ferment, and often went on strike. The agitation was answered by rifle shots and Cossack whips which were used to disperse the demonstrators. The extreme wing of the Socialist party resorted to terroristic acts. A tremendous sensation was caused by the assassination of Grand Duke Sergius, the governor-general of Moscow (February 4), one of the most detestable members of the house of Romanov. The grand duke, whose name was bound up with the expulsion of tens of thousands of Jews from Moscow in 1891 and with the cruel oppression of the Jewish colony still left there, was the victim of a bomb thrown by a non-Jew, the Social-Revolutionist Kalayev.

The surging tide of the revolution intimidated Nicholas II., and wrested from him still another concession. On February 18, 1905, three enactments were published: an imperial manifesto condemning the revolutionary "unrest" at a time when "the sanguinary war in the Far East" was going on, and calling upon all "well-intentioned persons" to wage war against "the internal sedition." A rescript addressed to Bulyghin, Minister of the Interior, announced the decision of the Tzar "to invite the worthiest men, invested with the confidence of the nation and chosen by the population, to participate in the consideration of legislative projects"—in other words, a popular representation with merely consultative rights. Finally, an ukase addressed to the Senate granted permission to private persons and institutions to lay before the Government their "views and suggestions relating to the perfection of the wellbeing of the state."

The progressive elements of Russia were not in a mood to be reconciled to the duplicity of these enactments in which threats and concessions followed upon one another, or to the pettiness of the concessions in themselves. They took, however, full advantage of the permission to "lay" their views before the Government, and indulged in an avalanche of resolutions and declarations, demanding the substitution of a parliamentary system of government for the existing system of autocracy. The Jewish institutions joined in this general campaign. The oldest Jewish organization, the "Society for the Diffusion of Enlightenment Among the Jews," in St. Petersburg, at a meeting, held on February 27, adopted the following resolution:

The proper organization of Jewish education such as would be in keeping with the social and cultural peculiarities of the Jewish people, will only be possible when the Jews will be placed on a footing of complete equality of rights with the rest of the Russian population. As a firm guarantee of the untrammelled cultural development and the complete equality of all nationalities, it is necessary that the legislative power and the administrative control of the country shall have the co-operation of popular representatives, to be elected upon the basis of the universal, direct, and secret vote of all citizens of the country, without any distinction of nationality, denomination or calling.

The need of a non-partisan political organization to direct the struggle for Jewish emancipation which was to be waged by all classes of Jewry—outside the small fraction which had already been united in the labor organization of the "Bund"—was universally felt.

Such an organization was formed at the conference of public-spirited Jews which took place in Vilna at the end of March, 1905. It assumed the name of "The League for the Attainment of Equal Rights for the Jewish People in Russia," and proclaimed as its object "the realization to their full extent of the *civil, political, and national rights* of the Jewish people in Russia." The complete civil emancipation of the Jews, the assurance of their proportionate participation in the Russian popular representation, "the freedom of national-cultural self-determination in all its manifestations," in the shape of "a comprehensive system of communal self-government, the freedom of language and school education"—such was the threefold program of the League.

It was the first attempt of a Jewish organization in modern history to inscribe upon its banner not only the demand for the civil and political, but also for the national emancipation of the Jewish people, the first attempt to obtain liberty for Jewry as a nationality, and not as a mere denominational group, forming part of the dominant nation, as had been the case in Western Europe during the nineteenth century. The central bureau of the League was located in St. Petersburg, composed of twenty-two elective members, half of whom lived in the capital (M. Vinaver, G. Sliosberg, L. Bramson, and others), and the other half in the provinces (Dr. Shmaryahu Levin, S. M. Dubnow,¹ M. Ratner, and others).

The first resolutions adopted by the League were in substance as follows:

To demand universal suffrage at the elections to the future parliament, with a guarantee of proper representation for the national minorities; to influence the Russian public to the end that the general resolutions demanding equality for all citizens should contain an explicit reference to the emancipation of the Jews; to call upon all the Jewish aldermen in the municipal Dumas to resign their posts, in view of the fact that under the law of 1892, which had deprived the Jews of their franchise at the municipal elections,² these aldermen had not been elected by the Jewish population, but had been appointed by the administration—an act which implied an insult to the civic and national dignity of the Jewish people.

[¹ The author of the present volume, who resided in Vilna at that time.]

[² See vol. II, p. 246.]

The last-mentioned clause of this resolution, adopted at the first conference of the League, proved effective. In the majority of cities, the Jewish members of the municipal Dumas began to tender their resignations, by way of protest against the disfranchisement of the Jews in the municipal self-government. At first, the authorities were somewhat embarrassed and made an attempt to appoint other Jews in lieu of those that had resigned, but seeing that the Jewish boycott continued, they became "reconciled" to the entire absence of Jewish representatives in municipal self-government. The protest of the Jewish aldermen was drowned in the general noise of protests and demonstrations which filled the air during the revolutionary year.

3. The "Black Hundred" and the "Patriotic" Pogroms

In this wise did the Jewish people, though chafing under thraldom and well-nigh crushed by it, strive for the light of liberty. But the forces of reaction were preparing to wreak terrible vengeance upon the prisoner for his endeavor to throw off his bonds. As the revolutionary tide, which had engulfed the best elements of the Russian people, was rolling on, it clashed with the filthy wave of the Black Hundred, which the underlings of Tzardom had called to the surface from the lowest depths of the Russian underworld. *Acheronta movebo* ^{1}—this threat was now carried out systematically by the Government of Nicholas II. in its struggle with the emancipatory movement. By letting loose the Russian "nether-world" against the liberal *intelligenzia* and the Zhyds,

[^{1} "I shall set the nether-world in motion."]

the reactionaries hoped to achieve three objects at once: to intimidate the liberals and revolutionaries; to demonstrate the unwillingness of the "people" to abolish autocracy in favor of constitutional government, and, finally, to discredit the entire revolutionary movement as "the work of Jewish hands." The latter end could, in the opinion of the reactionaries, be obtained best by convincing the Russian masses that "the enemies of Christ are the only enemies of the Tzar." An open anti-Jewish agitation was set in motion. Proclamations of the Black Hundred with the appeals, "Slay the students and the Zhyds!" "Remember Kishinev and Homel!" were scattered broadcast. The proclamation of the "Nationalist Society" of Kiev, Odessa, Kishinev, and other cities contained the following sentences:

The shouts "Down with autocracy!" are the shouts of those blood-suckers who call themselves Zhyds, Armenians, and Poles . . . . Be on your guard against the Zhyds! All the misfortunes in our lives are due to the Zhyds. Soon, very soon, the great time will come when there will be no Zhyds in Russia. Down with the traitors! Down with the constitution!

With the approaching Passover season, pogroms were openly organized. The papers were flooded with telegrams from many cities stating that riots were imminent. In some places the governors adopted measures to check the excesses of the savage crowd, but in many localities the pogroms were deliberately permitted or even directly engineered by the police. In the manufacturing city of Bialystok, the center of the Jewish labor movement, the Cossacks assaulted Jewish passers-by on the streets, invaded the synagogues and Jewish homes, cruelly maltreating their inmates and frequently searching them and taking away their money (April 9-10). During the Passover holidays, peasants made an attack upon the Jews in the town of Dusyaty, in the government of Kovno, looting their property and beating those that dared to oppose them. In the city of Melitopol, in the government of Tavrida, an intoxicated mob demolished and set fire to Jewish stores, and thereupon started to attack the houses of Christians, but the self-defence consisting of Jewish and Christian young men checked the pogrom (April 18-19). In Simferopol, in the same government, the Black Hundred spread a rumor that a Jewish boy, the son of a pharmacist, had desecrated a Christian ikon. A pogrom was set in motion which met with the resistance of the armed Jewish youth and was afterwards checked by the troops (April 22).

The most terrible outbreak took place in Zhitomir. In this quiet center of Volhynia the progressive elements of both the Jewish and the Russian population revelled in the joy of their political honeymoon. As had been the case in other large cities, here, too, the "bloody Sunday" of January called forth political strikes on the part of the workingmen, demonstrations on the part of the college youth, and the circulation of revolutionary appeals. The fact that the movement was headed by the Jewish youth was enough to inspire the Black Hundred to embark upon their criminal task. All kinds of rumors were set afloat, such as that the Jews had been firing at the Tzar's portrait on the field behind the city, that they were preparing to slaughter the Christians, and other absurd stories. At the approach of Passover, the pogrom organizers summoned to their aid a group of "Katzaps," Great-Russian laborers, from Moscow. The Jews, anticipating the danger, began to arm themselves in self-defence, and made their preparations openly. A clash between the "Black" and the "Red" was inevitable. It came in the form of a sanguinary battle which was fought on April 23-26, matching by its cruelty the pogrom at Homel, though exceeding it vastly by its dimensions.

In the course of three days, the city was in the hands of the black hordes who plundered, murdered and mutilated the Jews. They were fortified not only by quantities of alcohol, but also by the conviction that they were fighting for the Tzar against the "Sicilists,"¹ who clamored for "freedom" and a "republic." The Jewish self-defence performed prodigies of valor wherever they were not interfered with by the police and military, and died gallantly where the authorities actively assisted the savage work of the infuriated rioters. During the three pogrom days fifteen Jews were killed and nearly one hundred wounded, many of them severely. The casualties were mostly among young workingmen and handicraftsmen. But there were also some students among the victims, one of them a Christian, named Blinov, who stood up nobly for the assaulted Jews. The inhuman fiends fell upon Blinov, shouting: "Though you are a Russian, you are a Sicilist and worse than the Zhyds, now that you've come to defend them." The young hero was beaten to death, and the murderers were actively assisted by soldiers and policemen.

On one of those days, on April 25, a heart-rending tragedy took place in the town of Troyanov, in the government of Volhynia, not far from Zhitomir. Having learned of the massacre that was going on in Zhitomir, fourteen brave Jewish

¹ A mutilated form of "Socialists" which is in vogue among the ignorant Russian masses.

young men from the neighboring town of Chudnov armed themselves with cheap pistols, and proceeded to bring aid to their endangered fellow-Jews. On the way, while passing through Troyanov, they were met by a crowd of peasants and workingmen who had been aroused by a rumor that Jewish "slaughterers" were marching in order to exterminate the Russians. The infuriated mob fell upon the youths, and, in the presence of the local Jews, savagely killed ten of them, while the others were cruelly beaten. The following account of this ghastly occurrence was given by one of the survivors:

There were fourteen of us. We were on the way from Chudnov to Zhitomir. In Troyanov we were surrounded by Katzaps. They began to search us, taking away everything we had, and then started to beat us with hatchets and clubs. I saw my comrades fall down dead one after the other. Before the constabulary appeared, only four had remained alive, I and three other men. The constabulary ordered us to be carried to the hospital at Zhitomir, but on the way we were wrested by the Katzaps from the rural police and were tortured again . . . . I was roped and dragged to the priest. He begged that I should be left alone. The Katzaps made fun of him, dragged me out again, and started to beat me. The policemen began to tell them that "they would answer for me," since the constabulary had ordered them to get me to Zhitomir. "Well," said the Katzaps, "if that be the case, we will let him go, but before we do this, that hound of a Jew must have a look at his fellow-Zhyds." I was then dragged in an unconscious state to my comrades. I found myself in a pool of water. I had been drenched so as to make me regain consciousness. Then I beheld the dead bodies of my ten comrades . . . . No matter how long I may live, I shall never forget that sight . . . . One of them lay with his head chopped off; another with a ripped stomach . . . . cut off hands . . . . I fell into a swoon, and found myself here in this bed.

In the cemetery of Troyanov one may still behold the ten graves of the youthful martyrs who unselfishly went to the rescue of their brethren against beasts in human form, and were on the way torn to pieces by these beasts—ten graves which ought to become sacred to the entire Jewish people.

The Government reacted upon the Zhitomir massacre by an official communication in which the facts were deliberately garbled in order to prove that the Jews had called forth the pogrom by their conduct. It was alleged in this communication that, during their shooting exercises in the woods, the Jews had discharged their pistols at the portrait of the Tzar, had hurled insulting remarks at the police escort which was conveying a band of political prisoners, had issued a proclamation in the name of "the criminal party of the Social-Revolutionaries" in which the authorities of Zhitomir were accused of preparing the pogrom, and similar charges. The concrete object of the official communication is betrayed in its concluding part in which the governors are enjoined "to explain to the sober-minded section of the Jewish population that, in the interest of the safety of the Jewish masses, it is in duty bound to inspire their coreligionists who have been drawn into the political struggle with the consciousness of the absolute necessity of refraining from arousing by their behavior the hatred of the Christian population against them." Translated into plain terms, the Government order meant: "If you do not wish to have pogroms and massacres, then keep your hands off the liberty movement; but if you will persist in playing a part in it, then the Christian population will make short work of you, dealing with you as with enemies of the Fatherland."

Caught in the general revolutionary conflagration which flared up with particular violence in the summer of 1905, after the destruction of the Russian fleet by the Japanese near Tsushima, the Jews reacted upon the pogroms by intensifying their revolutionary activity and swelling the number of self-defence organizations. Russian Jewry played an active part in the two wings of the emancipation army, the Constitutional-Democratic as well as the Social-Democratic party, and was represented even in the extreme wing occupied by the Social-Revolutionaries. The majority of these Jewish revolutionaries were actuated by general Russian aspirations, and were often entirely oblivious of the national interests of Judaism. This, however, did not prevent the henchmen of the Tzar from visiting the "sin" of the revolution upon the Jewish masses. A vicious circle was the result of this policy: As victims of the old despotism, the Jews naturally threw in their lot with the revolution which promised to do away with it; thereupon uncivilized Russia vented its fury upon them by instituting pogroms which, in turn, pushed them more and more into the ranks of the revolution.

During the summer months of 1905, a new succession of pogroms took place, this time of the military variety. Wrought up over the defeats of the Russian army in Manchuria, and roused by the vile proclamations of the Black Hundred which pictured the Jews as the inner enemy, soldiers and Cossacks began to wreak their vengeance upon this inner enemy, assaulting and killing or wounding Jews on the streets of Minsk (May 26), Brest-Litovsk (May 29-31), Syedletz and Lodz (June 9). In the first three cities, the soldiers plundered and murdered only the Jews. In Lodz, they fired at a mixed Polish-

Jewish demonstration of workingmen. A regular butchery was engineered by the soldiery in Bialystok (June 30). During the entire day, the city resounded with the rifle shots of maddened soldiers who were firing into peaceful Jewish crowds. Fifty dead and a still larger number of wounded were the result of these military exploits.

During the same time a regularly organized pogrom occurred in the southern outskirts of Russia, in the city of Kerch, in the Crimea. On July 27, a peaceful political demonstration of the kind then generally in vogue took place in that city; among the participants were also the Jewish youth. By way of protest, the city-governor and gendarmerie chief organized a "patriotic" counter-demonstration, which was held a few days later, on July 31. Carrying a banner with the portrait of the Tzar and singing the Russian national hymn, the "patriotic" hordes, with the notorious local thieves and hooligans as the predominating element, sacked Jewish houses and stores, and, in the name of patriotism, looted Jewish property—even the so-called respectable public participating in the latter act. When the armed Jewish self-defence began to oppose the rioters, they were scattered by a volley from the soldiers, ten of them being killed on the spot. The subsequent inquiry established the fact that the pogrom had been fully prepared by the police and gendarmerie authorities, which had been in telegraphic communication in regard to it with the Police Department in St. Petersburg. It was a rehearsal of the monstrous October pogroms which were to take place a few months later.

4. The Jewish Franchise

In the midst of the noise caused by the revolution on the one hand and by the pogroms on the other, the question of popular representation, promised in the ukase of February 18, 1905, was discussed in the highest Government spheres of Russia. A committee, which met under the chairmanship of M. Bulyghin, was drafting a scheme of a consultative popular assembly; as far as the Jews were concerned, it was proposed to exclude them from the franchise, on the ground that the latter would not be compatible with their civil disfranchisement. This proposition, which was in entire accord with the general reactionary trend of Russian politics, called forth a storm of indignation in all circles of Russian Jewry. During the month of June protest resolutions against the contemplated measure were adopted by the Jewish communities of St. Petersburg, Riga, Kishinev, Bobruisk, Zhitomir, Nicholayev, Minsk, Vitebsk, Vilna, and other cities. Many resolutions were couched in violent terms betraying the outraged sentiments of Russian Jewry. As an illustration, the following extract from the Vilna resolution may be quoted:

In the proposed scheme of popular representation, we Jews, a cultured nation of six millions, are placed below the semi-savage aliens of Eastern Russia. The policy of pacification applied to other suppressed nationalities has given way to a policy of terrorization when the Jews are concerned. The mad system, consisting in the endeavor to irritate and infuriate the Jews by mediæval persecutions and thereupon wreak vengeance on them for the manifestation of that irritation, has now reached its climax . . . . We appeal to the Russian people, which is now called upon to renovate the antiquated political structure of the country . . . . We are of the hope that the malign vindictiveness toward the Jews on the part of the retiring bureaucracy, which is eager to carry over the ferments of corruption into the healthy atmosphere of the future popular representation, will not be realized.

Professor Trubetzkoy, who waited upon the Tzar on June 6, at the head of a combined deputation of Zemstvos and municipalities, pointed out in his famous speech that no one should be excluded from popular representation: "It is important that there should not be any disfranchised and disinherited." The Government was shaken in its resolution, and the Council of Ministers eliminated from the Bulyghin project the clause barring the Jews from voting, justifying this step by the undesirability "to irritate the Jews still further."

The Jewish question was also touched upon in the conferences at Peterhof, which were held during the month of July under the chairmanship of the Tzar, to formulate plans for an Imperial Duma. Naryshkin, a reactionary dignitary, demanded that "the dangerous Jewish nation" be barred from the Duma. But a number of other dignitaries—the Minister of Finance, Kokovtzev, the Assistant-Minister of the Interior, Trepov, and Obolenski and Chikhachev, members of the Council of State—advocated their admission, and the discussions were terminated by the brief remark of the Tzar: "The project [with the insertion of the Council of Ministers in favor of the Jews] shall be left unaltered."

By this action, the Government made itself guilty of a flagrant inconsistency. It conferred upon the Jews the highest political privilege—the right of voting for popular representatives—but left them at the same time in a state of complete civil disfranchisement, even with regard to such elementary liberties as the right of domicile, the right of transit, and so on. Only one month previously, on June 8, the Tzar had approved the "Opinion" of the Committee of Ministers—in pursuance of the ukase of December 12, 1904, the Committee had been busy discussing the Jewish problem—to the effect that the consideration of the question of ameliorating the condition of the Jews should be deferred until the convocation of the new Parliament. Evidently, the anti-Jewish conscience of the Tzar made it impossible for him to grant even the slightest relief to the Jews who from pariahs had been turned into revolutionaries.

CHAPTER XXXVI

THE COUNTER-REVOLUTION AND THE OCTOBER MASSACRES

1. The Fiendish Designs of the "Black Hundred"

Soon afterwards, on August 6, 1905, the so-called "Bulyghin Constitution" was made public, providing for a truncated Imperial Duma with a system of representation based on class qualifications and limited to advisory functions but without any restrictions as far as the franchise of the Jews was concerned. "Now," wrote the *Voskhod*, "the Jew has the right to be a popular representative, but he has no right to reside in the place in which the Imperial Duma assembles— in the capital." Russian Jewry, with the exception of its Left wing, was on the point of starting an election campaign to send its representatives to this mutilated Duma, in the hope of attaining through it to a more perfect form of representation, when the stormy course of events brought to the fore new threatening questions. This counterfeit of a national parliament failed to satisfy the Russian democracy, and the struggle with the Government broke out anew with unprecedented energy. Stormy political meetings were held at the universities and at the other institutions of higher learning, which, by an ukase of August 27, had been granted academic self-government. The autonomous professorial councils began to admit Jewish students to the schools, without any restrictive percentage, and the wave of an agitated Jewish youth was drawn into the whirling sea of the Russian student body.

A new succession of strikes followed, arranged by the students, workingmen, and railroad workers. A general Russian strike was being carefully prepared as a last resort in the struggle for a democratic constitution. The army of the emancipation movement was instituting a bloodless revolution, the temporary stoppage of all railroad movements and of all other activities in the country, in the hope of forcing Tzardom to an act of self-abnegation and the proclamation of civil liberties.

The month of September and the beginning of October were spent in these feverish preparations, but at the same time, the black army of absolutism was making its own arrangements for a sanguinary counter-revolution, for regular St. Bartholomew nights, directed against the participants in the emancipation movement, and particularly against the Jews. The plans of the emancipation army were universally known, but the terrible designs of the dark forces of reaction were effectively concealed. Only when the bloody undertaking was accomplished, was it possible to uncover the threads of the criminal pogrom organization, which led from the palaces of the Tzar and the highest dignitaries of state, by way of the Police Department, to the slums of murderers and hooligans. In the disclosures made by Lvov, in November, 1905, in his memorandum to Witte, the president of the Council of Ministers, the officials in the immediate environment of Nicholas II. who had organized the October pogroms were pointed out by name. They were the "patriotic" General Bogdanovich in St. Petersburg, who acted with the blessing of Archbishop ^{1} Vladimir and with the as-

[^{1} In Russian, *Mitropolit*, the highest ecclesiastical dignitary in the Greek-Orthodox Church. There are three Mitropolits in Russia, residing in Petrograd, Moscow, and Kiev.]

sistance of the Imperial camarilla and of many governors and governors-general in the provinces. During the month of September "fighting contingents" of the Black Hundred, whose number, as Bogdanovich boasted in the highest government spheres, amounted to one hundred thousand, were organized all over Russia. In every city the parts to be enacted by the administrators, the police and the pogrom hirelings from among the local riff-raff were carefully prepared and assigned. The pogrom proclamations were printed openly; the "manufacturing" center of this propaganda literature, as was afterwards disclosed in the Imperial Duma by deputy Urussov (formerly Assistant-Minister of the Interior), was located in the printing office of the Police Department. There can be no question that the Tzar was acquainted, if not with all the details of these preparations, at least with the general plan of arranging a counter-revolution by means of carefully engineered massacres of which the Jews were to become the chief victims. Millions of rubles for the organization of the pogroms were appropriated from a secret ten-million ruble fund, the disposition of which lay entirely in the hands of the Tzar.

Such were the conditions which ushered in the month of October, 1905. The first days of the month saw the beginning of the railroad strike; by the middle of the month it had already seized the entire country, accompanied in the industrial centers by a general strike in all lines of productive endeavor. In many cities, collisions took place between the revolutionaries and the military. At first, the Government made an attempt to resort to threats, and all over Russia rang the blood-thirsty cry of the Chief of Police Trepov: "No cartridges shall be spared!" But at the last moment, autocracy recoiled before the revolutionary tempest and gave way. On October 17, an imperial manifesto was issued, solemnly promising to bestow all civil liberties upon the Russian people—inviolability of person, freedom of conscience, liberty of speech, assemblage and organization, and a legislative Duma in which the representatives of all classes of the population were to have a voice. The manifesto made no mention, however, of the equality of all citizens before the law or of the bestowal of equal rights on the various nationalities, and even in the accompanying memorandum of Premier Witte, the author of the enactment of October 17, the subject was disposed of in a few nebulous phrases.

Nevertheless, even in this hazy form, the manifesto made a tremendous impression. Everybody believed that autocratic Tzardom had been vanquished by the army of liberty and that Russia had been finally converted from a state founded on police force into a body politic based on law. But, on the day following, all these hopes were cruelly shattered. On October 18, in hundreds of cities the carefully concealed army of counter-revolutionaries, evidently obeying a prearranged signal, crawled out from beneath the ground, to indulge in an orgy of blood, lasting a full week (October 18-25), which in its horrors finds no parallel in the entire history of humanity.

2. The Russian St. Bartholomew Night

The principal victims of this protracted St. Bartholomew night were the new Huguenots of the emancipation movement—the Jews. They were to pay the penalty for having assisted in wresting from the despotic Government the manifesto with its promise of liberties. In the course of one week, nearly fifty anti-Jewish pogroms, accompanied by bloodshed, took place in various cities (Odessa, Kiev, Kishinev, Kalarash, Simferopol, Romny, Kremenchug, Chernigov, Nicholayev, Yekaterinoslav, Kamenetz-Podolsk, Yelisavetgrad, Orsha, etc.), in addition to several hundred "bloodless" pogroms, marked in regular fashion by the destruction of property, plunder, and incendiarism. The pogroms directed against the Christian participants in the emancipation movement, such as intellectuals, students, etc., in Tver, Tomsk, and other interior Russian cities, amounted in all to a score or two. This disproportion alone shows the direction in which the organized dark forces were active. The strict uniformity and consistency in the carrying out of the counter-revolutionary conspiracy was too palpable to be overlooked.

The customary procedure was as follows: In connection with the manifesto of October 17, the progressive elements would arrange a street procession, frequently adorned by the red flags of the left parties and accompanied by appropriate acclamations and speeches expressive of the new liberty. Simultaneously, the participants in the "patriotic demonstration"—consisting mostly of the scum of society, of detectives and police officials in plain clothes—would emerge from their nooks and crannies, carrying the portrait of the Tzar under the shadow of the national flag, singing the national hymn and shouting, "Hurrah, beat the Zhyds! The Zhyds are eager for liberty. They go against our Tzar to put a Zhyd in his place." These "patriotic" demonstrators would be accompanied by police and Cossack patrols (or soldiers), ostensibly to preserve order, but in reality to enable the hooligans to attack and maltreat the Jews and prevent the victims from defending themselves. As soon as the Jews assembled for self-defence, they would be driven off by the police and troops. Thereupon, the "patriotic" demonstrators and the accomplices, joining them on the way, would break up into small bands and disperse all over the city, invading Jewish houses and stores, ruin, plunder, beat, and sometimes slaughter entire families.

The most terrible pogrom took place in Odessa. It lasted fully four days. The rioters were openly assisted by the police and troops, and were encouraged by the active support of city-governor Neidthart, and the criminal inactivity of the military governor, Kaulbars. The heroism displayed by the Jewish self-defence was strong enough to beat off the hooligans, but it was powerless to defeat the troops and police. Over three hundred dead, thousands of wounded or crippled Jews, among them many who lost their minds from the horrors, one hundred and forty widows, five hundred and ninety-three orphans, and more than forty thousand Jews materially ruined—such were the results of the battle which was fought against the Jews of Odessa during October 18-21.

Approximately along the same lines the pogrom campaign was conducted in scores of other cities, with a few lurid departures from the customary ritual, as, for instance, in Nyezhin, in the government of Chernigov, where the Jewish community, headed by the rabbi, was forced by the rioters, under the pain of death, to pronounce publicly the oath of allegiance to the Tzar. As a rule the pogroms which occurred in hundreds of cities, towns, and villages, were limited to the destruction of property, although even in small localities, such as in Semyonovka, in the government of Chernigov, the riots were occasionally accompanied by massacres. It may be added that the outbreaks were not confined to the Pale of Settlement. In a number of cities outside the Pale, such as in Saratov, Voronyezh, and other places with a small Jewish population, the Jewish communities were ruthlessly attacked.

Contemporary history is not yet in a position to depict all the horrors which were perpetrated upon the Jews in Russia in the latter half of October, 1905, or to trace with any amount of accuracy their underlying causes. Let us draw a veil over this bloody spectacle. There will come a time when the world will shudder on learning the truth about the bloody happenings and about the real culprits of this prolonged Bartholomew night at the beginning of the twentieth century.

The sinister counter-revolution which broke out on October 17, the day on which the manifesto of the Tzar was promulgated, threatened to drag the revolution into the abyss of anarchy. All were profoundly aroused by the perfidious Byzantine policy of Nicholas II., who with one hand waved the peace banner before the progressive section of the Russian people, and with the other plunged a knife into its heart—a knife which most of all was to slash Jewry. Not only the parties of the extreme Left, but even the Constitutionists who were willing to accept the promises of the October manifesto, had little faith in their ultimate realization. A reign of chaos ensued. The parties of the Left demanded now a democratic, now even a social, republic. The political and labor strikes, among them those arranged by the Jewish "Bund," assumed the character of anarchy. The peasant or agrarian movement burst forth, accompanied by the burning of manors and estates. Poland and the Baltic region were in the throes of terrorism. Moscow witnessed an armed uprising with barricades and with all the paraphernalia of a popular revolution (December, 1905). The Government quelled the Moscow rebellion, and resolutely adopted a policy of repression. Arrests, executions, punitive military expeditions, were the means by which the program of the Witte-Durnovo Cabinet was to be carried into effect.

The reactionary camarilla around the Tzar operated in full force, fanning the hatred against the Jews. On December 23, the Tzar received a deputation of the ringleaders of the Black Hundred, who had organized themselves in the "League of the Russian People." One of the speeches appealing to the Tzar to preserve autocracy was devoted to the Jewish question. The deputation begged the Tzar "not to give equal rights to the Jews." To this Nicholas replied laconically: "I shall think it over."

3. The Undaunted Struggle for Equal Rights

The terrible October calamities were faced by Russian Jewry in a spirit of courage and fortitude. It stood alone in its sorrow. The progressive elements of Russian society which were themselves in the throes of a great crisis reacted feebly upon the sufferings of the Jewish people which had become the scape-goat of the counter-revolution. The indifference of the outside world, however, was counteracted by the rise of the Jewish national sentiment among the better classes of Russian Jewry. One month after the pogrom bacchanalia, the "League for the Attainment of Equal Rights for the Jewish People" held its second convention in St. Petersburg. The Convention which lasted four days (November 22-25) gave public utterance to the feeling of profound national indignation. It voted down the motion to send a deputation to Count Witte, asking for the immediate grant of equal rights to the Jews. In the resolution repudiating this step the policy of the Government was characterized in these words:

The facts have incontrovertibly proved that the recent pogroms, appalling by their dimensions and by the number of their victims, have been staged with the open connivance and, in many cases, with the immediate assistance and sometimes even under the direction of the police and highest local administration; that the Government, not at all abashed by the monstrous crimes of its executive organs, the local representatives of State authority, has not removed from office a single one of the suspected functionaries, and has taken no measures to bring them to justice.

In view of the fact that Count Witte has repeatedly stated that the Government does not see its way clear to proclaim at the present moment the emancipation of the Jews, supposedly in the interest of the Jews themselves, against whom the agitation of the popular masses might be intensified by such a measure, whereas, in reality, the pogroms are a result of that very rightlessness of the Jews which is fully realized by the masses of the Russian people and by the so-called Black Hundred—the Convention resolves that the sending of a deputation to Count Witte and the entering into negotiations with him will achieve no purpose, and that, instead, all efforts shall be concentrated upon organizing Russian Jewry in the struggle for its equality of citizenship by joining the ranks of the general movement for liberty.

Imbued with the spirit of martyrdom, the Convention remembered the martyr Dashevski, the avenger of the Kishinev massacre,^{1} and passed a resolution to convey to the youthful sufferer, who was then languishing in a penal military company, its "enthusiastic greetings."

[^{1} See above, p. 81.]

In an outburst of national enthusiasm the Convention adopted the following bold resolution:

In the interest of realizing to their full extent the civil, political, and national rights of the Jewish nationality in Russia, the Convention resolves as follows:

To proceed without delay to call, on the basis of universal and equal suffrage, without discrimination of sex, and by a direct secret vote, an All-Russian Jewish National Assembly in order to establish, in accordance with the will of the entire Jewish population, the forms and principles of its national self-determination as well as the foundations of its internal organization.

It was the project of a national Synedrion, radically different in its conception from the Napoleonic Synedrion convened in 1807.

The third convention of the "League of Equal Rights" was held on February 10-13, 1906, during the election campaign to the first Imperial Duma. The proposal of the Left wing of the League to boycott the Duma, on the ground that it "will prove a bulwark of reaction"—a prediction which was fully justified by events—and to refrain from taking part in the elections, was voted down. On the contrary, a resolution was passed, calling upon the Jews to take a most active part in the elections, to nominate everywhere their own Jewish candidates, and, wherever this was impossible, to give their votes to the non-Jewish candidates on condition that they pledge themselves to support in the Duma the civil, political, and national rights of the Jewish people. The resolution, moreover, contained this clause: "To insist that the Jewish question in the Duma shall be settled unconditionally in connection with the fundamental articles of the Constitution and with the questions of elementary liberties to be granted to all citizens."

An election campaign was set in motion and carried on under the most difficult circumstances. The police authorities took advantage of the state of war which had been proclaimed in many places to interfere with a comprehensive pre-election propaganda, and at the same time the Black Hundred tried to intimidate the Jews by holding out the menace of pogroms during the approaching Passover season. In Poland, the anti-Semitic chauvinists threatened the Jews with all possible reprisals for their "audacious intention" to nominate their own candidates for the Duma, alongside of the candidates of the Christian Poles. Simultaneously, the Jewish group of the Left, the "Bund" and others, followed the policy of boycotting the Duma and did their best to interfere with the elections. However, all these apprehensions proved groundless. The Passover and election pogroms did not take place, and Russian Jewry displayed a vigorous activity in the elections, with the result that twelve Jewish deputies were sent to the first Duma. The most active among these deputies were M. Vinaver, one of the leaders of the general Russian Constitutional-Democratic party and president of the "League for the Attainment of Equal Rights"; Dr. Shmaryahu Levin, the well-known Zionist; L. Bramson, actively identified with Jewish educational activities, who was affiliated with the Russian Democratic group, known as the *Trudoviki*, or "Laborites." All the Jewish deputies were united on the nationalistic platform formulated by the "League for the Attainment of Equal Rights." By a resolution passed at the fourth Convention of the League, held on May 9-13, 1906, they pledged themselves to co-ordinate their actions in all questions pertaining to Jewish emancipation and to abide by a common discipline, without, however, forming a separate parliamentary fraction.

4. The Jewish Question Before the First Duma

The first Duma was convened on April 27, 1906, and barely three months later, on July 8, it was dissolved, or rather dispersed by the Tzar, for having displayed a spirit of excessive opposition. The prevailing element in the first Duma was the Constitutional-Democratic majority to which, by their political sympathies, the bulk of Russian Jewry and ten of its twelve representatives in the Duma—the other two stood a little more to the Left—belonged. It was natural for the Jews to expect that a Parliament of this complexion would have no difficulty in solving the question of equal rights for the Jews as one of the most fundamental prerequisites of civil liberty. Unfortunately, this expectation was not justified. The entire brief session of the Duma was spent in an uninterrupted struggle of the Opposition with the unscrupulous Government which was then headed by Goremykin, a hide-bound reactionary. True, in its reply to the speech from the throne, the Duma declared that "neither liberty nor order can be firmly established without the equality of all citizens before the law." But in the pronouncement of the Government of May 13 no word was said about this equality of citizenship. The Jewish deputy Vinaver delivered a powerful speech, in which, among other things, he spoke as follows:

From this platform, from which so much has been said about political liberties, we Jews, the representatives of one of the most tortured nationalities in the land, have not uttered a single word about ourselves, because we did not consider it seemly to speak here of civil inequality . . . . Now, however, it is becoming clear to us that the Government has made up its mind to continue on the same road on which it has gone until now, and we are, therefore, bound to declare that, so long as you will connive at civil slavery, there will be no peace in the land.

The mistake made by the Jewish deputies consisted just in the fact that they had not "uttered a single word" about themselves on a former occasion, in reply to the speech from the Throne which had equally failed to make the slightest mention of civil equality—practically affecting only the Jews—and that they did not utter that word with that feeling of righteous indignation to which the representatives of "the most tortured nationality" in Russia were morally entitled.

Later on, the debates in the Duma concerning the Jewish question were, by the force of events, concentrated upon the pogrom policy of the Government. On May 8 an interpellation was introduced regarding the complicity of the Imperial Police Department in instigating the pogroms of 1905. Stolypin, the Minister of the Interior, promised to reply to the interpellation, which was substantiated by documentary evidence, a month later. But before that term had elapsed a new sanguinary pogrom broke out in Bialystok.

In this center of the Jewish revolutionary and labor movement, where, in 1905, the police and troops had already twice staged a Jewish massacre, a new conspiracy was being hatched by the police and military against "the authors of the liberty movement." An accidental act of terrorism, the assassination of the Chief of Police by an unknown culprit, gave the police conspirators a proper occasion to execute their terrible design. On June 1, during a church procession, a pistol was discharged by an *agent provocateur* from among the Black Hundred, and at once a rumor spread like wildfire among the crowd that "the Jewish anarchists are firing at the Christians." The pogrom flared up on the spot. In the course of two days the mob was busy demolishing Jewish houses and stores and attacking the Jews, while at the same time the police and military were systematically firing at the Jews not only on the streets but also in the houses, in which the unfortunate tried to hide. The bestialities of Kishinev were enacted again. Entire families were slaughtered, human beings were tortured, and hacked to pieces; limbs were cut off from the body, nails driven into the heads. . . . . Eighty dead and hundreds of wounded Jews were the result of this new exploit of the counter-revolutionaries.

On June 2, the Imperial Duma received the heart-rending news of the Bialystok massacre, and right there, after the passionate speeches of Dr. Levin, Rodichev, and other deputies, passed a resolution to bring in an interpellation to be answered by the Government within a fixed date, and to appoint a parliamentary commission which was to investigate the events on the spot. Three Duma deputies left at once for Bialystok, and on their return submitted to the Duma an unvarnished account which incontrovertibly established the fact that the Bialystok crime had been carefully prepared as a counter-revolutionary act, and that the peaceful Jewish population had been pitilessly shot down by the police and soldiery.

On June 5, three days after the appearance of the bloody spectre of Bialystok in the Duma hall, a bill dealing with civil equality for the Jews came up for discussion. The burning problem involving the disfranchisement of six million human beings was discussed side by side with the question of a few petty class discriminations and with the entirely separate question of women's rights. The entire treatment of the subject by the deputies showed a distinct lack of warm-hearted sympathy. Only the speech of the Jewish deputy Levin reverberated with indignation, when he reminded the Russian Assembly that he himself, being a Jew, would in ordinary times be denied the right of residence in the capital, and that, as soon as the Duma would be dissolved, he, a representative of the people and a former legislator, would be evicted from St. Petersburg by the police. The bill was referred to a committee to receive its final shape.

After an interval of three days, on June 8, the Duma had again occasion to discuss the subject of pogroms. Premier Stolypin replied to the interpellation of May 8 concerning the complicity of the Government in the pogrom of 1905. His lame attempt to exonerate the authorities called forth a strong rebuttal from a former member of the Government, the erstwhile Assistant-Minister of the Interior, Deputy Urussov, who bravely disclosed the full truth. Fortified by documentary evidence, he proved the existence of a secret printing-press in the Police Department which was issuing "patriotic" proclamations calling upon the populace to exterminate the Jews. He quoted the words of the gendarmerie officer who was in charge of that particular activity: "A pogrom may be arranged on whatever scale you please, whether it be against ten people or against ten thousand," and he concluded his speech with these words: "The danger will not disappear, so long as the affairs of the state and the destinies of the land will be subject to the influence of people who, by their training, are corporals and policemen, and by their convictions pogrom makers." These words were accompanied by a storm of applause, and the Government bench was showered with cries, "Resign, you pogrom fiends!" The Duma finally adopted a resolution echoing these cries of indignation.

A more passionate tone characterized the discussions of the Duma during the days of June 23-26, in connection with the report of the parliamentary commission which had been appointed to investigate the Bialystok massacre. The Duma was scandalized by the lying official communication, in which the Jews were put forward as the authors of the pogrom, and by the shameful military order of the day, in which the troops of the Bialystok garrison were thanked "for their splendid services during the time of the pogrom." The speeches delivered by the Jewish deputies, by Jacobson, who had visited Bialystok as one of the members of the parliamentary commission, and by Vinaver and Levin, gave vent to their burning national wrath. The Russian Mirabeau, Rodichev, pilloried the highly placed instigators of the Bialystok butchery. On July 7, the Duma concluded the debate by adopting a resolution denouncing in violent terms the policy of the Government, a policy of oppression, frightfulness and extermination, which had created "a situation unprecedented in the history of civilized countries," and demanding, moreover, the immediate resignation of the reactionary Ministry.

5. The Spread of Anarchy and the Second Duma

Two days later, when the deputies appeared before the Duma, they found the building closed, and on the doors was displayed an imperial manifesto dissolving the Duma which "has encroached upon a domain outside its jurisdiction, and has engaged in investigating the acts of the authorities appointed by us." The sudden dissolution of the Duma was answered by the "Vyborg Manifesto" which was signed by the entire parliamentary Opposition, calling upon the people to refuse to pay taxes to furnish soldiers to a Government which had driven asunder their representatives. The manifesto was also signed by all the Jewish deputies who subsequently had to pay for it with imprisonment and the loss of their electoral rights.

The revolutionary terrorism which had subsided during the sessions of the Duma broke out with redoubled violence after its dissolution. Attempts upon the lives of high officials—the most terrible being the explosion of a bomb in the summer residence of Stolypin, who had been appointed Prime Minister at the dissolution of the Duma—"expropriations," *i. e.*, the plunder of state funds and private moneys for revolutionary purposes, anarchistic labor strikes, were the order of the day. The Government retorted with monstrous measures of oppression. A political court-martial was instituted which, in the course of five months (September, 1906–January, 1907) sentenced over one thousand people to death, among them many who were innocent or under age. Needless to say, a considerable portion of these victims were Jews.

Yet as far as the revolutionary attitude of the Jewish population was concerned, the Government was not satisfied to cope with it by "legal" executions, and therefore resorted, in addition, to the well-tried contrivance of wholesale executions, in other words, of pogroms. The chief of the political police in the city of Syedletz, Tikhanovich, engineered on August 27-28 a bloody military pogrom in that city, netting thirty dead and more than one hundred and fifty wounded Jews. The signal for the pogrom were shots fired at a sentry by an *agent provocateur*, whereupon the troops started an aimless musketry fire on the streets and even bombarded Jewish houses with grenades. Many soldiers, in a state of intoxication, committed incredible barbarities and looted Jewish property. Notwithstanding the official report of another agent of the local political police, Captain Pyetukhov, in which he asserted that the Jews had not given the slightest reason for the butchery and that the latter had been entirely engineered by the military and political authorities, the perpetrator of the pogrom, Tikhanovich, was not only allowed to go unpunished, but received from the governor-general of Warsaw an expression of thanks for his "energy and executive skill."

This being the attitude of the ruling spheres of Russia, it was out of the question to expect any initiative from that quarter in regard to the solution of the Jewish question. The Government of Stolypin, in a circular issued on August 24, 1906, had promised "to find out without delay which restrictions, being a source of irritation and manifestly obsolete, could be immediately repealed, and which others, affecting basically the relationship of the Jewish nationality to the native population, seem to be a matter of popular conscience, and should therefore be referred to the legislative institutions." The Council of Ministers laid before the Tzar a draft of moderate reforms in favor of the Jews, pointing to the necessity of appeasing the Jews who, as a result of their grievous restrictions, "had been forced to carry on a desperate struggle against the existing order." But these representations had no effect. Nicholas II. is reported to have said on that occasion: "So long as I am Tzar, the Zhyds of Russia shall not have equal rights." During that time, the power of the so-called "Second Government," the horrible camarilla around the Tzar, was in the ascendancy, and their mainstay were the Black Hundred now organized in the reactionary "League of the Russian People." These reactionary terrorists knew only of one way to solve the Jewish question—by exterminating the Jews.

There was only one ray of hope left—the second Duma which was to be convoked in February, 1907. The election campaign was carried on under Government pressure and was hampered by the threat of reprisals and pogroms on the part of the "Black." The elections resulted in a Duma with an anomalous complexion. The two extreme wings, the Socialists and Black Hundred, had gained in strength, whereas the Constitutional Democratic center had been weakened. The Jews had managed to elect only three deputies, apart from one Jewish Social-Democrat who ran on the ticket of his party. They were men of little renown, whereas as of the deputies of the first Duma who were prosecuted for signing the Vyborg Manifesto not one was elected.

The entire energy of the new Parliament spent itself in the struggle between its left and right wing. The Jewish question was entirely relegated to the "Committee on the Freedom of Conscience." The Government had brought in a bill repealing all denominational restrictions, "except those affecting the Jews," but the Committee decided to eliminate this discriminating clause and in this manner carry through the emancipation of the Jews under the guise of the "Freedom of Conscience."

But this time, too, the hope for Jewish emancipation proved an illusion. The Duma was soon dissolved, under the pretext that a revolutionary conspiracy of the Socialistic deputies had been uncovered. On June 3, 1907, another *coup d'état* took place. The former electoral law which made it possible for the Russian democracy and the oppressed nationalities to send their representatives to the Duma was arbitrarily changed by the Tzar in order to insure a conservative pro-Government majority in the Russian parliament. There followed an era of dismal reaction.

CHAPTER XXXVII

EXTERNAL OPPRESSION AND INTERNAL CONSOLIDATION

1. The New Alignments Within Russian Jewry

The terrible quatrennium of 1903-1906 had an extraordinarily quickening effect upon the national and political thought of the classes as well as of the masses of Russian Jewry. The year of Kishinev and Homel, when the rightless Jews were made defenceless; the year of the Russo-Japanese War, when these rightless and defenceless pariahs were called upon to fight for their fatherland against the enemy from without; the year of the revolution when after the sanguinary struggle for liberty the Jews received a "constitutional charter wrapped up in pogroms"; finally, the first year of the Duma when indignant utterances of the Jewish deputies from the platform of the Duma were accompanied by the moans of the wounded Jews of Bialystok—these terrible upheavals might have proved fatal to Russian Israel had it not, during the preceding period, worked out for itself a definite *nationalistic* attitude towards the non-Jewish world. There were several varieties of this national-political formula. At the one pole stood Zionism, with its theory of a new "exodus." At the other pole was the Social-Democratic party with its premise that "the blood of the Jew must serve as lubricating oil upon the wheels of the Russian Revolution." But even these two poles came somewhat closer to one another at the moment of the great national danger, converging, in spite of all their differences in program and tactics, toward the central line above which floated the banner proclaiming the fight for the civil, political, and national rights of the Jewish people. Disfranchised, battered by pogroms, victimized by tyrannous Tzardom, the Jews of Russia never thought of degrading themselves to the point of begging equal rights "in instalments." They demanded their rights in full, and demanded them not merely as "the Jewish *population*," but as the Jewish *people*, as an autonomous nation among other nations with a culture of its own. The doctrine of "National-Cultural Autonomism" ^{1} was crystallized in definite slogans. These slogans were proclaimed, as we have seen, by the "League for the Attainment of Equal Rights for the Jewish People," which united on its platform all political Jewish groups, with the exception of the Social-Democratic partisans.

The years of storm and stress also forced Zionism to recede from its original position of denying the possibility of a national struggle in the Diaspora. Meeting during the most exciting days of the Russian Revolution, the Seventh Zionist Congress at Basle, held in July, 1905, mourned the loss of its prematurely cut-off leader, Theodor Herzl, and adopted a resolution voicing its strict allegiance to the Palestine idea and rejecting the temptations of Territorialism. This led to a formal split within the party, the Territorialists, headed by Zangwill, seceding and forming an organization of their own.

A year later, in November, 1906, the Russian Zionists met at Helsingfors, and adopted the platform of a "synthetic Zion-

^{1} See above, p. 51 *et seq*.

ism," that is, a combination of the Palestine idea with the fight for national and cultural autonomy in the Diaspora. The guiding resolution of the Zionist Convention was couched in the following terms:

The Zionist organization of Russia sanctions the affiliation of the Zionists with the movement for liberty among the territorial nationalities of Russia, and advocates the necessity of uniting Russian Jewry upon the principles of the recognition of the Jewish nationality and its self-government in all the affairs affecting Jewish national life.

This slogan of "national rights" was followed by the Zionists during the elections to the first Imperial Duma. It was acted upon to a lesser extent by the two Socialistic factions affiliated with Zionism, the *Poale Zion* and the Zionistic Socialists ^{1}; both groups confined themselves to the demand of a minimum of cultural autonomy in the Diaspora, concentrating their entire energy upon emigration, whether it be into Palestine, as advocated by the *Poale Zion*, or into any other territory, as preached by the Zionistic Socialists. During 1905-1906, a new Socialistic party with strong nationalistic leanings came into existence. In distinction from the other two Socialistic factions, it demanded a maximum of national autonomy in the Diaspora, including even a Jewish Diet as the central organ of Jewish self-government. The members of this party called themselves "Saymists" (from *Saym*, "Diet"), or went by the name of the "Jewish Socialistic Labor Party."

In the midst of all these partisan platforms stood the "League for the Attainment of Equal Rights for the Jewish

[^{1} Called by their Russian initials S. S.]

People," disregarding all party and class affiliations.¹ During the revolutionary period, this organization endeavored to unite all public-spirited Jews in the general Russian and national Jewish struggle for liberty, but with the decline of the revolutionary movement, the centrifugal forces within the League began to assert themselves. The divergence of views and tactics among the various groups composing the League proved stronger than their common interest in the nearest aim, which, with the advent of the political reaction, had become more remote.

Thus it came about that, at the beginning of 1907, the "League for the Attainment of Equal Rights" fell asunder into its component parts. The first to secede from it was the Zionist party, which preferred to carry on its own *Gegenwartsarbeit* under a separate party flag—although, properly considered, a far-reaching activity on behalf of national-Jewish rejuvenation in the lands of the Diaspora was scarcely compatible with the fundamental principle of political Zionism, the "negation of the *Golus.*" The Helsingfors program of "synthetic Zionism," the child of the liberty movement, shrank more and more, as the hopes for a Jewish emancipation in Russia receded into the distance.

Out of the "League for Equal Rights" came further the "Jewish People's Group," a party which opposed the Zionist idea altogether and repudiated the attempt to find new Jewish centers outside of Russia. This group, headed by the well-known political leader, M. Vinaver, placed in the center of its program the fight for civil emancipation, in close contact with

¹ See above, p. 111 *et seq.*

the progressive elements of the Russian people, whereas in the question of national-Jewish interests it confined itself to the principle of "self-determination" and to the freedom of Jewish culture in general outlines, without putting forward concrete demands of Jewish autonomy. The People's Group counted among its adherents many representatives of the Jewish *intelligenzia* who had more or less discarded the idea of assimilation and had come to recognize the necessity of a minimum of "Jewish-national rights."

The third group, which also took its rise in the "League for Equal Rights," and received the name *Volkspartei*, or Jewish National Party, stood firmly on the platform of national Jewish policies. The underlying principle of this organization, or, more correctly, of this far-reaching social current, which has its origin in the historic development of the Jewish people, was the same principle of national-cultural autonomism which had long before the revolution pursued its own line of development parallel to Zionism.^{1} The simultaneous struggle for civil and national rights, the creation of a full-fledged national community, instead of the *Kultusgemeinde* of Western Europe, an autonomous national school, and the rights of both languages, the Hebrew and the Yiddish—such was, in general outlines, the program of the *Volkspartei*. At the same time, this party, taking the historic idea of the transplantation of Jewish centers in the Diaspora as its point of departure, recognized the emigration to America and the colonization of Palestine as great national factors destined to create two new centers of Judaism, one quantitatively powerful center in North Amer-

^{1} See above, p. 51.

ica, and a smaller national center, but qualitatively, from the point of view of cultural purity, more valuable, in Palestine.¹

Finally, the "League for Equal Rights" gave birth to a fourth party, the Jewish Democratic Group, which is distinguished from the People's Group by its stronger leaning towards the political parties of the Left, the Russian radicals and Socialists.

Since the dissolution of the "League," these four groups have, as a rule, united in various coalitions. They are all represented on the permanent council at St. Petersburg which, together with the deputies of the Imperial Duma, discusses Jewish political questions as they arise from time to time. Thus, there emerged in Jewish public life a form of representation reflecting the national and political ideas which had assumed concrete shape during the years of the Russian revolution and counter-revolution. The only organization standing outside these federated groups and their common platform of national Jewish politics is the Jewish Social-Democratic party, known as the "Bund," which is tied down by its class program and is barred by it from co-operating with the bourgeoisie, or a non-class organization, even within the domain of national Jewish interests.

¹ Beginning with the year 1905, the emigration to America once more assumed enormous proportions. During 1905-1906, the years of revolution and pogroms, nearly 230,000 Jews left Russia for the United States. During the following years the figure was somewhat lower, but still continued on a fairly high level, amounting to 50,000-75,000 annually. In Palestine, the colonization went apace, and with it the cultural activities. Several schools, with a purely national program, such as the gymnazia in Jaffa and Jerusalem, and other institutions, came into being.

2. The Triumph of the "Black Hundred"

All these strivings and slogans were severely hit by the *coup d'état* of June 3, 1907, when a large part of what the revolution had achieved was rendered null and void. Owing to the amendment of the suffrage law by this clumsy act of autocratic despotism, the constitution became the handmaid of Tzardom. The ruling power slipped into the hands of the Black Hundred, the extreme monarchistic groups, which were organized in the "League of the Russian People" and openly advocated the restoration of autocracy. The head of the League, Dubrovin, congratulated the emperor upon his act of violence of June 3, and was assured in reply that henceforth the "League of the Russian People" would be the "trusted bulwark" of the Throne. Nicholas might have said with greater justification that the Throne was the bulwark of the League of the Black Hundred, the hirelings of the reaction, who were supplied with millions of rubles from the imperial counter-revolutionary fund, the so-called "black money." Street heroes and pogrom perpetrators became the masters of Russian politics. The sinister forces began the liquidation of the emancipation movement. Day after day the newspaper columns were crammed with reports concerning the arrests of politically "undependable" persons and the executions of revolutionaries. The gallows and the jails became, as it were, the emblems of governmental authority. The spectacle of daily executions which continued for two years (1907-1909) forced from the breast of the grand old man, Leo Tolstoi, the desperate cry: "I cannot keep silent."

Yet Nicholas II. continued his rôle of hangman. While young men and women, among them a great number of Jews, met their fate on the scaffold, the rioters and murderers from among the Black Hundred, who during the days of October, 1905, alone had ruined hundreds of Jewish communities, remained unpunished. The majority of them were not even put on trial, for the local authorities who were charged with that duty were afraid lest the judicial inquiry might establish their own complicity in the pogroms. But even those who were prosecuted and convicted on the charge of murder and plunder were released from punishment by orders from St. Petersburg. As a rule, the local branch of the League of the Russian People would appeal to the Tzar to pardon the participants in the "patriotic demonstrations"—the official euphemism for anti-Jewish riots—and the invariable response was an immediate pardon which was ostentatiously published in the newspapers. The petitions to the Tzar applying for the pardon of convicted perpetrators of violence went regularly through the Minister of Justice, the ferocious reactionary and anti-Semite Shcheglovitov. No one doubted that this amnesty was granted by virtue of an agreement concluded in 1905 between the Government and the pogrom ringleaders, guaranteeing immunity to the anti-Jewish rioters.

A different treatment was meted out to the Jewish self-defence contingents, which had the courage to oppose the murderers. They were dealt with ruthlessly. In Odessa, a court-martial sentenced six young Jews, members of a self-defence group which was active during the October pogroms, to long terms of hard labor, characterizing the "crime" of these Jews in the following words: "For having participated in a conspiracy having for its object the overthrow of the existing order by means of arming the Jewish proletariat for an attack upon the police and troops." This characterization was not far from the mark. The men engaged in defending the lives of their brothers and sisters against the murderous hordes were indeed guilty of a criminal offence against the "existing order," since the latter sought its support in these hordes, of whom "the police and troops," as was shown by the judicial inquiries, had formed a part. The appeal taken from this judgment to the highest military court was dismissed and the sentence sustained (August, 1907). The Jews who had done nothing beyond defending life and property could expect neither pardon nor mitigation. This lurid contrast between the release of the pogrom perpetrators and the conviction of the pogrom victims was interpreted as a direct challenge to the Jewish population on the part of Nicholas II. and his frenzied accomplices.

The Black Hundred had a right to feel that it was their day. They knew that the League of the Russian People formed, to use the phrase then frequently applied to it in the press, a "Second Government," which wielded greater power than the official quasi-constitutional Government of Stolypin. The dregs of the Russian populace gave full vent to their base instincts. In Odessa, hordes of League members made it a regular practice to assault the Jews upon the streets with rubber sticks, and, in case of resistance, to fire at them with pistols. Grigoryev, the city-governor, one of the few honest administrators, who made an attempt to restrain this black terrorism, was dismissed in August, 1907,¹ with the result that

¹ When the same official waited upon the Tzar with his report concerning the events at Odessa, he was amazed to see the Tzar come out to him with the badge of the League of the Russian People upon his chest—the same badge which was worn by the rioters in Odessa. He was subsequently given to understand that the Tzar had done so demonstratively to show his solidarity with the hordes of the Black Hundred.

the assaults upon the Jews in the streets assumed an even more sanguinary character. All complaints of the Jews were dismissed by the authorities with the remark: "All this is taking place because the Jews were most prominent in the revolution."

The Government represented by Stolypin, which was anxious to save at least the appearance of a constitutional régime, was often forced to give way before the secret Government of the Black League, which commanded the full sympathy of the Tzar. By orders of the League, Stolypin decreed that one hundred Jewish students who had passed the competitive examination at the Kiev Polytechnicum should be excluded from that institution and that a like number of Russian students who had failed to pass should be admitted instead. The director and dean of the institution protested against this clumsy violation of academic freedom, but their protest was left unheeded, whereupon they tendered their resignation (September, 1907). Following upon this, the Ministry of Public Instruction, yielding to the pressure of the "Second Government," restored the shameful percentage norm, restricting the admission of Jews to institutions of higher learning, which, during the preceding years, had been disregarded by the autonomous professorial councils.

About the same time the Senate handed down a decision declaring the Zionist organization, which had been active in Russia for many years, to be illegal, and giving full scope to the police authorities to proceed with repressive measures against the members of the movement.

3. The Third, or Black, Duma

Such was the atmosphere which surrounded the elections to the third Imperial Duma in the fall of 1907. The reactionary electoral law of June 3 barred from the Russian Parliament the most progressive and democratic elements of the Empire. Moreover, by splitting the electoral assemblies into class and national curias, the Government succeeded in preventing the election of any considerable number of Jewish deputies. The elections took place under severe pressure from the authorities. Many "dangerous" nominees of the Left were arbitrarily put under arrest on framed-up political charges and, pending the conclusion of the investigation, were temporarily barred from running for office. In some places, the Black Hundred openly threatened the Jews with pogroms, if they dared to nominate their own candidates. As a result, only two Jewish deputies managed to get into the Duma—Friedman from the government of Kovno, and Nisselovich from Courland.

The third Duma, nicknamed the Black, assembled in November, 1907. It had an overwhelming majority of reactionaries and anti-Semites. This majority of the Right was made up of the coalition of the conservative Center, represented by the "Octobrist" party,¹ with the extreme Right wing, the Russian "Nationalists," and Black Hundred. Whenever the Jewish question came up for discussion, the reactionary bloc was always able to drown the voices of the weak opposition, the "Cadet" party (Constitutional Democrats), the *Trudoviki* ("the Labor Party"), and the handful of Socialists.

The attitude of this reactionary Duma toward the Jewish question was revealed at its early sessions when the bill concern-

[¹ So called because it based its program on the imperial manifesto of October 17, 1905. See above, p. 127.]

ing the inviolability of the person was the subject of discussion. The opposition demanded the establishment of the full freedom of movement as the most fundamental condition of the inviolability of the person, but the majority of the Right managed to insert in the bill the following stipulation: "No one shall be limited in the right of choosing his place of residence and in moving from place to place, except in the cases set forth in the law, and excepting the Jews who arrive in localities situated outside the Pale of Settlement" (1908). In this wise the Russian legislators cleverly succeeded in harmonizing the principle of the inviolability of the person with the life-long imprisonment of millions of people in the huge prison house known as the Pale of Settlement.

Their solicitude for the maintenance of this vast ghetto was so intense that the reactionary Government of Stolypin was often the butt of criticism because it did not always show sufficient regard for this holy institution. The fact of the matter was that in May, 1907, Stolypin had issued a circular ordering the governors to stop the expulsion from the interior governments of those Jews who had settled there before August, 1906, and possessed "a family and a domestic establishment" in those provinces, provided they were "harmless to the public order and do not arouse the dissatisfaction of the Christian population." As a result of this circular, several hundred, possibly several thousand, Jewish families were saved from expulsion. In consequence, the Right brought in an interpellation calling upon the Government to explain on what ground it had dared to issue this "charter of privileges" to the Jews. The interpellation, of course, proved effective, and the Government did its utmost to nullify the exemptive provisions of the circular. The anti-Semitic Duma betrayed the same spirit on another occasion by rejecting in the same year (1908) the bill, introduced by the Opposition, conferring the right of visiting the health resorts or watering-places upon all sufferers, without distinction of nationality.

Yet these legal discriminations were not the worst feature of the third Duma. Even more excruciating was the way in which the Right wing of the Russian Parliament permitted itself to make sport of Judaism and things Jewish. It almost seemed as if the devotees of autocracy, the members of the extreme Right, had come to the Russian Parliament for the express purpose of showering abuse not only on the Russian constitution but also on parliamentary government in general. The hirelings of Nicholas II. danced like a horde of savages over the dead body of the emancipation movement, singing hymns in praise of slavery and despotism. Creatures of the street, the reactionary deputies drenched the tribune of the Imperial Duma with mud and filth, and, when dealing with the Jews, they resorted to methods similar to those which were in vogue among their accomplices upon the streets of the devastated cities. The term *Zhyd* and the adjective *Zhydovski*, in addition to other scurrilous epithets, became the most favored terms of their vocabulary. They inserted formulas and amendments in various bills submitted to the Duma which were deliberately intended to insult the Jews. They called upon the Ministry of War to bring in a bill excluding the Jews from the army, in view of the fact that the Jewish soldiers had proved an element "which corrupts the army in the time of peace and is extremely unreliable in the time of war" (1908). They supported a law barring the Jews from the military

Academy of Medicine, on the ground that the Jewish surgeons had carried on a revolutionary propaganda in the army during the Russo-Japanese War (1910). The Octobrists demanded the exclusion of the Jews from the office of Justice of the Peace, for the reason that their admission was subversive of the principles of a "Christian State" (1909). The remark made on that occasion by Karaulov, a deputy of the Opposition, "Where there is no equality, where there are pariah nationalities, there is no room for a constitutional order," was met from the benches of the Right with the retort: "Thank God for it; we don't want it." A similar cynical outburst of laughter greeted the warning of Rodichev: "Without the abolition of the Jewish disabilities, there is no access to the Temple of Freedom."

The two Jewish Duma deputies did their utmost to get a hearing, but the Black Hundred generally interrupted their speeches by wild and offensive exclamations. In 1910, the Jewish deputy Nisselovich succeeded in obtaining the signatures of one hundred and sixty-six deputies for a legal draft, abrogating the Pale of Settlement. It was laid before the Duma, but resulted merely in fruitless debates. It was referred to a committee which quietly strangled the bill.

4. New Jewish Disabilities

Spurred on by the reactionary Duma, the Government went to even greater lengths in its policy of Jewish discrimination. Premier Stolypin, who was getting constantly nearer to the Right, was entirely oblivious of the promise, made by him in 1905, to remove immediately all restrictions which are "the source of irritation and are manifestly obsolete." On the contrary, the Ministry presided over by him was systematically engaged in inventing new grievous disabilities. The Jewish deputy Friedman was fully justified in declaring, in a speech delivered in February, 1910, that even "during the most terrible time which the Jews had to live through under Plehve no such cruelties and barbarities were practised as at the present moment." Wholesale expulsions of Jews from the cities situated outside the Pale of Settlement and from the villages within the Pale assumed the character of an epidemic. In the spring of 1910 the Government decided on sacrificing to the Moloch of Jew-hatred a whole hecatomb by expelling twelve hundred Jewish families from Kiev—a measure which aroused a cry of indignation beyond the confines of Russia. The acts of the Government were marked by a refinement of cruelty, for even little children, invalids, and aged people were pitilessly evicted. Particular enmity was shown in the ejection of Jews who had committed the "crime" of visiting summer resorts outside the city lines. The Senate handed down a decision to the effect that the Jewish soldiers who had participated in the defence of the besieged fortress of Port Arthur during the Japanese War were not entitled to the right of residence which had been granted by a former decree^1 to the Jewish soldiers who had taken part in the war.

The spiritual murder of Jewish school children was the function of the black Minister of Enlightenment, with the significant name of Schwartz. The school norm, which, before the revolution, had been applied merely as a Government order, without legislative sanction, was formulated by him into a law and ratified by the Tzar in September, 1908. Henceforth, all

^{1} See p. 98 *et seq.*

institutions of higher learning in the Empire were open to the Jews only in a proportion not exceeding three per cent. of the total number of students for the capitals, five per cent. for the educational establishments outside the Pale, and ten per cent. for the Pale of Settlement. In view of the fact that during the emancipation movement the influx of Jews to the higher schools had been very great, so that their number was now vastly in excess of the established norm, it would have become necessary for the higher schools to bar completely all new candidates until the number of Jewish students had been reduced to the prescribed percentage limits. For a while the Minister recoiled from taking this cruel step, and permitted for the next few years the admission of Jewish students within the limits of the percentage norm, calculating the latter in relation to the number of the *newly admitted* Christian students during a given year, without regard to the Jewish students admitted previously. Subsequently, however, many educational institutions closed their doors completely to the Jews, referring, by way of explanation, to the "completion of the norm" by the former pupils. Once more, bands of the "martyrs of learning" could be seen wending their ways toward the universities in foreign lands.

A year later, in 1909, the percentage restrictions governing the secondary schools were also placed on the statute books. The proportion of Jewish admissions was fixed between five and fifteen per cent.—*i. e.*, slightly in excess of the old norm—and was extended in its application to private educational institutions with the prerogatives of government schools. This law spelled ruin to many gymnazia and schools of commerce which, though directed by Christians, were almost entirely dependent on Jewish support, eighty per cent. of their school population consisting of Jews. As for the gymnazia maintained by Jews, with very few exceptions, they never were able to obtain from the Ministry the status of government institutions.

The educational Hamans, however, went a step further, and in March, 1911, secured an ukase of the Tzar extending the percentage norm to the "externs":^{1} henceforward Jews were to be admitted to the examination for the "certificate of maturity"^{2} or for the completion of a part of the curriculum only in a certain proportion to the number of Christian externs. In point of fact, however, there were no Christian externs, since only the Jews who had failed to find admission to the schools were forced to present themselves for examination as externs. In consequence, the enormous number of Jewish children who had been barred from the schools by the percentage norm were deprived of their right to receive a testimonial from a secondary school. This law was passed during a brief interruption in the sessions of the Duma and was never submitted to it. The deputies of the Opposition brought in an interpellation concerning this action, but the "Black Parliament" laid the matter on the table, and the law which lacked all legal basis went into operation.

Swayed more and more by the tendencies of a reactionary Russian nationalism, Stolypin's Government set out to uproot the national-cultural institutions of the "alien" races in Russia. The Poles, the Finns, and other nationalities became

[^{1} See vol. II, p. 351.]

[^{2} The name given to the graduation certificate of a gymnazium. In German it is similarly called *Reifezeugnis*.]

the victims of this policy. The lash of oppression was also applied to Jewish cultural life. In 1910, Stolypin issued a circular impressing Russian officialdom with the idea that the cultural and educational societies of the "aliens" contributed towards arousing in them "a narrow national-political self-consciousness" and towards "the strengthening of national separatism," and that for this reason all the societies of the Ukrainians and Jews which were established for the purpose of fostering a separate national culture should be prohibited.

5. The Spiritual Revival of Russian Jewry

This new blow was aimed right at the heart of Judaism. For after the revolution, when the political struggle had subsided, the Jewish *intelligenzia* directed its entire energy into the channel of national-cultural endeavors. Profiting by the law of 1906, granting the freedom of assemblies and meetings, they founded everywhere cultural, educational, and economic (co-operative and credit) societies. In 1908, the Jewish Literary Society was established in St. Petersburg, which soon counted over a hundred branches in the provinces. The same year saw the formation of the Jewish Historico-Ethnographic Society which began to publish a quarterly review under the name *Yevreyskaya Starina* ("Jewish Antiquity).^{1} The oldest educational organization among the Jews, the Society for the Diffusion of Enlightenment, enlarged its activity and was endeavoring to create a new type of national Jewish school.

A multitude of other cultural societies and circles sprang into life with the sanction of the authorities throughout the

[^{1} It was edited by the writer of the present work, S. M. Dubnow.]

length and breadth of the Pale. Everywhere lectures and conferences were held and heated debates were carried on, centering around national-cultural problems. Particularly passionate were the discussions about the position of Hebrew and Yiddish in public life, in school and in literature, leading to the alignment of two parties, the Hebraists and the Yiddishists. The lectures, conferences and debates themselves were generally carried on in one of these languages, mostly in the Yiddish vernacular.

In spite of their crudities, these partisan conflicts were a clear indication of the advance of national self-consciousness and of the desire for the upbuilding of a genuine Jewish life upon the concrete foundations of a cultural autonomy. Of course, anti-Semitic Tzardom could not be expected to sympathize with this inner regeneration of Jewry, and, as in the time of Plehve, it directed its blow at the Jewish-national organizations. Here and there the blow was effective. In 1911, the Jewish Literary Society, with its one hundred and twenty branches, which had displayed an energetic activity in the establishment of libraries and the arrangement of public lectures, went out of existence. In general, however, the attacks directed against the Jewish spirit proved much more difficult of realization than the attacks upon Jewish property. The cultural activities continued in their course, defying all external restrictions and persecutions.

The literary revival, which had started in the nineties, and was but temporarily interrupted by the stormy events of the revolutionary period, also came into its own again. The rejuvenation of both the national and the popular language, finding its expression in a widely ramified Jewish literature, proceeded along paralled lines. The periodical press in Hebrew, represented by the two dailies, *ha-Tzefirah* in Warsaw, and *ha-Zeman* in Vilna, and the monthly *ha-Shiloah* in Odessa, found its counterpart in a popular press in Yiddish, reaching hundreds of thousands of readers, such as the dailies *Fraind* ("The Friend," published since 1903 in St. Petersburg), *Haint* ("To-day"), *Moment*, and others, in Warsaw. In addition there was the Jewish press in Russian: the weeklies *Voskhod*, *Razsvyet*, *Yevreyski Mir* in St. Petersburg, and a few other publications.

In the domain of higher literary productivity, new forces were being constantly added to the old ones. Besides the great national bard Bialik there appeared a number of gifted poets: Shneor, the singer of "storm and stress," of doubts and negations, the romantically inclined Jacob Kohan, Fichman, Reisin, David Einhorn, and many other youthful, as yet scarcely unfolded talents. J. L. Perez found a rival in Shalom Asch, the portrayer of patriarchal Jewish life in the provincial towns of Poland (*Die Städtel*, "The Provincial Town," 1904), and the author of charming sketches from Jewish life, as well as a playwright of note whose productions have met with tumultuous applause both on the Jewish and the non-Jewish stage (*Moshiah's Zeiten*, "Messianic Times," *Gott von Nekomo*, "God of Revenge," *Shabbetai Zewi*, *Yihus*, "Blue Blood"). His numerous co-workers in Yiddish letters have devoted themselves with youthful enthusiasm to the cultivation of this branch of Jewish literature.

In Hebrew fiction a number of talented writers and a group of novelists, who publish their works mostly in the *ha-Shiloah*, came to the fore. The successor of Ahad Ha'am in the editorship of this periodical, Dr. Joseph Klausner, occupies a prominent place in Jewish literature as publicist, critic, and partly as historian. If we add to these talents the not inconsiderable number of writers who are domiciled in Galicia, Palestine, Germany, and America, and draw their inspiration from the vast Russian-Jewish reservoir, the growth of Jewish literature during the last decade stands forth in bold relief.

This progress of inner Jewish life in Russia is truly remarkable. In spite of the catastrophes which have descended upon Russian Jewry during the first decade of the twentieth century, the productivity of the Jewish national spirit has gone on unchecked, and the national-Jewish culture has struck out in all directions. The assimilationist positions, which have been generally abandoned, are only held by a few loyal devotees of a past age. It is true that the process of *elemental* assimilation, which penetrates from the surrounding atmosphere into Judaism through the medium of language, school and literature continues to affect Jewish life with the same force as of old. But there can be no doubt that it is effectively counterbalanced by the centripetal factor of a national culture which is becoming more and more powerful. Large as is the number of religious apostates who have deserted Judaism under the effect of external pressure, and of moral renegades who have abandoned the national ethical ideals of Judaism in favor of a new-fangled decadent æstheticism, it is negligible when compared with the compact mass of Russian Jewry and with the army of intellectuals whose national self-consciousness has been deepened by suffering. As in all previous critical moments in the history of the Jews, the spirit of the nation, defying its new tormentors, has grown stronger in the worn-out body.

The Hamans of Russia who have attempted to crush the Eternal People have failed as signally as their predecessors in Persia, Syria and Byzantium.

RUSSIAN JEWRY SINCE 1911

Being loath to cross the threshold of the present, we shall stop at the year 1911, terminating the first decade of the Thirty Years' War waged by Russian Tzardom against Jewry since 1881. The more recent phases of this war are still fresh in our memory. To put the new campaign of Jew-hatred in its proper light, it will suffice to point out its most conspicuous landmarks which stand out by their extraordinarily sinister features. In 1911, the organizations of the Black Hundred, with the help of their accomplices in the Duma and in the Government circles, manufactured the monstrous "Beilis case." The murder of a Russian boy in Kiev, of a family belonging to a band of thieves, and the discovery of the body in the neighborhood of a brickkiln owned by a Jew provided the anti-Semites with an opportunity to bring forward the old charge of ritual murder. In the beginning the Government was somewhat uncertain as to the attitude it should adopt towards the mysterious Kiev murder. But a political occurrence which took place at the time put an end to its vacillation. In September, 1911, Premier Stolypin was assassinated in a Kiev theatre in the presence of the Tzar and the dignitaries of State. The assassin, by the name of Bogrov, proved to be the son of a lawyer who was of Jewish extraction, though he had long before turned his back upon his people—a semi-anarchist, who at one time had been active as police agent for some mysterious revolutionary purposes. The Jewish extraction of the father of the assassin was enough to produce a paroxysm of fury in the camp of the anti-Semitic reactionaries who had lost in the person of Stolypin an exalted patron. In Kiev preparations were openly made for a Jewish massacre, but the Government was afraid that the proposed wholesale execution of Jews would mar the festive solemnity of the Tzar's visit to Kiev. The authorities made it known that the Tzar was not in favor of riots, and a bloody street pogrom was averted.

In its place, however, a bloodless pogrom, extending over two years, was arranged in the form of the Beilis case. Minister of Justice Shcheglovitov, a former Liberal, who had become a fanatical partisan of the Black Hundred, made up his mind to impart to the trial a glaring ritual coloring. The original Judicial inquiry having failed to uncover any traces of Jewish complicity, the Minister of Justice ordered a new special inquiry and constantly changed the personnel of the investigating and prosecuting officials, until he finally secured a bill of indictment in which the whole case was represented as a ritual crime, committed by the Jew Beilis with the participation of "undiscovered persons."

For two years, the Beilis case provided the pabulum for a wild anti-Semitic campaign which was carried on among the so-called better classes, on the streets, in the press, and in the Imperial Duma. The court trial which took place in Kiev in October, 1913, was expected to crown with success the criminal design harbored by the Minister of Justice and the Black Hundred, but the expectations of the Government were disappointed. In spite of a carefully selected court personnel, which consisted of anti-Semitic judges representing the Crown, and of sworn jurymen, ignorant peasants and burghers who believed in the ritual murder legend, Beilis was acquitted, and the authorities found it impossible to fasten the guilt upon the Jews.

Exasperated by the failure, the Government wreaked its vengeance upon the liberal-minded intellectuals and newspaper men, who, by their agitation against the hideous libel, had wrested the prey from the hands of the Black Hundred. Scores of legal actions were instituted not only against newspaper editors and contributors but also against the St. Petersburg Bar Association, which had adopted a resolution protesting against the method pursued by Shcheglovitov in the Beilis trial. The sensational case against the metropolitan lawyers was tried in June, 1914, one month before the declaration of the World War, and terminated in a verdict of guilty for twenty-five lawyers, on the charge of "having agitated against the Government."

The triennium preceding the World War witnessed the rise of a new danger for Judaism, this time coming from Poland. The extraordinary intensity of the national and religious sentiment of the Poles, accentuated by the political oppression which for more than a hundred years had been inflicted upon them, particularly by the hands of Russian despotism, has, during the last decade, been directed against the Jewish people. The economic progress made by the Jews in the two industrial centers of Russian Poland, in Warsaw and Lodz, gave rise to the boycott agitation. Polish anti-Semites proclaimed the slogan "Do not buy from Jews!", aiming the cry specifically against the "Litvaks," that is, the hundreds of thousands of

Russian Jews who, in the course of the last few decades, had been chiefly instrumental in the economic advancement of those two centers. The cloak beneath which this agitation was carried on was purely that of Polish nationalism: the Russian Jews were alleged, on the one hand, " to Russify Poland," and, accused, on the other hand, of an opposite tendency, of asserting themselves as the members of a separate Jewish nationality, with a press and a social organization of their own, which refuses to be merged in the Polish people.

The anti-Semitic movement in Poland, which began shortly after the revolution of 1905, assumed extraordinary dimensions in 1910-1911, when the boycott became a fierce economic pogrom, reaching its culmination in 1912, during the election campaign to the fourth Imperial Duma. The Jewish electors of Warsaw formed a majority, and were, therefore, in a position to send a Jewish deputy to the Duma. Yet out of consideration for the national susceptibilities of the Poles who insisted on sending as a representative of the Polish capital one of their "own," a Christian, the Jews were willing to accept a Polish candidate, provided the latter was not an anti-Semite. When, however, the Polish election committee, disregarding the feelings of the Jews, nominated the anti-Semitic candidate Kukhazhevski, the Jews gave their votes to the Polish Socialistic nominee Yaghello, who carried the election. This attitude of the Jews aroused a storm of indignation among the higher classes of Polish society. An anti-Jewish campaign, marked by extraordinary bitterness, was set in motion, and in the press and on the streets the Jews were nicknamed "Beilises," an echo of the ritual murder legend which had given rise to such horrors in ancient Catholic

Poland. The economic boycott was carried on with incredible fury, and in a number of towns and villages the cowardly enemies of the Jews, being afraid of attacking them openly, set fire to Jewish houses, with the result that in many cases entire families were consumed in the flames.

The *furor Polonicus* assumed more and more dangerous forms, so that at the beginning of the World War, in 1914, almost the entire Polish nation, from the "progressive anti-Semites" down to the clericals, were up in arms against the Jews. From this armed camp came the defiant war cry: "On the banks of the Vistula there is no room for two nationalities," thus sentencing to death the two millions of Polish Jewry who consider themselves a part of the Jewish, and not of the Polish nation. Out of this soil of national hatred crawled forth the snake of the terrible "military libel," which during the first year of the war drenched Polish Jewry in rivers of blood. Over the bleeding body of the Jewish people Polish and Russian anti-Semitism joined hands. Horrors upon horrors were perpetrated before which the ancient annals of Jewish martyrdom fade into insignificance.

* * *

Nearly twenty centuries have passed since the ancient Judæo-Hellenic Diaspora sent forth a handful of men who established a Jewish colony upon the northern Scythian, now Russian, shores of the Black Sea. More than a thousand years ago the Jews of Byzantium from one direction, and those of the Arabian Caliphate from another, went forth to colonize the land of the Scythians. The Jew stood at the cradle of ancient Kiovian Russia, which received Christianity from the hands of the Byzantines. The Jew witnessed the birth of Catholic Poland, and, during the stormy days of the Crusades, fled from the West of Europe to this haven of refuge which was not yet entirely in the hands of the Catholic Church. He has seen Poland in its bloom and decay; he has witnessed the rise of Muscovite Russia, tying the fate of one-half of his nation to the new Russian Empire. Here the power that dominates history opened up before the Jewish people a black abyss of mediævalism in the midst of the blazing light of modern civilization, and finally threw it into the flames of the gigantic struggle of nations. What may the World War be expected to bring to the World-Nation? Full of agitation, the Jew is looking into the future, and the question of his ancient prophet is trembling on his lips: "Ah Lord God! wilt Thou make a full end of the remnant of Israel?"^{1} . . . . Let the entire past of the Jewish people serve as an answer to this question—a people which, in the maelstrom of human history, has succeeded in conquering the two cosmic forces: Time and Space.

[^{1} Ezekiel XI, 13.]

BIBLIOGRAPHY

BIBLIOGRAPHY

VOLUME I

[*Yevr. Bibl.* = *Yevreyskaya Bibliotyeka;*
Yevr. St. = *Yevreyskaya Starina.*]

Chapter I.

The Jewish Diaspora in Eastern Europe

(pp. 13-38)

Latyschew, Inscriptiones antiquae orae Septentrionalis Ponti Euxini, vols. I-II, St. Petersburg, 1885, 1890 [R].

Reghesty i Nadpisi. Svod materialov dla istoriyi yevreyev v Rossiyi ("Documents and Inscriptions. Collection of Materials for the History of the Jews in Russia"). Vol. I, St. Petersburg, 1899, Nos. 1-218 [R].

Dubnow, "The Historical Mystery of the Crimea," *Yevr. St.*, 1914, No. 1.

Harkavy, Skazaniya Musulmanskikh pisatyeley o Slavianakh i Russkikh ("The Accounts of the Mohammedan Writers concerning the Slavs and Russians") St. Petersburg, 1870 [R].

———, Mitteilungen über die Chasaren, *Russische Revue*, 1877; also *Yevr. Bibl.*, vols. VII-VIII, St. Petersburg, 1878.

———, Altjüdische Denkmäler aus der Krim, St. Petersburg, 1876.

Firkovich, Abne Zikkaron. Matzebot 'al Kibre Bne Israel bi-Krim, Vilna, 1872.

Chwolson, Corpus inscriptionum hebraicarum. Grabschriften aus der Krim, St. Petersburg, 1882.

Petahiah of Ratisbon, Sibbub, edited by Grünhut, Jerusalem, 1904.

Benjamin of Tudela, Sefer ha-Massa'ot, ed. Grünhut, Jerusalem, 1903; ed. Marcus Adler, London.

Hoker, "The Jews in Kaffa under the Genoese Régime (1455)," *Yevr. St.* 1912, p. 66 *et seq.*

Sobranie russkih letopisey ("Collection of Russian Chronicles") [R]. Solovyov, Historiya Rossiyi ("The History of Russia"). Vol. I, Moscow, 1863-75 [R]

Chapter II

THE JEWISH COLONIES IN POLAND AND LITHUANIA

(pp. 39-65)

Volumina legum. Leges et constitutiones Regni Poloniae, vol. I, St. Petersburg, 1859 (*sub anno* 1347, 1420, 1496, 1505).

Bershadski, Russko-yevreyski arkhiv ("Russian-Jewish Archives"), St. Petersburg, vol. I (1882), Nos. 1-39, and vol. III (1903), Nos. 1-15.

Bersohn, Dyplomataryusz dotyczacy żydow w dawniej Polsce ("Diplomatic Documents relating to the Jews in Ancient Poland"), Warsaw, 1910, Nos. 1-4, 386-402 [P].

Hube, Constitutiones synodales provinciae Gnesnensis, St. Petersburg, 1856, pp. 68 70, 159-161.

Czacki, Rozprawa o Żydach ("An Inquiry concerning the Jews"), Cracow, 1860 [P].

Gumplowicz, Prawodawstwie Polskie względem żydów ("Polish Legislation relating to Jews"), Cracow, 1867 [P].

Sternberg, Geschichte der Juden in Polen, Leipzig, 1878.

Bershadski, Litovskiye yevreyi ("The Lithuanian Jews"), St. Petersburg, 1883 [R].

Schipper, Studya nad stosunkami gospodarczymi żydów w Polsce podczas średniowiecza ("A Study of the Economic Relations of the Jews in Poland during the Middle Ages"), Lemberg, 1911 [P].

Chapter III

THE AUTONOMOUS CENTER IN POLAND AT ITS ZENITH

(pp. 66-102)

Volumina legum (1859-1860), vol. I, pp. 309, 375, 506, 524-525, 550; vol. II, pp. 624, 690-692, 725, 1052, 1243; vol. III, pp. 289, 809-810; vol. IV, pp. 39-40.

BIBLIOGRAPHY

Bershadski, Russo-yevreyski arkhiv, vol. I, pp. 62-337; vol. II (St. Petersburg, 1882); vol. III (1903), pp. 36-260 [R].

Reghesty i Nadpisi, vol. I, pp. 95-871 [R].

Akty Vilenskoy komissiyi dla razbora drevnikh aktov ("Records of the Vilna Commission for the Examination of Ancient Documents"), vol. XXVIII, containing documents relating to Jews (Vilna, 1901), Nos. 1-278 [R].

Bersohn, Dyplomataryusz, Nos. 5-246, 351-356, 401-552 [P].

Schorr, "The Cracow Collection of the Jewish Statutes and Charters of the Fifteenth to the Sixteenth Century," *Yevr. St.*, vol. I, pp. 247 *et seq.*, vol. II, pp. 76, 223 *et seq.*

Czacki, Rozprawa o Żydach, pp. 44-54 [P].

Kraushar, Historya Żydów w Polsce ("History of the Jews in Poland"), vol. II, Warsaw, 1866, pp. 144-318 [P].

Gumplowicz, Prawodawstwie Polskie, etc., pp. 36-45, 50-52, 58-76, 103 [P].

Nussbaum, Historya Żydow ("History of the Jews"), vol. V, pp. 108-223 [P].

Bershadski, Litovskiye yevreyi, chapters V-VI [R].

Dubnow, "The Jews and the Reformation in Poland during the Sixteenth Century," *Voskhod*, 1895, Books V-VIII.

———, "The Victims of Fictitious Accusations during the years 1636-1639," *Voskhod*, 1895, Books I-II.

Perles, Geschichte der Juden in Posen, Breslau, 1865. Comp. Frankel's *Monatsschrift*, 1864-1865.

Balaban, "The Jewish Physicians in Cracow and Tragedies of the Ghetto," *Yevr. St.*, 1912, p. 38 *et seq.*

———, "Episodes from the History of Ritual-Murder Trials," *Yevr. St.*, 1914, p. 163 *et seq.*

———, "The Legal Status of the Jews in Poland during the Middle Ages and in more Recent Times," *Yevr. St.*, 1910-1911.

———, Dzieje Żydów w Krakowie ("History of the Jews in Cracow"), vol. I, Cracow, 1913 [P].

———, Żydyi lwowscy na przełomie XVI i XVII wieku ("The Jews of Lemberg on the Border-Line between the Sixteenth and Seventeenth Century"), Lemberg, 1906 [P].

Chapter IV

The Inner Life of Polish Jewry at Its Zenith

(pp. 103-138)

Dubnow, "Kahal Constitutions," etc., *Voskhod*, 1894, Books II-XII.

———, "Documents of the Council of Four Lands," *Yevr. St.*, 1912, pp. 70, 178, 453.

———, "The Record Book of the Lithuanian Provincial Assembly," *Yevr. St.*, 1909-1915.

———, Wa'ad Arba 'Aratzot be-Polen, article in *Sefer ha-Yobel* le-Rab Nahum Sokolow, Warsaw, 1904.

———, "Council of Four Lands," article in Jewish Encyclopedia, vol. IV, p. 304 *et seq.*

———, "The Inner Life of Polish Jewry during the Sixteenth Century," *Voskhod*, 1900, Books II and IV.

———, "The Vernacular of the Polish-Lithuanian Jews during the Sixteenth and Seventeenth Century," *Yevr. St.*, 1909, p. 1 *et seq.*

Harkavy, Hadashim gam Yeshanim. Appendix to Rabbinowitz's Hebrew translation of Grätz's History, vol. VII, Warsaw, 1899.

Schorr, Organizacya Żydow w Polsce ("The Organization of the Jews in Poland"), Lemberg, 1899.

——— Żydzi w Przemysłu ("The Jews in Pshemyshl"), 1903.

Perles, Geschichte der Juden in Posen, 1865.

Balaban, Żydzi lwowscy, etc.

———, Dzieye Żydów w Krakowie.

———, "Jacob Pollak, the Father of Polish Rabbinism, and His Age," *Yevr. St.*, 1912, p. 225 *et seq.*

———, "Die Krakauer Judengemeinde-Ordnung von 1595," *Jahrbuch der Jüdisch-Literarischen Gesellschaft*, vol. X, Frankfurt-on-the-Maine, 1913.

Horodezki, Le-Korot ha-Rabbanut, Warsaw, 1911, containing the biographies of Moses Isserles, Solomon Luria, Mordecai Joffe, Meir of Lublin, Samuel Edels, and others.

———, "Rabbi Nathan Shapiro, a Kabbalist of the Seventeenth Century," *Yevr. St.*, 1910, pp. 192 *et seq.*

———, "The Age of the Ascetic Kabbalah" (Isaiah Horvitz and his family), *Yevr. St.*, 1913, pp. 145, 367, 455.

Rabbinovich, "Traces of Free-thinking in Polish Rabbinism of the Sixteenth Century," *Yevr. St.*, 1911, p. 1 *et seq.*

Warchel, "Polish Jews at the University of Padua," *Kwartalnik historyi Zydow* ("Jewish Historical Quarterly"), Warsaw, 1913, No. 3.

Bruckner, "From the History of Polish Dissidents," *Ateneum*, Warsaw, 1898, No. 2.

Isaac Troki, Hizzuk Emunah, edited with German translation by D. Deutsch, Breslau, 1873.

Chapter V

The Autonomous Center in Poland During Its Decline

(pp. 139-187)

Nathan Hannover, Yewen Mezulah, Venice 1653. The other Jewish chronicles and records will be found in the collection of I. Gurland, Le-Korot ha-Gezerot 'al Israel, Parts I-VI, Cracow, 1887-1892, and the posthumous edition, Odessa, 1892.

Kostomarov, Bogdan Khmelnitzki, vols. I-III, St. Petersburg, 1884 [R].

Arkhiv Yugo-zapadnoy Rossiyi ("Archives of South-western Russia"), Part III, volume 3, Kiev 1876, containing the documents relating to the Haidamacks, with a preface by V. Antonovich [R].

———, Part V, volume II, Kiev 1890, concerning the censuses of the Jewish population of the South-western region, taken during the years 1765-1791 [R].

Volumina Legum, vols. IV-VIII, passim.

Bersohn, Dyplomataryusz, Nos. 247-350, 357-384.

Schorr, "The Cracow Collection, etc.," see bibliography to Chapter III.

Akty Vilenskoy kommissiyi (see bibliography to Chapter III), vols. XXVIII-XXIX, containing Jewish records, Vilna, 1901-1902.

Reghesty i Nadpisi, vol. I, Nos. 872:1111; vol. II; vol. III, Nos. 1850-2224, St. Petersburg, 1913.

Levin, Judenverfolgungen im Schwedisch-polnischen Kriege 1655-1659, Posen, 1901.

Dubnow, "The Ruzhan Martyrs of 1659," *Voskhod*, 1893, Book I.

Balaban, "The Jewish Physicians in Cracow, etc." (concerning Calahora), *Yevr. St.*, 1912, pp. 51-53.

———, Skizzen zur Geschichte der Juden in Polen, Berlin, 1911.

———, "From the Past of a Jewish Street in Lemberg," *Yevr. St.*, 1909, p. 237.

———, "The Ritual Murder Trial in Posen of 1736-1740," *Yevr. St.*, 1913, p. 469 *et seq.*

———, "An Episode from the History of the Ritual Murder Trials and of the anti-Jewish Literature in Poland," *Yevr. St.*, 1914, p. 318 *et seq.*

Galant, "The Ritual Murder Trial in Dunaigorod of 1748," *Yevr. St.*, 1911, p. 268.

———, "The Victims of the Blood Accusation in Zaslav of 1747," *Yevr. St.*, 1912, p. 202 *et seq.*

G. E., On the trials of Stupnitza and Voyslavitzá, *Yevr. St.*, 1912, p. 26 *et seq.*

The Papal Bulls concerning the Blood Accusation, Russian translation of Stern's book, pp. 29-105, containing Ganganelli's memorandum and the appended documents, Kiev, 1912.

Hekker, "Anti-Semitism in Poland during the Eighteenth Century," *Yevr. St.*, 1913, p. 439 *et seq.*

Concerning the Haidamack uprising and the massacre at Uman, see Gurland's Le-Korot ha-Gezerot and Reghesty i Nadpisi, *sub anno* 1768.

Chapter VI

THE INNER LIFE OF POLISH JEWRY DURING THE PERIOD OF DECLINE

(pp. 188-241)

Dubnow, "Records of the Council of Four Lands during 1621-1699," *Yevr. St.*, 1912, pp. 178, 453.

———, "The Record Book of the Lithuanian Provincial Assembly during 1623-1761," *Yevr. St.*, 1910-1915.

———, Article on the Provincial Assemblies, *Voskhod*, 1894, Books IV and XII.

Schipper, Beiträge zur Geschichte der partiellen Judentage in Polen im XVII-XVIII Jahrhundert bis 1764.

Grätz, Geschichte der Juden, vol. X, Index sub "Polen," particularly the chapter on Sabbatai Zevi.

———, Frank und die Frankisten, Breslau, 1868.

Dubnow, "Jacob Frank and his Christianizing Sect," *Voskhod*, 1883, Book I *et seq.*

———, "The History of Frankism according to newly discovered sources," *Voskhod*, 1896, Books III-IV.

Kraushar, Frank i Frankiści ("Frank and the Polish Frankists"), Cracow, 1895. Two volumes [P].

Balaban, "Notes on the History of the Frankist Sect," *He-'Atid*, vol. V, Berlin, 1913.

Horodezki, Mystisch-religiöse Strömungen unter den Juden in Polen im XVI-XVIII Jahrhundert, Leipzig, 1914.

Dubnow, "The Social and Spiritual Life of the Jews in Poland in the First Half of the Eighteenth Century," *Voskhod*, 1899, Books I-II.

———, "Introduction to the History of Hasidism," *He-'Atid*, vol. III, Berlin, 1911.

———, "The Rise of Hasidism and Tzaddikism. History of the Hasidic Schism. The Religious Struggle, etc.," *Voskhod*, 1888-1893.

Lewin, "Aliyyot Eliyyahu" (a biography of the Gaon of Vilna), Vilna, 1875.

Yatzkan, Rabbenu Eliyyahu (another biography), Warsaw, 1900.

Solomon Maimon, Lebensgeschichte, Berlin, 1792.

Chapter VII

The Russian Quarantine Against Jews

(pp. 242-261)

Reghesty i Nadpisi, vol. I, Nos. 462, 470, 527, 653, 654, 757, 877-878, 897-898.

Levanda, Sbornik zakonov o yevreyakh ot 1649 do 1873 ("Compendium of the Laws relating to Jews from 1649 to 1873"), Nos. 1-29.

Solovyov, Historya Rossiyi ("History of Russia"), Book III, edition 1910, p. 1345.

Dubnow, "Peter the Great and the Jews."

———, Article on the Moghilev massacre of 1655, *Pardes*, vol. III, Odessa, 1896.

Orshanski, Russkoye zakonodatyelstvo o yevreyakh ("The Russian Legislation relating to Jews"), St. Petersburg, 1877.

Golitzin, Istoriya russkavo zakonodatyelstva o yevreyakh ("History of the Russian Legislation relating to Jews"), St. Petersburg, 1886.

Kunin, "The Jews of Moscow in the Seventeenth Century," *Yevr. St.*, 1913, p. 96 *et seq.*

S. D., "The Expulsion of the Jews from Little Russia in the Second Quarter of the Eighteenth Century," *Yevr. St.*, 1913, pp. 193, 123 *et seq.*

———, "The Census taken of the Jews of Little Russia in 1736," *Yevr. St.*, 1913, pp. 400, 526.

———, "The Petition of the Nobility and the Elders of Little Russia for the Restoration of the Ancient Rights of Little Russia, presented to Catherine II. in 1764," *Kievskaya Starina*, 1883, Book 6.

Chapter VIII

Polish Jewry During the Period of the Partitions

(pp. 262-305)

Czacki, Rozprawa o Żydach (see bibliography to Chapter II), 9, pp. 117-134 [P].

Korzon, Wewnętvzne dzieje Polskie za Stanislawa Augusta ("The Inner History of Poland under Stanislav Augustus"), Cracow, 1882, vol. I, pp. 164-167, 230-232, 240 *et seq.* [P].

Solomon Maimon, Lebensgeschichte.

Okhotski, "Stories from Poland's Past," Russian translation, St. Petersburg, 1874, vol. I, pp. 54-55.

Volumina Legum (see bibliography to Chapter II), vol. VII, pp. 333, 352; vol. VIII, p. 95.

BIBLIOGRAPHY

Nussbaum, Szkice historyczne z życia żydow w Warszawie ("Historic Sketch from the Life of the Jews in Warsaw"), Warsaw, 1881, pp. 13-15 [P].

Smolenski, Stan i sprawa żydow polskich w XVIII wieku ("The Status and the Cause of the Polish Jews in the Eighteenth Century"), Warsaw, 1876 [P].

Maciejowski, Żydzi w Polsce, na Rusi i Litwie ("The Jews in Poland, Russia and Lithuania"), Warsaw, 1878 [P].

Bershadski, Litovskiye yevreyi ("The Jews of Lithuania"), St. Petersburg, 1883, pp. 46-48 [R].

Akty Vilenskoy kommissiyi (see bibliography to Chapter III), vol. 29, pp. 463-480 [R].

Hekker, "The Jews in the Polish Cities in the Second Half of the XVIII. Century," *Yevr. St.*, 1913.

Dubnow, "History of the Hasidic Schism," *Voskhod*, 1890-1891.

Fünn, Kiryah Neemanah (history of the Vilna community), Vilna, 1860, pp. 27, 130, 273.

Katz, "History of the Haskalah Movement in Russia," *Ha-Zeman*, 1903, vol. I, pp. 97-102.

Kraushar, Frank i Frankiści (see bibliography to Chapter VI), vol. I, pp. 139-149 [P].

Paperna, article on Hirshovitz's memorandum, *Voskhod*, Book VI, 1902.

Kraszewski, Polska w czasie trzech rozbiorów ("Poland during the Time of the Three Partitions"), vol. II, pp. 318-320; vol. III, pp. 108, 122 [P].

Gumplowicz, Stanislawa Augusta proekt reformy żydowstwa ("Stanislav Augustus' Project of Jewish Reform"), Cracow, 1875 [P].

Deiches, Sprawa żydowska podczas Sejmu Weilkiego ("The Jewish Cause at the Time of the Great, or Quadrennial Diet"), 1891.

Luninski, Berek Joselwicz, Warsaw, 1909 [P]. Comp. *Yevr. St.*, 1909, vol. 11, p. 128 *et seq.*

Moscicki, "Polish Jewry under the Sceptre of Catherine II," *Kwartalnik poświacony badaniu przeszłości żydow w Polsce* ("Quarterly devoted to the Study of the History of Polish Jewry"), Warsaw, vol. I, 1912. Pages 61-65 describe the attitude of the Jews in Vilna and Grodno in the Polish revolution of 1794 [P].

Skarbek, Dzieje ksiestwa Warszawskiego ("History of the Duchy of Warsaw"). Three volumes, Posen, 1860 [P].

Golitzin, Istoriya russkavo zakonodatyelstva (see bibliography to Chapter VII), pp. 1001 *et seq.*, containing a list of the laws passed by the Duchy of Warsaw during 1807-1812 [R].

Vishnitzer, "A Plan of Reforming Jewish Life in the Duchy of Warsaw and in the Kingdom of Poland," *Perezhytoye*, vol. I, pp. 166-171, St. Petersburg, 1908 [R].

Hessen, "In an Ephemeral Body Politic," *Yevr. St.*, 1910, p. 6 *et seq.*

Askenazy, "The Era of the Duchy of Warsaw," *Kwartalnik*, etc., 1912, vol. I [P].

Chapter IX

THE BEGINNINGS OF THE RUSSIAN RÉGIME

(pp. 306-334)

Shugurov, "History of the Jews in Russia," *Russki Arkhiv*, 1894, vol. I, pp. 163-167. The petition of the Moscow merchants is reprinted, *Voskhod*, 1895, Book I, pp. 31-33 of the second division [R].

Orshanski, Russkoye zakonodatyelstvo (see bibliography to Chapter VII), pp. 183-184.

Golitzin, Istoriya russkavo zakonodatelstva, p. 136 [R].

Levanda, Sbornik, etc. (see bibliography to Chapter VII), Nos. 30-47, 55.

Bershadski, "The Jewish Statute of 1804" (containing the official correspondence and plans relating to the Jewish question during 1797-1801), *Voskhod*, 1895, Books I-IV.

Dyerzhavin, Collected Writings, 1878, vol. VI, pp. 113-114, 124, 715; vol. VII ("Opinion concerning the Jews") [R].

Hessen, Yevreyi v Rossiyi ("The Jews in Russia"), St. Petersburg, 1906 [R].

Chapter X

THE "ENLIGHTENED ABSOLUTISM" OF ALEXANDER I.

(pp. 335-365)

Brafman, Kniga Kahala ("The Book of the Kahal"), vol. II, Nos. 335, 339, 340, 352.

Hessen, Yevreyi v Rossiyi, pp. 77-78, 322.

——, "The Deputies of the Jewish People," *Yevr. St.*, 1909, vol. II, pp. 19-20.

Gordon, "Note on the History of the Settlement of the Jews in St. Petersburg," *Voskhod*, 1881, Book II, pp. 29, 39-40.

Levanda, Sbornik zakonov, Nos. 59 (the Statute of 1804), 64, 69-70.

"The Report of the Jewish Committee in 1812," *Russki Arkhiv*, 1903, Book II, pp. 253-274.

Orshanski, Russkoye zakonodatelstvo, p. 271 *et seq.*

Golitzin, Istoriya russkavo zakonodatelstva, pp. 543 *et seq.*, 587, 590, 981, 985 [R].

Ginsburg, Otyechestvennaya Voyna 1812 goda i russkiye yevreyi ("The Patriotic War of 1812 and the Russian Jews," St. Petersburg, 1912 [R].

Nikitin, Yevreyi-zemledyeltzy ("The Jewish Agriculturists"), St. Petersburg, 1887 [R].

Helman, Bet Rabbi (a biography of Shneor Zalman and his children), Berdychev, 1901, fol. 47.

Chapter XI

THE INNER LIFE OF RUSSIAN JEWRY DURING THE PERIOD OF "ENLIGHTENED ABSOLUTISM"

(pp. 366-389)

Bershadski, "The Jewish Statute of 1804," *Voskhod*, 1895, Book VI, pp. 46-63.

Hessen, Yevreyi v Rossiyi, pp. 220, 237 [R].

Golitzin, Istoriya, pp. 348-355 [R].

Dubnow, "History of the Hasidic Schism," *Voskhod*, 1890, Books XI-XII; 1891, Book I.

———, "The Religious Struggle," *Voskhod*, 1893, Book I, pp. 37-49.

———, "The Intervention of the Russian Government in the War against Hasidism," *Yevr. St.*, 1910, Books I-II.

Hessen, Yevreyi v Rossiyi, p. 164 *et seq.* [R].

Fünn, Kiryah Neemanah (history of the Vilna community), Vilna, 1860, p. 134 *et seq.*

———, Safah le-Neemanim, Vilna, 1881, §§ 91, 94, 98.

Horodezki, "Levi Itzhok of Berdychev," *Yevr. St.*, 1909, vol. I, p. 205 *et seq.*

———, "Nahman of Bratzlav," *Ha-Goren*, IV (1903).

Zederbaum, Keter Kehunnah, Odessa, 1866.

Frenk, Yehude Polin bime Napoleon, Warsaw, 1912.

Calmanson, Essai sur l'état actuel des Juifs, Warsaw, 1796; comp. *Ha-Meassef*, 1809, pp. 286-291.

Nyevakhovich, Vopl dochery yudyeyskoy ("The Moan of the Daughter of Judah"), St. Petersburg, 1803. Reprinted in the collective volume published by the Russian-Jewish weekly *Budushchnost*, St. Petersburg, 1902 [R]. The same in Hebrew, under the title *Kol shaw'at bat Yehudah*, Shklov, 1804.

Stanislavski, "Mendel Lewin," *Voskhod*, 1881, Book III.

Chapter XII

The Last Years of Alexander I.

(pp. 390-413)

Levanda, Sbornik zakonov, *sub anno* 1815-1825.

Pen, "The Deputation of the Jewish People," *Voskhod*, 1905, Books 1-3.

Hessen, "The Deputies of the Jewish People," *Yevr. St.*, 1909, vol. II.

Way, Lewis, Memoires sur l'etat des Israélites, dediés et presentés a leurs Majestés imperiales et royales reunies au Congres d'Aix-la-Chapelle, Paris, 1819.

Lerner, Yevreyi v Novo-rossiyskom kraye ("The Jews in the New-Russian Region"), Odessa, 1901 [R].

Golitzin, Istoriya, etc., pp. 608, 686 [R].

Kozmin, "Past and Present of the Siberian Subbotniks (Sabbatharians)," *Yevr. St.*, 1913, Book I, p. 3 *et seq.*

Dubnow, "Historical Communications," *Voskhod*, 1901, Book IV, p. 37.

"A Inquiry into the Jewish Question," published by the Chancellery of the United Societies of the Nobility, St. Petersburg, 1910, vol. I, pp. 3, 18 [R].

Pestel, Russkaya Pravda ("Russian Truth"), edited by Shchogolev, St. Petersburg, 1906, pp. 50-52 [R].

Semyovski, Politicheskiya i obshchestvennyia idyeyi Dyekabristov ("The Political and Social Ideas of the Decembrists"), St. Petersburg, 1910, pp. 517-523 [R].

VOLUME II

CHAPTER XIII

The Military Despotism of Nicholas I.

(pp. 13-45)

Yevr. St., 1911, p. 589 (Nicholas' Opinions of the Jews).

———, 1909, p. 256 ff., (an account of Tziprinus, a Russian official, about the introduction of military service).

Levanda, Sbornik zakonov, Nos. 153, 154, 159, etc. (see Index s. v. "Recruits").

Volhynian Legends, *Yevr. St.*, 1911, p. 389.

Ginzburg and Marek, Yevreyskiya Narodniya Pyesni ("Jewish Folk-Songs"), St. Petersburg, 1901, p. 42 *et seq.* [R].

Recollections of former Cantonists in *Yevr. St.*, 1909, vol. II, pp. 115 *et seq.*; 1911, pp. 249 *et seq.*; 1912, pp. 54 *et seq.*

Hertzen, Byloye i Dumy ("Recollections and Reflections"), foreign edition, vol. I, 308 [R].

Korobkov, "Jewish Conscription during the Reign of Nicholas I.," *Yevr. St.*, 1913, Books I-II.

Nikitin, Mnogostradalnyie ("The Martyrs"), St. Petersburg, 1871.

———, Reminiscences, *Yevr. Bibl.*, St. Petersburg, 1873.

On the *Beholoh*, see Bogrov, Zapiski Yevreya ("Memoirs of a Jew"), St. Petersburg, 1874, p. 114 [R]; Smolenskin, Ha-To'eh, vol. II, p. 169; and Kotik, Meine Zichroines ("My Reminiscences"), Warsaw, 1913, pp. 99 *et seq.*

Levanda, Sbornik zakonov, *sub anno* 1827-1840.

Spravka po yevreyskomu voprosu ("Inquiry into the Jewish Question"), Part I, pp. 1-43 (containing archival documents on the work preliminary to the Statute of 1835).

Hessen, "The Memoranda Submitted by the Kahal of Vilna and L. Feigin," *Yevr. St.*, 1911, 96 *et seq.* and 394 *et seq.*

Yevr. St., 1909, p. 112, and 1911, pp. 417-418.

Chapter XIV

Compulsory Enlightenment and Increased Oppression

(pp. 46-87)

Dubnow, "Historical Communications," *Voskhod*, 1901, Books 4-5 (dealing with the work of the committee of 1840).

Georgievski, Doklad po voprosu ob obrazovaniyi yevreyev ("Report on the Question of Educating the Jews"), St. Petersburg, 1886. Not published [R].

Morgulis, Voprosy yevreyskoy zhizni ("Problems of Jewish Life"), St. Petersburg, 1889, pp. 33 *et seq.* [R].

Mandelstamm, Hazon la-Mo'ed ("A Vision for the Appointed Time"), Vienna, 1877. Part II [H].

Allgemeine Zeitung des Judentums, 1842-1848, articles describing Lilienthal's mission.

Scheinhaus, Ein deutscher Pioneer (on Lilienthal's mission), Berlin, 1911.

Tzinberg, "Levinsohn and his Time," *Yevr. St.*, 1910, pp. 520 *et seq.* Comp. *ibid.*, 1912, p. 91.

Levanda, Sbornik zakonov, Nos. 462, 475, 509-510, 575.

Die Juden in Russland, Hamburg, 1844.

Lerner, Yevreyi v Novorossiyi ("The Jews in New Russia"), Odessa, 1901, pp. 46 *et seq.* [R].

Loewe, Diaries of Sir Moses Montefiore, London, 1890. Hebrew edition, Warsaw, 1899.

Ginzburg, "A Forerunner of Baron Hirsch" (on Altaras), *Voskhod*, 1897, Book XI.

Leket Amarim ("Collection of Essays"), edited *Ha-Melitz*, St. Petersburg, 1889, pp. 81 *et seq*.

Nikitin, Yevreyi zemledyeltzy ("Jews as Agriculturists"), St. Petersburg, 1887, pp. 103 *et seq*. [R].

Spravka k dokladu po yevreyekomu voprosu ("Inquiry in connection with the Report on the Jewish Question"). Part V: The Ritual Murder Trials, edited by the United Societies of the Nobility, St. Petersburg, 1912 [R].

A memorandum on the Velizh case by the Senate. Not published.

Hessen, Velizhskaya Drama ("The Drama of Velizh"), St. Petersburg, 1905 [R].

Ryvkin, "The Velizh Case as reflected in local legends," *Perezhytoye*, vol. III, St. Petersburg, 1911 [R].

Dubnow's articles on Velizh, *Luah Ahiasaf*, 1895-1896; on Novaya Ushitza, *Perezhytoye*, vol. I (1909); on Mstislavl, *Voskhod*, 1899, Book 9.

Hessen, "The Mstislavl Disturbances," *Perezhytoye*, vol. II.

An-ski, "Some of the Legends Connected with the Mstislavl Incident," *ibid*.

Chapter XV

THE JEWS IN THE KINGDOM OF POLAND

(pp. 88-110)

S. Askenazy, "Concerning Jewish Affairs during the Era of Congresses," *Kwartalnik*, etc., vol. I, No. 3, Warsaw, 1913.

Vishnitzer, "Reform Projects in the Kingdom of Poland," *Perezhytoye*, vol. I, St. Petersburg, 1908.

Friedländer, David, Die Verbesserung der Israeliten im Königreich Polen, Berlin, 1819.

Inquiry into the Jewish Question, etc. (the utterances of Zaionchek), vol. I, 43.

The Legal Journal of the Kingdom of Poland (during the years indicated in the text).

Golitzin, Istoria Russkavo zakonodatyelstva o yevreyakh ("The History of Russian Legislation relating to Jews," pp. 1001-1005 [R].

Luninski, Berek Joselowicz, Warsaw, 1909.

"The Ritual Murder Trials during the Year 1816," *Yevr. St.*, 1912, pp. 144-163.

Nussbaum, Historya Żydow, V, 390-399 [P].

"From the History of the Rabbinical School in Warsaw," *Perezhytoye*, vol. I.

Kandel, "The Committee of Old Testament Believers," *Kwartalnik*, 1912, No. 12, pp. 85-103.

Jost, 11. II, 302 (on Chiarini).

Mstislavskaya, "The Jews in the Polish Insurrection of 1831," *Yevr. St.*, 1910.

Myakotin, "The Tovyanski Movement," *Voskhod*, 1888, Books 11-12.

Die Juden in Russland, Hamburg, 1844, pp. 35, 38-40 (on conscription in the kingdom of Poland).

CHAPTER XVI

THE INNER LIFE OF RUSSIAN JEWRY DURING THE PERIOD OF MILITARY DESPOTISM

(pp. 111-139)

Gottlober, Autobiography, in the Hebrew periodical *Ha-Boker Or*, 1880-1881.

Ginzburg, M. A., Abi'ezer (autobiography), Vilna, 1883.

Plungian, Ben Porat (biography of Menashe Ilyer), Vilna, 1858.

Hilman, Beth Rabbi (biography of Shneor Zalman and descendants), Berdychev, 1901.

Horodezki, Rabbi Nahum mi-Chernobyl u-Banaw ("R. Nahum of Chernobyl and his Descendants"), Berdychev, 1902.

Sternholz, 'Alim li-Tetrufah ("Leaves for Healing," letters of Rabbi Nahman of Bratzlav), Berdychev, 1896.

Nathansohn, Sefer ha-Zikronot ("Book of Recollections," on I. B. Levinsohn), Warsaw, 1878.

Wengeroff, P., Memoiren einer Grossmutter, Berlin, 1908.
Horodezki, "The Sadagora Dynasty," *Yevr. St.*, 1909, vol. II.
Zederbaum, Keter Kehunnah ("The Crown of Priesthood," on the Tzaddiks of Poland), Odessa, 1866.
Magid, "M. A. Ginzburg," St. Petersburg, 1897 [H].
Fünn, Safah le-Neemanim ("Speech of the Trustworthy"), pp. 149 *et seq.*, Vilna, 1881.
Gordon, "A. B. Lebensohn," *Yevr. Bibl.*, vol. VIII, St. Petersburg, 1880.

Chapter XVII

The Last Years of Nicholas I.

(pp. 140-153)

Levanda, Sbornik zakonov (for the years 1848-1854).
Ginzburg, "A forgotten Era," *Voskhod*, 1896, Book 2.
Ginzburg and Marek, Yevreyskiya Narodnya Pyesni ("Jewish Folk-Songs"), St. Petersburg, 1901, No. 53 [R].
Osip Rabinovich, "The Penal Recruit" and "The Inherited Candlestick," collected works, vol. I, St. Petersburg, 1880 [R].
Bogrov, "The Captured Recruit," *Yevr. Bibl.*, vol. IV, St. Petersburg, 1874, pp. 2-7, preface.
Friedberg, "The Captured Recruits," *Sefer ha-Shanah*, edited by Sokolow, vol. III, Warsaw, 1901.
Spiegel, "From the Diary of a Cantonist," *Yevr. St.*, 1911, pp. 249 *et seq.*
Itzkovich, "Reminiscences of a Cantonist," *Yevr. St.*, 1912, pp. 54 *et seq.*
Korobkov, "Jewish Conscription during the Reign of Nicholas I.," *Yevr. St.*, 1913.
On the Ritual Murder Trial of Saratov, see "Inquiry into the Jewish Question, etc." Part V, pp. 208-243 [R].
Trivus, "Ritual Murder Trials before the pre-Reformatory Courts," *Yevr. St.*, 1912, pp. 252-262 *et seq.*

Chapter XVIII

The Era of Reforms Under Alexander II.

(pp. 154-183)

Levanda, Sbornik zakonov (for the years 1855-1865).

"Inquiry into the Jewish Question," etc. Part I, pp. 55-102, 105, 112; Part III, pp. 10-17, 79-92 (discussion of the projected legal bills in the Council of State, etc.).

K stoletyu komityeta ministrov ("The Centenary of the Committee of Ministers"), St. Petersburg, 1902 [R]; the "resolutions" of Alexander II. are recorded in *Voskhod*, 1903, Book III.

"Some Resolutions of Alexander II. on the Jewish Question in 1861," *Yevr. St.*, 1912, p. 472.

Hessen, "An Attempt at Jewish Emancipation in Russia," *Perezhitoye*, vol. I, p. 153 ff.

Orshanski, Yevreyi v Rossiyi ("The Jews in Russia"), St. Petersburg, 1877 [R].

———, Russkóye zakonodatyelstvo o yevreyakh ("The Russian Legislation relating to Jews"), St. Petersburg, 1877, pp. 214, 309-334 [R].

Georgievski, Doklad po voprosu ob obrazovaniyi yevreyev ("Report on the Question of educating the Jews"), St. Petersburg, 1886, pp. 92, 134 *et seq*. [R].

Marek, Ocherki po istoriyi prosvyeshchenya v Rossiyi ("Sketches from the History of Enlightenment among the Jews of Russia"), Moscow, 1909 [R].

Kandel, "The Petition of 1857," *Kwartalnik*, 1913, 147-159.

Sternberg, Geschichte der Juden in Polen, Leipsic, 1878, Beilage G, pp. 186-191 (the Jewish agitation of 1859 in Warsaw, and Lelevel's reply).

Jutrzenka ("The Dawn"), Polish-Jewish weekly in Warsaw, for the years 1861-1863.

Berg, Zapiski o polskikh zagovorakh i powstaniakh ("Memoirs concerning Polish Conspiracies and Revolutions"), St. Petersburg, 1873 [R].

"The Experiences of a Jew during the Polish Insurrection of 1863," *Yevr. St.*, 1910, pp. 378-390.

Inquiry into the Jewish Question, Part VII, pp. 63, 70, 89, 95.

Spasovski, Zhizn i politika markiza Vyelepolskavo ("Life and Policies of Marquis Vyelepolski"), St. Petersburg, 1882 [R].

Chapter XIX

THE REACTION UNDER ALEXANDER II.

(pp. 184-205)

Spravka po yevreyskomu voprosu ("Inquiry into the Jewish Question"), Part VII, pp. 63, 70, 89, 95 [R].

Brafman, Kniga Kahala, 3d edition, St. Petersburg, 1888 [R].

"The Jewish Delegation in the Vilna Commission of 1869," *Yevr. St.*, 1912, pp. 187 *et seq.*; comp. *Perezhytoye*, II, pp. 306 *et seq.* and III, pp. 385 *et seq.*

"The Enactments against the Jewish Dress in 1871," *Yevr. St.*, 1912, pp. 334-338; comp. "The Struggle with the Jewish Dress," *Perezhytoye*, I, 2d Section, pp. 16-18.

Orshanski, "On the Nature of the Odessa Pogrom," in the collective volume *Yevreyi v Rossiyi* ("The Jews in Russia"), 1877, pp. 156 *et seq.* [R].

Margulis, "The Odessa Riots of 1871," in the collective volume *Yevreyski Mir* ("The Jewish World"), St. Petersburg, 1910.

Levanda, Sbornik zakonov, for the years 1865-1873.

For the additional laws for 1874-1880 see *Sobranie zakonov* ("Collection of Laws"), edited by the Government Senate. Comp. *Systyematicheski ukazatyel literatury o yevreyakh* ("A Systematic Index of the Literature dealing with the Jews"), St. Petersburg, 1892, pp. 59-60.

"Analysis of the Legislation relating to the Jews during the past Decade," *Yevr. Bibl.*, vol. VII, 1879.

The memorandum of Nyekhludov "On the Emancipation of the Jews" is found in *Spravka po yevreyskomu voprosu*, Part VII, pp. 103-122; appeared also as a separate publication, St. Petersburg, 1907.

On the Municipal Statute of 1870 and on the Conscription Statute of 1874, see *Spravka*, Part II, pp. 127-138, 142-209.

An account of the Congress of Berlin, based on the French text of the Proceedings, *Spravka*, Part III, pp. 151-154; see also *Yevr. Bibl.*, vol. VI, 1878, p. 145 *et seq.* [R].

On the Jews in the Russo-Turkish War of 1877, see Criticus (penname of S. M. Dubnow) in *Voskhod*, 1891, Book I, pp. 32-38.

The full proceedings of the Kutais case are found in a supplement to *Yevr. Bibl.*, vol. VI, pp. 1-188.

Chwolson, Upotreblayut-li yevreyi khristianskuyu krov? ("Do the Jews use Christian Blood?"), 2d edition, with a reply to Kostomarov, St. Petersburg, 1879 [R].

Borissov, "Ippolit Lutostanski," Kiev, 1912 [R].

Chapter XX

The Inner Life of Russian Jewry During the Reign of Alexander II.

(pp. 206-242)

S. Ginzburg, "A forgotten Era," *Voskhod*, 1896, Books III and V.

Margulis, article on "N. I. Pirogov," in *Voprosy yevreyskoy zhizni* ("Questions of Jewish Life"), St. Petersburg, 1889.

Criticus (pen-name of S. M. Dubnow), "I. S. Aksakov and the Jews," *Voskhod*, 1887, Book II.

Dostoyevski, Yevreyski vopros ("The Jewish Question"), in his collected writings, edited by Marx, vol. XI, pp. 85-102; also in his *Dnyevnik pisatyela* ("The Diary of an Author," autobiographical sketches), during 1873-1877, in various places [R].

Orshanski, Yevreyi v Rossiyi ("The Jews in Russia").

Margulis, Voprosy yevreyskoy zhizni, pp. 149-195, on the Crown rabbis and teachers of the sixties.

Tarnopol, Opyt osmotrityelnoy reformy v oblasti iudaizma ("Attempt at Cautious Reforms in the Domain of Judaism"), Odessa, 1868, [R].

Gumplovich's article is found in *Jutzenka* ("The Dawn"), 1891, No. 19 [P].

BIBLIOGRAPHY

Leon Rosenthal, Toldot Hebrat Marbe Haskalah be-Israel ("History of the Society for the Diffusion of Enlightenment among the Jews"), two volumes, St. Petersburg, 1885-1890; comp. Criticus, *Voskhod*, 1891, Books X-XI.

Levanda, "The Establishment of the First Periodical of Russian Jewry," *Voskhod*, 1881, Book VI.

The Letters of Ossip Rabinovich, published in *Yevr. St.*, 1911, p. 71 *et seq.*

Dubnow, "The Change of Tendencies in Jewish Journalism," in "Letters on Ancient and Modern Judaism," St. Petersburg, 1907, pp. 205-226 [R].

Frumkin, "From the History of the Revolutionary Movement among the Jews during the Seventies," *Yevr. St.*, 1911, pp. 221 *et seq.*, 513 *et seq.*

Tzinberg, "The First Socialistic Periodicals in Hebrew Literature," *Perezhytoye*, I, pp. 233-263.

Sosis, "Social Currents during the Period of Reforms," *Yevr. St.*, 1914.

Mandelkern, "Micah Joseph Lebensohn," *Ha-Asif*, III, 1886.

Brainin, "Micah Joseph Lebensohn," *Voskhod*, 1902, Book III.

———, "Abraham Mapu," Warsaw, 1900 [H].

Cantor, "Gordon and His 25 years of Activity," *Voskhod*, 1881, Books XI-XII.

S. D. (= S. Dubnow), "The Jewish Nyekrassov" (on J. L. Gordon), *Voskhod*, 1884, Book VII.

Iggerot Jelag ("Letters of J. L. Gordon"), two volumes, Warsaw, 1894.

Bienstock, "A Festival in Yiddish Literature" (a biography of Abramovich), *Voskhod*, 1884, Book XII.

Frischmann, "Mendele Mokher Sforim," in Introduction to the collected Hebrew works of Abramovich, vol. II, Odessa, 1911.

Brainin, "Perez Smolenskin," Warsaw, 1896 [H].

M. Kahan, Me-'Ereb 'ad 'Ereb, vol. I, Vilna, 1904, pp. 186-244. The same volume also contains an analysis of Lilienblum's work and of the literary currents of the seventies in general.

Gottlieb, "P. M. Smolenskin" ("Gallery of Jewish Worthies"), Part II, St. Petersburg, 1899 [R].

Lilienblum, Hattot Ne'urim ("Sins of Youth"), Vienna, 1876; also in his collected works, Cracow, 1910-1912, vol. II.

Klausner, "Moshe Leib Lilienblum" (a biographical analysis, prefacing the first volume of Lilienblum's collected works).

Hessen, "O. Rabinivich and I. Orshanski" ("Gallery of Jewish Worthies"), Part I, St. Petersburg, 1898 [R].

"Ilya Grigorievich Orshanski, an Autobiographical Sketch," *Yevr. Bibl.*, vol. VI, pp. 1-43, St. Petersburg, 1878.

Yampolski, "Recollections of I. G. Orshanski," *Yevr. St.*, 1911, p. 55 *et seq.*

Volynski, "The Portrayer of Russian Jewry" (on the stories of Levanda), *Voskhod*, 1888.

"From the Correspondence of L. O. Levanda," *Yevr. Bibl.*, vols. IX-X, St. Petersburg, 1901-1903, containing also some letters from Bogrov; Comp. *Yevr. St.*, 1913, pp. 279-281.

Wengeroff, Memoiren einer Grossmutter, vol. II, Berlin, 1910, containing valuable material for the understanding of the transition period of the fifties and sixties.

Chapter XXI

The Accession of Alexander III and the Inauguration of Pogroms

(pp. 243-258)

Razsvyet, 1881, pp. 494, 650, 653; 846, 1255-57.

Yevr. St., I. pp. 9193; II. pp. 207 ff.

Chronique du movement socialiste en Russie, 1878-1887. *Byloye* (historical journal), 1907, Book VI, p. 305.

Chapter XXII

The Anti-Jewish Policies of Ignatyev

(pp. 259-283)

Pravityelstvyenny vyestnik (1881), No. 98.

Razsvyet, No. 19.

Yevr. St., V, p. 346.

Archives of Historical Society.

Voskhod (1881), Book V, p. 83 (II part).

Sagasty's letter, *Razsvyet*, 1881, p. 1105; Campos' letter, *ibid.*, p. 1143.

"Inquiry into the Jewish question" (ed. by the Council of the United Nobility, St. Petersburg, 1910), Part II, pp. 125-126; *Russian Jew. Encycl.*, I, pp. 826-827.

Dr. Mandelstamm's Reminiscences, *Perezhitnoye*, vol. IV, p. 53 *et seq.* (St. Petersburg, 1913).

Report of the Gubernatorial Commissions on the Jewish Question, vols. I-II, St. Petersburg, 1884.

Istoria Revolutzionnavo Dvizhenia v Rossiyi ("The History of the Revolutionary Movement in Russia"), St. Petersburg, 1906, pp. 260-262.

Die Judenpogromen in Russland, I, pp. 46-66 (Koln, 1910).

Chapter XXIII

New Measures of Oppression and Public Protests

(pp. 284-308)

"Historical review of the activities of the Committee of Ministers," vol. IV, p. 183 (St. Petersburg, 1902).

Voskhod, 1903, Book III, p. 154.

Razsvyet (1882), No. 3 (supplement), and No. 4, p. 125.

Yevr. St. (1909), I. pp. 93-97.

Judische Welt (Yiddish monthly, St. Petersburg, 1912), No. 2.

Archives, Nos. 10, 12, 13, 15.

Chapter XXIV

Legislative Pogroms

(pp. 309-323)

Yevr. St., I, pp. 265-267.

Russian Jew. Encycl., I, p. 829.

Historical Review of the activities of the Commission of Ministers, IV, pp. 20-21, 183.

Voskhod, 1903, Book III, p. 155.

Razsvyet, No. 20.
Razsvyet, 1882, pp. 1125, 1417.
"Diary of a Palestinian Immigrant," *Voskhod Chron.*, 1882.
Yevr. St., 1915, pp. 100, 201 ff.
Voskhod, 1883, Book I, p. 69 (II part).

Chapter XXV

Inner Upheavals

(pp. 324-335)

Razsvyet, 1882, pp. 506, 1301.
Voskhod Chron., 1882, p. 645.
Bez Illuzii ("Without Illusion"), *Razsvyet*, 1881, p. 1988; 1882, p. 152 ff.
Dubnow, *Razsvyet*, 1881, Nos. 34, 35.
Gordon, Kol Schire Jelag, I, pp. 115-116, St. Petersburg, 1884.
Dubnow, "The Question of the Day," *Razsvyet*, 1881, Nos. 34-35.
Hamzefot, Chto Zhe Dielat? ("What is to be done?"), *Razsvyet*, 1882, Nos. 2-5.
Razsvyet, 1881, Nos. 41-42, "The General Jewish Question and Palestine."
Ben-Zion (Priluker), Yevreyi Reformatory ("Jewish Reformers"), St. Petersburg, 1882.

Chapter XXVI

Increased Jewish Disabilities

(pp. 336-357)

"Inquiry into the Report on the Jewish question," vol. II, pp. 20-21.
Pahlen's Commission, pp. 175, 251 *et seq.*
Yevr. St., I, p. 88 *et seq.*
Gieorgievski, Doklad po voprosu ob obrazovani Yevreyev ("Report on the question of the Education of Jews"), St. Petersburg, 1886.
Pozner, Yevrei v Obshchey Shkolie ("Jews in Secular Schools"), St. Petersburg, 1914, pp. 58-59.

"History of Ministers' Commission" (Government publication), vol. IV, p. 433, St. Petersburg, 1902.

"Review of the Last Year" (Annual reviews of the first books of the *Voskhod* for 1884-1889; especially 1884, Book I, pp. 27, 30-31, 36-37; 1885, Book I, p. 47 *et seq.*).

Voskhod, 1891, Book II, p. 40 (II part).

Frederic, "The New Exodus," London, 1902, pp. 175, 248-252.

Frug, "Two Generals" (a page of reminiscences), *Yevreyskaya Zhizn*, 1915, No. 14.

Mysh, Rukovodstvo k zakonodatielstvu o Yevreyakh v Rossiyi ("Guide to the Laws about Jews in Russia"), p. 384, St. Petersburg, 1892.

Yevreyskaia Bibl., vol. IV, p. 469, St. Petersburg, 1901.

Usov, Yevreyi v Armii ("Jews in the Army"), St. Petersburg, 1911, pp. 14-92.

Chapter XXVII

Russian Reaction and Jewish Emigration

(pp. 358-377)

Voskhod Chron. (1883), Nos. 19, 20; 1884, Book VI, p. 30 *et seq.* (II part).

Orshanski, "Review for the Last Lear," Voskhod, 1884, Book II, pp. 40-49.

Pahlem Commission, pp. 78-79.

Margulis, "Reminiscences," *Yevreyski Mir* (1909), Book VI; *Voskhod* (1895), Book I, p. 50 (II part).

Pozner, Yevreyi v Vysshey Shkolie ("Jews in Higher Institutions"), p. 56.

"Russian Jews in America: Results of the Emigration Movement." *Voskhod*, 1890, Book X.

"Jewish Agricultural Colonies in America," *Voskhod*, 1891, Books I-IV.

Fornberg, Yevreyskaya Emigratzia ("Jewish Emigration"), Kiev, 1908.

Lilienblum, Derekh la-'avor Golim, Warsaw, 1893.

M. Kahan, Me-'Erev 'ad 'Erev ("From Evening to Evening"), vol. II, Vilno, 1904.

Khisin, "From the Diary of a Palestinian Emigrant," *Vohkhod*, 1889, Books I-XXII.

Sapir, "Zionism," Vilno, 1903, *Yevr. St.*, 1915, Books I-II.

Chapter XXVIII

Judæophobia Triumphant

(pp. 378-398)

H. Frederic, "The New Exodus: A Study of Israel in Russia," p. 173 (London, 1892; the author visited Russia in 1891, and heard about the Tzar's resolution from a man who saw the document).

Voskhod Chron., 1890, No. 21 (p. 528), 23 (p. 569), 30 (pp. 475, 752).

Voskhod (1891), Book I, p. 63 (II part); II, pp. 42-47.

"Judenpogromem in Russland," I, p. 119.

"Spravka k dokladu po yevreyekomu voprosu ("Inquiry of the Report on the Jewish Question"), II, pp. 138-140.

Letters from V. Solovyev to F. Getz (St. Petersburg, 1909), pp. 27-40, 55 *et seq.*

Chapter XXIX

The Expulsion from Moscow

(pp. 399-413)

"Mysterious References to the Work of the Councils," *Voskhod Chron.*, 1891, No. 11, p. 288, and No. 12, p. 315.

Voskhod (1895), Book I, p. 50 (II part).

Archives of the Jew. Hist. Soc. (interview between Baron Günzburg and the Minister of Finance in September, 1891).

Weber-Kempner, La Situation des Juifs en Russie. Rapport addressé au Gouvernement des États-Unis (Paris, 1892), p. 17.

Goldovski, "Jews in Moscow."

"Beyond the Border," *Voskhod* (1891), Books IV-XI, pp. 5-6.

Chapter XXX

Baron Hirsch's Emigration Scheme and Unrelieved Suffering

(pp. 414-429)

Istoricheski Obzor Dieyatielnosti Comitieta Ministrov ("Historical Study of the Activity of the Ministers' Committee"), vol. IV, p. 184 (St. Petersburg, 1902).

Jew. Encycl., VI, p. 415.

Russian Jew. Encycl., VI, p. 564.

Voskhod (1888), No. 2.

A. White, Jewish Colonization and the Russian Persecution, New Review, London, 1891, No. 27, August, pp. 97-105.

Voskhod, 1891, Books IV-IX.

Lietopisiets, "Beyond the Border."

Lapin, Nastoyashchiye i Budushchiye Colonisatsii v Argentinie ("The Present and Future Colonisation in Argentine"), St. Petersburg, 1894.

Fornberg, Yevreyskaya Emigratzia ("Jewish Emigration"), Kiev, 1908.

Jewish Colonisation Association Rapports de L'administration Centrale, Paris, 1891-94.

M. Kahan, Me-'Erev 'ad 'Erev, I, pp. 55-118, Vilno, 1904.

Berkenheim, "Colonisation Movement," *Voskhod*, 1895, Books I, V, VII, XI.

Katzenelson, "The Martyrdom in the Moscow Synagogues," *Yevr. St.*, 1909, I, pp. 175-186.

Goldovski, "Jews in Moscow," *Byloye*, 1907, Book IX, 161-163.

Yevr. St. (1911), IV, p. 109 *et seq.*

Dubnow, Novieyshaya Istoria Yevreyev ("The New History of the Jews"), p. 552 (1914 ed.).

Voskhod Chron., 1894.

VOLUME III

CHAPTER XXXI

THE ACCESSION OF NICHOLAS II.

(pp. 7-39)

Voskhod, 1896, Book I, p. 38 (II part).

Yevr. St. (1914), VIII, p. 400.

Judenpogromen in Russland, vol. I, p. 98.

"Memoirs of the commission on the Jewish question under Plehve" (1903-1904), pp. 6-7 (not published).

Archives of Jew. Hist. Soc., coll. S. P. E., No. 134, I.

Byloye (1907), Book IX, p. 162.

Levine, Svornik Zakonov o Yevreyakh ("Collection of Laws about Jews"), St. Petersburg, 1902.

Voytanski, Yevreyi v Irkutskie ("Jews in Irkutsk"), 1915, pp. 30, 264.

Yevr. Bibl., IX, p. 467 *et seq.* (St. Petersburg, 1901, London ed.).

Pozner, Yevreyi v Obshchey Shkolie ("Jews in Secular Schools"), St. Petersburg, 1914, pp. 89-92, 105, 119-129, 127-129.

Budushchmost (weekly), 1902, Nos. 5-6.

Russian Jew. Encycl., IV, pp. 661-664.

CHAPTER XXXII

THE NATIONAL AWAKENING

(pp. 40-65)

Theodor Herzl, Zionistische Schriften, vol. I, Berlin, 1905.

Friedemann, Das Leben Th. Herzl's, Berlin, 1904.

R. Gottheil, Zionism, Philadelphia, 1914.

Protokolle der Zionisten-Kongresse 1897-1901 (*Die Welt*, official party organ, 1897-1902, Vienna).

Voskhod (weekly), 1897-1902.

Ha-Shiloah (Ahad Ha'am's monthly), Berlin-Odessa, 1896-1902.

Max Nordau, Zionistische Schriften, Köln, 1909.

BIBLIOGRAPHY

Dubnow, Letters about the Old and New Judaism, St. Petersburg, 1907, pp. 164 *et seq.*, 181 ff., 230 *et seq.* (The first two "letters" were translated into German, Jud. Verlag, Berlin, 1903.)

Ahad Ha'am, 'Al Parashat Derakhim, vols. I-III, 1895-1904 (partly in English and partly in German translation).

J. Klausner, Dukhovny Sionisme ("Spiritual Zionism"), St. Petersburg, 1900.

Frumkin, "Sketches from the History of the Jewish Workingmen's Movement, 1885-97," *Yevr. St.*, 1913.

Geschichte vun d. Judische Arbeiter-Bewegung in Russland (Yiddish), Geneva, 1900.

Medem, Natzionalnost i Proletariat ("Nationalism and the Proletariat") in Kastelanski's collection, Formy natzionalnavo dvizhenia v sovremiennykh gosudarstvakh ("The Forms of the National Movement in Contemporary Governments"), St. Petersburg, 1910, pp. 772 *et seq.*

"Bund" in *Russian Jew. Encycl.*, vol. V, p. 93 *et seq.*

M. Philippson, Neueste Geschichte d. Jüdischen Bewegung, Berlin, 1911.

Borokhov, Klassovye momenty natzionalnavo voprosa ("Classic Moments of the National Question"), St. Petersburg, 1906.

J. Klausner, Novoyevreyskaya literatura ("The New Jewish Literature"), 2d edition, Odessa, 1912; M. Pines, Historie de la Litterature Judéo-Allemande, Paris, 1910.

CHAPTER XXXIII

THE KISHINEV MASSACRE

(pp. 66-86)

Die Judenpogromen in Russland, vol. II, pp. 6-8.

Voskhod (weekly), 1903, pp. 11 *et seq.*, 16 *et seq.*, 18, 20, 22, 24, 25, 28, 31, 32, 33, 38.

Urusov, Zapiski Gubernatora ("A Gubernator's Memoirs"), St. Petersburg, 1907.

Chemu uchit pokushenie Dashevskavo? ("What Do We Learn from Dashevski's Temptation?"), London, 1903, edition of *Molodoi Israel* ("Young Israel").

Yevr. St. (1915), VIII, p. 412.

Protokoll d. VI Zionisten-Congresses, 1903.

Chlenov, Sion i Africa na Vi Congressie ("Zion and Africa at the VI Congress"), Moscow, 1905.

Dubnow, "Historical Moment," *Voskhod*, 1903, Nos. 21-22.

Chapter XXXIV

CONTINUED POGROMS AND THE RUSSO-JAPANESE WAR

(pp. 87-104)

Voskhod, 1905, pp. 3-35.

Memoirs of Pahlen, governor of Vilna, Geneva, 1904 ("Bund" edition).

Voskhod Booklets, 1904, IX, pp. 134 *et seq.*, 140 *et seq.*, 146 *et seq.*

Fornberg, Yevreyskaya Emigratzia ("Jewish Emigration"), p. 19, Kiev, 1908.

Chapter XXXV

THE REVOLUTION OF 1905 AND THE FIGHT FOR EMANCIPATION

(pp. 105-123)

Voskhod, 1905, Nos. 3-35.

Chapter XXXVI

THE COUNTER-REVOLUTION AND THE OCTOBER MASSACRE

(pp. 124-142)

Voskhod, 1905, No. 47; 1906, Nos. 10, 14, 18-21, 26, 42, 47, 49, 50.

"Sources for the History of the Russian Counter-Revolution," vol. I, St. Petersburg, 1908 (Pogroms according to official documents).

Judenpogromen, vol. I, pp. 187-223, 267-327, 383-400; vol. II, pp. 8-536.

Archives of the League of Equal Rights, St. Petersburg, 1906.

Vinaver, Yevreyski Vopros v Gosudarstvyennoy Dumie ("The Jewish Question in the Duma"), in *Svoboda i Ravienstvo*, 1907, Nos. 2-3.

Yevreyskaya Zhizn (weekly), 1906, Nos. 25-28, 32.

L. Wolf, The Legal Sufferings of the Jews in Russia, London, 1902, pp. 49-50.

CHAPTER XXXVII

EXTERNAL OPPRESSION AND INTERNAL CONSOLIDATION

(pp. 143-169)

Formy natzionalnavo dvizhenia v sovremiennykh gosudarstvakh, St. Petersburg., 1910, pp. 399-423, 778-783.

Dubnow, "Letters," St. Petersburg, introduction and pp. 294-361.

Svoboda i Ravienstvo, 1907, Nos. 30-32, 38, 39, 40, 41, 43-45, 46.

Stenographic Reports of the Duma for 1908-1909.

"A Study of Internal Affairs," in *Yevr. Mir.*, 1909, Book I.

Russian Jew. Encycl., vol. VII, p. 374.

J. Klausner, Novoyevreyskaya Literatura ("The New Jewish Literature"), 2d edition, Odessa, 1912.

M. Pines, Histoire de la Litterature Judéo-Allemande, Paris, 1910.

INDEX

INDEX

Aaron (I.), king of Khazars, I 26

Aaron (II.), king of Khazars, I 26

Aaron, rabbi of Tulchyn, I 148

Aaron, of Karlin, hasidic leader, I 234

Aaron Samuel Kaidanover, see Kaidanover

Abderrahman III., caliph of Cordova, I 24

Abraham, son of Isaac, Polish minter, I 42

Abraham Prokhovnik, see Prokhovnik

Abrahams, Israel, quoted, I 160

Abramius, Russian priest, objects to erection of synagogue, I 252

Abramovich, Shalom Jacob (*Mendele Mokher Sforim*), Hebrew and Yiddish writer, II 231 ff, III 60 f

Abydos, near Constantinople, seat of Sabbatai Zevi, I 206, 219

Adam, see Lebensohn, Abraham Baer

Adamovich, Mary, alleged victim of ritual murder, II 73

Adrianople, Sabbatai Zevi active in, I 207

Agriculture, among Jews in Lithuania, I 60, 68, II 72 in Poland, I 68, 264, II 89 championed by Nota Shklover, I 338; by Isaac Baer Levinsohn and by Maskilim in general, II 126 promoted by Russian Government, I 342 f, II 20, 61, 71 hampered by it, II 48, 197, III 10, 24 f; see also Colonization

Ahad Ha'am, pen-name of Asher Ginzberg, II 423 Hebrew writer and thinker, II 423, III 59 f exponent of Spiritual Zionism, II 48 ff associated with Palestinian colonization, III 49 founder of Order *Bne Moshe*, III 49 participates in Zionist Convention, III 51 founder and editor of *Ha-Shiloah*, III 58, 162 f

Ahijah, the prophet, alleged teacher of *Besht*, I 228

Aix-la-Chapelle, Jewish question discussed at Congress of, I 398 f

Akhal-Tekke, oasis in Central Asia, offered to Jews for settlement, II 306

Akmolinsk, territory of, in Siberia, II 367

Aksavok, Ivan, Russian publicist, advocates limited emancipation of Jews, II 208 defends pogroms, II 278

Aktziznik, Russian name for farmer of excise dues, II 186, 241

Albedinski, governor-general of Warsaw, suppresses pogrom, II 282

Albo, Joseph, philosophic work of, studied in Poland, I 133 f

Alexander the Great, indirectly responsible for Jewish immigration into Eastern Europe, I 13 f

Alexander (Yaghello), grand duke of Lithuania (1492-1506) and king of Poland (1501-1506), grants autonomy to Karaites, I 64 f favors Jewish capitalists, I 65, 71 expels Jews from Lithuania, and confiscates their property (1495), I 65 allows Jews to return to Lithuania and restores their property (1503), I 65, 70 f attended by Jewish body-physician, I 132

Alexander I, emperor of Russia (1801-1825), I 335-413 receives report of "Jewish Committee," I 341 f sanctions Jewish Statute of 1804, I 342 agrees to postponement of expulsion from villages, I 347 invites Jews to send deputies, I 351 establishes friendly relations with Napoleon, I 350 f orders again expulsion from villages, I 361 again postpones it, I 352 Hasidim indebted to, I 356 releases Shneor Zalman, hasidic leader, I 378 praises patriotism of Jews, I 358 accords friendly reception to Jewish deputations, I 358, 359, 392 f appealed to by Christian residents of Vilna and Kovno against Jews, I 369 f orders investigation of ritual murder, II 74 issues decree forbidding charge of ritual murder, II 74 grants autonomy to Poland, II 88 appoints his brother Constantine military commander of Poland, II 16

INDEX

receives report on Jews of Poland, II 94
appealed to by Poles against Jews, II 97, 99
vetoes Polish law barring Jews from liquor trade, II 94
reaction under, I 390 ff, 395 ff
favors conversion of Jews, I 396
establishes "Society of Israelitish Christians," I 396 f
refuses to dissolve it, I 400
sanction severe measures against "Judaizers," I 403
receives memorandum of Lewis Way on Jews of Russia, I 398
renews oppression of Jews, I 404
decrees expulsion from villages in White Russia, I 406
appoints new "Jewish Committee," I 407
objects to residence of Jews in Russian Interior, I 409
contemplates introduction of military service among Jews, II 15
favors agriculture among Jews, II 197, III 24; see I 363 ff
beginnings of revolutionary movement under, I 410
Alexander II., emperor of Russia (1855-1881), II 154-242
decendants of Jewish converts prominent during reign of, I 388

releases imprisoned Jewish printer, II 124
confirms sentence of Jews accused of ritual murder, II 152
pardons them later, II 153
abolishes juvenile conscription, II 155 f
sanctions opening of Russian Interior to first guild merchants, II 162; to university graduates, II 166, 348; to artisans, II 170
promotes handicrafts among Jews, II 346 f
Jewish trade school named after, III 13
does not favor agriculture among Jews, II 197
refuses right of universal residence to "Nicholas Soldiers," II 171 ff; finally grants it, II 29, 172
restricts appointment of rabbis and teachers, II 175
sanctions removal of Jewish disabilities in Poland, II 95, 181 f
admits Jews to bench, III 26
receives memorandum from Brafman, II 187
approves of popular representation, II 245
grants liberties to Zemstvos, II 386
assassinated, II 243, 279

influence of, on succeeding reign, II 349
laws in favor of Jews enacted by, repealed by successor, II 399
Jewish policy of, declared ineffective, II 271, 309
era of, depicted by Mendele Mokher Sforim, III 61

Alexander III., emporor of Russia (1881-1894), II 243-429
prejudiced against Jews while yet crown prince, II 202, 203, 244
influenced by Pobyedonostzev, II 245
holds conferences to decide policy of state, II 244
promises to maintain autocracy, II 246
receives Jewish deputation, II 260 f
endorses Ignatyev's anti-Jewish policy, II 272
appoints Gubernatorial Commissions, II 272
regrets necessity of suppressing pogroms, II 284
disregards Jews in coronation manifesto, II 338
bent on limiting admission of Jews to schools, II 339 f, 349
closes Jewish school of handicrafts, II 347

supports anti-Jewish minority of Pahlen Commission, II 370
affected by "miraculous" escape in railroad accident, II 378
condemns Jews for Crucifixion, II 379
reads and supports anti-Semitic papers, II 380
disregards Solovyov's appeal in favor of Jews, II 390
appealed to by Mayor of London in favor of Jews, II 390
angered by London appeal, II 393
United States Congress decides to appeal to, II 395
endorses emigration of Jewish proletariat, II 414
favors liquor state monopoly as anti-Jewish measure, III 22
refuses petition of Jewish soldiers to remain in Moscow, II 404
expels heads of Moscow Jewish community, II 424
threatens to sell at auction Moscow synagogue, II 424, III 12
causes expulsion of Jews from Yalta, II 429, III 18
death of, II 429
Jewish sect promises to name children after, II 334

INDEX

Alexandria, Egypt, emigration from, to South Russia, I 16

Alexandra (government of Kherson), pogrom at, III 100

Alexandrovka, village in Podolia, II 301

Alexeyev, member of Russian Senate, investigates condition of Jews, I 347 f, 352

Alexeyev, burgomaster of Moscow, opposes Jews, II 400 f

Alexis Michaelovich, Russian Tzar, annexes Little Russia, I 152 f, 244

invades Polish provinces, I 245

expels Jews from Moghilev, I 153

persecutes Jews of Vilna, I 154

imposes death penalty on converts to Judaism, I 253

Alexis, son of Nicholas II, birth of, occasions manifesto, III 98

Alexius, Russian priest, converted to Judaism, I 36

Alfasi, work of, studied in Poland, I 118

Algiers, emigration of Russian Jews to, II 69

Aliens, Jews in Russian law designated as, II 367

Allgemeine Zeitung des Judentums, quoted, II 55

founded by Ludwig Philippson, II 67, 219

hails end of persecution in Russia, II 67

Alliance, the Holy, inaugurates European reaction, I 390

assembles in Aix-la-Chapelle, I 398

Alliance Israélite Universelle, headed by Crémieux, II 153

suspected by Russian anti-Semites, II 189, 194

assists Russian-Jewish emigrants, II 268 f, 297

establishes agricultural settlement in Palestine, II 322

Alma, locality in Crimea, I 26

Altaras, Isaac, of Marseilles, visits Russia, II 69

Alter, Isaac Itche Meier, hasidic leader in Poland, II 122

Alubika, locality in Crimea, I 26

Alus, locality in Crimea, I 26

America, see Argentina and United States

American Hebrew, The, quoted, II 296

Amoraim, names of, collected by Polish rabbi, I 200

Amsterdam, emissary of Sabbatai Zevi active in, I 204

Jews of, petition Peter the Great, I 246

Ananyev (government of Kherson), pogrom at, II 251

Anapa, see Gorgippia

Andreas, of Brixen, alleged victim of ritual murder, I 179

Andrusovo, Treaty of (1667), provides for cession of Polish territory to Russia,

I 159; and release of prisoners, I 245

Anna (or Anne), Russian empress, permits retail trade to Jews, I 251
expels Jews from Little Russia, I 254
attended by Jewish body-physician, I 258

Anti-Semitism, in Poland, I 281 f, II 94 ff, III 166 ff
German A., referred to by Russian dignitaries, II 309
contrasted with Russian, III 6 f
in Russia, condemned by Russian writers, II 208
denounced by Solovyov, II 387
effect on Zionism, III 48 f

Anti-Trinitarians, Christian rationalistic sect in Poland, I 79, 136

Antwerp, Russian Jews in, II 420

Apostol, see Daniel Apostol; see also Conversion

Apter, Joshua Heshel, hasidic leader, II 121

Arabs, backward condition of, II 375
Jews in Palestine buy land from, II 422

Arakcheyev, Alexis, Russian reactionary, I 395, 406, II 19

Arbeiter Stimme, socialistic organ in Yiddish, III 56

Archangel, government of, II 367

Arendar, name explained, I 93
position of, I 93, 112, 265 f
in the Ukraine, I 141 f, 152
maltreated by Poles, I 169 f

Arendator, see Arendar

Argentina, emigration of Russian Jews to, II 413, 416 ff, 419

Arians, heterodox Christian sect in Poland, I 91, 136, 164
Isaac Troki argues with, I 137

Aristotle, studied in Polish yeshibahs, I 120, 126

Arisu, Slavonic tribe, I 26

Armenians, in Crimea, I 34
in Lemberg, I 53

Armleder, persecution of, drives Jews to Poland, I 50

Army, Jews volunteer in Polish A., I 152, 293 ff, II 105 f
Jews assist Polish A., in defence of country, I 147 f, 154, 293
Jews barred from advancement in Russian A., II 157, 354
number of Jews disproportionately large in Russian A., II 355 ff, 394.
promotion of Jews in Russian A., limited to rank of sergeant, II 157
Third Russian Duma proposes exclusion of Jews from, III 155 f
See Military Service, Recruits, and Soldiers

INDEX

Aronovich, Joseph, Polish-Jewish patriot, I 394

Artemisia, name of Jewess in Crimea, I 16

Arthur, president of United States, submits to Congress papers relating to Russian Jews, II 294

Artisans, Jews form 50% of A., in Poland, I 264

excluded from Christian tradeguilds, I 266

form special estate in Russia, I 308

form part of "burgher class," II 405

encouraged in Jewish Statute of 1804, I 344

opposed by Christian tradeguilds, I 360

exempted from military service, II 20

granted right of residence outside Pale, II 161, 168, 170

fictitious A., in St. Petersburg, II 343 f

restricted to products of their own workmanship, II 347

wives of, forbidden to engage in trade, II 385

attempt to withdraw from, right of residence outside Pale, II 399

school for A., closed, II 347

bank for A., opposed, III 25 f

expelled from Moscow, II 402, III 14

Baron Hirsch's gift in favor of, declined, II 415

Asefat Hakamim, Hebrew magazine, II 223

Ash, Shalom, Yiddish novelist and playright, III 162

Asher, rabbi in Cracow, I 104 f

Ashkenasi, Solomon, Polish court physician, I 132

Asia, Central, steppes of, suggested for settlement of Russian Jews, II 285, 306

Asia Minor, emigration from, to Black Sea coast, I 13 f, 16

establishment of Jewish state in, advocated, I 412; see also Turkey

Assimilation, see Polonization and Russification

"Assortment" (classification), of Jews, decreed by Nicholas I., II 64 ff, 141 ff

reflected in manifesto of Alexander II., II 157

Astrakhan (city), ancient Khazar capital situated near, I 19

Astrakhan (government), mosques destroyed in, I 254

opened to Jewish agriculturists, I 342

villages in, forbidden to Jews, I 343

Jews compared with Kalmycks in, II 367

Atyeney ("Athenaeum"), Russian magazine, defends Jews, II 208

Augustus II., king of Poland (1697-1704), I 167
- ratifies Jewish privileges, I 168
- expels Jews from Sandomir, I 173

Augustus III., king of Poland (1733-1763), I 167
- ratifies Jewish privileges, I 168, 180
- appealed to by Jews of Posen, I 175
- acquits Jews of ritual murder charge, I 176
- grants safe conduct to Frankists, I 215
- acts as God-father to Frank, I 218

Austria, Jews flee from, to Poland, I 66

Polish Jews export goods to, I 67

Polish Jews pass, on way to Palestine, I 209

shares in partitioning of Polish territory, I 186, 262, 274, 371

Frank stays in, I 220

Berek Yoselevich arrested in, I 297

wages war against duchy of Warsaw, I 303

forbids Jews to communicate with Paris, I 346 f

represented at Congress of Aix-la-Chapelle, I 398 f

Jews of, forbidden to settle in Russia (1824), I 409

grants emancipation to Jews, II 30

imposes military duty on Jews, II 30

Jewish policy of, serves as model for Russia, II 46, 49

Israel of Ruzhin escapes to, II 121

Parliament of, meets in Kremsier, II 177

Jewish socialists expelled from, II 224

Russian-Jewish students in, II 351

Government of, supports plans of Baron Hirsch, II 416

anti-Semitism rampant in, III 42

Autocracy, upheld by Alexander III., II 246; by Nicholas II., III 8
- re-establishment of, favored by Black Hundred, III 149

Autoemancipation, doctrine of, propounded by Leo Pinsker, II 330 ff
- contrasted with emancipation, II 331

Autonomism, national-cultural, doctrine of, propounded by Dubnow, III 41, 51 ff
- adopted as political platform, III 144

INDEX

Autonomy, Jewish, in ancient Tauris, I 16

granted, or confirmed, by kings of Poland, I 52, 53, 62, 72 f, 83 f, 98, 104, 105

rise and development of, I 103 ff, 188 ff

magna charta of (1551), I 105 ff

curtailment of, advocated by Poles, I 273, 280 f, 282

Jews of Poland plead for preservation of, I 291

recognized by Russian Government (1776), I 308 ff

curtailed by it (1795), I 319 f

recognized in modified form in Statute of 1804, I 344

larger amount of, demanded by Jews, I 349

abolition of, recommended by Council of State (1840), II 49

abolished by Nicholas I. (1844), II 59 ff

scheme of, proposed for kingdom of Poland, II 92

abolished in Poland (1822), II 102

abolition of last remnants of, recommended by Committee of Russian Government, II 195

St. Petersburg Jews, plead for, II 370

demanded by adherents of national-cultural Autonom-

ism, III 53 f; by "Bund," III 57; by Vilna community, III 109; by League for Equal Rights, III 112; by Russian Jewry in general, III 161; see also Kahal

Azariah, alleged biblical prophet, quoted to substantiate ritual murder libel, II 73

Azov, Sea of, Jewish settlements on shores of, I 14 f

movement of Khazars towards, I 19

Baal-Shem, name explained, I 223

Joel, I 203

founder of Hasidism acting as, I 224

Israel Baal-Shem-Tob, see Israel

Bab Al-Abwab (now Derbent), city in Caucasia, I 26

Babunj, land of, synagogue destroyed in, I 22

Babylonia, Judaism of, influences Khazars, I 20

scholars of, invited by Khazars 21, I 27

Poland compared with, I 122

Baer, of Lubavici, head of *Habad* sect, II 117

Baer, of Mezherich, disciple of Israel *Baal-Shem-Tob*, I 227, I 229 f, I 232

disciples of, carry Hasidism to North, I 234; establish Hasidism in Poland, I 33, 34 great-grandson of Israel of Ruzhin, II 120

Bagdad, caliphate of, relation of Khazars to, I 22

city of, threatened by Russians, I 26 f

Gaon of, communicates with Jewish scholars in Russia, I 33

Bahurs, or Yeshibah students, supported by Jewish communities in Poland, I 116

large number of in Lithuania, II 113

affected by *pilpul* method, I 119

study Aristotle, I 120

Bak-Tadlud, city in Caucasia, I 26

Bakchi-Sarai, Tartar capital, I 35

Bakst, professor, attends Jewish conference in St. Petersburg, II 304

opposes Jewish emigration from Russia, II 306

Balkan Peninsula, movement of Khazars towards, I 20

Balta (Podolia), pogrom at, II 299 ff, 314, 316, 321

rabbi of, pleads for rioters, II 316

visited by governor-general, II 316 f

Jewish community of, sends deputation to St. Petersburg, II 316 f

Baltic Provinces, number of Jews in, II 168

new Jewish settlers expelled from, II 32

Jews barred from (1835), II 40

expulsion of old settlers from, repealed, II 428

in throes of terrorism (1905), III 130; see Courland and Livonia

Bank, St. Petersburg lawyer, member of Jewish deputation to Alexander III., II 261

Baptism, see Conversion

Bar (Podolia), massacre at, I 149

Polish conference of, I 183

Bar, the Russian, established 1864, II 173

Jews admitted to, II 73

excluded from, II 352 f; III 26 f

Bar Association of St. Petersburg protests against Beilis case, II 166

Baranov, Russian Senator, dispatched to White Russia, I 406

"Bare-Footed Brigade," the, nickname for tramps, II 253

active in pogroms, 253, 256

Bartnit, city in Crimea, I 26

Baruch, see Boruch

INDEX

Bashi-Buzuks, Turkish irregular troops, II 253

pogrom makers compared with, II 253, 289

Basil, the Macedonian, emperor of Byzantium, persecutes Jews, I 23

Basil, Christian martyr, I 17

Basil, grand duke of Moscow, I 242

Basle, Council of, adopts canonical laws against Jews, I 63

Zionist Congresses at, III 44 f, 84 f, 144

"Program," III 44; modified by Ahad Ha'am, 50

Basurman, Russian name for non-Orthodox, I 35

Batory, Stephen, king of Poland (1576-1586), forbids charge of ritual murder and desecration, I 89, 96

ratifies and amplifies Jewish privileges, I 89

defends Jews of Posen, I 90

patronizes Jesuites, I 90 f

grants license to Jewish printer, I 131

attended by Jewish body-physician, I 132

recaptures city of Polotzk, I 243

Bavaria, Wagenseil, anti-Jewish writer, native of, I 138

Max Lilienthal, native of, II 52

Beaconsfield, Earl of, champions equal rights for Jews, II 202

hostile to Russia, II 288

Beards, shaving of (and of earlocks), recommended by Polish reformers, I 282, and by Kalmansohn, I 385

"bearded regiment" in Warsaw, II 106; see Earlocks

Beilis, Mendel, accused of ritual murder, III 82, 164 ff

nickname for Jews in Poland, III 167

Bekri, Al-, Arabic writer, quoted, I 21

Belza, Polish judge, arranges libel against Jews, I 101

Belzhytz (Province of Lublin), Jacob of, author of polemical treatise in Polish, I 136

Bench, the Russian, Jews excluded from, II 352 f, III 26

Benckendorff, chief of Russian gendarmerie, II 21

Benedict XIV., appealed to by Jews of Poland, I 179

Benjacob, bibliographer in Vilna, II 136

Benjamin, king of Khazars, I 26

Benjamin of Tudela, Jewish traveller, I 32; II 233

Benjamin II. (Joseph Israel), Jewish traveller, II 233

Benjamin III., name of fictitious traveller in Yiddish and Hebrew novel, II 233

Berdychev (government of Kiev), Levi Itzhok, hasidic leader, resident of, I 232 f, 382

Jews of, release fellow-Jews from prison, I 266

Jews of, support Polish cause, I 292

Tobias Feder, Hebrew writer, of, I 388

Max Lilienthal accorded friendly reception at, II 56

Halperin, resident of, member of Rabbinical Commission, II 57

Mendele Mokher Sforim, resident of, II 232

pogrom at, averted by Jewish self-defence, II 256 f

visited by White, representative of Baron Hirsch, II 418

Jewish community of, signs petition for equal rights, III 108

Berdychevsky, Micah Joseph, Hebrew writer, III 60

Berek, Kahal elder, I 172

Berek Yoselovich, see Yoselovich

Bergson, Jacob, prominent Jew of Warsaw, II 103

Berkovich, Joseph, son of Berek Yoselovich, calls for Jewish volunteers to Polish army, II 105

Berlin (Germany), Mendelssohn circle in, centre of enlightenment, I 238

attracts Jewish students from Poland and Russia, I 239, 388, II 114

"Berliner" synonymous with heretic, I 278, 384

enlightenment of, hated by hasidic leaders, I 383

influences Warsaw, I 300 f, 384 f

epidemic of conversions in, I 388

Congress of, II 202

Jewish socialists in, II 223

stock-exchange of, affected by pogrom at Rostov, II 358

refugees from Moscow arrive in, II 408

Russian Jews emigrate to, II 420

place of publication, I 386; III 51, 52, 58, 60

Berlin, Shmerka, of Velizh, accused of ritual murder, II 75, 77

Berlin, Slava, wife of former, arrested on same charge, II 77

Berlin, Jewish scholar, member of Jewish deputation to Alexander III., II 261

Berliner, A., quoted, I 179

Bernardine Monks, in Poland, active in ritual murder libel, I 100 f, 177

Bersohn, Polish-Jewish writer, quoted, I 105

INDEX

Berthenson, I., converted Jew, Russian court physician, II 214

Besht, see Israel Baal-Shem-Tob

Bessarabetz, anti-Semitic paper in Kishinev, III 169 ff

Bessarabia, included in Pale (1835), II 40

Jewish agricultural colonies in, II 72

expulsions from, II 385

anti-Semitic agitation in, III 69 ff

von Raaben, governor of, III 74, 77

Urussov, governor of, III 93, 97; see Kishinev

Bezalel, Jewish tax-farmer in Poland, I 167

Bezalel, of Kobrin, Hebrew author, I 201

Bialocerkiew, see Byelaya Tzerkov

Bibikov, governor-general of Kiev, criticises Jews in official report, II 47

arrests Israel of Ruzhyn, II 120 f

Bialik, Hayyim Nahman, Hebrew poet, III 63, 162

composes poem on Kishinev massacre, III 79 f

Bialystok, province of, annexed by Prussia (1795), I 297

Bialystok (city, government of Grodno), Samuel Mohilever, rabbi of, II 378

Poles threaten massacre of Russians and Jews in, I 357

Jewish labor movement in, III 55

pogroms at, III 114 f, 120, 136 f; discussed by First Russian Duma, 137 f

Bible, studied by Khazars, I 21

taught in Yiddish translation in Poland, I 114

study of, encouraged by Isaac Baer Levinsohn, II 126

Bible Society, of London, model of Russian Bible Society, I 396

Lewis Way, representative of, champions cause of Russian Jews, I 397

Bible Society, the Russian, established under Alexander I., I 396

Bielsk (Lithuania), Jew of, accused of ritual murder, I 87

Bielski, Polish chronicler, quoted, 180

"**Bilu**," society of Palestinian pioneers, organized in Kharkov, II 321 f

Bismarck, German chancellor, favors equal rights for Jews, II 202

Black Death, the, stimulates immigration of Jews into Poland, I 50
penetrates to Poland, I 52
ravages of 1648 compared with those of, I 157

Black Hundred, the, patronized by Nicholas II., III 113, 151
deputation of, received by Nicholas II., III 131
supposed to number 100,000, III 126
organized as "League of Russian People," III 141
gain in Second Duma, III 142
triumph of, III 149 ff
active in organizing pogroms, III 113 ff, 124 ff, 126 ff, 136
engineer Beilis case, III 164 ff
take advantage of Jewish rightlessness, III 132
intimidate Jews during elections, III 134, 153
insult Jewish deputies in Duma, III 156; see League of the Russian People

Black Sea, the, ancient Jewish settlements on shores of, I 13 ff
Khazars move in direction of, I 19, 28
Petahiah of Ratisbon travels to, I 33
establishment of Jewish colonies in neighborhood of, advocated, I 331

Blaine, James G., American Secretary of State, expresses resentment at persecution of Russian Jews, II 395 f

Blinov, Russian student, killed while defending Jews, III 116

Blondes, David, Jewish barber in Vilna, accused of ritual murder, III 37

Board of Deputies, Jewish organization in London, pleads for Russian Jews, II 262

Bobovnya (government of Minsk), Jewish convert from, slanders Jews, II 80
Jewish community of, protests against denial of Jewish franchise, III 121

Bobrov, District of (government of Voronyezh), Judaizing sect spreads to, I 401

Bogdanov, Russian soldier, accuses Jews of ritual murder, II 151

Bogdanovich, Russian general, organizes pogroms, III 125 f

Bogolepov, Minister of Public Instruction, bars Jews from schools, III 27 f
assassinated by Russian terrorist, 29

Bogrov, Grigory, Russian-Jewish writer, II 241 f

INDEX

Bogrov, assassinates Stolypin, III 164 f

Bohemia, visited by Pethahiah of Ratisbon, I 33

oppressed Jews of, emigrate to Poland, I 41

Jews from, form community in Cracow, I 104

Magdenburg Law adopted in many parts of, I 41

talmudic learning carried from, to Poland, I 122

Mordecai Jaffe, native of, famous rabbi in Poland, I 127

Jews of, apply to Polish rabbis for religious guidance, I 125

Boleslav the Pious (*Polish*, Boleslav Pobozny), of Kalish, prince of Great Poland, grants charter to Jews, I 45 ff

charter of, ratified by successors, I 51, 59; embodied in Polish code of law, I 71

Boleslav the Shy (*Polish*, Boleslav Wstydliwy), Polish prince, encourages immigration of Germans, I 44

Bona Sporza, Polish queen, sells office of state, I 76

Bonaparte, see Napoleon

Border Zone, along Polish-Prussian and Polish-Austrian border (Twenty-one-Verst

Zone), barred to Jews by Polish Government (1823), II 95

law excluding Jews from, repealed by Alexander II., II 95, 181

along Western Russian border (Fifty-Verst Zone), villages in, barred to new Jewish settlers (1835), II 40, 366

expulsion of Jews from entire B. Z. ordered, II 63; but not executed, II 64

new attempt to expel Jews from, II 385

Borispol (government of Poltava), pogrom at, II 267

Borki (government of Kherson), railroad accident to Alexander III., in neighborhood of, affects his policies, II 378

Borukh Leibov, Jewish tax-farmer, I 249

publicly executed, I 251 ff

Borukh Shklover, translates Euclid into Hebrew, I 381

Borukh of Tulchyn, hasidic leader, I 232

succeeded by Joshua Heshel, II 121

Bosporan Era, The, I 15

Bosporus, the Cimmerian, or Taurian, also called Panticapaeum (now Kerch), ancient Jewish community in, I 14 f

Greco-Jewish inscription found in, I 15
bishop of, instructed to convert Jews, I 18

Boycott, economic, against Jews in Poland, III 166 ff

Brafman, Jacob, Jewish apostate, accuses Jews of forming illegal Kahal organization, II 187 ff
author of "Book of the Kahal," I 189
accuses *Alliance Israélite* of heading world Kahal, II 189
accuses Society for Diffusion of Enlightenment of forming part of Kahal, II 216
influences Russian authorities, II 190, 193 ff, 240
example of, followed by Lutestanski, II 202

Bramson, L., member of Central Committee of League for Equal Rights, III 112
deputy to First Russian Duma, III 134

Bratzlav (Podolia), Polish deputy from, objects to extension of Jewish rights, I 288
Nahman of, leader of "Bratzlav Hasidim," I 382 f; II 121 f
former name for government of Pololia, I 317

Breslau, Church Council of, adopts anti-Jewish restrictions, I 47 ff; ratified by Church Council of Kalish, I 57
visited by Solomon Maimon, I 239

Brest-Kuyavsk, name explained, I 75
anti-Jewish riot in, I 75
home of Jacob Koppelman, Hebrew author, I 133

Brest-Litovsk, name explained, I 75
Jews of, form important community, I 59, 73
Jewish community of, represented in Polish Federation of Kahals, I 110; and later in Lithuanian Federation, I 112
Jewish community of, headed by Saul Udich (Saul Wahl), I 94
Michael Yosefovich, taxfarmer, native of, I 72
Mendel Frank, rabbi of, I 73, 104
supposed former rabbi of, accuses Jews of ritual murder, I 173
Jews expelled from (1495), I 65
Jews of, express loyalty to Sigismund I., I 81
Jews of, protected by Sigismund III., I 94

INDEX

Jews of, import goods to Moscow, I 243

Starosta of, upholds authority of Kahal, I 190

Kahal of, upbraided by Polish authorities for delaying elections, I 192

pogroms in (17th century), I 99, 161 (May, 1905), III 119

Briskin, Arye, Jewish apostate, informs against Jews of Mstislavl, II 85

British East Africa, see Uganda

British Government, The, see England

Brodski, Jewish merchant of Kiev, offers to establish trade bank, III 25 f

Brody (Galicia), rabbis assembled at, excommunicate Frankists, I 214; and Hasidim, I 237

Besht settles in, 223

Jewish merchants of, settling in Odessa, spread Haskalah, II 133

rallying-point of pogrom refugees, II 268 f, 321

Bruchsaal (Germany), Alexander I., receives Jewish deputation at, I 359, 391

Bruhl, Polish Prime Minister, I 180

Brunn, capital of Moravia, Jacob Frank settles in, I 219

Brussels, newspaper in, defends Russian Government, II 393 place of publication, II 173

Bryce, James, English statesman, addresses London protest meeting against pogroms, II 290

Buarezm, see Khwarizm

Buchner, Abraham, Polish assimilationist, II 103 f

Buckee, influences Russian-Jewish *intelligenzia,* II 209

Buda (Ofen), Hungary, Church Council of, passes anti-Jewish restrictions, I 49; ratified by Council of Kalish, I 57

Budak, city in Crimea, I 26

Budberg, Russian Minister for Foreign Affairs, member of Committee to consider Jewish legislation, I 347

Budek, Polish priest, foments anti-Jewish agitation in Cracow, I 56

Budny, Simon, Polish theologian, holds disputations with Jews, I 136

Budushchnost ("The Future"), Zionist weekly in Russian, III 59

Buenos Ayres, Russian Jewish immigrants settle in, II 421

Bukovina, The, I 150

Hasidism gains footing in, II 121

Bulan, King of Khazars, embraces Judaism, I 21, 25

Bulgar, The, Slav tribe, I 26

Bulgaria, on the way to Khazaria, I 25

called upon by Congress of Berlin to grant equality to Jews, II 202

villages in, attacked by Bashibuzuks, II 253, 289

Bulgarin, Thaddeus, Russian anti-Semitic writer, II 139

Bulyghin, Russian Minister of Interior, receives rescript from Nicholas II. concerning Duma, III 110

Chairman of Committee to discuss Jewish franchise, III 121

recommends denial of Jewish franchise, III 122

"the Bulyghin Constitution" published, III 124

"Bund," League of the Jewish Workingmen of Lithuania, Poland, and Russia, organized (1897), III 56 ff

holds secret conventions, III 56 f

demands Jewish-national rights, III 57

arranges demonstrations, III 68; and strikes, III 130

held responsible for pogroms, III 89

boycotts First Duma, III 134

refuses co-operation with other Jewish parties, III 111, 148;

see Revolutionary Movement and Socialism

Burghers form estate in Poland, I 44

hostile to Jews, I 70

enter into relations with, I 84 f

receive civil rights from Polish Diet, I 279

form estate in Russia, I 308

restricted in right of transit, I 322

bear burden of conscription, II 23, 29; later relieved, II 200

subject to corporal punishment, II 405

artisans included in estate of, II 405

segregation of Jews as unsettled B. proposed by Nicholas I., 142 f

Burgomaster, office of, barred to Jews, II 199, 425

Burtas, Slav tribe, I 26

Butrymovich (*Polish,* Butrymowicz), Polish deputy, member of Jewish Commission, I 264, 287 f

offers plan of Jewish reform, I 271, 274, 281 ff, 283

his plan used as a model, I 326 f, 385

Byelaya Tzerkov (*Polish,* Bialocerkiew), Treaty of (1651), readmits Jews to Ukraina, I 152

INDEX

Byzantine Sea, The, see Black Sea

Byzantium, Empire of, influences Jewish colonies in Tauris, I 17 ff

Jews persecuted in, I 23 f

Jews emigrate from, to Tauris, I 28

relation of, to Khazars, I 19 ff

defeats Khazars in Crimea, I 28

relation of, to Russia, I 30

relations of Hasdai Ibn Shaprut with, I 24

Cabala, firmly entrenched in Poland, I 134 f

attracts Solomon Luria, I 126

esteemed and defended by Joel Sirkis, I 130, 133

vies with Rabbinism, I 199

study of, forbidden before the age of forty, I 214

adopted by sect of Frankists, I 214

studied by Elijah of Vilna, I 235

preached by Nohum of Chernobyl, I 382

Cabala, Practical, name explained, I 134

spreads in Poland, I 134 f, 202 ff

introduced from Italy, I 208

studied and pursued by Besht, I 222 f, 224

Cadets, The, see Constitutional Democrats

Calahora, Arie-Leib, Jewish martyr in Posen, I 174 f

Calahora, Mattathiah, Jewish martyr in Cracow, I 164 f

Calahora, Solomon, Polish court physician, I 132

Caliphate, Eastern, or Caliphate of Bagdad, checks movement of Khazars, I 19

relation of, to Khazars, I 22

Caliphate, of Cordova, connected by Hasdai ibn Shaprut with other lands, I 24

Calvinists, in Poland, welcome invading Swedes, I 155

Candia, Delmedigo, author, born in, I 134

Campe, German author, work of, translated into Hebrew, II 134

Canada, Jewish emigration from Russia to, II 421

immigration of Dukhobortzy, Russian sect, to, III 10

Candidate, learned degree in Russia, term explained, II 165

Candle Tax, see Tax

Canterbury, Archbishop of, sends representative to London protest meeting against pogroms, II 289

joins pogrom relief committee, II 291

Cantonists, or juvenile recruits, name explained, II 19 institution by Nicholas I., II 19 sent to outlying Russian provinces, II 24 f hunters, or "captors," of, II 23 martyrdom of, II 24 ff forced conversion of, II 26, 45 institution of, not extended to Poland, II 109 abolished by Alexander II., II 156; see Conscription, Military Service, Recruits, and Soldiers

Capistrano, papal legate, "Scourge of the Jews," I 62

Capitals, the Russian (St. Petersburg and Moscow), Jewish first and second guild merchants permitted to visit (1835), II 40

Jewish physicians, though admitted into Interior, excluded from (1865), III 167

admission of Jews to schools of, restricted to 3%, II 350

admission of Jews to universities of, restricted to 2%, III 29

Capiton, Christian martyr, I 17

Carlowitz, Treaty of (1699), returns Podolia to Poland, I 208

Carmelites, Church of, in Posen, holds demonstration against Jews, I 95

monk, member of, accuses Jews of ritual murder, I 100 bring law suit against Jews of Posen, I 174

Caro, Joseph, author of *Beth-Yoseph*, I 123 author of Shulhan-Arukh, see Shulhan-Arukh

Carpathian Mountains, The, Besht retires to, I 223

Casimir the Great (1333-1370), king of Poland, rejuvenates country, I 50 f ratifies and amplifies Jewish charter of Boleslav, I 51 f annexes Red Russia, I 42, 53 grants autonomy to Jews of Lemberg, I 53 infatuated with Jewess, I 53 f charter of, ratified by Vitovt, I 59 referred to as patron of Jews, II 98

Casimir IV., king of Poland (1447-1492), pursues liberal policy towards Jews, I 61 f grants Jews new charter, I 61 f attacked by archbishop of Cracow, I 62 forced to rescind Jewish privileges, I 63 fines magistracy of Cracow for permitting riots against Jews, I 64 charter of, ratified by Sigismund II., I 83

INDEX

Casimir the Just, Polish ruler, Jews active as ministers during reign of, I 42

Caspian Sea, The, called Sea of Jorjan, I 23

Khazars settled on shores of, I 19, 26; dislodged from, I 28

Castellan, title of Polish official, explained, I 287

Catherine I., empress of Russia, changes and deports Jewish tax-farmer (1727), I 249

Catherine II., The Great (1762-1796), empress of Russia, fictitious ukase of, permitting pogroms, I 183 refuses to admit Jews into Russia, I 259 f; and into Little Russia, I 260 f attitude of, towards Jews of annexed Polish provinces, I 306 ff appealed to by the Jews of White Russia, I 311 f attitude of, towards Jews, changes for worse, I 314 ff lays foundation of Pale of Settlement, I 314 ff favors removal of Jews from villages, I 319, 366 curtails Jewish autonomy, I 319, 366 endeavors to destroy "Jewish separateness," I 367 admits Jews to South Russia, I 316

substitutes term "Yevrey" for "Zhyd," I 320

Caucasus, The, ancient trade route leading through, I 23 Khazars originate from, I 19 Khazars occupy cities in, I 26 Jewish agriculturists permitted to settle in (1804), I 342; but not in villages of, I 343 "Judaizers" deported to, I 403 ritual murder trial in, II 204

Censorship, over Hebrew books, exercised by Council of Four Lands, I 195 f

Government C. advocated by Polish reformers, I 723, 281 disregard of, severely punished, II 123

enforcement of, advocated by I. B. Levinsohn, II 130

hasidic books subjected to, II 212

Russian C., hampers Maskilim in Vilna, II 136

interferes with Jewish press, I 219 f

suppresses *ha-Emet,* II 223; *Voskhod,* 407, III 98; *Novosti,* II 407

rages throughout Russia, II 371

suppresses news of pogroms, II 302, 358; and of Moscow expulsion, II 407 prevents Russian press from expressing sympathy with Jews, II 387

forbids Russian press to publish collective statements concerning Jews, II 387

confiscates pamphlet defending Jews, II 388

grants full scope to anti-Semitic press, III 31; see also Printing

Census, of the Jewish population, in Poland (1764), I 197

in White Russia (1772), I 307

in Russia (1816-1819), I 390

Jews of Vilna released from municipal C. (1682), I 166; see Statistics

Central Committee, see Committee

Champagny, French Cabinet Minister, conducts negotiations with Polish Government, I 299

Charles IX., French king, succeeded by Henry, Polish king, I 89

Charles XII., Swedish king, invades Poland, I 154 ff, 169

Charnetzki, Polish general, massacres Jews, I 155 f

Charter, granted to Jews by Leshek, prince of Poland (905), I 40

issued by Boleslav of Kalish (1264), I 45 ff

included in Polish code of law (1505), I 71

ratified and amplified by Casimir the Great, I 51 f; burned, I 61

issued by Vitovt, grand duke of Lithuania (1388), I 59 f

granted by Casimir IV. (1447), I 61 f

granted to Jews of Lithuania by Sigismund I (1540), I 81

ratified by Sigismund II. (1548), I 83 f

old Ch's. ratified by Stephen Batory, I 89; by Vishniovetzki, I 160; by Augustus II., I 168; by Augustus III., I 168, 180

Ch. of Jewish autonomy issued by Sigismund II. (1551), I 105 ff

Ch. demanding admission of Jews into Russia sent by Sigismund II. to Ivan the Terrible (1550), I 243

granted to Jews of Cracow by John Casimir (1661), I 159

"Golden Ch." by Catherine the Great, permitting pogroms, I 183

Theodor Herzl seeks to obtain Ch. from Sultan, III 84

offered by British Government for colonization of Uganda, III 84; see also Statute

INDEX

Chartoriski (or Chartoryski), Adam, member of Committee for Amelioration of Jews, I 335

chairman of Committee to consider Jewish question in Poland, II 89, 91

opposes liberal project of Novosiltzev, II 93

Chatzki, Thaddeus, Polish historian, makes special study of Jewish problem, I 263 ff

proposes Jewish reforms, I 271, 288

suggestions of, adopted by others, I 327, 385

Chatzkin, Russian-Jewish journalist, II 207

Chazars, see Khazars

Chekhovich, Martin, Polish theologian, holds disputations with Jews, I 136 f

Chenstokhov (*Polish*, Czenstochowa), province of Piotrkov, Jacob Frank imprisoned in, I 218 f

occupied by Russian troops, I 219

pogrom at, III 36 f

Cherkaski, Count, burgomaster of Moscow, favors limitation of Jews in municipal government, II 199

Cherkassy (government of Kiev), hasidic center, II 120

Chernigov (city), Jews of, exterminated, I 149

pogrom at, III 128

ritual murder at Gorodnya, in neighborhood of, I 247

home of Isaac, early Russian-Jewish scholar, I 33

home of Litman Veigin, merchant, II 38

Chernigov (province or government), subject to Poland, I 140

closed to Jews (1649), I 151

opened again to Jews (1651), I 152

Jews of, exterminated, I 157

ceded to Russia (1667), I 159

few Jews left in, I 246

made part of Pale (1794), I 317, II 40

pogroms in localities of, II 257, 267, 315, 411, III 129

court of, sentences rioters, II 315

Jews expelled from villages of, II 341

governor of, misapplies laws relating to Jews, II 341

governor of, permits Jews to open stores on Christian holidays, II 411

localities in:

Gorodnya, I 247

Karpovich, II 315

Konotop, II 257

Nyezhin, II 267, III 129

Semyonovka, III 129

Starodub, II 411

Chernikhovski, Saul, Hebrew poet, III 64

Chernobyl (government of Kiev), hasidic center, I 232, 382

"dynasty" of, widely ramified, I 332, II 119 ff

Chernovitz (Bukowina), Sadagora, in neighborhood of, hasidic center, II 121

Chernyshev, Count, governor-general of White Russia, assures Jews of former liberties, I 306 f

sets apart Jews as an estate, I 309

Chernyshevski, radical Russian author, influences Jewish *Intelligenzia*, II 207, 209 effect of, on Lilienblum, 237

Chersonesus, near Sevastopol, bishops of, force Jews into baptism, I 17

scene of rivalry between Jews and Byzantines, I 30

Chetvertinski, Count, betrays Jews of Tulchyn, I 147 f

Chiarini, Abbé, Polish anti-Semitic writer, II 104

Chigirin (province of Kiev), home of Khmelnitzki, I 144

Chikhachev, Russian Navy Minister, favors emigration of Jews from Russia, II 419

Chikhachev, member of Council of State, favors Jewish franchise, III 12

Chlenov, Zionist leader, III 47

Chmelnicki, see Khmelnitzki

Chresta, name of Greco-Jewish woman, I 15

Christianity, propaganda of, in Tauris, I 17 f; among Khazars, I 20

fusion of Judaism and Ch. attempted by Jewish sect in Russia, II 335; see Church and Conversion

Chudnov (Volhynia), young Jews of, martyred, III 117

Chufut-Kale (Crimea), harbors old Karaite community, I 35

Church, the Greek-Orthodox, persecutes Jews in Byzantine empire, I 18

Pobyedonostzev reports on affairs of, III 9

Church, the Roman-Catholic, in Poland, spreads hatred of Jews, I 44, 47 ff

gains strength under Yaguello, I 54 f

opposes Casimir IV., I 62 f

hostile to Jews during Reformation, I 79, 85 f

agitates against Jews, I 99 ff

prompts anti-Jewish legislation of Polish Diets, I 160

responsible for anti-Jewish riots, I 161

Jews forbidden to leave houses during Ch. processions, I 160

INDEX

Church Council, or Synod, of Breslau (1266), introduces canonical laws into Poland, I 47 f

of Buda (1279), passes anti-Jewish restrictions, I 49

of Constance (1420), attended by Polish ecclesiastics, I 57

of Kalish (1420), ratifies former canonical enactments against Jews, I 57 f

of Piotrkov (1542), adopts "Constitution" against Jews, I 82 f, 171

of Lovich (1720), forbids building of new synagogues, I 171

of Plotzk (1733), insists on necessity of Jewish suffering, I 171

Chwolson, Daniel, professor, converted Jew, member of Committee to investigate ritual murder, II 151

disproves ritual murder, II 205

member of Executive Committee of Society for Diffusion of Enlightenment, II 214

Cilicia (Asia Minor), harbors Jewish communities, I 14

Cimmerian Bosporus, see Bosporus

Cincinnati, Max Lilienthal, rabbi of, II 59

"Circular Jews," name explained, II 404

privileges of, withdrawn, II 428

City Government, see Municipalities

Civil Service, Jews barred from by Church councils, I 49

Jews in Russian army promised admission to, II 29

possessors of learned degrees admitted to, II 165

Jewish physicians admitted to, II 167; barred from, III 27

Jews in general barred from, II 352; III 26; see Tax-Farmer

Clement XIII., pope, protects Polish Jews, I 180

Clement XIV., see Ganganelli

Cohen, Jacob Joseph, disciple of Besht, I 227, 230 f

stirs wrath of Elijah Gaon, I 237

Cohen, Joshua Falk, rabbi of Lublin, I 111 f

presides over Council of Four Lands, I 128

head of talmudic academy in Lemberg, I 128

Cohen, Naphtali, Polish rabbi, engages in magic and enters into relations with Sabbatians, I 204

Cohen, Nehemiah, Messianic propagandist, I 207

Cohen, Sabbatai, called *Shak*, of Vilna, author of commentary on *Shulhun Arukh*, I 130

issues epistle picturing persecutions of 1648, I 157 f

Colchians, tribe, I 15

Colonies, Jewish, in South Russia, visited by emissary of Baron Hirsch, II 418

pogroms in, II 271; III 35

Colonization, of Jews, undertaken by Russian Government in New (South) Russia, I 352 363 ff; II 70 ff; checked by Government, II 365

in White Russia, II 72

in Siberia, II 71

in Palestine, II 321 f; III 42, 46, 49; promoted by Baron Rothschild, II 375

in United States, II 328, 374

in Russia, proposed by Baron Hirsch, II 415; and by ICA of Paris, III 10; but discouraged by Russian Government, III 24 f

in Argentina, II 416, 421; see Agriculture

Commerce, Jews as mediators in, between Europe and Asia, I 23

Jews engage in, with Slav countries, I 39

Jews in Polish C., I 264, 266 f

Polish kings encourage Jews in, I 85

Sigismund III. confirms Jewish rights of (1588), I 93

Jews restricted in, in Posen, I 74 f; Lemberg, I 75; Cracow, I 98; Vilna, I 99

restrictions in, imposed upon Jews by Polish Diets (1538), I 78; (1768), I 182; (1643), I 99

anti-Jewish restrictions in, demanded by Synod of Piotrkov (1542), I 82; and by Polish journalist (1798), I 281

Russian Government permits Jews to engage in, at fairs of Little Russia and Kharkov government, I 250 ff

Little Russians plead for admission of Jews in interest of, I 260 f

Jews in Russian C., I 359 f; II 366

deprecated by I. B. Levinsohn, II 126; and other Maskilim, II 137

attitude of Russian Government towards Jewish C., II 185

Jews with higher education granted unrestricted right of (1904), III 98; see also Economic Life and Merchants

Commission, "C. for Jewish Reform," appointed by Polish Diet (1790), I 287 ff

project of, submitted to Diet and postponed, I 289
resumes labors but fails, I 290
Butrymovich, member of, I 264
project of, adopted by Friesel, Russian governor of Vilna, I 326 f

Commission, "High C. for revision of current Laws concerning Jews" ("Pahlen C."), appointed 1883, II 336
composition of, II 336
examines material of "Gubernatorial Commissions," II 337, 363
futility of, II 337
serves as screen for anti-Jewish legislation, II 338
discusses projected educational restrictions against Jews ("school norm"), II 339; votes against them, II 349
conclusions of, II 363 ff
deprecates Jewish disabilities, II 364, 366
refers to revolutionary leanings of Jews, II 364 f
criticize Jewish separation and exploitation, II 365
describes poverty of Jews, II 366 f
favors gradual emancipation of Jews, II 368 f
minority of, favors continuation of repression policy, II

369; supported by Alexander III., II 370
invites Jewish experts, II 369 f
disbanded, II 380

Commissions, the Gubernatorial, appointed to counteract "injurious influence" of Jews (1881), II 272 ff
circular of Ignatyev concerning appointment of, II 273; quoted by Cardinal Manning, II 289
anti-Jewish recommendations of, II 275
influence Central Committee for Revision of Jewish Question, II 277, 309
material of, examined and discarded by Pahlen Commission, II 337, 363
charges of, denied by Jewish Conference, II 307

Commission, the Rabbinical, see Rabbinical Commission

Committee, to consider Jewish questions, appointed by Polish Government (1815), II 89 f; (1825), II 103 f
to investigate ritual murder (1864), II 151
to investigate Brafman's charges against Kahals (1866), II 189 f, 240
Russo-Jewish C. in London, II 388 f

Central C. of ICA in St. Petersburg, II 420
secret C. under Plehve plans Jewish counter-reforms (1891), II 399
C. of governors and high officials appointed with anti-Semitic instructions (1904), III 93

Committee for Amelioration of Jews, called "Jewish Committee" (1802), I 335 ff
appointment of, causes alarm among Jews, I 336
invites deputies from Jewish Kahals, I 337
Nota Shklover invited to assist, I 338
elaborates plan of Jewish reform, I 338; and submits it to Kahals, I 339
conflicting tendencies within, I 339 f
submits report to Alexander I., I 341 f
supplies basis for Statute of 1804, I 342
reappointed 1809, advises against expulsion of Jews from villages, I 352 ff, 405
reappointed 1823, plans to reduce number of Jews in Russia, I 407 f
drafts principal enactments concerning Jews, II 31
suggest expulsion of Jews from Courland, II 32

frame Statute of 1835, II 34
appointed 1871, II 191
charged to consider Kahal organization and economic exploitation, II 193 ff

Committee for Radical Transformation of Jews, appointed 1840, II 49 f, 157
presided over by Kisselev, II 50, 157
considers plan of "assorting" Jews, II 64 ff
Moses Montefiore permitted to communicate with Nicholas I. through, II 68
suggests modification of conscription system, II 155
resuscitated (1856), II 161
discusses right of residence outside Pale, II 161 ff, 163 ff, 169
favors opening of Interior to retired soldiers, II 171
suggests law demanding secular education of teachers and rabbis, II 175

Committee for Revision of Jewish Question, appointed 1881, II 277
suggests unpopulated localities for Jewish settlement, II 285
plans expulsion of Jews from villages, II 285
frames "Temporary Laws" of 1882, II 309 ff

INDEX

Committee of Ministers approves measures against "Judaizers," I 402

approves expulsion of Jews from villages of White Russia, I 406

instructed to provide relief for expelled Jews, I 406

advised to stop expulsion, I 407

formulates function of "Jewish Committee," I 408

question of admitting artisans into Interior transferred to, II 169 f

modifies "temporary Rules" of Ignatyev, II 311 f, 318

objects to pogroms, II 312 f

advocates school norm for Jews, II 339, 349

discusses emigration to Argentina, II 419

entrusted by Nicholas II. with execution of constitutional reforms, III 106

presided over by Witte, III 107

discusses Jewish question, III 123; see Council of Ministers

Committee on Freedom of Conscience, appointed by Second Duma, favors Jewish emancipation, III 142

Conference of Jewish Notables, in St. Petersburg (September, 1881), II 277; (April, 1882), II 304 ff

refuses to regulate emigration, II 307

disastrous results of decision of, II 321

Congregation of New Testament Israelites, Judeo-Christian sect in Kishinev, II 335

Congregational Board, supersedes Kahal in Poland, II 102 f

(of Warsaw), objects to separate Jewish regiment, II 106

sends deputation to St. Petersburg to plead for equal rights, II 110

president of, arrested by Russian Government, II 181

Congress, of Aix-la-Chapelle, discusses Jewish question, I 398 f

of Berlin, demands equal rights for Balkan Jews, II 202

of Vienna, see Vienna, Congress of

Jewish C. proposed by Pinsker, II 331

of Medicine, in Moscow, III 15

Zionist C., III 41, 44 f, 84 f, 144

of United States, see United States

of Poland, see Poland, kingdom of

Congressional Record, quoted, II 294, 296, 395

THE JEWS IN RUSSIA AND POLAND

Conscription, see Cantonists, Military Service, and Recruits

Constance, Synod of, attended by Polish clergy, I 57

Constantine, Old, see Constantinov

Constantine Pavlovich, grand duke, Russian heir-apparent, II 13, 129

proclaimed emperor but resigns, II 13

appointed commander of Poland, II 13, 16, 91

suggests expulsion of Jews from border zone, I 408

expels Jews from villages, II 31

Isaac Baer Levinsohn submits memorandum to, II 129

Constantinople, capital of Byzantium, I 17

captured by Turks, I 35

patriarchs of, carry on Christian propaganda in Tauris, I 18

Church of, hopes for conversion of Khazars, I 20

Spanish exiles in, I 27

Abydos, seat of Sabbatai Zevi, in neighborhood of, I 206

Jewish pilgrims on way to Palestine arrive in, I 209

Ignetyev, Russian ambassador at, II 259

Constantinov, Old, or Staro-(Volhynia), Cossack massacre at, I 149

"protest" against conscription at, II 21 f

Constitution, "anti-Jewish C.," passed by Polish Diet of 1538, I 77 f

adopted by Piotrkov Church Council of 1542, I 82 f

Polish C. of May 3, 1791, 289 f

introduced by Napoleon into duchy of Warsaw, I 398

violated by Government of duchy, I 299 ff

"Jewish C." of 1804, I 342 ff

Constitutional Democratic Party, the (Cadets), in Russia, mistrusts Government, III 130

forms majority in First Duma, III 135

loses in Second Duma, III 142

weak in Third Duma, III 153

Jews in, III 119

Vinaver, leader of, III 134

majority of Jewish deputies belong to, III 135

Contra-Talmudists, name for Frankists, I 214 f

Conversion, of Jews, to Christianity, recommended by patriarch of Constantinople and bishop of Bosporus, I 18, 20

forced upon Jews of Byzantium, I 23

forcible C. of children punished by Polish law (1264), I 47
of Jewish Messianic pilgrims in Palestine, I 210
of Jacob Frank and followers, I 217 f; deplored by Besht, I 229
carried on through military service, II 26 f, 45, 156 f
feared by Jews of Vilna, II 54 f
endeavors of Russians towards, stopped, II 173 f
of Haskalah pioneers, II 132
of disillusioned *intelligenzia*, II 327
as result of expulsions in St. Petersburg, II 344; and Moscow, II 425; see Society of Israelitisch Christians
C. epidemic in Berlin, I 388
forced by Ivan the Terrible upon Jews of Vitebsk, I 154; and upon Jews of Polotzk, I 243
Russian Government aims at, I 396 ff; II 44 f, 188
of Khazars, to Judaism, I 20
attempted C. of Vladimir, I 30
of Turkish Sabbatians, to Mohammedanism, I 210

Converts, to Christianity, permitted by King John Casimir to return to Judaism, I 151
accuse Jews of ritual murder, I 173 f; II 73, 80

inform against Hebrew books, II 42
in city of Saratov, II 150
individual converts:
Abraham Yosefovich, I 73
Berthenson, II 214
Bogrov, II 242
Brafman, II 187 ff
Briskin, II 85
Chwolson, II 151, 205, 214
Efron-Litvin, III 38
Grudinski, II 80
Horvitz, II 202, 244
Kronenberg, II 178
Nyevakhovich, I 388
Peretz, I 388
Pfefferkorn, II 189
Priluker, II 335
Savitzki, II 73
Serafinovich, I 173 f
See also, Judaizers

Cordova, Caliphate of, see Caliphate

Coronation Diets, see Diets, Coronation

Cosmopolitanism, advocated by Jewish socialists, II 222; by Levanda, II 240; by Bogrov, II 241

Cossacks, name explained, I 142
origin of, I 142 ff
Ukrainian C's., I 142
Zaporozhian C's., see Zaporozhians
massacre Jews (1637), I 144; (1648), I 144 ff, 154, 246

exclude Jews from their country (1649), I 151
readmit Jews to their territory (1651), I 152
ally themselves with Russia (1654), I 152 ff
invade Polish territories, I 154, 156, 244 ff
rise against Poles and Jews, I 182 ff
Jews visit territory of, despite prohibition, I 246
C's. of Little Russia plead for admission of Jews, I 250
See also Khmelnitzki

Costanda, military governor of Moscow, inaugurates expulsion of Jews, II 401

Council, Church C., see Church Council

Council of Ministers, in duchy of Warsaw, opposes Jewish emancipation, I 299
in Russia, Nicholas I. appends resolution to report of, II 62
reports to Tzar on Jewish agricultural colonization, II 71
recommends appointment of "High Commission" on Jewish question, II 336
passes anti-Jewish laws, II 338
not consulted in expulsion from Moscow, II 402
favors grant of franchise to Jews, III 122
presided over by Witte, II 125
suggests moderate Jewish reforms to Nicholas II., II 141

Council of State, in Poland, discusses Jewish question, II 93 f
formation of, in Russia, I 335
bars Jews from Russian Interior, I 316
condemns expulsion of Jews from White Russian villages, I 407; II 34
objects to further expulsions, II 34 f
discusses right of residence outside Pale, II 35 f, 161 ff, 163 ff, 169 f
recommends alleviation in military service, II 36
disagrees on expulsion from Kiev, II 36 f
passes Statute of 1835, II 37
receives memoranda on Jewish question, II 38
discusses Jewish question and suggests measures (1840), II 47 ff
discusses exact limits of Pale, II 70
acquits Velizh Jews of ritual murder charge, II 81 ff
convicts Jews of Saratov, II 152
discusses Jewish separatism, under influence of Brafman's charges, II 190

recommends appointment of Commission of Amelioration of Jews, II 191, 193

material on Jewish question prepared for, II 336

plans of Pahlen Commission said to have been brought before, II 320

disregarded by Alexander III. in issuing "Temporary Rules," II 312, 386; in passing anti-Jewish restrictions, II 338; in passing school norm, II 349; in expulsion from Moscow, II 402

confirms exclusion of Jews from Zemstvos, II 386

members of, favor Jewish franchise, III 122

Courland, added to Pale, I 321

Jews settled in, I 341

new Jewish settler expelled from, II 32

Lipman Levy, Russian financial agent, native of, I 248

Mordecai Aaron Ginzburg, Hebrew writer, resident of, II 133

Nisselovich, Duma deputy for, III 153

Courts, Jews of Poland exempted from jurisdiction of municipal and ecclesiastic C's., I 45 f, 51 f, 84, 94, 103

cases between Jews tried by royal C's., or Voyevoda C.

(in Lithuania, Starosta C.), I 45 f, 51 f, 59 f

"Jewish Judge," Polish official nominated by Jews, attached to Voyevoda C., I 46, 52, 192

Voyevoda C. tries cases between Jews and Christians, I 84, 191; acts as Court of Appeals, I 191; Kahal elders attached to, I 84

tax-farmer Yosko and employees placed under jurisdiction of royal C., I 71

Jews on noble estates placed under C's. of nobles, I 84

Municipal C's. claim jurisdiction over Jews, I 93 f

ritual murder cases tried by C's. without proper jurisdiction, I 95 f

civil and partly criminal cases between Jews tried by C. of rabbis and Kahal elders, I 83, 105 f

Kahal C. granted right of imposing *herem* and other penalties, I 73, 105 f

Kahal C. granted exclusive jurisdiction in cases between Jews, I 191

Kahal C. consists of rabbis as judges and Kahal elders as jury, I 191

Council of Four Lands acts as C., I 111; appoints provincial judges, I 111

Kahal C. of Vilna issues *herem* against Hasidim (1772), I 237

Kahals recognized as C's. by Russian Senate (1776), I 309

cases between Jews tried by C's. of District and Gubernatorial Kahals, I 309

Gubernatorial Kahals act as C's. of Appeal, I 309

cases between Jews and Christians tried by municipal C's., I 309

Senate questions legality of special Jewish C's. (1782), I 310

Jews admitted to membership in municipal C's. (1783), I 310

cases between Jews tried by municipal C's. (1786), I 313

Jews represented on municipal C's. by elective jurymen, I 313

Kahal C's. limited to spiritual affairs (1786), I 313; (1795), I 319

Jews of Lithuania plead for preservation of Kahal C's. (1795), I 320

Statute of 1804 places Jews under jurisdiction of Russian C's., I 344

Jews continue to resort to Kahal C., I 367; see Kahal, Jewish Judge, and Rabbi

Cox, Samuel S., of New York, protests in Congress against pogroms, II 294 ff

Cracow, leading city of Little Poland, I 42, 110, 196

capital of Western Galicia, I 53

election diets held in, I 98

superseded as Polish capital by Warsaw, I 85

conquered by Swedes, I 154

surrendered by Shlakhta, I 155

Province of, annexed by Austria, I 297

Jewish refugees from Crusades seek shelter in, I 41

Jewish Community of, represented on Council of Four Lands, I 110

Jewish communities in Province of, destroyed, I 156

Jewish charter ratified by Casimir the Great, in, I 51

Jews of, receive charter from John Casimir, I 159

anti-Jewish riots in, I 56 f, 63 f, 75 f, 102, 161, 166

Jews of, subjected to commercial restrictions, I 74 f, 98

restrictions for Jews of, demanded by Church Synod, I 82

ghetto established in, I 64, 85

ritual murder trial in, I 164 f

host trial in, I 101 f

INDEX

"Judaizing" tendencies in, I 79 f

anti-Semitic writers in, 96 f

Oleshnitzki, archbishop of, I 62

Gamrat, bishop of, I 79

Kmita, Voyevoda of, I 76

Hebrew printing-press in, I 131, 195

Delacruta, Cabalist, resident of, I 134

Horowitz, Isaiah, Cabalist, studies in. I 135

Pollak, Jacob, head of yeshibah in, I 122

Spira, Nathan, head of yeshibah in, I 135

Rabbis of:

Asher, I 104

Fishel, I 105, 132

Heller, I 158

Isserles, I 123

Kaidanover, Samuel, I 200

Meir of Lublin, I 129

Meisels, II 179

Peretz, I 104

Sirkis, I 133

Crémieux, Adolf, president of *Alliance Israélite,* corresponds with Lilienthal, II 67

petitions Alexander II. on behalf of Jews accused of ritual murder, II 153

criticized by governor-general of Kiev, II 194

Crimea, The, name defined, I 13

Greeks in, I 13 f

conquered by Khazars, I 19 f

last refuge of Khazars, I 28

known as Khazaria, I 28 f

ruled by Pechenegs and Polovtzis, I 29

conquered by Tatars, I 33

Tataric Khanate of, I 35 f, 142

Tatars of, ally themselves with Cossacks, I 143 ff

Kaffa, Genoese colony in, I 33 f

list of cities in, I 26

visited by Petahiah of Ratisbon, I 33

Taman peninsula, in neighborhood of, I 23

Jews in, I 14 ff, 33 ff

Karaite communities in, I 35

Jews of, settle in Kiev, I 30; in Lithuania, I 35

expelled Lithuanian Jews emigrate to, I 65

Jewish State in, suggested, I 412; see Tavrida, government of

Crimean War, stops plan of Jewish "Assortment," II 143

effect of, on Jewish situation II 149 f, 154

Crown, the, signifying Poland as contrasted with Lithuania, 1 72, 88, 110, 113, 127, 162, 193

Crown Rabbis ("official," or *kazyonny*, rabbis), name explained, II 176
forced upon congregations, II 176
act as Government agents
See Rabbis

Crown Schools, see Schools

Crusades, the, stimulate immigration of Jews into Poland, I 33, 41
give rise to Teutonic order, I 63
victims of Cossack massacres (1648) compared with those of, I 156

Cyril, Christian missionary, disputes with Jews, I 18

Daitzelman, Jewish merchant in Nizhni-Novgorod, victim of pogrom, II 361

Dakota, North and South, Jewish agricultural colonies in, II 374

Damascus, ritual murder trial of, II 68

Daniel Apostol, Hetman of Little Russia, pleads for admission of Jewish salesman, I 250

Dantzic, annexed by Prussia, I 292

Danube, The, Jewish emigration form provinces of, to Poland, I 41

Dardanelles, The, commerce between Genoa and Crimea through, I 34

Darkest Russia, periodical published in England, II 381

Darshanim (Preachers), in Poland, I 201 f

Darvin, Charles, influences Russian-Jewish *intelligenzia*, II 209

Dashevski, Pincus, assaults Krushevan to avenge Kishinev massacre, III 81 f
trial of, induces Plehve to forbid Zionism, III 82
receives greetings of Russian-Jewish convention, III 132

Davidov, Russian military leader, praises Jews, I 357

Davis, Noah, Judge, speaks at New York protest meeting, II 297

Decembrists (*Russian*, Dyekabrist), Russian revolutionaries, name explained, I 410
suppressed by Nicholas I., II 13
attitude of, towards Jews, I 409 ff

Dekert, John, mayor of Warsaw, champion of burgher class, I 286

Delacruta, Mattathiah, Italian Cabalist in Cracow, I 134

INDEX

Delmedigo, Joseph Solomon, called *Yashar*, of Candia, arraigns Polish Jews for opposing secular culture, I 134

Dembrovski, Polish bishop, arranges disputations between Frankists and Talmudist, I 214 f

orders burning of Talmud, I 215

Demiovka, suburb of Kiev, pogrom at, II 254 f

De non Tolerandis Iudaeis, right of excluding Jews

in Warsaw (and other Polish cities), I 85

in Kiev, I 94 f

abolished in Zhitomir, Vilna (and other cities), II 172

abolished throughout Poland (1862), II 181

Denis, Greek-orthodox priest, converted to Judaism, I 36

Department of Law, part of Council of State, considers Jewish legislation, II 34 ff

Deputation of the Jewish People, The, created by Alexander I., I 392 ff

disbanded in 1825, I 395

instrumental in stopping ritual murder trial in Grodno, II 74

induces Alexander I. to veto prohibition of liquor trade in Poland, II 94

Derbent, see Bab Al-Abwab

Diaspora, Jewish, neglected by Zionism, III 52

as conceived by National-Cultural Autonomism, III 53 ff

as conceived by Russian-Jewish historians, II 65

Diet, The, in Poland, term defined, I 76

controlled by Shlakhta, I 58, 77, 160

authority of, undermined by *liberum veto*, I 92, 168

Jews represented at, by "syndics," I 111

anti-Jewish tendency of, I 76 f, 160

preceded by anti-Jewish propaganda, I 165

counteracts benevolent intentions of kings, I 160

censures King Sobieski for interest in Jews, I 167

condemns anti-Jewish riots, I 166 f, 171

fixes amount of Jewish head-tax, I 194

granted right to elect government, I 263

Jews admitted to Warsaw during sessions of, I 268 ff

re-established in duchy of Warsaw, I 298

Coronation D's., name explained, I 98

Jewish privileges ratified at, I 98, 160, 168

Election D's., name explained, I 98

Individual Diets, according to years:

1423 (of Varta), restricts financial operations of Jews, I 58

1454 (of Nyeshava), rescinds Jewish privileges, I 63

1496 (of Piotrkov), confirms restrictions of Nyeshava Diet, I 64

1521 (of Piotrkov), limits commerce of Lemberg Jews, I 75

1538 (of Piotrkov), passes anti-Jewish "constitution," I 77; confirmed by Diet of 1562, 1565 and 1768, I 87

1548 (of Piotrkov), Sigismund II. ratifies Jewish charter at, I 83

1618, discusses passionately Jewish question, I 97

1643 (of Warsaw), restricts profits of Jews, I 99

1658 (of Warsaw), expels sectarians from Poland, I 91

1670 (of Warsaw), restricts financial operations of Jews, I 160

1693 (of Grodno), arraigns Bezalel, Jewish tax-farmer, I 167

1717 (of Warsaw), increases Jewish head tax, I 169; protests against anti-Jewish riots, I 171

1740, rejects resolution turning Jews into serfs, I 170

1764 (of Warsaw), alters system of Jewish taxation, I 181, 197; prohibits conventions of Jewish District elders, I 198

1768 (of Warsaw), renews commercial restrictions of 1538, I 182, 267; admits Jews temporarily to Warsaw, I 268

1788-1791, see Diet, Quadrennial

1808, elections to, force Government to take up Jewish question, I 299

1818, first D. of kingdom of Poland, displays anti-Jewish attitude, II 96, 99

1831, releases Jews from conscription, II 107

Diet, The Quadrennial, or Great (1788-1791), name explained, I 263

reflects liberal ideas, I 278

INDEX

elaborates modern constitution, I 263

equalizes burgher class, I 278

discusses agrarian question, I 279

prepares for struggle with Russia, I 279

attitude of, towards Jewish question, I 263 ff, 279 ff, 285, 288 ff

refers Jewish question to special commission, I 264, 279, 287, 327

finance committee of, reports on Jews, 263 ff

Chatzki, Polish historian, member of, I 263, 288

Butrymovich, champion of Polish Jews, member of, I 264, 274, 280 f, 285, 289

Chatzki and Butrymovich submit proposals to, I 271

Jews admitted to Warsaw during, I 285

notified of anti-Jewish demonstration in Warsaw, I 286; and investigates it, I 287

literature centering around, I 279 ff

appealed to by Simeon Wolfovich against Kahals, I 276

project of Jewish reforms submitted to king during, I 284

Dietines, the, Polish provincial diets, I 76

provide occasions for anti-Jewish riots, I 170

serve as pattern for Jewish D., I 113, 196 f

Jewish D., called officially "synagogues," I 196

Dilke, Sir Charles, English Under-Secretary of State, interpellated about pogroms, II 262

Dillon, Eliezer, army purveyor, represents Jews before Russian Government, I 358

member of Deputation of Jewish People, I 392 f

Disabilities, see Restrictions

Disputations, religious, between Jews and Christians, I 136 f

between Frankists and orthodox Jews, I 214 f, 216 f; attended by Besht, I 229

Disraeli, see Beaconsfield

Distillers, Jewish, admitted to Russian Interior, II 170

Distilling, see *Propinatzya*

Dlugosh, Jan, called Longinus, Polish historian, quoted, I 57

Dnieper, the, river, Petahiah of Ratisbon reaches banks of, I 33

Jews disappear from left bank of, I 157

Jews decimated on right bank of, I 157

southern basin of, subject to Poland, I 140
left bank of, called Little Russia, ceded to Russia, I 159
Jews penetrate into Little Russia "from other side of," I 253
Cossacks beyond Falls of, I 143 ff
uprising against Poles and Jews on right bank of, I 182
Cossack army "on both sides of," plead for admission of Jewish salesmen, I 250
central river of Pale, I 317
See Moghilev on the Dnieper

Dniester, The, river, Moghilev on, I 98

Dobrolubov, Russian critic, influences Jewish *intelligenzia,* II 207, 209

Doctor, official title of rabbis in ancient Poland, I 72, 104, 109

Dolgoruki, Count, governor-general of Moscow, friendly to Jews, II 400 f

Dombrovski, Polish revolutionary leader, I 303

Domestics, Christian, the keeping of, prohibited by Church Council of Breslau (1266), I 49
by Synod of Piotrkov (1542), I 82

by "Lithuanian Statute" (1566), I 87
by Diet of Warsaw (1670), I 160
prohibition of, in Russia, suggested by Dyerzhavin, I 333, and Golitzin, 404
prohibited by Russian Senate (1820), I 404 f
prohibited for permanent employment (1835), II 40
Christians of Pereyaslav call upon Jews to refrain from, II 266
Pobyedonostzev deplores influence of Jews on their D., III 9

Domestics, Jewish, outside Pale, Jewish merchants allowed limited number of, II 162
Jewish university graduates allowed two, II 166, 344
fictitious D. in St. Petersburg, II 344 f

Dominican Order, the, church of, in Posen, collects regular fine from Jews, I 55
priest of, in Cracow, causes execution of Jews, I 164
general of, in Rome, calls upon head of, in Cracow, to defend Jews, I 165

Don, the, river, Khazars move towards, I 19
Territory of D. Army closed to Jews, II 346

INDEX

Dondukov-Korsakov, governor-general of Kiev, criticizes Jews, II 193 f

Drabkin, rabbi of St. Petersburg, reports conversation with Ignatyev, II 305

Drenteln, governor-general of Kiev, ferocious Jew-baiter, abets pogroms, II 252, 254 recommends severe repression of Jews, II 276 upbraids Jews of Balta, II 316 f misconstrues "Temporary Rules" against Jews, II 341

Dresden, Jews of, appeal to Augustus III. against ritual murder libel, I 176

Dress, Christian, forbidden to Jews by "Lithuanian Statute" (1566), I 87 deprecated by rabbis (1607), I 112 prescribed for Jewish visitors to Russian Interior (1835), II 40 prescribed for Jewish members of municipalities (1804), I 345 German D. adopted by "Berliners," I 384 Russian D. preferred by Jews to German D., I 350; see Dress, Jewish

Dress, Jewish (hat or badge), prescribed by Synod of Breslau (1266), I 48

by Synod of Buda (1279), I 49 by Synod of Kalish (1420), I 57 by Diet of Piotrkov (1538), I 78 by Synod of Piotrkov (1542), I 83 abandoned by some Jews in Warsaw, I 300 f defended by Polish rabbi, I 283 Jews of Warsaw demand equal rights as reward for discarding, I 385 f prohibition of, recommended by Butrymovich, I 281; by Polish nobility of Lithuania, I 326; by Friesel, governor of Vilna, I 327; and Dyerzhavin, I 333 tax imposed on, in Russia (1843), I 110; extended to Poland (1845), I 110 Russian Council of State finds principal source of Jewish separatism in (1840), II 48; and suggests prohibition, II 49; but modifies view (1870), II 190 f governors-general advised of impending prohibition of, II 66 prohibition of, enacted (1850), I 144; and extended to female attire (1851), I 144 prohibition of, remains ineffective, I 144 f

Alexander II. displeased with, in Poland, II 190

luxury in, forbidden (1566), I 87; deprecated by Abraham Hirshovich, I 284; by I. B. Levinsohn, II 128; by Christians of Pereyaslav, II 266

white D. favored by early "Hasidim," I 209, 231, 237; objected to by assembly of rabbis, I 237; see Dress, Christian

Dreyfus Affair, the, exploited by Russian press, III 32

witnessed by Doctor Herzl, III 42

Druskeniki (government of Grodno), Conference of "Lovers of Zion" at, II 377

Drusus, name of Greek Jew, I 15

Dubnow, S. M., author of present work, quoted, I 114, 163, 235 champions national rejuvenation of Judaism in Russia, II 327

formulates theory of Spiritual Nationalism, or National-Cultural Autonomism, III 52

member of central committee of League for Equal Rights, III 42

editor of periodical *Yevreyskaya Starina*, III 160

Dubossary, ritual murder libel at, III 70 f

pogrom at, frustrated by Jews, III 71

Dubrovin, head of Black Hundred, received by Nicholas II., III 149

Dubrovna (government of Moghilev), Voznitzin, captain of navy, converted to Judaism at, I 252

Duchy of Warsaw, see Warsaw, Duchy of

Dukhobortzy, Russian sect, flees from persecution to Canada, III 10

Duma, Imperial Russian, plans for, formulated, III 122; and published, III 124

manifesto of October 17 promises establishment of, III 127

First D., elections to, III 133

League for Equal Rights participates in elections to, III 133 f

Zionists participate in elections to, III 145

boycotted by Left, III 134

Jewish deputies to, III 134

Jewish question before, III 135 ff

pogroms discussed by, III 126, 136 ff

appoints commission to investigate Bialystok pogrom, III 137

INDEX

adopts resolution condemning pogroms, III 139

dissolved, III 139

Second D., convoked, III 141

only three Jewish deputies elected to, III 142

Jewish question referred by, to committee, III 142

dissolved, III 142

Third D., called the Black, III 153

only two Jewish deputies elected to, III 153

violently anti-Semitic, III 153 ff

discusses Beilis case, III 165

Fourth D., anti-Semitic agitation in Poland during elections to, III 167

Jewish D. deputies co-operate with joint Jewish Council in St. Petersburg, III 148

Dunaigrod (Podolia), ritual murder trial at, I 178

Durnovo, Russian official, investigates ritual murder trial at Saratov, II 150

Durnovo, Russian Minister of Interior, fanatic reactionary, II 379

bars Jews from local self-government (Zemstvos), II 386; and municipal self-government, II 425

suggests expulsion of Jews from Moscow, II 402

revokes decree of 1880, causing expulsion of "circular Jews," II 428

continues in office under Nicholas II., III 9, 16

member of Witte cabinet, III 31

Dusyaty (government of Kovno), pogrom at, III 115

Dvina, river, Jews drowned by Russian troops in, I 243

Dyekabristy, see Decembrists

Dyelanov, Minister of Public Instruction, decrees "school norm," limiting admission of Jews to schools and universities, II 349 ff

applies school norm leniently, III 27 f

Dyen ("The Day"), Russian-Jewish weekly, II 218, 220, 238

Dyerzhavin, Gabriel, member of Russian Senate, becomes interested in Jewish question, I 327

meets Jews for first time on tour to White Russia, I 328

meets modernized Jewish physician in White Russia, I 386

pursues anti-Jewish purpose on tour, I 329 f

prepares elaborate "Opinion" on Jews, I 330 ff

appointed Minister of Justice, I 335

"Opinion" of, studied by Committee for Amelioration of Jews, I 335 f

retires, I 337

example of, followed later in White Russia, 405

Earlocks (*Peies*), discarded by modernized Jews, I 384

cutting off of, recommended in Poland, I 385

wearing of, prohibited by Nicholas I., II 144 f

See Beards

Easter, Russian, duration of, II 249

season of pogroms, II 248, 299; III 34, 71 ff, 96 f, 114 f, 134

Economic life, of Jews, in Poland, I 42, 44 f, 67 f, 160, 264 ff, 270

in Polish Silesia, I 42

in Lithuania, I 60

in Russia, I 353 f, 359 ff

in White Russia, I 310 ff; II 14

in Russian South-west, II 193 f

in Kiev, II 264

undermined under Nicholas I., II 70, 72

improved under Alexander II., II 185 f

E. importance of Russian Jews pointed out by Vorontzov, II 64 f; by Pahlen Commission. II 366; and by foreign press, II 408

Russian Jews accused of E. exploitation, II 193 f, 270 ff

restricted under Alexander III., II 318, 346 ff

E. misery of Russian Jews, II 318, 366 f

collapse of, under Nicholas II., III 22 ff

in America, II 374

E. boycott in Poland, III 166 ff

Edels, Samuel, called Maharsho, famous Polish talmudist, I 129 f

Education, Jewish, see Heder and Yeshibah

modernization of, in Poland, urged by Kalmansohn, I 385; by David Friedländer. II 90; by Polish assimilationists, II 101

criticized by Russian Council of State, II 48

negative effects of, pointed out by author, II 113

national E. demanded by Zionist Convention at Minsk, III 45

fostered by Society for Diffusion of Enlightenment, III 160

autonomy of, demanded by League for Equal Rights, III 112

progress of, in Palestine, III 148

See School

Education, Secular, promotion of, among Jews, urged by Russian dignitaries, I 327, 333

championed by Frank, Jewish physician, I 331; by I. B. Levinsohn, II 128; and by Maskilim of Vilna, II 137

encouraged by Alexander I., I 344 f; by Nicholas I., II 20, 57 f; and by Alexander II., II 163 ff, 166, 175, 216

shunned by Russian Jews, I 350, 380; II 48, 53 ff, 175

spreads under Alexander II., II 176 f, 216

promoted by Society for Diffusion of Enlightenment

spread of, among Jews feared by Russian authorities, II 339, 348

disparaged in general by Pobyedonostzev, II 348

Educational Restrictions, demanded by Alexander III., II 349

issued by Minister of Instruction (1887), II 350

disastrous effects of, II 350 f

compel Jewish youth to study abroad, II 351; III 31

stimulate emigration, II 373

applied with increasing rigor under Nicholas II., III 27 ff

abolished in institutions of higher learning (1905), III 124

restored (1907), III 152

placed on Statute books in 1908, III 157 f

See Enlightenment, School, and University

Efron-Litvin, converted Jew, anti-Semitic playwright, III 38

Egypt, emigration of Jews from, into Tauris, I 16

Sabbatian propaganda in, I 205

Eibeschiitz, upheld by Polish rabbis in struggle with Emden, I 204

Einhorn, David, modern Jewish writer, III 162

Eisenbaum, Anton, Polish-Jewish assimilationist, head of rabbinical seminary, II 103

Eisenmenger, anti-Jewish writer, II 104

Eisenstadt, Michael, represents Kahals before Russian Government, I 393

Ekaterinoslav, see Yekaterinoslav

Ekron, Jewish colony in Palestine, II 375

Eliezer, Bohemian scholar, quoted, I 43

Elijah, the prophet, believed to associate with Besht, I 228

Russian church festival in honor of, II 358

Elijah of Vilna, called the Gaon, idolized by rabbis of Lithuania and other countries, I 235 f

familiar with Cabala, I 235

studied secular sciences, I 235 f

tolerant towards pursuit of secular sciences, I 381

avoids *pilpul* and cultivates method of textual analysis, I 236

introduces method into yeshibahs of Lithuania, I 380; particularly into yeshibah of Volozhin, I 381

fragmentary nature of literary work of, I 236

rigorist in religious practice, I 236

opposes Hasidism, I 236

causes issuance of *herem* against Hasidism, I 237

reaffirms *herem*, I 373

checks growth of Hasidism in Vilna, I 372

refuses to see Shneor Zalman, I 374 f

death of, I 375

Hasidim of Vilna rejoice over death of, I 375

Elimelech of Lizno, hasidic leader, I 232

Elizabeth Petrovna, Russian empress (1741-1761), persecutes non-Orthodox, I 254

decrees expulsion of Jews from entire Russian empire (1727), I 255

refuses plea of Ukrainians and Livonians for admission of Jews, I 257

pens famous resolution against Jews (1743), I 257

decrees again unconditional expulsion of Jews (1744), I 257 f

dismisses Sanches, Jewish court physician, I 258

policy of, followed by Catherine II., I 259

Elizabethgrad, see Yelisavetgrad

Emancipation (Equal Rights), introduced by Napoleon into duchy of Warsaw, I 298

not applied to Jews, I 298 f

Warsaw Jews apply to Polish Government for, I 299

opposed by Polish Council of Ministers, I 299

suspended by duke of Warsaw for ten years, I 299

17 Jews of Warsaw apply for, as reward for assimilation, I 300

refused by Polish Minister of Justice, I 300 f

representatives of Warsaw community plead for, I 301 f

opposed by Polish Senate, I 302

Warsaw Jews apply to Nicholas I. for, II 110

INDEX

granted to Jews of Poland by Alexander II (1862), II 181 ff

promised to Jews by early Russian revolutionaries, I 413

prominent St. Petersburg Jews apply to Alexander II. for, II 159 f

recommended by Stroganov, governor-general of New Russia, II 168 f

advocated by Russian-Jewish press, II 219 f, 238, 332

claimed by Young Israel, heterodox Jewish sect, II 334

recommended by Pahlen Commission, II 364, 368

urged by Guildhall meeting in London, II 391

demanded by Russian lawyers and writers for all citizens, III 105

partial E. promised by Russian Government, III 106

unrestricted E. demanded by Russian Jews, III 108 ff

demanded by Society for Diffusion of Enlightenment, III 111

urged by League for Equal Rights, III 111 f

adopted for all citizens by First Duma, III 135

bill providing for E. of Jews referred by First Duma to Committee, III 137 f

opposed by Nicholas II., III 141

bill providing for, passed by Committee of Second Duma, III 142

forms platforms of Jewish people's group, III 146 f

See League for Attainment of Equal Rights

Emden, Jacob, opposed by Polish rabbis in fight with Eibeshutz, I 204

Emigration, of Jews, from Lithuania, prevented by Sigismund I. (1540), I 81

from Poland, caused by Khmelnitzki massacres (1648 ff), I 157

from Russia, caused by persecutions and pogroms, II 268, 327 ff, 413, 420; III 96

causes shortage of Jewish recruits, II 356

prompts imposition of military fine, II 373, 414

stimulated by educational restrictions, I 373

welcomed by Russian Government as solution of Jewish problem, II 419 f; III 10

encouraged by Russian Government, II 285, 414, 417 f, 420

old Russian law prohibiting E. not enforced, II 69, 285

Plehve promises to support E., III 83

to Algiers, proposed by French Jews, II 69

to Argentina, II 413, 416 ff, 419 f

to Canada, II 421

to Palestine, I 269 f; II 321 f, 419 ff, 421 ff; advocated by *Poale Zion*, III 145; importance of, recognized by Russian Jewry, III 54, 147

to United States, II 297 f, 320 f, 373 ff, 409, 413, 420 f; III 96, 104; calls forth protest of U. S. Government, II 396; importance of, recognized by Russian Jewish parties, III 54, 145, 147

Emigration, Regulation of, attempted by emigrant societies, II 297 f

urged by Mandelstamm and part of Jewish press, II 298

feared by prominent St. Petersburg Jews, II 298

deprecated by *Voskhod* as subversive of emancipation, II 298 f

rejected by Jewish Conference in St. Petersburg (April, 1882), II 307; disastrous results of rejection, II 420

proposed by Baron Hirsch, II 416, 419

sanctioned by Russian Government, II 420

Encyclopedists, French, praise polemical treatise of Isaac Troki, I 138

England, represented at Congress of Aix-la-Chapelle, I 398

Parliament in, discusses pogroms, II 262 f, 281 f, 287 ff, 388 ff

prominent men in, approach Nicholas I. on behalf of Russian Jews, II 63

Priluker, Russian Jew, missionary in, II 335

Russian-Jewish students in, II 351

offers Uganda to Zionists, III 85

See London

Enlightenment, see Haskalah

Equal Rights, see Emancipation

Ephes-Dammim, name of biblical place, used as book title, II 131

Ephesus, city in Asia Minor, Jewish community in, I 14

Epstein, Samuel, represents Jews before Russian Government, I 393

Eshet Hayil, term explained, II 113

Estate, Real, see Property, Real

Estherka, concubine of Casimir the Great, I 53 f

INDEX

Euclid, geometry of, translated into Hebrew, I 381

Euler, German mathematician, criticizes dismissal of Jewish court physician in St. Petersburg, I 258

Europe, Eastern, beginnings of Diaspora in, I 13

Euxine Colonies, see Black Sea

Evangelists, Protestant sect in Poland, I 91

Evarts, William M., American Secretary of State, makes representations to Russian Government, II 293

Eve, daughter of Jacob Frank, head of Frankist sect, I 220

Excise Farmers, called *aktzizniks*, II 186

Excommunication, see *Herem*

Execution, or forcible seizure, term explained, II 20

Exilarchs, heads of Babylonian Jewry, I 20

Exploitation, economic, Russian Jews accused of, II 193 used as pretext for pogroms, II 261 f, 264, 270 ff, 315 handicrafts stigmatized as, I 347

Expulsion, of Jews, by Polish Government from Lithuania (1495), I 65

from Sandomir, I 173

from Warsaw, I 260, 286 f

by Russian troops, from invaded Polish cities (1654), I 153 f, 245

by Russian Government, from Little Russia (1727), I 249 f, 253 ff

from Russia in general (1741), I 255; (1744), I 257 f

from Courland and Livonia (1829), II 32

from Port Arthur and Kuantung Peninsula (1904), III 94

from Russian Interior (outside of Pale), in general, I 402 f; II 264, 399, 428; III 95, 154, 157; foreign Jews expelled from, II 262, 293, 345

from Kharkov, II 319

from Moscow, II 264, 319, 396 f, 399 ff, 402, 408, 424 f; III 14 f

from Oryol, II 264

from Riga, II 256

from St. Petersburg, II 319, 344, 399, 410

from Pale of Settlement; Fifty-Verst Zone, I 408; II 62 ff, 385

from Kiev, II 31, 33, 263 f, 319, 346; III 157

from Nicholayev, II 32

from Sevastopol, II 32

from Yalta, II 428 f; III 18 f

from villages, I 319, 323 f, 326, 343, 345 ff, 349, 351 f, 354 f, 405 ff; II 30 f, 32 f, 35, 48, 310 f, 318 f, 385; III 17, 157

For particulars see special headings; see also Residence, Right of, and Temporary Rules

Externs, *extra muros* pupils, result of educational restrictions, II 351; III 31

school norm applied to, without sanction of Duma, III 159

join revolutionary ranks, III 31

Factor, Polish name for agent, I 170; II 55

Fair, commercial, Jews permitted to visit F's.

of Little Russia, for wholesale trade (1728), I 250; and for retail trade (1734), I 251

of government of Smolensk (1731), I 251

of government of Kharkov, for retail trade (1734), I 251

of Warsaw (1768), I 268

of Nizhni-Nevgorod, Kharlov, and other cities (1835), II 40

Jews travel to F's. abroad, particularly Leipsic, I 359

Polish F's. provide occasion for Jewish conferences, I 109 f

F. of Lublin, chief meeting-place of Council of Four Lands, I 109

F. of Lantzkrona, mystical services of Frankists during, I 213, 215

F's. of Brody and Zelva, rabbis assembled at, excommunicate Hasidim, I 237

Farrar, Canon, addresses Mansion House Meeting in London, II 290

Feder, Tobias, Hebrew writer, I 388

criticizes translation of Bible into Yiddish, I 388

Feigin, Litman, of Chernigov, submits memorandum on Jewish question to Council of State, II 38 f

Feldshers, Jewish, name explained, II 167

granted right of universal residence (1879), II 167

admission of, into army restricted, II 319

Fergusson, English Under-Secretary for Foreign Affairs, replies to interpellation concerning Russian Jews, II 382

Fez (Morocco), Alfasi native of, I 118

Fichman, modern Hebrew writer, III 162

Fifty-Verst Zone, see Border Zone

Finkelstein, Nahum, delegate of Jews wishing to engage in agriculture, I 363

INDEX

Finns, oppressed by Russian Government, III 159

Fishel, Moses, chief-rabbi of Cracow, I 105

studied medicine in Padua, I 132

Foreign Jews forbidden to settle in Russia (1824), I 409

expelled from Russia, II 262, 293, 345

Foster, John W., United States Minister to Russia, reports about pogroms, II 260

Fox, Polish tailor, starts anti-Jewish riot at Warsaw, I 286 f

Fraind, Yiddish daily in St. Petersburg, III 162

France (and French), Napoleon's policy towards Jews of, I 298

Jews killed by French for loyalty to Russia (1812), I 358

represented at Congress of Aix-la-Chapelle, I 398

high officials of, favor immigration of Russian Jews to Algiers, II 69

Polish-Jewish patriots, pursued by Russia, flee to, I 298; II 105, 109

French witness protest against pogroms, II 326

Russian Jews, in search of university education, go to, II 351

Dreyfus Affair in, III 32, 42; see Paris

Franchise, Jewish, discussed by Russian officials, III 121

proposed denial of, elicits protests from Jewish communities in Russia, III 121; and representatives of Russian people, III 122

finally granted, III 122

Frank, physician in White Russia, adherent of Mendelssohn, suggests Jewish reforms, I 331, 386

Frank, Helena, English translator of Peretz' works, III 62

Frank, Jacob, Polish-Jewish sectarian, born in Podolia, I 211

settles in Wallachia, I 212

travels as salesman in Turkey, I 212

joins, and later heads, Turkish Sabbatians, I 212

banished by Polish authorities to Turkey, I 213

regarded as reincarnation of Sabbatai Zevi, I 214

reappears in Podolia, I 216

submits to preliminary baptism in Lemberg, I 217

appears for final baptism in Warsaw, I 217 f

Polish king acts as godfather of, I 218

poses as Messiah, I 218
arrested in Warsaw, I 218
imprisoned in Chenstokhov, I 219 f
freed by invading Russian troops, I 219
escapes to Brünn (Moravia), I 219
moves to Vienna, I 220
settles in Offenbach (Germany), I 220
supported in Offenbach by adherents in Poland, I 283
See Frankists

Frank, Mendel, rabbi of Brest, receives large powers from Polish king, I 73, 104 f

Frankfort-on-the-Main, Naphtali Cohen, Polish Cabalist and Sabbatian, settles in, I 204
Offenbach, in neighborhood of, residence of Jacob Frank, I 220
Oppenheim, Jewish painter, resident of, II 67
place of publication, II 202

Frankists, adherents of Jacob Frank, hold mystical services and engage in excesses, I 213 f
excommunicated by rabbis, I 214
address themselves to Demboviski, Catholic bishop, I 214
denounce Talmud and recognize Trinity, I 214
call themselves "Contra-Talmudists," and "Zoharists," I 214
bishop arranges disputation between, and rabbis, 214 f
acknowledged victorious in disputation and awarded fine, I 215
obtain safe-conduct from Polish king, I 215
offer to embrace Christianity, I 216
hold second disputation with rabbis, I 216 f
accuse Jews of ritual murder, I 216 f
large number of, baptized at Lemberg, I 217
remain loyal to Frank, I 218, 283
follow Frank to Chenstokhov, his place of imprisonment, I 219
settle with Frank in Offenbach, I 220
Sabbatian movement compromised by, I 222
shunned and despised by Poles, I 283
ultimately absorbed by Poles, I 230

Frederic, Harold, quoted, II 378

Freeman, see Lieberman, A.

Frederick of Austria, Jewish charter of, used as model by Polish rulers, I 45

INDEX

Frederick II., The Great, annexes Polish territory, I 262

Frederick Augustus, Saxon king, made ruler of duchy of Warsaw, I 297

receives report of Council of Ministers, opposing Jewish emancipation, I 299

issues decree, postponing Jewish emancipation for ten years (1808), I 299

receives anti-Jewish report from Polish Senate, I 302

Frelinghuysen, Frederic T., American Secretary of State, expresses regret at treatment of Russian Jews, II 294

Friedlaender, Israel, quoted, II 235

translator of Dubnow, III 52

translator of Ahad Ha'am, III 60

Friedländer, David, submits memorandum to Polish Government, suggesting reform of Polish Jewry, II 90 f

followers of, in Warsaw, plead for secular culture, I 386

Friedman, Jewish deputy to Third Duma, III 153

complains about Jewish disabilities, III 157

Friesel, governor of Vilna, invites Polish nobility of Lithuania to express opinion on Jews, I 325 f

submits opinion of nobility to Senate with his own memorandum, 326

urges Jewish cultural reforms, 327

Frischman, David, Hebrew writer, III 60

Frug, Simon, Russian and Yiddish poet, III 63

resides in St. Petersburg as "flunkey," II 345

glorifies emigration, II 330

pictures despair of Russian Jewry, II 371

appeals for victims of Kishinev massacres, III 78

Fünn, Samuel Joseph, Jewish historian and writer, II 136

editor of *Pirhe Tzafon,* II 136; and *ha-Karmel,* II 217

Gabbaim, directors of Kahal institutions, I 107

"gentlemen in waiting" of Tzaddiks, II 120

Galatia (Asia Minor), Jewish communities in, I 14

Galatovski, Ukrainian writer, quoted, I 205

Galicia, divided into Eastern and Western, I 53

annexed by Austria (1772), I 187, 262

Sabbatian propaganda in, I 208, 210 f

intellectual development of Jews in, contrasted with North-west, I 221

Besht, founder of Hasidism, active in, I 223

Hasidism spreads in, I 229, 274

type of Tzaddik in, I 233

rabbis of, excommunicate Hasidim, I 237

Tzaddik of Sadagora (Bukovina) attracts Hasidim from, II 121

I. B. Levinsohn associates with Maskilim of, II 125 f; contrasted with them, II 127

Haskalah carried from, to Odessa, II 133

Hebrew publications of, imitated in Vilna, II 136

Meisels, rabbi of Cracow, joins Polish patriots in, II 179

Baron Hirsch establishes schools in, II 416

Hebrew writers in, III 163; see Russia (Red), Lemberg, and Yaroslav

Galicia, Eastern, see Russia, Red Uniat Church in, I 141

Galilee, Jewish colonies in, II 375

Gamrat, Peter, bishop of Cracow, condemns woman to death for adhering to Jewish doctrine, I 79

leads agitation against Jews, I 81 f

Ganganelli, cardinal, later Pope Clement XIV., defends Polish Jews against ritual murder charges, I 179 f

Gania, Cossack leader, perpetrates Jewish massacre in Niemirov, I 146

Gans, David, work of, copied by Halperin, Polish-Jewish chronicler, I 201

Gaons, heads of Babylonian Jewry, I 20

Gaon of Bagdad corresponds with early Russian rabbis, I 33

Gaon of Vilna, see Elijah of Vilna

Gapon, Russian priest and demagogue, III 106

Gatchina, near St. Petersburg, secret conferences of high Russian dignitaries held at, II 244 f

Jewish deputation received by Alexander III. at, II 261

Geiger, Abraham, quoted, I 136

corresponds with Lilienthal, II 67

Gemara, term explained, II 114; see Talmud

Gendarmerie, see Police

Genoa, commercial colony of, in Crimea, I 33 f

Germany, Poland commercially dependent on, I 39; and religiously, I 40 f, 44

INDEX

Polish rulers welcome settlers from, I 43 f; bestow upon them autonomy (Magdeburg Law), I 44

Jews of, carry on commerce with Slav countries, I 39

Jewish delegation from, pleads for admission of Jews to Poland, I 40

Jews of, immigrate to Poland, I 33, 41, 66

anti-Jewish hatred in Poland fed from, I 57; fostered by German burghers in Poland, I 95

Polish-Jewish pilgrims to Palestine pass through, I 209

Jacob Frank settles in, I 220

Jews of Slav lands culturally dependent on, I 33; invite rabbis from, I 43

Jews of, apply to Polish rabbis for religious advice, I 125

grandfather of Solomon Luria native of, I 124

Haskalah originates in, I 239, 384 ff

Polish Jews contrasted with Jews of, I 386

Hebrew publications of, imitated in Vilna, II 136

Russian-Jewish students in, II 381

Hebrew writers in, III 163

Doctor Herzl negotiates with emperor of, III 46

penalty of *Spiessruten* introduced into Russia from, II 85

See Prussia and Berlin

Gershon Kutover, see Kutover

Gershuni, member of Social-revolutionary party, III 67

Ghederah, Jewish colony in Judea, II 375

Gher (Poland), see Goora Kalvaria

Ghetto, separate Jewish quarter in cities, creation of, demanded by Polish Church, I 48, 57

in Cracow, I 64, 85

in Moghilev (on the Dnieper), I 98 f

in Posen, I 85

in Vilna, I 99

in Warsaw, I 269

former Moscow Gh. called Glebov Yard, II 403

Gicatilla, Joseph, Cabalist, work of, published in Poland, I 134

Giers, De, Russian minister for Foreign Affairs, discusses Jewish question with American Government, II 293, 396

Ginzberg, Asher, see Ahad Ha'am

Ginzburg, Mordecai Aaron, Hebrew writer, II 133 f

translates German works into Hebrew, II 134

influences formation of neo-Hebraic style, II 134

Giovio, Paolo, Italian scholar, I 242

Gladkov, instigator of pogrom in Starodub, II 411 f

Gladstone, English Prime Minister, cultivates friendly relations with Russia, II 287 f appealed to by Mansion House Meeting on behalf of Russian Jews, II 290 answers interpellation concerning Russian Jews, II 291 f

Glebov Yard, former Ghetto in Moscow, raided by police, II 403

Glogau (Germany), Solomon Maimon buried in, I 240

Gmina, Polish name for Congregation, II 102

Gnesen (Province of Posen), oldest Polish diocese, I 47 seat of Polish primate, I 82 Council of Breslau demands introduction of canonical laws into diocese of, I 47 f archbishop of, attends Synod of Constance and presides over Synod of Kalish, I 57 John Casimir, primate of, becomes Polish king, I 151

God, conception of, by Besht, I 225 f

Goeje, De, quoted, I 23

Goethe, impressed by autobiography of Solomon Maimon, I 240

Goetz, F., author of pamphlet defending Jews, II 389

Gogol, Russian writer, anti-Jewish tendency of, 138 f

"Going to the People," phase of Russian revolutionary movement, term explained, II 222 practised by Russian-Jewish *intelligentsia*, II 222

Golitzin, Count, Minister of Ecclesiastic Affairs, associate of Alexander I. in Christian mysticism, I 392, 396 president of Russian Bible Society, I 396 all Jewish matters transferred to, I 394 communicates with Kahals through "Deputies of Jewish People," I 394 receives protest of deputies against blood accusation, II 74 prohibits blood accusation by decree, II 74 f extends prohibition of blood accusation to Poland, II 99 advises dissolution of Society of Israelitish Christians, I 400 orders investigation of "Judaizing heresy," I 401 accuses Jews of proselytizing, I 404 suggests prohibition of keeping Christian domestics, I 404 discharged, I 395

INDEX

Gonta, Cossack leader, engineers Jewish massacre, I 184 ff

Goora Kalvaria (*Polish*, Gora Kalwarza; *Yiddish*, Gher), hasidic dynasty of, popular in Warsaw, II 122

Gorchakov, viceroy of Poland, receives deputation of revolutionary Poles, II 180

opposes Jewish rights at Berlin Congress, II 202

Gordin, Jacob, founds anti-talmudic sect, II 333 f

becomes Jewish playwright in America, II 325

Gordon, Judah Leib, Hebrew poet, champion of Haskalah, II 228

secretary of Society of Diffusion of Enlightenment, II 229

attacks traditional Judaism, II 129 ff

champions emigration from Russia, II 328

dies (1892), III 63

Goremykin, Minister of Interior, pursues reactionary policy, III 9, 16, 135

Gorgippia (Crimea), now called Anapa, ancient Jewish settlement in, I 14

Gorodnya (near Chernigov), alleged ritual murder at, reported to Peter the Great, I 247 f

Gotovtzev, Assistant-Minister of Interior, chairman of Central Committee for Revision of Jewish Question, II 227

Gotz, member of Social Revolutionary party, III 67

Government (province), governor, and governor-general, terms explained, I 308

Grace, William R., mayor of New York, presides at protest meeting, II 296

Granville, Lord, English Secretary for Foreign Affairs, receives Anglo-Jewish deputation on subject of pogroms, II 262 f

receives resolutions of Mansion House Meeting, II 290

Grazdanin ("The Citizen"), anti-Semitic Russian paper, II 380, 381, 412

Great Poland, see Poland, Great

Greeks, immigration of ancient Greeks into Tauris and Crimea, I 13 f

export grain from Tauris and Crimea, I 14

Jews follow in wake of, I 14

language of, spoken by Jews of Tauris, I 16

compete with Jews in Odessa, II 191

make pogrom upon Jews of Odessa, II 192 f

Greek-Orthodox Church, oppressed in Poland, I 91 f; and Ukraine, I 140 ff

"Gregor, Horowitz & Kohan," semi-Jewish firm of Russian army purveyors, II 202, 244

Greig, Russian Admiral, member of Council of State, pleads for Jews, II 37

Gresser, city-governor of St. Petersburg, persecutes Jews, II 343 f

issues ordinance concerning Jewish names, II 397 f

deports Moscow fugitives, II 410

Grigoryev, member of Committee for Amelioration of Jews, pleads for maintenance of Pale, I 196

Grigoreyev, city-governor of Odessa, dismissed for restraining "Black Hundred," III 151

Grodno (city), meeting-place of Polish Diet, I 76

important Jewish community in, I 59, 73

Jews of, expelled, I 65; and allowed to return, I 70 f

Jews of, assure Sigismund I. of loyalty to country, I 81

Poles of, antagonistic to Russia (1812), I 357

Jews of, entrusted with police duty, I 357

blood accusation in, II 73, 80

Jewish community of, represented on Polish Council, (*Waad Arba Aratzoth*), I 110; and later on Lithuanian Council, I 112

Mordecai Jaffe rabbi of, I 127

Sundel Sonnenberg, army purveyor and Jewish deputy, native of, I 358

Grodno (province, or government), annexed by Russia (1795), I 297

included in Pale (1795), I 317; (1835), II 39

invited by Russian Government to send deputies, I 349

Jews expelled from villages of (1827), II 30 f

placed under military dictatorship of Muravyov, II 188

Cities in:

Druskeniki, II 377

Ruzhany, I 162

Zelva, I 237

Grudinski, convert, accuses Jews of ritual murder, II 80

Gruzenberg, Russian-Jewish lawyer, acts as counsel for Blondes, accused of ritual murder, III 37

defends Dashevski, assailant of Krushevan, III 82

defends Jews of Kishinev, III 91

INDEX

Gruzin (Crimea), I 26

Gudovich, Count, governor-general of South-west, rebuked for interfering with Jewish deputation to Paul I., I 325

Guido, papal legate, convenes Church Council of Breslau, I 47

Guilds, mercantile, in Poland, I 44; see Merchants trade Guilds, in Poland, I 44; see Trade-Unions

Guizolfi, Zechariah, Italian Jew, owns Taman Peninsula, I 36 corresponds with Ivan III. of Moscow, I 36

Guizot, French Premier, supports schemes of Russian-Jewish emigration to Algiers, II 69

Gumbiner, Abel, head of yeshibah in Kalish, Hebrew author, I 200

Gumplovich, Polish-Jewish writer and assimilator, II 213

Günzberg, Baron Joseph Yozel, leader of St. Petersburg community, petitions Alexander II. on behalf of victim of ritual murder accusation, II 152

petitions Alexander II. for privileges to Jews, II 159 f

founder of Society for Diffusion of Enlightenment, II 214

Günzburg, Baron Horace, son of former, waits on Vladimir, brother of Alexander III., II 260

member of Jewish deputation to Alexander III., 261

calls conference of notables in St. Petersburg, II 277, 304

acts as link between Jews and Pahlen Commission, I 337

petitions Government to allow Jews purchase of land for personal use, III 24

Gurko, governor-general of Odessa, suggests restrictive school-norm for Jews, II 339

Gurnitzki, Lucas, Polish writer, quoted, I 79 f

Gymnazium, secondary school, name explained, II 164

right of residence outside Pale proposed for graduates of, II 164

restrictive percentage at, intensified, III 29, 158; but not applied to girls, III 30

award of graduation certificates restricted in case of Jews, III 159

Pro-gymnazium, name explained, III 29

See Education and School

Gzheslik, Jewish tailor, accused of desecrating host, I 101

Ha-Asif, Hebrew Periodical, II 372, III 58

Habad, adherents of "rational Hasidism," term explained, I 234

centered in White Russia, I 234, II 117

Polish Tzaddiks compared with those of, II 123

See Shneorsohn, Zalman

Haber, title of Jewish educated layman, I 117

Ha-Emet, socialistic periodical in Hebrew, II 223

Hague Conference, the, calling of, prompts Nicholas II. to stop pogroms, III 35 f

Haidamacks, rebellious Ukrainian peasants, name explained, I 182, II 138

massacre Jews (1648), I 49; (1734 and 1750), I 182; (1768), I 182 ff

massacres of, described by Gogol, II 138 f

Haimovich, Avigdor, rabbi of Pinsk, informs against Hasidim, I 377 f

Haint, Yiddish daily in Warsaw, III 162

Ha-Karmel, Hebrew weekly, in Vilna, II 217

Ha-Kol, Hebrew periodical in Königsberg, II 223

Halevi, David, called *Taz*, rabbi of Lemberg and Ostrog, I 130

author of commentary on *Shulhan Arukh*, I 130

receives letter and present from Sabbatai Zevi, I 206 f

Halevi, Isaiah, son of former member of Polish-Jewish delegation to Sabbatai Zevi, I 206

Halperin, banker of Berdychev, member of rabbinical commission, II 57

Halperin, Jehiel, rabbi of Minsk, Hebrew chronicler, I 200 f

Ha-Maggid, Hebrew weekly, II 217

Hamburg, Solomon Maimon resides in, I 239

Moscow refugees in, II 420

Ha-Melitz, Hebrew weekly, in St. Petersburg, edited by Zederbaum, II 204, 217 f

publishes Lilienblum's articles, II 236

champions "Love of Zion" movement, II 332

becomes daily, II 372, III 58

Handicrafts; see Artisans

Hannover, Nathan, of Zaslav, historian, describes Council of Four Lands, I 111

pictures Jewish intellectual life in Poland, I 116 ff

gives account of Khmelnitzki massacres, I 157

Hanukkah, king of Khazars, I 26

INDEX

Hardenberg, Prussian representatives at Congress at Aix-la-Chapelle, I 399

Harkavy, quoted, I 23

Harrison, President of United States, publishes diplomatic papers bearing on Russian Jews, II 294, 394

describes, in message to Congress, plight of Russian Jewry, II 408 f

Hasdai Ibn Shaprut, of Cordova, corresponds with king of Khazars, I 24 ff

Ha-Shahar, Hebrew monthly, edited by Smolenskin, II 218, 234

publishes Gordon's epics, II 229

champions "Love of Zion" movement, II 332

Ha-Shiloah, Hebrew monthly, edited by Ahad Ha'am, and later by Klausner, III 58, 162 f

Hasidim, adherents of Judah Hasid, I 209

emigrate to Palestine, I 209 ff

adherents of Hasidism; see Hasidism

struggle between H. and old-orthodox (*Mithnagdim*), I 238, 274, 278, 375 f

H. of Vilna rejoice over death of Gaon, I 375

granted right of secession by Statute of 1804, I 356, 379

H. of Old-Constantinov "protest" against Nicholas I., II 22

H. of Poland refuse to discard Jewish dress, II 145

Hasidism, founded by Besht, I 222

doctrine of, expounded by Besht, I 22, 224 ff

counteracts Rabbinism, l 224 f; and Messianism, l 222; and Asceticism, I 227

propagated by Besht's apostles, I 229 ff

opposes Haskalah, I 238 f

bitterly opposed by Elijah of Vilna, I 236 ff, 372 ff

spread of, I 231 f

triumph of, I 371 f

growth of, under Alexander I., I 381 ff

stagnation of, under Nicholas I., II 116 ff

in North (White Russia and Lithuania), I 381 f, II 117 f

in South (Ukraina), I 382 f, II 119 ff

in Poland, I 384, II 122 f

retrogressive character of, I 278, II 124

encourages use of alcohol, II 124 f

restrictions against, suggested by Friesel, governor of Vilna, I 327 denounced by rabbi of Pinsk, as dangerous to Russian Government, I 378

extermination of, recommended by Kalmansohn, I 385

criticized by David Friedländer, II 90

attacked, or silently opposed, by I. B. Levinsohn, II 127 f

subjected to rigorous censorship (1864), II 212

literature of, declared by I. B. Levinsohn as dangerous to State, II 130

See Hasidim, Tzaddiks, and Shneor Zalman

Haskalah, attempt to harmonize Jewish and secular culture, term explained, II 125

originated by Mendelssohn in Germany, I 238 f, II 125

opposed by Rabbinism and Hasidism, I 238 f

hated by Nahman of Bratzlav, I 333

Solomon Maimon influenced by, I 239

effect of, on Jews of Warsaw, I 284, 384 ff

championed by Jacques Kalmansohn, I 385

need of, for Polish Jews, emphasized by David Friedländer, II 90; and followers, I 386

advocated by Frank in White Russia, I 331, 386

carried to St. Petersburg, I 386 ff

Max Lilienthal appeals to adherents of (Maskilim), II 53

preached by Isaac Baer Levinsohn, II 125 ff

center of, in Odessa, II 132 f

center of, in Vilna, II 134, 136 f

aims of adherents of, in Vilna, II 136 f.

persecuted adherents of, escape through baptism, II 132

adherents of, lean on Russian Government, II 137

Russian H. compared with German, II 137 f

becomes more aggressive, II 210, 224

stimulates neo-Hebraic style and literature, II 132 ff, 210

advocated by Jewish press, II 217, 332 f

championed by M. L. Lilienblum, II 236

adherents of, portrayed by Mapu, II 228

See Education, Neo-Hebraic Literature, and School

Ha-Tzefirah, Hebrew weekly in Warsaw, advocates Haskalah, II 333

edited by Sokolow, III 60

becomes a daily, II 372, III 58, 162

Hausfreund, Yiddish periodical, III 59

Hayyun, emissary of Sabbatai Zevi, I 204

Hazakah, priority of possession, term explained, II 188 grant of, must be sanctioned by Kahal, I 190, II 188 matters relating to, decided by Council of Four Lands, I 111

Ha-Zeman, Hebrew daily in Vilna, III 162

Hebrew, language, importance of, emphasized by Smolenskin, II 134 f position of, in Jewish life, forms party issue, III 161 promoted by Zionism, III 45 restoration of, II 133, 135, 225 modern H. (Neo-Hebraic) literature, beginnings of, I 388 f rise of, II 132 ff renaissance of, II 224 ff, III 58 ff, 162 f cultivated by Haskalah, II 132-ff, 210, 224 H. writers hail form Lithuania, II 238 H. press, beginnings of, II 217 f preaches Haskalah, II 217 recent revival of, III 58 f See also Language

Heder, traditional Jewish school, imparts elementary education, I 114 Bible and Talmud principal subjects of instruction at, I 114, 121

secular subjects excluded from, I 277 left to private initiative, but supervised by Kahal, I 114 pupils of, examined weekly by head of yeshibah, I 118 attendance at, compulsory for boys, I 114, 121 negative effects of, I 277 shortened attendance at, suggested by Dyerzhavin, I 333 criticised by Russian Council of State, II 49 abolition of, suggested by Lilienthal, II 53 defended by Rabbinical Commission, II 57 placed under Government supervision (1842), II 56; (1856), II 176 keepers of (Melammeds) required to possess secular education (1844), II 58 recognized by ukase of 1879, II 177 6,000 H's. in Russian Southwest, II 194 legalized and restricted to religious subjects (1893), II 427 f See Education, School, and Yeshibah

Heder, for poor children, called Talmud Torah, maintained by public funds, I 114 f

pupils of, examined weekly by trustee, I 118
provided for, by Council of Four Lands, I 195
established in Moscow, III 13

Helena, Russian princess, sympathizes with "Judaizing heresy," I 36

Helfman, Hesia, participates in plot against Alexander II., II 244

Heliconias, name of Greek-speaking Jew, I 115

Heller, Lipman, rabbi of Cracow, describes persecutions of 1648, I 58

Helsingfors (Finland), Russian Zionists hold Convention at, III 144 f

"H. Program" gradually weakened, III 146

Heniochi, tribe, I 15

Hennadius, archbishop of Novgorod, combats "Judaizing heresy," I 37

Henry of Valois, elected king of Poland, I 89

Heracles, name of slave freed by Crimean Jewess, I 15

Herem (Excommunication), right of, granted by Polish kings to rabbi of Brest (1531), I 73, 105; to rabbis of Great Poland (1551), I 106; to Kahals of Lithuania (1672), I 190

proclaimed against Sabbatians by rabbis assembled at Lemberg (1722), I 211; (1725), I 211
issued against Frankists by rabbis assembled at Brody. I 214
issued against Hasidim by rabbinical court of Vilna (1722), I 237; by rabbis assembled at Brody, I 237; and at Zelva (Grodno), I 237: reaffirmed by Elijah of Vilna (1796), I 373 f
new H. against Hasidim contemplated by Kahal of Vilna (1797), I 375
issued by Kahal of Vilna against Simeon Volfovich (1788), I 276
Jews of Minsk complain about abuse of (1782), I 275
prohibited by Statute of 1804, I 344
prohibition of, occasionally disregarded, I 367
power of, criticised by Polish assimilationists, II 101
secret exercise of, alleged by Brafman, II 188

Hernish, Stanislav, Polish-Jewish patriot, II 105
refutes Polish attacks upon Jews, II 109

Hershel, Ostropoler, See Ostropoler

INDEX

Hershko, name of Jewish "arendar," I 266

Hertzen, Alexander, liberal Russian writer, describes sufferings of cantonists, II 24 f influences Russian-Jewish *intelligenzia*, II 207

Herzl, Theodor, aroused by Dreyfus Affair, III 42 f publishes *Judenstaat*, III 43 compared with Pinsker, III 43 revives hopes of *Hobebe Zion*, III 43 f speeches of, discussed in Russia, III 47 author of *Altneuland*, III 48 visit of, to Russia, III 82 ff negotiates with Plehve, III 83 f; and Lansdorf, III 84 greeted enthusiastically by Russian Zionist, III 84 criticized by non-Zionists, III 84 lays Uganda project before Sixth Zionist Congress, III 84 death of, mourned by Seventh Zionist Congress, III 144

Hetman, name explained, I 143, 192, 250 head of Cossacks, I 143 Khmelnitzki elected to post of, I 144

H. of Lithuania sends instructions to Kahal of Brest, I 192

H. of Little Russia pleads for admission of Jews, I 250, 260

Hezekiah, king of Khazars, I 26

Hirsch, Baron Maurice, II 413 proposes to establish arts and crafts schools in Russia, II 415 proposal of, declined by Russian Government, II 415 representatives of, offer Pobyedonostzev large contribution, II 415 applies funds intended for Russia to schools in Galicia, II 416 sends expedition to Argentina, II 416 sends Arnold White to Russia, II 416 ff founds Jewish Colonization Association, II 414, 419 obtains permission of Russian Government to regulate emigration, II 420 issues appeal, warning against emigration, II 420 scheme of, results in failure, II 421, III 10

Hirsh Kaidanover, see Kaidanover

Hirshovich, Abraham, Polish court broker, submits project of Jewish reforms to King Stanislav Augustus, I 284

Historiography, Jewish, in Russia, III 65

Hobebe Zion, see Zionism

Hollaenderski, Polish-Jewish patriot and writer, lives as exile in Paris, II 109

Holland, Peter the Great in, I 246

Antonio Sanchez, Russian court physician, invited from, I 258

See Amsterdam

Horodno, Nehman of, disciple of Besht, I 227

Homel (government of Moghilev), massacre under Khmelnitzki at (1648), I 149

pogrom at (1903), III 87 ff

self-defence organized by Jews of, III 87 f

pogrom at, condoned by governor of Moghilev, III 89

misrepresented in official documents, III 89

described as act of revenge by Jews, III 101

tried by Russian court, III 101 ff

Jewish community of, signs petition for equal rights, III 108

Horowitz, Isaiah, Cabalist, author of *Sheloh*, I 135

Horowitz, Sheftel, son of former, rabbi of Posen and Hebrew author, I 135

author of liturgy describing catastrophe of 1648, I 158

Horvitz, Russian-Jewish writer, attacked by Russian periodical, II 207 f

defended in public protest of Russian writers, II 208

Host Desecration, Charge of, causes death of Jews in Posen (1399), I 55, 95 174; and Sokhachev (1556), I 86 f

forbidden by Sigismund II. (1566), I 88; and Stephen Batory (1576), I 89

used as pretext to expel Jews of Cracow (1635), I 101

of frequent occurrence at end of 17th century, I 172

Hoym, Prussian minister, carries out Jewish reforms in annexed Polish provinces, I 385

Hugo, Victor, protests against Jewish persecutions in Russia, II 326

Hungary, geographical position of, I 25, 150

adopts Magdeburg Law, I 44

Church Council (of Buda) in, I 49

Louis of, king of Poland, persecutes Jews, I 54

Husiatyn (Galicia), place of publication, I 123

Huss, influence of, penetrates into Poland, I 57

adherents of, persecuted, I 62

Ibn Fakih, Arabic geographer, quoted, I 23

INDEX

Ibn Khordadbeh, Arabic geographer, quoted, I 23

Ibn Shaprut, see Hasdai I

Ibn Sharzi, Arabic writer, quoted, I 23

Ignatyev, Nicholas Pavlovich, Russian statesman, militant pan-Slavist, II 259

ambassador at Constantinople, II 259

nicknamed "Father of Lies," II 259

member of reactionary "Sacred League," II 248

appointed Minister of Interior, II 259

ascribes pogroms to revolutionary propaganda, II 259 f

changes attitude, II 261

refuses to submit memorandum in defence of Jews to Tzar, II 262

shows indifference to pogrom victims, II 263

ascribes pogroms to economic exploitation of Jews, II 271 f

issues circular condemning economic activities of Jews, II 273

influences Central Committee for Revision of Jewish Question, II 277

receives deputation of Jewish Notables, II 277

calls upon Jews to leave Russia, II 285, 297

Ignatyev directed to appoint Gubernatorial Commissions, II 272, 363

circular of, read to Gubernatorial Commissions, II 274; quoted by Cardinal Manning at London protest meeting, II 289

disregards protests in England, II 292

permits holding of Jewish Conference in St. Petersburg, II 304

holds Jews responsible for pogroms, II 305

considers settlement of Jews on steppes of Central Asia, II 306

suggests "Temporary Rules," II 311

makes concessions to Committee of Ministers, II 311, 318

connivance at pogroms causes downfall of, II 314

downfall of, checks plan of Jewish emigration from Russia, II 414

Illarion, Metropolitan of, preaches hatred against Jews, I 31

Illustratzia, Russian magazine, attacks Jews, II 207 f

causes public protest of Russian literateurs, II 208

Ilovaiski, professor, of Moscow, opposed to Jews, II 387

Ilya (government of Vilna), home of Menashe Ilyer, II 114

Ilyer, Menashe (Manasseh), Talmudist with modern tendencies, II 114 ff

acquires modern culture, II 114

criticises spiritual leaders, II 115

book of, burned, II 115

pleads for modifications of religious law, II 115

unappreciated by contemporaries, II 116

Imperial Messenger (*Pravityelstvenny Vyestnik*), official organ of Russian Government, minimizes pogroms, II 255

warns against pogrom protests, II 291

foreshadows new pogroms, II 299

criticised by *Moscow News*, II 299

Informing and Informers, see Mesirah

Inkerman, Heights of, near Sevastopol, Jewish soldiers killed at, II 149

Inns (and Taverns), keeping of, forms important Jewish pursuit, I 265, 362

Jews in White Russia forbidden from, I 311

permitted by Senate, I 312

forbidden by Statute of 1804, I 342 f

See Arendar, Propinatzia, and Villages

Innocent IV., pope, bull of, condemning ritual murder libel (1247), referred to, I 179

Intelligenzia, Jewish, in Russia, assimilation of, II 206 ff

in league with Russian Government, II 211 f

indifferent to things Jewish, II 212

Society for Diffusion of Enlightenment acts on behalf of, II 215

disillusionment of, II 324 ff

Interior, Russian, the (Russian empire outside Pale of Settlement), barred to Jews of annexed White Russia (1790, 1791), I 316

Jewish manufacturers, merchants, and artisans permitted to sojourn temporarily in (1804), I 344

Governments of Astrakhan and Caucasia in, opened to Jewish agriculturists (1804), I 342 f

Council of State considers admission of Jewish merchants into, II 35 f; negatived by Nicholas I., II 36

INDEX

Jews admitted into, on temporary "furlough" (1835), II 40

Jews, illegally residing in, severely punished (1838), II 42

prominent Jews of St. Petersburg plead for opening of (1856), II 160

admission of Jews into, discussed by Council of State and "Jewish Committee," II 161 ff

Jewish guild merchants admitted into (1859), II 162

Jews with learned degrees admitted into (1861), II 166

Jews with higher education admitted into (1879), II 167

Jewish artisans (mechanics and distillers) admitted into (1865), II 170

Jews begin to settle in, II 171

Alexander II. refuses to admit "Nicholas soldiers" into, II 171; but yields (1867), II 172

discharged Jewish soldiers barred from (1874), II 354 f

"Jewish Committee" discusses admission of Jews into (1880), II 196 ff

five "Gubernatorial Commissions" advocate opening of, II 275

"illegal" Jews in, persecuted, II 342 ff, 385

old settlers from among "illegal" Jews permitted to remain in (1880), II 404

admission of Jews to schools in, restricted to 5% (1887), II 350; restriction placed on Statute books (1908), III 158

admission of Jews to universities in, restricted to 3% (1898), III 29

pogrom in (Nizhni-Novgorod), II 360

Government endeavors to annul admission of privileged Jews into, II 399

expulsion of Jews from, II 428

barred to Jews (under Nicholas II.), III 20 f

Jewish soldiers forbidden to spend furlough in (1896), III 21

Jews in, forbidden to acquire real estate in villages (1903), III 81

attempt to expel families of mobilized Jewish soldiers from, III 95

Jewish veterans of Russian-Japanese War and families of other privileged Jews admitted into (1904), III 98 f

pogroms in (October, 1905), III 130

expulsion of Jews from (under Nicholas II.), III 157

See Pale of Settlement, and Residence, Right of

Ionian Islands, emigration from, to Black Sea settlements, I 13 f

Iphicleides, name of Greek-speaking Jew, I 15

Isaac, king of Khazars, I 26

Isaac, of Chernigov, corresponds with Gaon in Bagdad, I 33

Isaac, Jewish physician at Polish court, I 132

Isaac ben Jacob, see Alfasi

Isaacs, Henry, Lord Mayor of London, disapproves of protest meeting against pogroms, II 382

Ishmaelites, see Muhammedans

Ispravnik, title of Russian official, II 301, 409

Israel, son of Shakhna, succeeds his father as rabbi of Lublin, I 123

Israel, of Ruzhany, executed on ritual murder charge, I 162 f

Israel, Baal-Shem-Tob, called Besht, founder of Hasidism, I 222 ff

born in Podolia, I 222

sent to heder, I 222

neglects studies, I 222

strange conduct of, I 222

studies Practical Cabala, I 222 f

settles in Brody, I 223

marries sister of rabbi, I 223

retires to solitude in Carpathian mountains, I 223

occupies humble position in Tlusta (Galicia), I 223

considered an ignoramus, I 223

begins to practise as *Baal-Shem*, I 223

reputed as miracle-worker, I 224

called "good *Baal-Shem*," or *Baal-Shem-Tob*, I 224

disparages exclusive Talmud study, I 224, 226

recognizes authority of Cabala, I 224

objects to Cabalistic ascesticism, I 224, 226

inculcates cheerfulness, I 225

emphasizes faith and prayer, I 225, 226 f

settles in Medzhibozh (Podolia), I 225

doctrine of, I 225 f

evolves belief in *Tzaddik*, I 227

disciples of, I 227 f

acknowledged by rabbi of Brody, I 228

sends epistle to Palestine, I 228

believed to associate with biblical prophets, I 228

popular discourses of, I 228

laments conversion of Frankists, I 229

takes part in Frankist disputation, I 229

INDEX

sayings of, cellected by disciple, I 230, 237

See also Hasidism and Hasidim

Israel, of Kozhenitz, leader of Hasidim in duchy of Warsaw, I 384

successors of, II 122

Israel, of Ruzhin (government of Kiev), hasidic leader, keeps magnificent court, II 120

arouses suspicions of governor-general, I 120 f

arrested, I 121

flees to Sadagora (Bukovina), I 121

dynasty of, branches out, I 221

contests supremacy of Joshua Heshel Apter, II 121

Isserles, Moses (*Remo*), son of Kahal elder in Cracow, I 123

pupil of Shakhna of Lublin, I 123

judge and head of yeshibah in Cracow, I 123

writes commentary on *Turim*, I 123

adds notes to *Shulhan Arukh*, I 124

makes *Shulhan Arukh* great factor in Polish Jewry, I 130

differs from Solomon Luria, I 126

disparages mysticism, I 126

favors moderate philosophy, I 126

studies Maimonides' *Moreh*, I 126, 132

teacher of Mordecai Jaffe, I 127

method of, contrasted with that of Jaffe, I 128

method of, looked down upon by Meir of Lublin, I 129

unequalled by successors, I 199

Istumin, Pobyedonostzev's agent in Moscow, II 401

Italy, influence of, extends to Crimea, I 34

Guizolfi, Jew from Italy, owns Tanan Peninsula, I 36

Master Leon, Jew from, physician at Moscow court, I 37

Jews of, apply to Polish rabbis for religious advice, I 125

Jewish physicians in Poland originate from, I 132, or receive medical training in, I 132

Delacruta, founder of Polish Cabala, born in, I 134

work of Recanati, Italian Cabalist, studied in Poland, I 134

Calahora, native of, executed in Cracow, I 164 f

Judah Hasid studies Practical Cabala in, I 208

Polish-Jewish pilgrims to Palestine pass through, I 209

Itche (Isaac) Meier Alter, head of Gher Hasidim, has many adherents in Warsaw, II 122

Ityl, ancient name for Volga, I 19, 26

name of Khazar capital, I 19

Itzele, Rabbi, see Zelikin

Itzhaki, Itzhok (Isaac), head of Volozhin yeshibah, member of Rabbinical Commission, II 57

Ivan III., grand duke of Moscow, I 29

assisted by Crimean Jews in negotiations with Khan, I 35

corresponds with Guizolfi, Italian Jew, I 36

orders burning of "Judaizers," I 37

executes his Jewish body-physician, I 37

Ivan IV., The Terrible, Tzar of Moscow, I 29

refuses to admit Lithuanian Jews into Russia, I 243

orders drowning of Jews of Polotzk, I 243

Izyaslav, former name for government of Volhynia, I 317

Jacob Itzhok (Isaac), of Lublin, pioneer of Hasidism in Poland, I 384

Jacob (Nahman), of Belzhytz, Polish court physician, I 136

author of polemical treatise against Christianity, I 136 f

Jacob Zelig (Selek, or Jelek), presents petition of Polish Jews to pope, I 179 f

Jacob Ben Asher, author of *Turim*, work of, studied in Poland, I 118

Jacobs, Joseph, quoted, II 287

Jacobsohn, deputy to First Duma, reports on Bialystok pogrom, III 139

Jaffa (Palestine), Jewish agricultural settlements in neighborhood of, II 322

representative of Odessa Palestine Society in, II 422

gymnasium in, III 148

Jaffe, Mordecai, native of Bohemia, I 126

pupil of Isserles, I 126

rabbi of various Polish communities, I 126

presides over Council of Four Lands, I 126

author of elaborate code, entitled *Lebushim*, I 126 f

method of, differs from that of Caro and Isserles, I 27; looked down upon by Meir of Lublin, 129

comments on Maimonides' *Moreh*, I 132

pupil of Delacruta, Cabalist, I 134

author of cabalistic commentary, I 134

unequalled by successors, I 199

Japanese, expel Russians from Kuantung (Shantung) Peninsula, III 94

destroy Russian fleet, III 110
Jews accused of alliance with, III 95 f

Jastrow, Marcus, preacher in Warsaw, active in Polish Insurrection, II 179 ff
rabbi in Philadelphia, II 179

Jehiel Michael, rabbi and head of yeshibah in Niemirov, killed in massacre (1648), I 146

Jelek, see Jacob Zelig

Jeremiah, the prophet, teachings of, attacked by Judah Leib Gordon, II 230

Jerome, The Holy, quoted, I 17

Jerusalem, referred to by Khazar king, I 27; and Khazar Jews, I 30

Polish-Jewish pilgrims arrive in, I 205

Gymnazium in, III 148

Jesuits, patronized by Stephen Batory, I 90
establish academy at Vilna, I 90 f
grow in influence, I 91
derive financial benefit from ritual murder libel, I 96
hostile to Jews, I 97, 99 f
effect of, on Polish people, I 171
invited in Posen to exorcise evil spirits, I 203
students of colleges of, assault Jews, I 95, 161; but in Vilna protect Jews, I 166

college of, in Vitebsk supplies anti-Jewish information, I 330

Jewish Chronicle, of London, quoted, II 262, 290, 292, 382

Jewish Colonial Trust, created by Zionists, III 45
financial weakness of, III 46
sale of shares of, forbidden in Russia, III 83

Jewish Colonization Association (ICA), founded by Baron Hirsch in London, II 414, 419
Central Committee of, established in St. Petersburg, II 420
transplants Jews to Argentina, II 421
refused permission to settle Jews as farmers in Russia, III 10

Jewish Historico-Ethnographic Society, in St. Petersburg, founded 1908, III 160
publishes periodical, III 160

Jewish Judge, attached to court of voyevoda, I 46
nominated by Jewish elders, I 191
appointed by voyevoda, I 46, 191
functions of, I 46, 191
tries cases between Jews, I 46, 52

sits in Kahal chamber, near synagogue, I 46, 52, 191

officiates in presence of Kahal elders, I 191

guided, in part, by Jewish law, I 191

Jewish Literary Society, in St. Petersburg, founded in 1908, III 160

dissolved (1911), III 161

Jewish National Fund, created by Zionists, III 45

collections for, forbidden in Russia, III 83

Jewish National Party (Volkspartei), in Russia based on principle of National-Cultural Autonomism, III 147

recognizes Jewish centers in America and Palestine, III 147 f

Jewish People's Group, in Russia, opposes Zionism, III 146

satisfied with minimum of Jewish national rights, III 147

Jewish Publication Society of America, referred to, III 51, 60, 62

Joel Baal-Shem (miracle worker), of Zamoshch, I 203

John, Russian ecclesiastic, preaches hatred against Jews, I 31

John Albrecht, king of Poland (1492-1501), establishes ghetto in Cracow, I 64

permits expelled Lithuanian Jews to settle in Poland, I 65

grants right of distilling (*propinatzya*) to nobles (1496), I 67

attended by Jewish body-physician, 132

John Casimir (1648-1668), concludes peace with Khmelnittzki, I 151

permits baptized Jews to return to Judaism, I 151

anxious to compensate Jews for past sufferings, I 158

grants right of free commerce to Jews of Cracow, I 159

grants privileges to other communities, I 159

John Sobieski (1674-1696), protects Jews against enemies, I 165 f

protects Jews of Vilna, I 166

Jorjan, Sea of, see Caspian Sea

Joseph, king of Khazars, replies to letter of Hasdai Ibn Shaprut, I 25 ff

Joseph II., emperor of Austria, engages in "reformatory" experiments, I 262

project of Jewish reforms in Poland influenced by policy of, I 271, 273

Toleration Act of (1782), II 30

Joseph Israel, see Benjamin III

INDEX

Joseph Kalish, Polish minter, I 42

Joseph, N. S., secretary of Russo-Jewish Committee in London, II 388

Josephus, historian, quoted, I 14 f

Joshua Heshel Apter, see Apter

Jost, refutes anti-Semitic book of Abbé Chiarini, II 104, quoted, I 390

Journal De St. Petersbourg, Russian official organ, refutes charge of pogroms, II 287 f

Jud, Der, Yiddish weekly in Warsaw, III 59

Judæophobia, name for Russian anti-Semitism, II 247 growth of, II 378 ff contrasted with German anti-Semitism, II 6

Judah Ha-Nasi, compiler of the Mishnah, II 114

Judah Hasid, founds sect in Poland, I 208 f heads pilgrims to Palestine, I 209 dies in Jerusalem, I 210

Judah Leib, father of Jacob Frank, I 211 settles with son in Wallachia, I 212

"**Judaizing Heresy**," originated in Novgorod by Zechariah (15th century), I 36 carried to Moscow (1480), I 36

finds adherents at court, I 36 leaders of, burned at stake, I 37 checked, I 37 instils fear of Jews, I 37, 242, 249 spreads in Central Russia (1796), I 401 f severe measures adopted against (1823), I 402 f quoted by Senate as proof of Jewish proselytism, I 404 Reformation in Poland regarded as, I 79 f Christian rationalists in Poland nicknamed "Judaizers," I 136

Jude, Der, German-Jewish periodical, published by Riesser, II 219

Judea, part of Hellenistic Orient, I 14 Jewish colonies, in, II 375

Judicial Authority, see Courts

Jüdisch-Deutsch, see Yiddish

Jüdische Bibliothek, Yiddish periodical, edited by I. L. Peretz, III 59.

Jüdische Volksbibliothek, Yiddish periodical, edited by Shalom Aleichem, III 59

Jüdischer Verlag, in Berlin, referred to, III 52

Jüdisches Volksblatt, Yiddish weekly in St. Petersburg, III 58 f

Justinian, emperor of Byzantium, persecutes Jews, I 18

Jutrzenka ("The Dawn"), organ of Polish-Jewish assimilationists, II 213

Kaffa (now Theodosia), Crimea, maintains commercial relations with Kiev, I 33

becomes Genoese colony and international emporium, I 33 f

Jews flock to, I 34

taken by Turks (1475), I 34

Khoza-Kokos, Jewish native of, exercises great influence, I 35

Jews, expelled from Lithuania, emigrate to, I 65

Kahal (Jewish community), under Polish régime, forms cultural, national, and civil entity, I 103

signifies "community" and "communal administration," I 105

autonomy of, recognized by Casimir the Great, I 52

fully established by Sigismund II. (1551), I 106 f

organization of, I 106 f

elections to, I 192

oligarchic character of, I 192 f

functions of, I 107 f

acts as fiscal agency, I 107, 181; and valued as such by Government, 189 f

manages Jewish institutions, I 107

executes civil acts, I 107, 190

supervises elementary education, I 114 f

has separate judiciary, I 83, 191

elders of, attached to general courts, I 84

K. chamber serves as a seat of judiciary, I 191 f

relation of, to Polish authorities, I 191

federation of K's., I 104, 108 f, 112, 193, 196 f

Conferences (or *Waads*), of federated K's., I 108 ff

relation of K's. to one another, I 193

minor K's. called *Pri-Kahalki*, I 108, 193

autonomy of, stimulates learning, I 121; exerts beneficient effect on Jewish life, I 189

Polish Jews exhorted by rabbis to obey K's., I 188 f

Blackmailed by Polish officials, I 169

K. of Brest ordered by authorities to hold elections (1719), I 192

K. of Lemberg receives constitution from voyevoda (1692), I 191 f

court of Vilna K. excommunicates Hasidim (1772), I 237

INDEX

K. of Vilna engages in litigation with rabbis, I 275 f
financial indebtedness of K's., I 290
degeneration of, I 274 ff
Jews of Minsk complain against (1782), I 275
Simeon Volfovich of Vilna urges abolition of (1788), I 276
abolition or curtailment of, urged by Poles, I 280 ff
weakening of, recommended by Kalmansohn (1796), I 385
defended by Hirsch Yosefovich, rabbi of Khelm, I 283
supervision over, recommended by Abraham Hirschovich, I 284
abolition of, recommended by Committee of Polish Government (1815), II 89
abolition of, favored by Polish-Jewish assimilationists, II 101
criticised by David Friedländer, II 90
abolished in Poland (December 20, 1821-January 1, 1822), II 102
superseded by "Congregational Board," II 102 f
See also Autonomy and Courts

Kahal (Jewish Community), under Russian régime, attitude of Government towards, I 308 ff

admission of Jews to city government conflicts with separate organization, I 308
Jews of annexed White Russia in K's. (1772), I 308
sanctioned by Senate (1776), I 309
granted right to issue passports, I 309
charged with collection of state taxes, I 309
endowed with judicial powers, I 309
Government changes attitude towards, I 310
confined to religious and fiscal functions (1786), I 313
deprived of civil and judicial powers (1795), I 319
promise of Government to maintain judicial powers of, violated, I 320
preservation of, due to fiscal considerations, I 320, 366
establishment of, in Courland, due to same motives (1799), I 321
curtailed status of, recognized in Statute of 1804, I 344
admission to city government fails to weaken power of, I 368 ff
Government forced to extend functions of, I 367
Government communicates with K's., I 336, 339

K. of Minsk decides to send delegation to St. Petersburg (1802), I 336

K's. invited by Government to elect deputies (1803), I 337; (1806), I 349

ordered to assist Jews expelled from villages (1810), I 351

represented at army headquarters (1812), I 358

elected representatives of K's., called "Deputation of Jewish People," act as advisory council to Government (1818-1825), I 393 ff

K. of Grodno entrusted with police duties (1812), I 357

Alexander I. receives K. of Kalish, I 358

Alexander I. assures K's. of his high favor (1814), I 359

K. of Minsk inquires about attitude of Vilna Gaon towards Hasidism, I 373

Gaon issues appeal to K's. against Hasidism (1796), I 373

Hasidim kept within K. by Statute of 1804, I 379

demoralized by hasidic schism, I 371, 379

suppression of, advocated by nobility of Lithuania (1800), I 326; and Dyerzhavin (1800), I 332

made responsible for supply of recruits (1827), II 19 f

K's. directed to elect recruiting trustees, II 19

trustees of, turned into police agents, II 22 f

K. of Vilna complains to Council of State about oppression of Jews, II 38 f; pleads for abolition of cantonists, II 36 f

functions of, regulated by Statute of 1835, II 41

Council of State criticises power of (1840), II 47; and suggests dissolution of, II 49

abolished by Nicholas I. (December 19, 1844), II 59 ff

retained as fiscal and recruiting agency, I 60 ff

demoralized condition of, II 112

elders of, made personally responsible for quota of recruits (1850), 147 f

misdeeds of, portrayed by Mapu, II 227; by Gordon, II 230; by Bogrov, II 241

Brafman accuses Jews of secret continuation of, in Russia, II 188; and of organizing international "World K.," II 189

minutes of K. of Minsk serve as incriminating material, II 189

Brafman's "Book of K." printed and distributed by Government, II 190; serves as material for "Jewish Committee," II 193; influences reports of governors, II 194

Russian officials repeat Brafman's charges concerning K's., II 194 f

Alliance Israélite of Paris accused of constituting World K., II 189, 194

Society for Diffusion of Enlightenment accused of forming part of, II 216

Jewish Conference in St. Petersburg solemnly denies charges concerning K. (1882), II 307 f

Pahlen Commission questions Jewish experts in regard to (1888), II 369 f

See also Municipality and Autonomy

Kaidanover, Aaron Samuel, rabbi of Cracow, Hebrew author, I 200

Kaidanover, Hirsch, son of former, Hebrew author, I 202

Kakhanov, governor-general of Vilna, rebukes Jewish deputation of welcome, II 383

Kalarash (government of) pogrom at, III 128

Kalayev, Russian revolutionary, assassinates Grand Duke Sergius, III 110

Kalinovski, Polish commander, defeated by Cossacks, I 145

Kalish, leading city of Great Poland, I 42

Synod of, issues canonical laws against Jews, I 57, 62

surrenders to Swedes, I 155

city and province of, annexed by Prussia, I 292

Jews settle in, I 41

Jews of, petition Casimir IV for renewal of charter, I 61

communities in province of, destroyed, I 156

Alexander I. receives Kahal of, I 358

Abel Gumbiner, head of yeshibah in, I 200

Warta, in province of, place of Polish Diet, I 58

Kalkreuth, Count, patron of Solomon Maimon, I 240

Kalman, Jewish printer in Lublin, I 131

Kalmansohn, Jacques, author of pamphlet advocating Jewish reforms in Poland, I 385

Kalmanovich, Jewish lawyer, acts as council for Jewish victims of Kishinev pogrom, III 91; and of Homel pogrom, III 102

Kalmycks, tribe of, I 367

Kamenetz-Podolsk (Podolia), Dembrovski, bishop of, arranges disputation at, I 214 f

Talmud burned at, I 215
Vilna Gaon appeals against Hasidim to Kahal of, I 373
pogrom at, III 128

Kaniev (Ukraina), Starosta of, maltreats Jews, I 169

Kant, Immanuel, praises Solomon Maimon, I 240

Kantakuzenka (government of Kherson), pogrom at, III 33

Karabchevski, Russian lawyer, acts as council for Jewish victims of Kishinev pogrom, III 91

Karaites, in Byzantine empire, I 28
in Crimea, I 28 f
in Chufut-Kale (Crimea), I 35
in Lithuania, I 60
K. of Lithuania, receive autonomy from Casimir IV., I 61
autonomy of K's. of Troki confirmed by Alexander Yaguello, I 64
form separate municipality in Troki, I 73
K's. of Tavrida granted equal rights, I 318 f; II 160
excluded from bar but unofficially admitted, II 352 f
Isaac Troki, Karaite, author of anti-Christian treatise, I 137 f
Simha Pinsker, historian of, II 160

Karaulov, deputy to Third Duma, defends Jews, III 156

Karlin, near Pinsk (government of Minsk), Hasidim establish themselves in, I 372
Aaron of, hasidic leader, I 234
Solomon of, hasidic leader, I 372

"**Karliners,**" nickname for Hasidim in Lithuania, I 372, 375

Karnyeyev, governor of Minsk, inquires into condition of peasantry, I 322 f

Karpov, member of "Jewish Committees," advocates Jewish emancipation, II 196 ff

Karpovich (government of Chernigov), pogrom at, II 315

Kattowitz (Prussia), conference of "Lovers of Zion," at, II 376

Katzaps, nickname for Great-Russians in Little Russia, II 248; III 115, 117

Katzenellenbogen, Saul, rabbi of Vilna, objects to heterodoxy of Menashe Ilyer, II 115 f

Kauffmann, governor-general of Vilna, appoints commission to investigate Brafman's charges, II 189

Kaulbars, military governor of Odessa, fails to check pogrom, III 129

Kazan (Central Russia), Jews of Vitebsk exiled to (1654), I 154

INDEX

cantonists stationed in, II 25
suicide of cantonists in, II 27
mosques destroyed in government of, I 254

Kazimiezh (*Polish*, Kazimierz), suburb of Cracow, established as Jewish ghetto, I 64
Jews of, restricted in business, I 75

Kedars, name for Polovtzis, conquerors of Crimea, I 29

Kempster, United States commissioner, sent to Russia, II 407

Keneset Israel, Hebrew periodical, II 372, III 58

Kerch, pogrom at, III 120; see Bosporus

Kertz, Crimean city, probably identical with Kerch, I 26

Khagan, title of Khazar king, I 20 ff

Khappers, Yiddish name for recruiting agents, II 23

Kharkov (city), Jews permitted to visit fair of (1835), II 40
Jews expelled from, II 319
merchants of, protest against exclusion of Jews, II 319
Bilu, organization of Palestine pioneers, formed in, II 321

Kharkov (government), Jews permitted to visit fairs of (1734)*, I 251
Gubernatorial Commission appointed for, I 273

governor of, condemns Jews, II 276; advocates schoolnorm, II 339

Khazars, various forms of name, I 18
appear in Caucasus, I 19
establish kingdom on Volga, I 19
penetrate as far as Kiev, I 19
establish another center in Crimea, I 19 f
church attempts conversion of, I 20
converted to Judaism, I 20 f
invite teachers from Babylonia, I 21
inner life of, I 22
Jewish merchants travel through kingdom of, I 23
Jews of Byzantium flee to, I 23 f
Hasdai Ibn Shaprut corresponds with king of, I 24 ff
K's. defeated by Russians, I 28
withdraw to Crimea, I 28
K's. in Crimea destroyed by Russians and Byzantines, I 28
relatives of last king of, flee to Spain, I 28
Jews from kingdom of, attempt conversion of Vladimir, I 30
settle in principality of Kiev, I 31

---

* The text has 1774 by mistake.

civilizing influence of, on Kiev, II 252

Khazars, Sea of, name for Caspian Sea, I 23

Khazaria, name for Crimea, I 28 ff

Khelm (province of Lublin), bishop of, imprisons Jews on charge of host desecration, I 86

rabbi of, author of Polish pamphlet defending Jews, I 283

Kherson (city), visited by White, emissary of Baron Hirsch, II 418

Kherson (government), seat of Zaporozhian Cossacks, I 143

Jews settled as agriculturists in, I 363 f, II 71

included in Pale (Statute of 1835), II 40

pogroms in, II 251, 304, III 33, 100

governor of, deplores effect of Jews on their domestics, I 404

Localities in:

Alexandria, III 100

Anayev, II 251

Borki, II 378

Kantakuzenka, III 33

Khlopitzki, Polish dictator, declines offer of Jewish volunteers, II 105

Khlops, nickname for Polish peasants, I 140, 182; see Serfs

Khmelnitzki (*Polish,* Chmelnicki), **Bogdan,** I 144 ff

elected Hetman by Cossacks, I 144

forms alliance with Tartars of Crimea, I 144

defeats Polish army, I 145

heads rebellion of Ukrainians against Poles, I 145

organizes massacre of Jews, I 145

sends detachment of Cossacks against Niemirov, I 146

derides Polish generals, I 149

besieges Lemberg, I 150 f

demands delivery of Jews, I 151

receives ransom and withdraws, I 151

defeated by Poles, I 152

signs Treaty of Byelaya Tzerkov (1651), I 152

enters into negotiations with Tzar Alexis, I 152 f

extent of K. massacres, I 157

recollection of K. massacres stirs later Ukrainians, I 182, 185

reports of K. massacres arouses Sabbatai Zevi, I 205

K. massacres described by Gogol, II 139; and Bogrov, II 242

See Cossacks

INDEX

Kholonyevski, member of Polish Diet, objects to extension of Jewish rights, I 288

Khomyakov, Russian poet, condemns régime of Nicholas I., II 141

Khovanski, governor-general of White Russia, ordered to provide livelihood for Jews expelled from villages, I 406 recommends discontinuation of expulsion, I 407 recommends proceedings in ritual murder trial of Velish, II 76 ff believes to have discovered monstrous crime, II 78 asks governors of Pale for incriminating material, II 80 censured by Nicholas I., II 80 exposed as Jew-baiter by Council of State, I 81

Khoza Kokos, Jew of Crimea, agent of Grand Duke Ivan III. of Moscow, I 35 arranges alliance between grand duke and Khan of Crimea, I 35 writes to Ivan III. in Hebrew, I 35

Khwarism, city in Asia, I 26

Kiev (city), Khazars make raids on, I 19 captured by Lithuanians (1320), I 94 forms part of Polish empire, I 94, 140

incorporated, together with Little Russia, in Russian empire (1654), I 94 ceded to Russia by Poland (1667), I 159 Metropolitan of Greek-Orthodox Church resides in, III 125 Jews settle in, I 31 Jews and Khazars in, II 252 Khazar Jews appear in, to convert Prince Vladimir (986), I 30 f Greek-Orthodox priests in, preach hatred against Jews, I 31 pogroms at (12th century), I 32 Jews of, protected by Prince Svyatopolk II., I 32 fire at, damages Jews (1124), I 32 "Jewish Gate" at, mentioned in Russian Chronicles, I 32 visited by early Jewish travellers, I 32 f Jews, fleeing from Germany, settle in, I 33 Moses, rabbi of, mentioned in early Hebrew sources, I 33 "Skharia," Jew of, settles in Novgorod (15th century), I 36 burghers of, obtain right of excluding Jews (1619), I 95 Jews permitted to settle in (1794), I 317, II 31

Nicholas I. orders expulsion of Jews from (1827), II 30 ff authorities of, secure postponement of expulsion, II 33 Nicholas I. insists on expulsion from, II 36 closed to Jews by Statute of 1835, II 40 Jews permitted to visit K. temporarily, II 172 privileged categories of Jews settle in (under Alexander II.), II 264 Government agents prepare pogrom at (after accession of Alexander III.), II 248 pogrom at (April, 1881), II 251 ff, 287; tried in court, II 264 "illegal" Jews expelled from (May, 1881), II 263 f wholesale expulsions of Jews from (1882), II 319; (1886), II 346 Jews of, subjected to raids, or *oblavas*, II 346; III 20 wives of Jewish artisans in, forbidden to trade, II 385 visited by White, emissary of Baron Hirsch, II 418 persecution of Jews in (under Nicholas II.), III 19 f Jews made to pay for night raids, III 20 Government frustrates project of trade bank in, III 25 f

Russian Nationalist Society of, incites to pogroms, III 114 pogrom at (October, 1905), III 128 Jewish students excluded from Polytechnicum at (1907) III 152 1200 Jewish families expelled from (1910), III 157 Stolypin assassinated at (1911), III 164 impending pogrom at, stopped, III 165 Beilis ritual murder case in, III 165 f Jewish printing-press in, II 43; transferred to Zhitomir, II 43 Jewish printers of Slavuta imprisoned in, II 123 Censorship Committee in, ordered to examine Jewish books, II 44 Professor Mandelstamm, resident of, II 298, 304, III 47 Dashevski, avenger of Kishinev pogrom, student in, III 81 *Jüdisches Volksblatt* appears in, III 59

Kiev (province, or government), subject to Poland, I 140 estate in, owned by Polish nobles, I 140 ceded to Russia (1667), I 159 part of, annexed by Russia (1793), I 292

INDEX

Jews of, flee to Tatars (1648), I 145

Jews forbidden to settle in (1649), I 151

Jews in part of, exterminated, I 157

few Jewish survivors in, I 246

Haidamacks massacre Jews in (1768), I 183 f

included in Pale (1794), I 317; (1804), I 342; (1835), II 40

Jewish deputies from, arrive in St. Petersburg (1803), I 337

Jews of, invited to send delegates to city of Kiev (1807), I 349

Hasidism spreads in, I 382; II 119 f

Jews expelled from villages in (1830), II 32; expulsion postponed until 1835, II 33

number of Jewish artisans in, II 168

Poles and Jews forbidden to acquire estates in (1864), II 173

economic activity of Jews in, II 194

pogroms in (1881), II 256 f

Court of Appeals of, tries Homel pogrom, III 101

Localities in:

Berdychev, II 256 f

Chernobyl, I 382, II 119

Ruzhin, II 120

Shpola, III 33

Smyela, II 256

Uman, I 184 f, 383, II 122

Bibikow, governor-general of, condemns Jews, II 47; arrests Israel of Ruzhin, II 120 f

Vasilchikov, Count, favors transfer of Jewish artisans to Russian Interior, II 168

Dondukov, Korsakov, points out economic danger of Jews, II 193 f

Drenteln, fierce anti-Semite, II 276, 316 f, 319, 341

Kiev, principality of, claims overlordship over Russian lands, I 29

influenced by Byzantium, I 29 ff

passes under sovereignty of Tatars, I 33; see Kiev (city)

Kievlanin, anti-Semitic paper in Kiev, III 20

Kings, Polish, favor Jews because of financial advantages, I 69

elected by Poles, I 89

keep Jewish body-physicians, I 132

counteracted by Diets, I 160

lose their authority, I 168

Kirgiz, tribe, placed in Russian law above Jews, II 367

Kiselev, count, appointed chairman of Committee for Radical Transformation of Jews (1840), II 50, 157

addressess circular to governors-general concerning projected Jewish reforms (1845)*, II 65 f

receives petitions in favor of Jews from Moses Montefiore, II 688

advocates mitigation of Jewish restrictions (1856), II 157

Kishinev, modern Jewish school in, II 52

Jews of, accord friendly reception to Max Lilienthal, II 56

"Congregation of New Testament Israelites" in, II 225

"Smugglers," anti-Semitic play, produced in, III 38

pogrom at (1903), III 69 ff; stirs Jewish national sentiment, III 82; avenged by Jewish youth, II 81, 132; stimulates emigration, III 85; intensifies animosity of Nicholas II., III 93; tried in court, III 90 ff

authorities of, impeached before Senate, III 92

Jews accused of seeking to avenge K. massacre, III 95, 101

fear of new pogrom at, causes emigration, III 96 f

Russian Nationalist Society of, incites to pogroms, III 114

pogrom at (October, 1905), III 128

Jewish community of, protests against denial of Jewish franchise, III 121

Kitovich, Polish writer, accuses Jews of ritual murder, I 180

Klaus, name for hasidic house of prayer, II 124

Klausner, Joseph, Hebrew writer, editor of *ha-Shiloah,* III 58, 163

Klopstock, German poet, imitated in Hebrew, II 135

Kmita, Peter, voyevoda of Cracow, accepts bribes from Jewish merchants, I 76

Kobrin (province of Grodno), Bezalel of, Hebrew author, I 201

Kochubay, Minister of Interior, appointed chairman of Committees for Amelioration of Jews (1802), I 335 f

instructs governors to allay fears of Jews, I 336

assisted by Speranski, I 340

recommends postponement of expulsion of Jews from villages, I 347

assists settlement of Jewish agriculturists in New Russia, I 363

* The text has 1815 by mistake.

INDEX

accepts dedication of pamphlet by Nyevakhovich, I 387
recommends severe measures against "Judaizers," I 402

Koenigsburg (Prussia), visited by Solomon Maimon, I 239
visited by Menashe Ilyer, II 114
Jewish socialists arrested in, III 223 f
Hebrew periodicals published in, II 223

Kohan, Jacob, Hebrew poet, III 162

Kohen, Sabbatai, see Cohen

Kokovtzev, Minister of Finance, favors Jewish franchise, III 122

Kol Mebasser, Yiddish periodical, II 218

Kollontay (*Polish*, Kollontaj), radical member of Polish Diet, I 280
suggests abolition of Jewish autonomy, I 282
assists Jews in struggle for rights, I 291

Kolomea (Galicia), capital of Pokutye province, I 150

Konigsberg, see Koenigsberg

Konotop (government of Chernigov), pogrom at, intensified by Jewish self-defence, II 257

Koppelman, Jacob, Hebrew author, I 133

Koretz (Volhynia), Phineas of, disciple of Besht, I 227

Korff, Baron, advocates admission of Jewish artisans into Russian Interior, II 170

Korobka, or basket tax, name explained, II 61; see Tax

Korolenko, Russian writer, signs protest against Jewish persecutions, II 387
writes public letter in defence of Jews, II 388
portrays Kishinev massacre, III 76 f

Korostyshev, hasidic center, II 120

Korsun (province), Poles defeated by Cossacks at (1648), I 145

Kosciuszko, spelling and pronunciation of name, I 292
leads Polish uprising of 1794, I 292
liberal and democratic, I 292 f
permits formation of Jewish regiment, I 294
announces it in special army order, I 294 f
captured by Russians, I 296
Zayonchek, general under, I 296, II 91

Kosovo (Galicia), Besht settles in, I 223
Nahman of, disciple of Besht, I 227

Kostantinia, Sea of, name for Black Sea, I 26

Kostomarov, Russian historian, defends ritual murder libel, II 205

Kotzebue, governor-general of New Russia, fails to check Odessa pogrom (1871), II 192

Kotzk (*Polish*, Kock), near Warsaw, Berek Yoselevich killed in vicinity of, I 303 hasidic dynasty of, II 122

Kovalevski, Minister of Public Instruction, advocates admission into Russian Interior of graduates of secondary schools, II 164

Kovno (city), Jews of, barred from city government (1805), I 370 growth of pauperism in, III 24 "Bund" holds convention in (1899), III 57 Jewish community of, signs petition for equal rights (1905), III 108 Abraham Mapu, Hebrew writer, native of, II 226 ff Isaac Elhanan Spector, rabbi of, II 304

Kovno (government), part of, called Zhmud, I 293, II 133 formed originally part of government of Vilna, I 317 constituted 1872, I 317 forms part of Lithuania, II 39

vitally affected by expulsion of Jews from border zone (1843), II 63 placed under military dictatorship of Muravyov (1863), II 188 Lutostanski, anti-Semitic writer, priest in, II 203 Friedman from, deputy to Third Duma, III 153 Localities in: Dusyaty, III 115 Salant, II 133 Vilkomir, II 236

Kozhenitz (Poland), Israel of, hasidic leader in Poland, I 384, II 122

Kozhmyan, member of Polish Council of State, objects to emancipation of Jews, II 93

Kozlovska, witness in ritual murder case of Velizh, II 82

Kozodavlev, Russian assistant-minister of Interior, member of "Jewish Committee," I 352

Kozubales, tax to Catholic academies in Poland, I 161, 166

Kramshtyk, president of Warsaw community, arrested for participating in Polish Insurrection, II 181

Krasinski, Vincent, Polish general, author of pamphlet on Jews of Poland, II 96 f

INDEX

Kraushar, quoted, I 136

Krechatinikov, Russian general, captures Haidamack leaders, I 186

Kremenchug (government of Poltava), pogrom at (October, 1905), III 128

Kremenetz (Volhynia), Jewish community of, represented on Council of Four Lands, I 110

massacre at (1648), I 149

Mordecai Jaffe, rabbi of, I 127

native place of Isaac Baer Levinsohn, II 125 ff *

Kremsier (Moravia), meeting-place of Austrian Parliament, II 179

Kreslavka (government of Vitebsk), Frank, Jewish physician, resident of, I 331, 386

Krestentzya, form of lease, forbidden to Jews, I 404 f

Kretingen (province of Zhmud), Berek Yoselovich born at, I 293

Krochmal, Nahman, Galician thinker, associates with Isaac Baer Levinsohn, II 126

work of, compared with that of Levinsohn, II 127

Kronenberg, convert, protests against Polish anti-Semitism, II 178

Kronenstadt, fortress near St. Petersburg, place of imprisonment, II 42

Krueger, Russian official, accuses Jews of Saratov of ritual murder, II 151

Krushevan, journalist and petty official in Kishinev, III 69

editor of *Bessarabetz*, III 69 ff

carries on violent agitation against Jews, III 69 ff

invited by Plehve to publish *Znamya*, anti-Semitic paper, in St. Petersburg, III 70

accuses Jews of ritual murder, III 71

incites to pogroms, III 71

wounded by Dashevski, III 81 f

Krushnitza, ancient Polish capital, Jew elected king at, I 40

Krysa, Leib, represents Frankists at religious disputation, I 217

baptized, I 217

Kuantung (Shantung) Peninsula, Jews expelled by Russians from, III 94

Kukhazhevski (*Polish*, Kucharzewski), Polish anti-Semitic candidate to Russian Duma, defeated by Warsaw Jews, III 167

Kulak, Russian name for village boss, II 318, 325

* P. 125, line 3 from below, read "Volhynia," instead of "Podolia."

Kupernik, Jewish lawyer, acts as council for victims of Homel pogrom, III 102

Kursk (government), number of artisans in, II 168

Kut, Crimean city, I 26

Kutais (city in Caucasia), ritual murder case at, II 204

Kutaysov, Count, declares pogroms result of Jewish "exploitation," II 271

Kutover, Gershon, rabbi of Brody, brother-in-law of Besht, I 223

receives message from Besht in Palestine, I 228

Kuty (Galicia), Besht settles in neighborhood of, I 228

Kuyavia, former Polish province, I 75; II 90

Ladi (government of Moghilev), residence of Shneor Zalman, founder of *Habad*, and his successors, I 234; II 117

Lakh, Ukrainian nickname for Pole, I 142, 184

Lambat, Crimean city, I 26

Lamsdorff, Russian Minister of Foreign Affairs, has interview with Herzl, III 84

Landed Property, see Villages

Landau, Adolph, Russian-Jewish publicist, II 221

Language, use of Polish L., abandonment of Yiddish, and restriction of Hebrew advocated by Poles (1788-1791), I 273, 281

use of Polish in business [and elimination of Hebrew and Yiddish] advocated by Friesel, governor of Vilna (1800), I 327

use of Russian, Polish, or German in legal documents and in business suggested by Dyerzhavin (1800), I 333

Russian, Polish, or German made obligatory for Jewish schools and for public documents and business [Statute of 1804], I 345

reading and writing knowledge of Russian, Polish, or German required for Jewish members of municipalities [Statute of 1804], I 345

Jewish deputies plead for use of Hebrew in business, I 349 f

followers of David Friedländer call upon Polish Jews to abandon Yiddish and adopt L. of country, I 386

Statute of 1835 requires use of Russian, or other local dialect, for public and business documents, and forbids Hebrew categorically, II 40

Kahal elders required to read and write Russian [1835], II 41

INDEX

Isaac Baer Levinsohn calls on Jews to study L. of country, II 126

Jews of Poland forbidden use of Hebrew and Yiddish in civil affairs, legal documents, and business correspondence [Act of 1862], II 182

Jews of Poland retain use of their L., II 195

freedom of L. demanded by League for Equal Rights [1905], III 112

fight between Hebrew and Yiddish (1908), III 161

See Hebrew, Polish, Russian, and Yiddish

Lanskoy, Minister of Interior, favors admission into Russian Interior of Jewish graduates of secondary schools, II 164

corresponds with officials concerning admission of Jewish artisans into Russian Interior, II 168

Lantzkorona (*Polish*, Lanckorona, Podolia), assembly of Frankists at fair of, I 213, 215

Lapin, Shalom, of Grodno, suspected of ritual murder, II 73

Lapkovski, Benish, from government of Vitebsk, elected Jewish deputy, I 393

Laski, John, Polish chancellor, edits Polish code of laws, I 71

Laschenko organizes pogrom at Ananyev, government of Kherson, II 251

Lavrov, Russian revolutionary in London, II 223

Layze (Lazarus), son of Jewish arendar, I 266

Lazhentzka, Dorothy, of Sokhachev, sentenced on charge of having sold host to Jews, I 86

League for the Attainment of Equal Rights for the Jewish People in Russia, the, organized in Vilna (1905), III 111

program of, III 111 f

establishes Central Bureau in St. Petersburg, III 112

conventions of, III 131, 133 f

protests against pogroms, III 132

sends greetings to Dashevski, avenger of Kishinev pogrom, III 132

decides to call All-Russian Jewish National Assembly, III 133

Jewish Duma deputies accept program of, III 134

presided over by Vinaver, III 134

represents doctrine of National-Cultural Autonomism, III 144

stands above class and party affiliations, III 145 f

disintegration of, III 146 f

League of Jewish Socialists, in London, II 223

League of Jewish Workingmen, see "Bund"

League of Russian People, organization of Black Hundred, III 141

favors re-establishment of unlimited autocracy, III 149

secures pardon for pogrom makers, III 150

forms "Second Government," III 141, 151

badge of, demonstratively worn by Nicholas II., III 151

See Black Hundred

"Learned Jew" (*Uchony yevrey*), Russian title for Jewish Government expert, II 239

Lebensohn, Abraham Baer (called "Adam"), Hebrew poet, II 134 f

prominent in Maskilim circle of Vilna, II 136

Lebensohn, Micah Joseph, son of former, Hebrew poet, II 226

Legal Profession, see Bar

Leipsic, Russian-Jewish merchants visit fair of, I 359 f

place of publication, II 135

Lekkert, Hirsch, shoots at governor of Vilna, III 67

Lelevel (*Polish*, Lelewel), Polish historian, issues manifesto to Jews, II 107 f

calls upon Poles to be friendly to Jews, II 178

eulogized by Jews at memorial service, II 180

Lemberg (Lvov, *Polish*, Lwow), leading city of Red Russia, I 74, 196

anti-Jewish riots in (1463), I 63 f

Jews of, restricted in commerce, I 74

besieged by Khmelnitzki (1648), I 150 f

authorities of, refuse to deliver Jews, I 151

Jesuit college students in, attack Jews, I 161

Jews of, organize self-defence, I 161; but are massacred (1664), I 162

Pikolski, monk in, conducts agitation against Jews, I 174

Jews of, receive communal autonomy (1356), I 53; granted communal constitution (1692), I 191

rights of Kahal elders upheld by voyevoda of, I 190

Jewish community of, represented on Council of Four Lands, I 110

rabbis assembled at, excommunicate adherents of Sabbatai Zevi, I 211
disputation betwen Frankists and Orthodox at, I 216 f, 229
conversion of Frankists at, I 217
Isaiah Horowitz (*Sheloh*) educated in, I 135
Rabbis of:
Joshua Falk Cohen, head of yeshibah, I 128
David Halevi (Taz), I 130, 206
Meir of Lublin, I 129
Hayyim Rapoport, I 216
Solomon, I 115

Le Nord, newspaper in Brussels, organ of Russian Government, II 393

Lenchitza (*Polish*, Leckyca, province of Kalish), Jews of, executed on ritual murder charge, I 100
Solomon Ephraim of, criticises yeshibahs, I 119 f

Leon, Jewish physician, executed by Ivan III., I 37

Leshek, Polish prince, receives Jewish delegation from Germany, I 40

Leshek The White, Polish ruler, favorable to Jews, I 42

Lesnaya (White Russia), battle at, I 248

Lessing, referred to by Nyevakhovich, Russian-Jewish writer, I 387

Levanda, Leon (Lev), Russian-Jewish writer, native of Lithuania, II 238
teacher in Jewish Crown school, II 239
"Learned Jew" in Vilna, II 239 f
novels by, II 239 f
joins Palestine movement, II 240, 332
corresponds with Bogrov, II 241

Levendahl, Russian official, inspires Kishinev massacre, III 71, 77

Levi Itzhok, of Berdychev, hasidic leader, I 232 f
saintliness of, I 233, 382
Hebrew author, I 382

Levin, Shmaryahu, member of Central Committee of League for Equal Rights, III 112
deputy to First Duma, III 134
denounces Bialystok pogrom, III 137, 139
demands equal rights for Jews, III 137

Levinsohn, Isaac Baer, called "the Russian Mendelssohn," II 125 ff
born in Volhynia, II 125
associates with Maskilim of Galicia, II 125 f

author of *Te'udah be-Israel*, II 126; conclusions of, II 126

author of anonymous anti-hasidic satire, II 127

author of *Bet Yehudah*, II 127 f

suggests plan of Jewish reforms, II 128; and modifications in Jewish religious life, II 129

keeps in contact with Russian dignitaries, II 129 f

receives subsidies from Russian Government, II 129, 132

advocates prohibition of "harmful" books, II 129 f

naiveté of, II 130

publishes refutation of blood accusation, II 131

author of apologetic treatise *Zerubbabel*, defending the Talmud, II 131

compared with scholars in other lands, II 131

dies unappreciated, II 132

Levita, Benedict, of Cracow, granted monopoly of importing Hebrew books, I 131

Levy, Lipman, financial agent at Russian Court, I 248

Lewin, L., quoted, I 111

Lewin, Mendel, of Satanov (Podolia), Hebrew writer, I 388

Liberum Veto, Polish parliamentary law, source of anarchy, I 92, 168

Lieberman, A. (Freeman), Jewish socialist, II 223 f

Lieders, Russian viceroy in Poland, arrests Jewish leaders, II 181

Lieven, Russian Minister of Public Instruction, receives memorandum from Isaac Baer Levinsohn, II 129

Lifschitz, Gedaliah, of Lublin, Hebrew author, I 133

Lilienblum, Moses Leib, advocates religious reforms, II 236

joins Russified *intelligentsia*, II 237

writes "Sins of Youth," II 237

joins "Love of Zion" and later Zionist movement, II 237, 328 f, 376, III 42, 49

Lilienthal, Max, native of Bavaria, II 52

director of modern Jewish school in Riga, II 52

commissioned by Russian Government to carry out school reforms, II 53

visits Vilna, II 54; meets with approval of local Maskilim, II 136 f

meets with opposition in Minsk, II 55

presents report to Uvarov, Minister of Public Instruction, II 55

tours Russian South and South-west, II 56

INDEX

assured by Jewish communities of co-operation, II 56

campaign of, hailed by Jewish leaders of western Europe, II 67

not supported by Isaac Baer Levinsohn, II 136

emigrates to America, II 59

quoted, II 55

Lippomano, papal nuncio, instigates host trial of Sokhachev, I 86 f

Liquor, use of, encouraged by Hasidim, II 124 f

Liquor Trade, see Propination

Literature, rabbinic L. in Poland, I 121 ff; see also Hebrew, Yiddish, and Russian

Lithuania, Kiev incorporated in, I 94

Volhynia annexed by, I 59

"Union of Lublin," between Poland and L. (1569), I 88

annexed by Russia (1795), I 297

Jews emigrate from Crimea into, I 35

important Jewish communities in, I 59

Jews of, obtain charter from Vitovt (1388), I 59

favorable economic condition of Jews in, I 60, 72 f

Jewish tax farmers in, I 72, 94

Karaites in, I 60

Jews expelled from (1493), and allowed to return (1503), I 65, 70 f

Jews of, suspected of sheltering proselytes, I 80; and of planning to leave country, I 81

cleared of suspicion by royal charter (1540), I 81

"Lithuanian Statute" (1566) imposes restrictions on Jews, I 87

blood accusations in, I 87 f, 96, 162 ff

"Union of Lublin" affects unfavorably Jews of, I 88

Ukrainian rebels penetrate into, I 149

invaded by Russians (1654 ff), I 153 ff, 156, 264

Jews, persecuted by Cossacks, flee to, I 157

Jewish cultural center moves to, I 159 f

Jewish conditions in, described by Solomon Maimon, I 239 f

Jews of, barred from Russia, I 243 f; yet penetrate into Moscow, I 245

numbers of Jews in, I 263 f

included in Pale (1795), I 317; (1804), I 342; (1835), II 39

Polish nobility of, advocate Jewish reforms (1800), I 325 f

Jews establish woolen mills in, I 363

Jewish agricultural colonies in, II 72

Jews admitted to municipal government in, I 369; but speedily disfranchised, I 370

Jews of, loyal to Russia in Polish insurrections of 1861 and 1863, II 107, 182 f

Russian authorities of, believe Brafman's charges against Jews, II 189

pogroms checked in, II 267, 276

Jewish labor movement in, III 55

Jews of, called Litvaks, object of Polish anti-Semitism, III 166 f

Jewish communities of, represented on Council of Four Lands, I 110; but later form separate Council (1623), I 112, 193 f, 195

Michael Yosefovich appointed "senior" of Jews of, I 72

Kahals of, granted right of *herem* (1672), I 190

different intellectual development in, I 221

strong position of Rabbinism and Talmudism in, I 199 f, 221, II 113

Elijah of Vilna, champion of Rabbinism in, see Elijah of Vilna

yeshibahs of, adopt method of Elijah of Vilna, I 381 f

Messianism preached among Jews of, I 208

Hasidim penetrates into, I 230 ff, 237

type of Hasidism in, I 232 f

rabbis of, oppose Hasidism, II 233, 237 f

Kahals of, appealed to against Hasidism, I 373

Hasidism weak in, I 274, 372

Hasidim of, denounced to Russian authorities, I 376

spirit of denunciation (*mesirah*) among Jews of, I 377 f

disintegration of Kahals in, I 275 f

Jews of, plead for preservation of Kahal courts, I 320

greater political sense among Jews of, I 379

rabbis of, arbitrate between Kahal and rabbi of Vilna, I 276

rabbis of, appeal to I. B. Levinsohn to refute blood accusation, II 131

opposition to secular learning among Jews of, II 114 f

Haskalah movement in, see Haskalah and Vilna

Hebrew writers originate from, II 238

Little Poland, see Poland, Little

Little Russia, see Russia, Little

INDEX

Livadia, summer residence of Alexander III., II 429, III 18

Livonia, inhabitants of, demand admission of Jews, I 256

Empress Elizabeth refuses to admit Jews into, I 257

Jews expelled from (1744), I 257

Jewish newcomers expelled from (1829), II 32; see Baltic Provinces

Lizno (Galicia), Elimelech of, hasidic leader, I 232

Lobanov-Rostoveki, chairman of Committee for Amelioration of Jews (1871), II 191

Lobzovo, near Cracow, residence of Estherka, favorite of Casimir the Great, I 53

Lodz, Jewish labor movement in, III 55

pogrom at, III 119 f

economic success of Jews in, stimulate Polish boycott, II 166

Loewenthal, professor, sent by Baron Hirsch to Argentina, II 416

Lokhvitz (province), massacre at (1648), I 145

London, Moses Montefiore of, goes to Russia, II 68

M'Caul, missionary in, II 131

Jewish Socialist Society in, II 223

Mansion House Meeting held in (February 1, 1882), II 288 ff

Lord Mayor of, presides at meeting, II 288; and joins pogrom committee, II 291

bishop of, joins pogrom committee, II 291

secret circular of Plehve circulated in, II 381

new protest meeting planned in, II 382

Guildhall Meeting held in (December 10, 1890), II 388 ff

effect of protest meeting in, felt in St. Petersburg, II 397 f

Moscow refugees in, II 408

Jewish Colonization Association in, II 414, 419

Fourth Zionist Congress held in, III 45

L. Times publishes account of pogroms and persecutions, II 287; attacks Russia, II 381, 389 f; publishes secret letter of Plehve, III 77

Longinus, see Dlogosh

Lopukhin, Russian prosecutor-general, receives denunciation against Hasidim, I 375 f

Loris-Melikov, Russian statesman, favors popular representation, II 245

discusses Jewish question with American Minister, II 293

Louis of Hungary, Polish king (1370-1382), persecutes Jews, I 54

Louisiana, Jewish agricultural colonies, in, II 374

"Love of Zion," see Zionism

Lovich, Synod of (1720), forbids building or repairing of synagogues, I 171

Lozno (government of Moghilev), residence of Shneor Zalman, founder of *Habad*, I 234, 330, 372, 376, 378, II 117

Lubavichi (government of Moghilev), residence of Shneor Zalman's successors, II 117

Lubbock, Sir John, protests against pogroms, II 288

Lubenski, Polish Minister of Justice, objects to emancipation of Jews, I 300 f

suggests law barring Jews from liquor trade, I 304

Lublin, leading city of Little Poland and capital of Poland, I 42, 110

"Union of" (1569), I 88

Lublin (province), annexed by Austria (1795), I 297

ritual murder cases in, I 96, 100

Crown Tribunal in, tries ritual murder cases, I 96, 100, 172

conference of rabbis and Kahal elders meet at, I 109 f, 123

Council of Four Lands meets periodically at, I 110, 152, 194

community of, receives royal permission to open yeshibah (1567), I 115

printing-press in, I 131, 196

disputations between Jews and Christians at, I 136

Gedaliah Lifschitz, Hebrew author, of, I 133

Jacob Itzhok, hasidic leader, of, I 384

Martin Chekhovich, Christian theologian, of, I 136

Rabbis of:

Shalom Shakhna, father of Polish Talmudism, I 105, 122 f

Israel, son of former, I 123

Joshua Falk Cohen, I 112, 128

Solomon Luria (*Maharshal*), I 125

Mordecai Jaffe, I 127

Meir of (*Maharam*), I 128 f, 199

Samuel Edels (*Maharsho*), I 129

Towns in:

Shchebreshin, I 158

Voistovitza, I 178

Zamoshch, I 203

Lubliner, Polish-Jewish writer and patriot, II 109

INDEX

Lubny (province of Poltava), Cossack massacres at (1637), I 144; (1648), I 145

Lubomirski, Polish Crown Marshal, imposes tax on Jews sojourning in Warsaw, I 268 f

Lueger, anti-Semitic burgomaster of Vienna, III 32

Luga (government of St. Petersburg), Alexander I. causes expulsion of Jews from, I 409

Lukasinski, Valerian, Polish army officer, defends Jews, II 97 f

Lukov (province of Shedletz), I 287

Luria, Isaac (Ari), name explained, I 134

influence of Cabala system of, on Poland, I 134, 202

study of writings of, forbidden before age of forty, I 214

writings of, studied by Besht, I 223

prayer-book of, accepted by Hasidim, I 231

Luria, Solomon (Reshal or Maharshal) native of Posen, I 124

rabbi in Ostrog and Lublin, I 125

follows casuistic method of Tosafists, I 125

criticises *Shulhan Arukh*, I 125

gravitates towards mysticism, I 126

criticises study of Aristotle in yeshibahs, I 120

leaves profound impress on posterity, I 199

Lutherans, Isaac Troki argues with, I 137; see Reformation

Lutostanski, Hippolyte, accuses Jews of ritual murder, II 203 f

receives acknowledgment from Alexander III., 203, 244

Lutzk (Volhynia), Crimean Jews settle in, I 35

important Jewish community in, I 59

Karaites in, I 60

Jews of, expelled (1495), I 65

Lvov, see Lemberg

Lvov, Russian statesman, discloses connection between Government and pogroms, III 125 f

Lyck (Prussia), *ha-Maggid*, published in, II 217

Lysyanka (province of Kiev), massacre at, I 184

Maeotis, see Azov, Sea of

"Magdeburg Law," name explained, I 44

granted to Germans in Poland, I 44

bestowed on city of Lemberg, I 53

granted to Karaites of Lithuania, I 61; and confirmed, I 64

taken advantage of by Polish estates to oppress Jews, I 74

Jews exempted from jurisdiction of, I 94

Jewish Kahal forms counterpart to, I 103; see also Autonomy

Magister, Russian university degree, explained, II 165

Magistracies, see Municipalities

Maimon, Solomon, born in Lithuania, I 239

receives talmudic education, I 239

studies in Germany, I 239 f

student of Kantian philosophy, I 240

writes "Autobiography," I 240

quoted, I 221

Maimonides, philosophic writings of, studied by Moses Isserles, I 126; and Mordecai Jaffe, I 132

studied and interpreted by Solomon Maimon, I 240

influences Shneor Zalmon, I 382

does not appeal to Nahman of Bratzlav, I 383

invoked by Maskilim in support of secular learning, II 126

quoted, II 119

Makarov (government of Kiev), hasidic center, II 120

Makov, chairman of Commission for Revision of Laws concerning Jews, II 336

Malakh, Hayyim, Sabbatian propagandist, I 208

joins Judah Hasid, I 209

heads party of pilgrims to Palestine, I 209

holds Sabbatian services in Jerusalem, I 210

Melchevski, Polish bishop, invites David Friedländer to render opinion on Polish-Jewish question, II 90

Maliss, Eda, victim of pogrom, II 302

Manasseh, I., and II., kings of Khazars, I 26

Manassein, Minister of Justice, excludes Jews from Russian bar, II 352

Mandelstamm, successor to Max Lilienthal, II 118

Mandelstamm, professor, of Kiev, insists on necessity of organizing emigration, II 298

attends conference of Jewish notables in St. Petersburg, II 304

denounces Ignatyev's offer to settle Jews in Central Asia, II 306

supports Zionist leaders in Western Europe, III 47

INDEX

Manifesto, name explained, II 246

coronation M. of Alexander II. abolishes Jewish conscription, II 155 f

M. of Alexander III. promising to uphold autocracy, II 246

coronation M. of Alexander III. disregards Jews, II 338

M. of Nicholas II., on birth of heir-apparent Alexis, offers trifling alleviations to Jews, III 98

M. of October 17, promising Constitution, III 127; followed by pogroms, III 127 ff

Vyborg M., see Vyborg

Mankup (Mangup), Crimean city, I 26

Manning, cardinal, protests at Mansion House Meeting against pogroms, II 289 f

joins pogrom committee, II 291

expresses sympathy with Guildhall Meeting, II 390

Mansion House Meeting, see London

Mapu, Abraham, Hebrew writer, II 226 ff

Margolis, M., Jewish expert, invited by Pahlen Commission, II 369

Marini, general of Dominican Order, deprecates persecution of Polish Jews, I 165

Mark (Mordecai), victim of blood accusation, I 100

Markovich, Moses, "general syndic" of Polish Jews, I 160

Marriage, among Jews, restrictions placed upon, by Polish Diet (1775), I 267; disregarded, I 268

limitation of number of M's proposed by Poles, I 282

age of, restricted by Russian law (1835), II 40

early M's in vogue, II 112

Marseilles, Altaras of, visits Russia, II 69

Masalski, bishop of Vilna, employs Berek Yoselovich. I 294

Maskilim. see Haskalah

Massacres, see Pogroms

Masudi, Arabic writer, quoted, I 23 f

May Laws, see Temporary Rules

Maximova, witness in ritual murder case, II 82

Mazovia, Polish principality and province, I 42, 85

annexed by Prussia (1795), I 297

M'Caul, London missionary, attacks Talmud, II 131

Me'assef, Hebrew periodical, I 386; II 137

Meat Tax, see Tax

Meath, Earl of, addresses Guildhall Meeting, II 391

Mechanics, see Artisans

Mechislav, prince of Great Poland, forbids violence against Jews, I 42

Mechislav (Meshko), Polish king, mentioned on coins, I 42

Medicine, see Physicians

Medzhibozh (Podolia), Besht settles in, I 225 visited by his disciples, I 228 residence of Borukh Tulchinski, I 384; and his disciples, II 121

Meir of Lublin (*Maharam*), rabbi and scholar, I 128 f leaves profound impress on posterity, I 199

Meir, of Shchebreshin, describes Cossack persecutions, I 158

Meir, of Tarnopol, Hebrew author, I 201

Meisels, Berush, rabbi in Cracow, and member of Austrian parliament, II 179 rabbi in Warsaw, and active in Polish Insurrection (1863), II 179 ff

Melammed, see Heder

Melitopol (government of Tavrida), pogrom at, III 115

Melitzah, conventionalized Hebrew style, II 225, 228

Menahem, king of Khazars, I 26

Mendel, chief rabbi of Great Poland, I 104

Mendel Kotzker, hasidic leader, II 122

Mendel, of Lubavichi, see Shneorsohn

Mendel, of Vitebsk, hasidic leader, I 234

Mendele Mokher Sforim, see Abramovich

Mendelssohn, Moses, "Father of Enlightenment," I 238, II 125

"**Enlightenment**" of, contrasted with Russian Haskalah, II 137

followers of, among Polish and Russian Jews, I 239, 331, 384, 385, 387

Isaac Baer Levinsohn, called "the Russian M.," II 125

Bible translation of, rendered into Russian, II 118

David Friedländer, pupil of, approached by Polish Government, II 90

attacked by Smolenskin, II 235

Wessely, associate of, II 135

Mengli-Guiray, Khan of Crimea, communicates with prince of Moscow through Jewish agents, I 35 f

Menorah, represented on tombstones in Tauris, I 16

Merchants, the, form separate estate in Russia, I 308 exempted from military service, II 20

INDEX

called to military service (1874), II 200
few first-guild Jewish M's. in Pale, II 162
Jewish M. permitted temporary visit to Interior (1835), II 40
admission of, into Interior voted down by Council of State, II 35 f; discussed by Committee for Amelioration of Jews, II 161 f
Jewish first-guild M's. admitted into Interior (1859), II 62, 343
attempt to exclude Jewish M's. from Interior (under Alexander III.), II 399
permitted to remain in Moscow, III 14; but restricted in rights, III 15
See Commerce

Meshcherski, Count, editor of anti-semitic weekly *Grazhdanin*, II 380, 413

Meshko, see Mechislav

Mesirah ("Informing") develops among Jews under Russian rule, I 377
discharged rabbi of Pinsk engages in, I 377 f
in Novaya Ushitza, II 84 f, 121
in Mstislavl, II 85 ff

Messianism, preached in Poland, I 204 ff
superseded by Hasidism, I 222

defended by Smolenskin, II 235
"Love of Zion" viewed with suspicion by Orthodox as rival of, II 377
Messianic character of Political Zionism, III 48

Methodius, Slavonian missionary, engages in disputation with Jews, I 18

Metternich, represents Austria at Congress of Aix-la-Chapelle, I 399

Mezherich (or **Mezhirich**), Volhynia, hasidic center, I 229 f
Baer of M., called "Mazhiricher Maggid," I 227, 229 f, 384, II 120

Michinski, Sebastian, Polish anti-Semitic writer, I 97

Mickiewicz, see Mitzkevich

Mikhailishok (government of Vilna), residence of Abraham Lebensohn, II 134

Mikolski, Polish priest, favors Frankists, I 216

Mikweh Israel, agricultural settlement in Palestine, II 322

Miletus (Asia Minor), Jewish community in, I 14

Military Service (or **Conscription**), Jews of Poland free from, I 304
payment of ransom in lieu of, confirmed by Polish law (1812), I 304; (1817), II 95; (1831), II 107

imposed on Jews of Poland (1843), II 109
imposed on Jews of Austria, II 30
merchants in Russia exempted from, by paying conscription tax, I 318; II 15
merchants subjected to (1874), II 200
imposition of, on Jews planned by Alexander I., II 15
conceived by Nicholas I. as means of de-Judaization, II 15
danger of imposition of, on Jews set forth by Novosiltzev, II 16
Jews alarmed by rumors concerning imposition of, II 17
imposed upon Jews by conscription ukase of August 26, 1827, II 18 ff, ukaso reaffirmed in Statute of 1835, II 41
juvenile M. S., see Cantonists
certain classes of Jews exempted from, II 20
weight of, falls principally on burghers, II 29
horrors of, II 24 ff, 27 ff, 145 ff
Jews of Old-Constantinov "protest" against, II 21 f
early marriages due to fear of, II 28
alleviations in, proposed by Council of State and rejected by Nicholas I., II 36
ineffectiveness of, in reforming Jews pointed out by Council of State (1840), II 48
term of, reduced for graduates of Crown schools (1844), II 58
Jewish agriculturists exempted from, II 71
shunned by Russians in general, II 146
evaded by Jews, II 146
barbarous penalties decreed for evasion of (1850), II 147 f
severities of, repealed by Alexander II. (1856), II 155 ff
tax in lieu of, proposed for graduates of secular schools and rejected (1859), II 164
newly regulated by Law of 1874, II 199 ff
discriminations against Jews in new M. S. Statute of 1874, II 200 f, 355
evasion of, punished by fining family of recruit (1886), II 356
fine for evasion of, stimulates emigration, II 373, 414
Jewish emigrants relieved from, II 420
See Army, Recruits, and Soldiers
Milton, indirect effect of, on Hebrew literature, II 135

INDEX

Minor, rabbi of Moscow, refuses blackmail offer of Lutostanski, II 203

dismissed from office and exiled by Russian Government, II 423 f

Minsk (city), Jews of, complain against abuses of Kahal, I 275

Kahal of, decides to send deputation to Tzar, I 336

Jews of, communicate with Jews of Vilna concerning Hasidism, I 373

Max Lilienthal opposed by Jews of, II 55

visited by Alexander II., II 187

minutes of Kahal of, used by Brafman as incriminating material, II 189

growth of pauperism in, III 24

Convention of Russian Zionists at, III 45, 51, 59

pogrom at, III 119

Jewish community of, protests against denial of Jewish franchise, III 121

Jehiel Halperin, rabbi of, I 200

Naphtali, resident of, Hebrew author, I 201

Pollak, resident of, offers to establish agricultural farms, III 25

Minsk (province, or government), annexed by Russia (1793), I 292

included in Pale (1794), I 316 f; (1804), I 342; (1835), II 39

famine in, I 322 f

Polish nobles of, propose restrictions for Jews, I 322 ff

Jewish deputies from, active in St. Petersburg, I 337

Jews of, asked to elect delegates, I 349

massacre of Jews and Russians threatened by Poles in, I 357

Solomon of Karlin killed by troops in, I 372

placed under military dictatorship of Muravyov, II 188

Brafman, accuser of Jews, native of, II 187

Localities in:

Bobovnia, II 80

Mir, II 113

Nesvizh, I 239

Mint, Polish, administered by Jews, I 42

Mir (government of Minsk), yeshibah at, II 113

Mishnah, term explained, II 114

Mithnagdim, name of opponents of Hasidim, I 238, 372

oppose Hasidim, I 274, 278, 372, 375

Mitropolit, highest ecclesiastic title in Russia, III 125

Mitzkevich (*Polish*, Myckiewicz), **Adam**, Polish poet friendly to Jews, II 108

Mizrahi, Orthodox Zionists, III 47

Mladanovich, Polish governor of Uman, betrays Jews, I 184 killed by Haidamucks, I 185

Mocatta, Moses, English translator of Isaac Troki's work, I 130

Modebadze, Sarre, Gruzinian girl, alleged victim of ritual murder, II 204

Moghilev, on the Dnieper (city), I 98

Jews of, transferred to outskirts of city (1633), I 98; and barred from Christian neighborhood (1646), I 98 f

Jews of, expelled by invading Russians (1654), I 153; and massacred by Russian soldiers, I 154, 245

echo of Sabbatian propaganda, in, I 205

rabbinical conference at, protests against Hasidism, I 238

Kahal of, appealed to by Vilna Gaon against Hasidism, I 373

Shmerling, deputy from, dies at St. Petersburg Conference (1882), II 304

pogrom at (1904), III 100 f; avenged by Jewish youth, III 107

Moghilev (government), forms part of White Russia, I 187, 262, 307

communities of, form federation, I 196

Polish Jewish prisoners of war from, form nucleus of Moscow community, I 245

Jews of, visit Smolensk and Moscow, I 315

made part of Pale (1794), I 317; (1835), II 40

Jewish deputies from, arrive in St. Petersburg (1803), I 337

Jews of, invited to send delegates (1807), I 349

Jews from apply to be settled as agriculturists in New Russia, I 363

Jews elected to municipal offices in, I 368

Jews expelled from villages of (1823), I 406

governor of, reprimanded for accusing Jews falsely, II 87

governor of, decrees "polite manners" for Jews, II 383

governor of, censures Jews of Homel, III 89

Localities in:

Dubrovna, I 252

Homel, III 87 ff

Ladi, I 239, II 117

Lozno, I 234, II 117

Lubavichi, II 117

Monostyrchina, II 86

Mstislavl, II 85 ff, 383

Moghilev, on the Dniester (Podolia), I 98

INDEX

Mohammedans, king of Khazars invites representative of, I 21

destroy Synagogue and are punished by Khazar king, I 22

protected by Khazars against Russians, I 26

persecuted in Russia, I 254

excluded from Russian bar, II 252 f

Mohilever, Samuel, rabbi of Bialystok, joins "Love of Zion" movement, II 376 f

Moldavo-Wallachia, Jews export goods from Poland to, I 67 f

Moldavia, Lithuanian Jews accused of sending proselytes to, I 81

Moment, Yiddish daily in Warsaw, III 162

Monastyrchina (government of Moghilev), Itzele of, pleads for Jews, II 86

Montagu, Sir Samuel, of London, expelled from Moscow, II 345

Montefiore Sir Moses, corresponds with Max Lilienthal, II 67

visits Russia and pleads for Jews, II 68

fund in honor of, established by "Lovers of Zion," II 376

Moravia, Jacob Frank moves to, I 219

Kremsier, city in, II 179

Moravski, Polish Minister of War, objects to Jewish volunteers, II 105

Mordecai (Motele), of Chernobyl, hasidic leader, II 119

Mordvinov, member of Council of State, saves Jews of Velizh from ritual murder charge, II 81 f

Morenu, title of ordained rabbi, I 117

Moscow, Principality (Tzardom) of [Muscovy], growth of, I 29

Jews of Tauris brought into contract with, I 33

Crimean Jews render services to rulers of, I 35 f

closed to Jews, I 60, 242

Little Russia incorporated in (1654), I 94, 153; (1657), I 159

Jews barred from (1610), I 244

rulers of Muscovy invade Polish provinces, I 153 f, 244; and troops of, expel or massacre Jews, I 154, 243, 245 f

See Moscow (city)

Moscow (city), "Judaizing heresy" spreads in, I 36 f

Jewish court-physician burned in, 37

Jewish merchants from Poland and Lithuania penetrate into, I 242 f

Ivan the Terrible refuses to admit Jews to (1550), I 243

influx of Poles and Jews into, I 244

Polish-Jewish prisoners of war permitted to stay in, I 245

Jewish cloth merchants permitted to visit, I 245

Jews barred from (1676), I 245

Borukh Leibov pays visit to, I 251; and converts Voznitzin to Judaism, I 251 f

Jewish merchants of White Russia pay visits to, I 315

Russian merchants of, protest against admission of Jews, I 315

Jewish merchants excluded from (1790, 1791), I 316

Jewish merchants permitted temporary sojourn in (1835), II 40

Jewish physicians, though admitted to Interior, excluded from, II 167

burgomaster of, objects to admission of Jews to city government, II 199

Jews expelled from (under Ignatyev), II 264, 319

Russian merchants plead for admission of Jews to, II 319

Sir Samuel Montagu, of London, expelled from, II 345

admission of Jews to schools and university of, restricted to 3% (1887), II 350; restriction placed on statute books (1908), III 157 f

Jews harassed in, II 385, 397

Russian celebrities of, sign protest against Jewish persecution, II 387

Dolgoruki, governor-general of, lenient towards Jews, II 401

Grand Duke Sergius appointed governor-general of, II 400

Alexeyov, burgomaster, of, agitates against Jews, II 400 f

Istomin, agent of Pobyedonostzev, appointed to important post in, II 401

ukase, expelling Jews from city and government of, decreed (March 28, 1891), II 402; wording of ukase affected by hope for foreign loan, II 408

"illegal" Jews raided and imprisoned, II 403

Alexander III. pays visit to, II 404

discharged Jewish soldiers forbidden to remain in, II 404

Jewish artisans and tradesmen expelled from, II 404 f

horrors of expulsion from, II 405 f

news of expulsion from, suppressed in Russian press, II 407; reported in foreign press, II 407 expulsion from, witnessed by United States commissioners, II 407; causes protest of President Harrison of United States, II 408 f

expulsion from, affects unfavorably Russian loan in Paris, II 408

M. refugees deported from St. Petersburg, II 410

expulsion of Jews from, continued, II 413; causes emigration to Western Europe and America, II 410, 413, 420

visited by White, representative of Baron Hirsch, II 418

synagogue of, closed (1892), II 423

Minor, rabbi of M., and Schneider expelled from, II 423 f

conversion of synagogue of, into charitable institution ordered by Alexander III., II 424

"Marranos" in, II 425

request of Jews of, to open synagogue for Coronation services, refused, II 112

complete fashioning of synagogue of, ordered (1897), III 13 f

Jewish merchants left in, persecuted and expelled, III 14 f

new settlement of Jewish merchants in, prohibited (1899), III 15

International Congress of Medicine held in, III 15

Jewish community of, signs petition for equal rights, III 109

Grand Duke Sergius, governor-general of, assassinated, III 110

Russian laborers from, assist in Zhitomir pogrom, III 115

armed uprising in (December, 1905), III 131

Troitza monastery, in vicinity of, II 203

Minor, rabbi of, II 203, 423 f

Pobyedonostzev, professor at University of, III 245

Russ, newspaper in, deprecates sympathy with pogrom victims, II 278

headquarters of People's Freedom, revolutionary party, II 279 f

Moscow News criticises *Imperial Messenger* for connivance at pogroms, II 279

Bogolyepov, professor in, anti-Jewish minister of Public Instruction, III 27 f

Mitroplolit, head of Russian Church, resides in, III 125

Moser, see Mesirah

Moses, king of Khazars, I 26

Moses, of Kiev, early Jewish scholar, corresponds with Gaon in Bagdad, I 133

Moses, rabbi of Great Poland, confirmed in office by Polish king (1518), I 104

Moses Ben Abraham, rabbi, author of Polish pamphlet defending Jews, II 98

Moskal, nickname for Russians among Poles, III 36

Motele, see Mordecai

Moyetzki, Polish priest, anti-Jewish writer, I 96

Moyshe (Moses), Jewish martyr in Zaslav, I 177

Mstislavl (government of Moghilev), anti-Jewish riot at, stopped by Peter the Great, I 248

Jews of, accused of mutiny (1844), II 85 ff

Jews of, threatened with public whipping, II 383

Munich (Bavaria), Max Lilienthal born in, II 52

Municipalities (Magistracies), autonomy of Polish M. guaranteed by Magdeburg Law, I 44

subject Jews to economic restrictions, I 70, 74 f

of several cities combine against Jews, I 75

form compacts with Kahals, I 84 f

obtain right of excluding Jews, I 85

arrogate jurisdiction over Jews, I 93 f

Jews engaged in litigations with, I 171

Jews placed under control of (1768), I 267

Russian Government regulates relation of Jews to (1785 ff), I 308 ff

Jewish merchants of White Russia admitted as members of (1783), I 310, 367 f

Jews complain against oppression of, I 311 f

hostility of Christian burghers bars Jews from, I 320, 369 ff

Jewish membership in, restricted to one-third, I 368; (1836), II 41; (1870), II 199, 425

Jews of Lithuania declared eligible to (1802), I 369

Jews of Lithuania barred from (1805), II 41

participation of Jews in, discussed by special Government Committee, II 198 f

Jews of Pereyaslav invited to resign from, II 266

Jews take conspicuous part in, II 425

Jews deprived of votes in (1892), II 425 f

local authorities ordered to appoint Jewish members, II 426

League for Equal Rights calls on Jewish appointees in, to resign (1905), III 112

INDEX

Jewish Government appointees resign, III 113
combined deputation of Zemstvos and M. favors universal suffrage, III 122
See Kahals and Zemstvos

Muravyov, Minister of Justice, misrepresents facts of Homel pogrom, III 101

Muravyov, Michael, governor-general of Vilna, subdues Poles, II 183
appointed military dictator of six governments, II 188
pursues policy of Russification, II 188, 239

Muravyov, Nikita, leader of "Northern" revolutionaries, I 410
limits political rights of Jews to Pale, I 413

Musar (Ethical Literature), name explained, I 201
flourishes in Poland, I 201 f

Muscovy, see Moscow, principality of

Mysticism, see Cabala

Nagatava, agricultural Jewish colony, pogrom at, III 35

Nahman, of Belzhytz, see Jacob of Belshytz

Nahman, of Bratzlav, hasidic leader, I 382
makes pilgrimage to Palestine, I 383
deprecates rationalism, I 383

dies at Uman, I 383
grave of, visited annually by devotees, II 122
adherents of, persecuted by other Hasidim, II 122

Nahman, of Horodno, disciple of Besht, I 227

Nahman, of Kosovo, disciple of Besht, I 227

Nahum, see Nohum

Names, Jews of St. Petersburg ordered to use mutilated first N. (1890), II 397 f
Jews prohibited from using Russian first N. (1893), II 427

Naphtali, of Minsk, Hebrew author, I 201

Napoleon, creates duchy of Warsaw, I 297 f
"Code of N." introduced into duchy of Warsaw, I 298
"suspensory decree" of (1808), duplicated in duchy of Warsaw, I 299
announces to Jews of Europe convocation of "Great Synhedrion," I 346
marches towards Russia (1806), I 347
influence of, over Jews feared by Russian Government, I 347
presented by Russian authorities to Jews as enemy of Judaism, I 348

denounced by Holy Synod as "savior" of Jews, I 348 f wins friendship of Alexander I., I 350 f invades Russia (1812), I 354 meets with sympathy of Poles, I 355 Russian Jews prejudiced against, I 356 f marches through Palestine, I 383

Narodnaya Vola ("The People's Freedom"), revolutionary party, II 279; see Revolution

Narodnichestov ("Populism"), II 222; see Revolution

Narol (Volhynia), massacre at (1648), I 149

Naryshkin, Russian dignitary, opposes Jewish suffrage, III 122

Nathan, successor of Nahman of Bratzlav, II 122

Nationalism, Jewish, preached by Smolenskin, II 233 ff growth of, in Russia, II 372 rise of, III 40 ff National-cultural Autonomism (spiritual nationalism), II 327, 332, III 41, 51 ff, 144 effect of, on Jewish Labor Movement, III 57 national emancipation (and self-determination) demanded by League for Equal Rights, III 112, 133

calling of Russian-Jewish National Assembly decided upon by League, III 133 national-cultural Jewish institutions prohibited and suppressed, III 160 f strength of, III 163

Nationalist Society, organization of Russian Black Hundred, III 114

Neidthart, city-governor of Odessa, assists pogrom, III 129

Nekhludov, member of Committee for Amelioration of Jews, favors emancipation of Jews, II 196 ff

Nemirov, see Niemirov

Neo-Nebraic Literature, see Hebrew

Nesselrode, Russian Minister of Foreign Affairs, forwards memorandum on Jews to Congress of Aix-la-Chapelle, I 398 discusses plan of settling Russian Jews in Algiers, II 69

Nestor, Russian chronicler, refers to Jews, I 31

Nesvizh (government of Minsk), Solomon Maimon born in vicinity of, I 239 Simeon Volfovich, opponent of Vilna Kahal, imprisoned in, I 276 Eliezer Dillon, Jewish deputy, native of, I 358

INDEX

Netter, Charles, sent by *Alliance Israélite* to help emigrants in Brody, II 269

Neue Freie Presse, Vienna daily, Dr. Herzl acts as correspondent of, in Paris, III 42

Neuman, rabbi in St. Petersburg, member of Executive Committee of Society for Diffusion of Enlightenment, II 214

Nevel, Jews, driven from villages, huddled together in, I 407

New Israel, Jewish sect in Odessa, II 334 f

New Jersey, Jewish agricultural colonies in, II 374

New Russia, see Russia, New

New York, Max Lilienthal accepts post as rabbi in, II 59 Joseph Jacobs settles in, II 287

Cox, Congressman from, addresses Congress on persecutions in Russia, III 284 f

protest meeting against pogroms held in, II 296 f

Jewish emigrants settle in, II 374

Shalom Aleichem dies in, III 62

place of publication, II 290, 297

Nicholas I., emperor of Russia (1825-1855), II 13-153

policy of, foreshadowed by Alexander I., I 390

character of reign of, I 391, II 13, 140 f

era of, depicted by Mendele Mokher Sforim, III 61

coronation of, celebrated by Hebrew poet, II 135

ascends throne through resignation of brother, II 13

suppresses uprising of Decembrists, I 410, II 13

characterizes Jews as "leeches," II 14

plans to de-Judaize Jews through military conscription, II 15 f

signs Conscription Ukase (August 26, 1827), II 17

decrees expulsions of Jews, II 30 ff

rejects plea for postponement of expulsion, II 33

rejects recommendations of Council of State in favor of Jews, II 35 ff

signs "Statute concerning Jews" (1835), II 39

sentences Jews with expired passports to penal service, II 42

subjects Hebrew books to censorship (1836), II 42 ff

dissolves "Society of Israelitish Christians," I 400

interested in conversion of Jews, II 44 f

appoints Committee for Radical Transformation of Jews (1840), II 49
places Jewish schools under Government supervision (1842), II 56
orders opening of Government schools for Jews (1844), II 57 f
expels Jews from 51-verst zone (1843), II 62
approached on behalf of Jews during stay in England, II 63
German Jews plan gift to, II 67
receives Moses Montefiore, II 68
prohibits Jews from leaving Pale, II 70
interested in spreading agriculture among Jews, II 71 f, 197, III 24
closes synagogues in Velizh on ritual murder charge (1826), II 78
believes ritual murder accusation, II 78 f
warns Commission of Inquiry, at Velizh, against exaggerations, II 80
sanctions acquittal of Velizh Jews (1835), II 82
reiterates belief in ritual murder, II 83
inflicts severe punishment on Jews of Mstislavl, II 86

deports Jewish printers to Siberia, 123
orders "assortment" of Jews (1851), II 142 f
prohibits Jewish dress (1851), II 144 f
issues draconian conscription measures (1850), II 147; (1853), 148 f
appoints committee to investigate blood accusation (1854), II 151, 203
eclipsed by Alexander III., II 354
See "Nicholas Soldiers"

Nicholas II., emperor of Russia (1894-1917), III 7-169
reign of, characterized, III 7
ascends throne, III 7
pledges himself to uphold autocracy, III 8
thanks Jews for address of welcome, III 8
surrounds himself with reactionaries, III 9
influenced by Pobyedonostzev, III 9 f
objects to abrogation of Pale, III 11
Jews of Moscow restrained from celebrating coronation of, III 12
economic collapse of Russian Jewry during reign of, III 22 ff
Jews barred from liquor trade, III 22

INDEX

calls Hague Conference, III 35
disappoints hopes of liberals, III 66
appoints Plehve, III 67
hatred of, toward Jews, intensified by Kishinev massacre, III 93
grants trifling privileges to Jews on birth of heir-apparent, III 99
makes partial concession to revolution (1904), III 106
orders shooting of demonstrators (January, 1905), III, 106 f
forced to make further concessions (February 18, 1905), III 110
patronizes Black Hundred, III 113 f
receives deputation of Zemstvos and municipalities, III 122
defers consideration of Jewish question, III 123
abets counter-revolutionary pogroms (October, 1905), III 127
pursues double-faced policy, III 130
receives deputation of Black Hundred, III 131
dissolves First Duma, III 135, 139
objects to mitigation of Jewish disabilities, III 141

changes electoral law, III 142
expresses confidence in Black Hundred, III 149
pardons pogrom perpetrators, III 150
wears ostentatiously badge of Black Hundred, III 151
ratifies restrictive school norm of 1887 (1908), III 157
extends school norm to Jewish "externs" (1911), III 159
witnesses assassination of Stolypin at Kiev, III 164
checks pogrom at Kiev, and stirs up Beilis case, III 165
"Nicholas Soldiers," term explained, II 29
forbidden to live outside Pale, II 29
permitted to live outside Pale (1867), II 29, 172
Nicolayev (government of Kherson), Jews expelled from (1829), II 32 f
excluded from Pale and closed to Jews (1835), II 4
included in Pale by Alexander II., II 172
pogrom at (April 19, 1899), III 34 ; (October, 1905), III 128
Jewish community of, protests against denial of Jewish franchise, III 128
Niemen, river, Lithuanians settled on banks of, I 59
part of Jewish Pale, I 317

Niemirov (Podolia), Khmelnitzki massacre at (1648), I 146 f

pogrom at, commemorated annually, I 152

Jacob Joseph Cohen, rabbi of, I 227, 230

name of, used as substitute for Kishinev, III 79

Nietzscheanism, preached by Hebrew writer, III 60

Nikitin, Russian-Jewish writer, quoted, I 315

Nisselovich, Jewish deputy to Third Duma, III 153

collects signatures for abrogation of Pale, III 156

Nissi, king of Khazars, I 26

Nizhni-Novgorod, Jews permitted to visit fair of (1835), II 40

pogrom at (1884), II 360 f

Nobility, in Poland, see Shlakhta

Nohum, of Chernobyl, hasidic preacher and leader, I 232, 382; II 119

Nordau, Max, Zionist discourses of, discussed in Russia, III 47

denies future of diaspora, III 52

Norov, Minister of Public Instruction, suggests admission into Russian Interior of Jewish graduates of Russian schools (1857), II 163

North-West (Lithuania and White Russia), rabbinism of, contrasted with Hasidism of South-west (Ukraina and Poland), I 199, 221, 274

Hasidism weak in, I 371 f; and different from Hasidism of South-west, I 233 ff

Kahals in, stronger than in South-west, I 274, 379

Notkin, see Shklover

Novaya Ushitza (Podolia), Jews of, accused of collective crime, II 84 f

Israel of Ruzhin implicated in case against Jews of, II 121

Novgorod, Jews of Kiev emigrate to, I 36 f

Jews of Vitebsk exiled by Russians to (1654), I 154

Novgorod-Seversk, former name of government of Poltava, I 321

included in Pale (1794), I 317

Novo-Moskovsk (government of Yekaterinoslav), pogrom at (1883), II 360

Novoshelski, burgomaster of Odessa, favors admission of Jews to municipal government, II 199

Novosiltzev, Nicholas, Russian Commissary in Poland, II 16

warns against imposing conscription on Jews, II 16 f

INDEX

proposes plan of reorganization of Polish Jews, II 92 f
plan of, discussed and rejected by Polish Council of State, II 93 f
Novosti ("The News"), liberal paper in St. Petersburg, II 379
suppressed for expressing sympathy with Moscow exiles, II 407
Novoye Vremya ("The New Time"), St. Petersburg daily, adopts anti-Semitic policy, II 205
becomes organ of reaction, II 247
advocates repression of Jews, II 278, 381
commends pogrom at Warsaw, II 282
exerts anti-Jewish influence on Government circles, II 380
read by Alexander III., II 380
attacks Rothschild of Paris, II 410
utilizes Dreyfus Affair for attack upon Jews, III 32
report of Shpola pogrom in, quoted, III 33
Suvorin, publisher of, produces anti-Semitic play, II 38
libels Jews in Russo-Japanese war, III 95
Nyeshava (*Polish*, Nieszawa), Diet of, adopts anti-Jewish "Statute" (1454), I 63

"Statute" of, confirmed by Piotrkov Diet (1496), I 64
Nyevakhovich, Judah Leib (Lev), author of Russian pamphlet on Jewish question, I 386 f
becomes Russian playwright, I 388
embraces Christianity, I 388
descendants of, occupy prominent Government positions, I 388
Nyezhin (government of Chernigov), pogrom at (1881), II 267; October, 1905), III 129

Obadiah, king of Khazars, I 26
invites Jewish sages from Babylonia, I 21
Oblavas, or raids, on Jews of Moscow, II 403
on Jews of Kiev, III 20
Obolanin, procurator-general of Senate, gives anti-Jewish instructions to Dyerzhavin, I 229
Obolenski, member of Council of State, favors Jewish franchise, III 122
Octobrists, conservative Russian party, name explained, III 153
demand exclusion of Jews from office of Justice of Peace, I 156
Odessa, Jewish families in, converted to Christianity, I 400

Jewish model school in, II 52, 133, 137
Lilienthal kindly received by Jews of, II 56
Bezalel Stern, resident of, appointed on Rabbinical Commission, II 57
center of Haskalah, II 132 f
pogrom at (1871), II 191 ff, 215 f; effects of, II 216, 239
burgomaster of, advocates admission of Jews to municipal government, II 199
Pirogov, school superintendent of, encourages Jewish cultural aspirations, II 207, 209
branch of Society for Diffusion of Enlightenment established in, II 215 f; discontinued as result of pogrom, II 216
ha-Melitz, published in, II 217
Jewish periodicals in Russian published in, II 219
Smolenskin removes to, II 234
Lilienblum settles in, II 237
Osip Rabinovich, founder of Russian-Jewish literature, resides in, II 238
Government emissaries prepare pogrom in, II 248
pogrom at (May, 1881), II 257 f
Jewish students of, organize self-defence, II 258
"New Israel," Judeo-Christian sect, founded in, I 334

center of "Love of Zion" movement, II 376
headquarters of Palestine Relief Society, II 422
Jews of, warned by city-governor, II 383
visited by White, representative of Baron Hirsch, II 418
growth of pauperism among Jews of, III 24
pupils of Jewish Agricultural School in vicinity of, barred from land ownership, III 25
Order *Bne Moshe* founded by Ahad Ha'am in, III 49
ha-Shiloah edited in, III 58, 162
Jews of, organize self-defence (1904), III 96
Grigoryev, city-governor of, prevents pogrom, III 97; dismissed, III 151
chief-of-police of, fired at by Jew, III 107
Jewish community of, signs petition for equal rights, III 109
Russian Nationalist Society of, incites to pogrom, III 114
pogrom at (October, 1905), III 128 f
Jewish self-defence of, sentenced by court-martial, III 150 f
Jews of, assaulted by Black Hundred, III 151

governor-general of, condemns Jews, II 276

Gurko, governor-general of, suggests restrictive school norm, II 339

governor of, recommends forbidding Jewish emigrants to return to Russia, II 414

Odoyevski, Count, advises Catherine II. concerning admission of Jews into Russia, I 259

Ofen, see Buda

Offenbach (Germany), Jacob Frank settles in, I 220

Olbia, on Black Sea, Jewish settlement in, I 14

Old-Constantine (Staro-Constantine), see Constantinov

"Old Testament Believers," term of assimilated Polish Jews, II 96, 100 ff

Oleshnitzki, Zbignyev, archbishop of Cracow, denounces Casimir IV. for protecting Jews, I 62

starts campaign against Jews, I 62 f

dictates anti-Jewish "Statute" of Nyeshava, I 63

Omsk, Territory of (Siberia), lands in, set aside for Jewish colonists, II 71

Oppenheim, German-Jewish painter, stops painting ordered for Nicholas I., II 67

Orlov (government), "Judaizers" in, I 402

Orlov, Count, president of Council of State, urges punishment of Jews accused of ritual murder, II 162

Crsha (government of Moghilev), pogrom at, III 128

Orshanski, Ilya (Elias), Russian-Jewish writer, II 238 f

Orshanski, Dr., brother of former, reports interview with Ignatyev, II 284 f, 297

Oryol (city), Jews expelled from. II 264

anti-Semitic play produced at, III 38 f

Ostrog (Volhynia), Jewish community of, represented on Council of Four Lands, I 110

Cossack massacre at (1648), I 149

bombarded by Russian army (1792), I 292

Jewish conference at (1798), I 324

Rabbis of:

Solomon Luria (*Reshal*), I 125

Samuel Edels (*Maharsho*), I 129

David Halevi (*Taz*), I 130

Naphtali Cohen, I 204

Ostropol, Samson of, Cabalist and martyr, I 148 f

Ostropoler, Hershel, "court-fool" of Tzaddik Borukh Tulchinski, I 348

Ostrov, at extreme end of Jewish Pale, II 70

Ostrovski, Anton, commander of National Guard in Warsaw, II 106

defends Jews, II 107

Ottocar, of Bohemia, Jewish charter of, serves as model for Boleslav of Kalish, I 45

Otyechstvennyia Zapiski ("Records of the Fatherland"), radical Russian magazine, records Jewish question as economic problem, II 325 quoted, II 325

Oxman, Jewish informer, II 84

Padua, Polish Jews study medicine at University of, I 105, 132

Pahlen, Count, chairman of "Pahlen Commission," II 336 f

Pahlen, governor of Vilna, suggests removal of Jewish disabilities, III 93

Pale of Settlement (Russian, *cherta osyedlosti*), foreshadowed in decree of May 7, 1786, restricting Jews to annexed White Russia, I 314 f

enlarged as result of second partition of Poland (1793), I 316 f

formally sanctioned by Law of June 23, 1794, I 317

enlarged as result of third partition of Poland (1795), I 317 f

Courland added to (1795), I 321

defined in Statute of 1804, I 342

Kiev excluded from (1827), II 31 ff

Courland [and Livonia] excluded from (1829), II 32

Sevastopol and Nicholayev excluded from (1829), II 32

accurately defined in Statute of 1805, II 39 f

Nicholas I. watches over strict maintenance of, II 70

number of Jews and Jewish artisans in, II 168

Commission for Amelioration of Jews considers thinning out of (1871), II 193

gubernatorial commission appointed for every government of (1881), II 273

Ignatyev refuses to add to, II 285, 306

Rostov and Taganrog excluded from (1887), II 346

admission of Jews to schools in, restricted to 10% (1887), II 350; restriction placed on Statute books (1908-1909), III 157 f

admission of Jews to universities in, restricted to 7%, III 29

INDEX

disproportionately large number of Jewish recruits in, II 355 f

congestion in cities of, II 385

Jews in, compared with prisoner in cell, II 389

Moscow refugees driven into, II 406

visited by United States commissioners, II 407

visited by Arnold White, emissary of Baron Hirsch, II 417

Yalta excluded from (1893), II 428 f

governor of Vilna recommends abrogation of, III 11

zealously maintained under Nicholas II., III 16, 20 f

growth of pauperism in, III 23 f

localities in, barred to Jews in 1882, reopened to them (1903), III 80 f

preservation of, affirmed by Third Duma (1908), III 154

one hundred and six Duma deputies favor abrogation (1910), III 156

exclusion of Jews from villages in, see Villages

See also Interior, and Residence, Right of

Palestine, Teutonic Order originates in, I 63

Cabalists of, influence Polish Jewry, I 134

Sabbatian propaganda carried on in, II 205

mass emigration of Polish Jews to (1700), I 209 f

Shneor Zalman accused of collecting money for, I 376

Nahman of Bratzlav makes pilgrimage to, I 383

Lelevel, Polish historian, promises Polish help in restoration of, II 108

restoration of Jews to, preached by Smolenskin, II 236; advocated by Levanda, II 240

Bilu pioneers emigrate to (1882), II 321 f

beginnings of Jewish colonization in, II 322

"Lovers of Zion" establish colonies, in, III 42

Jewish national center in, championed by Lilienblum, II 328 ff; and, as an alternative, by Pinsker, II 331

expulsion from Moscow stimulates emigration to, II 416

attempt at mass emigration to (1891), II 421 f

feeble results of colonization in, III 42

colonization of, made part of Basle program, III 44

modern Hebrew writers in, III 163

See also Zionism

Palestinophilstvo, Russian name for "Love of Zion," II 328: see also Zionism

Pan, noble landowner in Poland, name explained, I 93

Panticapaeum, see Kerch

Pardes, Hebrew annual, III 58

Paris, Sanchez, Jewish court-physician in St. Petersburg, removes to, I 258

Berek Yoselovich pays visit to, I 294

"Jewish Parliament" meets in, I 346 ff; III 53

Rothschilds of, II 69, 375, 407, 410

Lelevel, Polish historian, refugee in, II 107

Polish refugees in, II 108

anti-Semitism among Polish refugees in, II 109

Alliance Israélite Universelle in, II 189, 194, 297, 322

Plehve's secret circular made known in, II 381

Moscow refugees arrive in, II 408

Jewish Colonization Association in, sends deputation to Pobyedonostzev, III 10

Herzl resides in, III 42

Paskevich, Russian viceroy in Poland, pacifies Poland (after 1831), II 109

Moses Montefiore communicates with, II 68

Altaras of Marseilles negotiates with, II 69

Passek, governor-general of White Russia, questioned by Senate concerning Jewish law courts, I 310

restricts Jews of White Russia in economic pursuits, I 310 f

Passover, Christian, see Easter

Passover, lawyer, member of Jewish deputation to Alexander III., II 261

Passports, Jews with expired P's. severely punished, II 42

Jews found without P's. sent into army, II 148 f

Jewish P's. examined in St. Petersburg, II 343

Jewish emigrants relieved from tax on, II 418

disabilities imposed by P. Regulations of 1894, II 427

Paul IV., pope, encourages anti-Jewish policy in Poland, I 86

Paul I., emperor of Russia (1796-1801), I 321-334

includes Courland in area of Jewish settlement, I 321

imposes restrictions on Jews of government of Minsk, I 323

Jews of Volhynia prepare to send deputation to, I 324 f

dispatches Dyerzhavin to White Russia, I 328 f

releases Shneor Zalman from prison, I 376

receives denunciation against Hasidim, I 378

INDEX

Arakcheyev prominent in military affairs during reign of, I 395

Pavlovsk, District of (government of Voroneyezh), "Judaizing" sect spreads in, I 401

Pavluk, Cossack leader, instigates attacks upon Jews, I 144

Pavolochi (province of Kiev), Jews of, accused of ritual murder, I 178

Pecheneges succeed Khazars in Crimea, I 29

Pechera Monastery, in Kiev, Abbot of, preaches hatred toward Jews, I 31

"People's Freedom" (in *Russian*, Narodnaya Vola), revolutionary party, responsible for assassination of Alexander II., II 279

pursues anti-Jewish policy, II 279 f

Perekop, gulf and isthmus of, I 13, 29

Peretz, rabbi of Bohemian Community in Cracow, I 104

Peretz, Abraham, of St. Petersburg, assists Jewish deputies, I 338

acts as Jewish Maecenas, I 386

converted to Christianity, I 388

Peretz, Gregory, son of former, Russian revolutionary, I 412

Pereyaslav (province, or government of Poltava), Cossack massacre at (1648), I 145

pogrom at (1881), II 265 f

Perez, I. L., editor of Yiddish magazine, III 59

Yiddish and Hebrew writer, III 61 f, 162

Perl, Joseph, Hebrew writer in Galicia, II 126 f

Perm (Central Russia), Jewish cantonists driven to, II 25

Perovksi, Russian statesman, considers emigration of Russian Jews to Algiers, II 69

Persia, Khazars make inroads into, I 19

Jewish merchants travel through, I 23

Pestel, Paul, leader of early Russian revolutionaries, I 410

discusses Jewish problem, I 410 ff

favors establishment of separate Jewish Commonwealth, I 412

Peter, Carmelite monk in Lublin, alleged victim of ritual murder, I 100

Peter I., The Great, emperor of Russia (1688-1725), extends influence of Russia over Poland

refuses to admit Jews into Russia, I 246 f

prejudiced against Jews, 1 247 f

stops military riot against Jews, I 248
admits Jewish financiers to St. Petersburg, I 248
quoted in favor of barring Jews from Russia, II 35 f
originator of penalty by *Spiessruten*, II 85

Peter II., emperor of Russia (1727-1730), permits Jews to visit fairs in Little Russia, I 250

Peter III., emperor of Russia (1761), dethroned by Catherine II., I 259

Peterhof, near St. Petersburg, Plehve killed on way to, III 97 Jewish franchise discussed at conferences in, III 122

Petersburg, see St. Petersburg

Pethahiah, of Ratisbon, Jewish traveller, I 29 refers to Russia, I 32 f

Petrograd, Greco-Jewish inscription kept in Hermitage at, I 15 Russian *Mitropolit* resides at, II 125; see St. Petersburg

Pfefferkorn, Jewish convert, II 189

Phanagoria (Taman Peninsula), Jews settled in, I 14, 18

Philadelphia, Marcus Jastrow accepts post of rabbi in, II 179 place of publication, III 51

Philippson, Ludwig, founder of *Allgemeine Zeitung des Judentums*, II 67

corresponds with Max Lilienthal, II 67
serves as model for Russian-Jewish publicists, II 219

Philipson, David, quoted, I 54

Philosophy, Jewish, studied in Poland, I 132 f
opposed by Joel Sirkis, I 133
reflected in doctrine of Besht, I 225 f
imbedded in doctrine of Shneor Zalman, I 374, 382
opposed by Rabbinism, I 381
regarded as destructive by Nahman of Bratzlav, I 383

Phineas, of Koretz, disciple of Besht, I 227 descendants of, II 123

Photius, Patriarch of Constantinople, hopes for conversion of Crimean Jews, I 18

Physicians, Jewish, in Poland, attacked by Christian physician, I 96
originally natives of Spain or Italy, I 131 f
study at University of Padua, I 105, 132
at Polish court, I 132, 136
at Russian court, I 258
in White Russia, I 331, 386
admitted to residence in Russian Interior and to civil service (1861), II 165, 167
excluded from civil service, III 27

INDEX

Physicians, Jewish, in Russian army:

number of, restricted, II 319 f

first to be mobilized in Russo-Japanese war, III 94 f

families of mobilized P. expelled, III 95

accused of revolutionary propaganda, III 156

Piast, progenitor of Piast dynasty in Poland, I 40

Piatoli, secretary of Polish king, assists Jews, I 291

Pidyon, contribution of Hasidim, term explained, II 119

Pikolski, monk at Lemberg, conducts agitation against Jews, I 174

Pilpul, method of talmudic dialectics, fostered in Poland, I 119 f

carried from Bohemia to Poland, I 122

opposed by Solomon Luria, I 256

grafted upon by Cabala, I 135, II 117

shunned by Elijah of Vilna, I 236

Pinkasevich, Jacob, Jewish martyr in Posen, I 175

Pinsk, important community in Lithuania, I 73

Jewish community of, represented in Lithuanian *Waad*, I 112

Avigdor, rabbi of, I 377 f

Pinsker, Leon, editor of *Sion*, II 220

author of *Autoemancipation*, II 330 f

ideas of, affect "Love of Zion" movement, II 332

becomes its leader, II 376, III 42, 49

elected president of Society for Granting Relief in Syria and Palestine, II 422

contrasted with Herzl, III 43

Pinsker, Simha, father of former, teacher in Odessa school, II 133

Piotrkov, Diet of (1496), confirms anti-Jewish Statute, I 64; restricts commercial rights of Lemberg Jews (1521), I 75

Sigismund II. confirms liberal Jewish Statute at Diet of (1548), I 83

Church Synod of, passes anti-Jewish "Constitution" (1542), I 82 f

Crown Tribunal of, tries ritual murder cases, I 95 f; and Jews accused of blasphemy, I 164 f

Jewish communities in province of, destroyed, I 156

Tobias Feder, Hebrew writer, native of, I 388

Pirhe Tzafon, Hebrew periodical in Vilna, II 136

Pirogov, Nicholas, Odessa physician, friend of Jews, II 207, 209

Piryatin (province of Poltavia), Cossack massacre at (1648), I 145

Pisarevski, instigator of Kishinev pogrom, commits suicide, III 91

Pisaryev, radical Russian writer, influences Russian-Jewish *intelligentzia,* II 209 influences M. L. Lilienblum, II 238

Plehve, Russian assistant-minister of Interior, II 379 chief of political police, II 381 objects to Jewish participation in Zemstvos, II 386 chairman of secret anti-Jewish Committee, II 399 suggests expulsion of Jews from Moscow, II 402 bars Jews from municipal government, II 425 appointed Minister of Interior, III 16, 67 plans to check revolution by pogroms, III 68 f subventions Krushevan's anti-Semitic paper, III 70 sends telegram to stop Kishinev massacre, III 75, 97 stifles press protests against Kishinev massacre, III 77 suspected of sending orders encouraging massacre, III 77 forbids Jewish self-defence, III 80, 90 forbids Zionism, III 82 f negotiates with Herzl, III 83 f plans regulating Jewish legislation, III 92 f stops expulsion of families of mobilized Jews, III 95 assassinated, III 97 urges Russo-Japanese War as anti-revolutionary measure, III 98 death of, predicted in *Voskhod,* III 98 investigation of Homel pogrom started during lifetime of, III 101

Plotzk (*Polish,* Plock), city in Poland, I 243 city and province of, annexed by Prussia (1793), I 292 Synod of, passes anti-Jewish resolution (1733), I 171 archbishop of, endorses project of Jewish reforms, I 292

Poale Zion, *see* Zionism

Pobyedonostzev, Constantine Petrovich, professor at Moscow University, II 245 tutor of Alexander III., II 245 head of Holy Synod, II 245 defends autocratic régime, II 245 member of reactionary Sacred League, II 248 disparages popular education, II 348 f

inspires educational restrictions for Jews, II 349
utilizes railroad accident at Borki for purposes of reaction, III 378
opposes Jewish participation in Zemstvos, II 386
endorses expulsion of Jews from Moscow, II 401
receives gift for ecclesiastic schools from Baron Hirsch, II 415
receives White, emissary of Baron Hirsch, II 417
recommends him to officials, II 418
condemns Jews as parasites, II 417
bars Jews from municipal self-government, II 425
all powerful under Nicholas II., III 9
continues fight against Jews, III 9 f
Podol, Jewish quarter in Kiev, pogrom in, II 252 ff
Podolia, part of Red Russia, I 53
subject to Poland, I 140
uprising against Poles in (1648), I 145
regained by Poland (1667), I 159
annexed by Turkey (1672), I 208
returned to Poland (1699), I 208

strip of, annexed by Austria (1772), I 187
annexed by Russia (1793), I 292
included in Pale (1794), I 317; (1804), I 342; (1835), II 39
Jews prohibited from selling cloth in, I 75
Jews massacred by Cossacks in (1648), I 146 ff, 157
part of, forbidden to Jews (1649), I 151
Jews massacred by haidamacks (1768), I 183 ff
Talmudic culture deteriorates in, I 199
Sabbatian movement propagated in, I 208, 210 f
Jacob Frank active in, I 211, 212 f, 216
rabbis of, summoned to disputation with Frankists, I 214 f
difference of intellectual development in, I 221
Besht, founder of Hasidism, active in, I 222, 224 f, 228
Hasidism spreads in, I 229, 274
type of Tzaddik in, I 233
conquered by Hasidim, I 371, 383
Kahal of, appealed to by Vilna Gaon against Hasidism, I 373
remains hotbed of Hasidism, II 121 f

Jews of, suffer from civil war in Poland (1792), I 292

Shlakhta of, suggests anti-Jewish measures (1798), I 324

Jews of, decide to appeal to Paul I., I 325

Jews of, send delegate to St. Petersburg (1803), I 337

Jews of, invited by Government to elect deputies (1807), I 349

Jews of, protest against discrimination in municipal government, I 369

Jews of, indifferent towards Polish insurrection (1831), II 107

Jewish economic activity in, II 194

pogroms in (1881), II 256; (1882), 299 ff, 304

governor of, favors emigration of Jewish proletariat, II 414

Localities in:

Balta, II 299 ff

Bratzlav, I 288, 383

Kamenitz, I 215, 324

Lantzkorona, I 213

Moghilev (on the Dniester), I 98

Satanov, I 213, 388

Pogroms (under Polish régime), occasioned by Black Death, I 52

at Cracow, I 56 f, 63 f, 97, 102, 161, 166

at Lemberg, I 64

at Posen, I 64, 75, 90, 95, 166

at Brest-Kuyavsk, I 75

at Brest-Litovsk, I 99

at Vilna, I 94, 99

at Warsaw (1790), I 285 ff

occasioned by meetings of provincial diets, or dietines, I 170

perpetrated by Polish irregular troops (1656), I 155 f

suppressed by Sigismund I., I 76

energetically opposed by Stephen Batory, I 90

forestalled by Sigismund III., I 97

prevented by Vladislav IV., I 98

forbidden by diet of Warsaw (1717), I 171

perpetrated by theological students (*Schülergelauf*), I 161

student P's. forbidden by Mechislav III. (1173), I 42; and condemned by Polish diet, I 166 f

Pogroms (in the Ukraina), under Pavluk, Cossack leader, (1637), I 144

under Khmelnitzki, Cossack leader, (1648), I 145 ff

by Haidamacks (1768), I 183 f

at Uman, I 184 f

INDEX

Pogroms (under Russian régime), term explained, II 191

perpetrated in Poland by invading Russians (1563), I 243; (1654), I 153 f, 245

checked by Peter the Great (1708), I 248

at Odessa (1871), II 191 ff; halts assimilation endeavors, 215 f; depicted by Smolenskin, II 245; produces staggering effect on Orshanski, II 239

initiation of policy of (1881), I 247

carefully prepared by Government agents, II 248

Katzaps, or Great Russians, imported for perpetration of, II 248, 256, 359, III 115

at Yelisavetgrad (April, 1881), II 249 ff

in district of Yelisavetgrad and government of Kherson, II 251

at Kiev (April, 1881), II 251 ff; effects of, minimized by Government press, II 255 f; tried in court, II 264 f

new P's. in South Russia, II 256 ff

averted at Berdychev by Jewish self-defence, II 256 f

at Odessa (May, 1881), II 257 f; Jewish self-defence punished, II 264

believed by peasants to have been ordered by Tzar, II 257

ascribed by Government to Russian revolutionary propaganda, II 259 f, 269, 279

later attributed by it to Jewish economic exploitation, II 261, 315

Government indifferent towards victims of, II 263

perpetrators of, receive slight sentences in court, II 264

outbreak of new P's. in South Russia (summer 1881), II 265 ff

suppressed in Lithuania and White Russia, II 267, 276

replaced there by incendiary activities, II 267

give rise to emigration movement, II 267 f

at Warsaw (December, 1881), II 280 ff; effect of, on Europe and America, II 283; London, II, 287; welcomed by Government "Jewish Committee," II 310

Alexander III. regrets necessity of suppressing. II 284

Jews hold public mourning for victims of, II 286

cause agitation in England, II 287 f

Mansion House Meeting in London protests against (February 1, 1882), II 288 ff committee to aid victims of, organized in London, II 290 f

perpetrators of, arrested, II 291

at Balta (March, 1882), II 299 ff; horrors of, II 302 f, terrifies Government, II 314; tried in court, II 315 f; produces emigration panic, II 321

discussed by Jewish Conference in St. Petersburg, II 306 f

justified in report of "Jewish Committee," II 309

policy of, abandoned by Government, II 311 ff

perpetrators of, receive severe sentences, II 315 f

Russian press and literature react feebly on, II 325 f

effect of, on Russian-Jewish *intelligentsia*, II 326

outbreak of new P's. in South Russia (1883), II 358 ff

at Rostov (May, 1883), II 358; news of, suppressed, II 358

at Yekaterinoslav (July, 1883), II 358 ff

at Nizhni-Novgorod (1884), II 360 ff; prompted by greed and prospect of immunity, II 361

referred to by Pahlen Commission, II 367

at Starodub (government of Chernigov, 1891), 411 ff; displeases Government, II 412

bred in public houses, III 23

outbreak of new P's. in Russian South and South-west (1897), III 32 ff

stopped by Government on account of Hague Conference, II 35

at Chenstokhov (by Poles), stopped by Russian Government (1902), III 36

planned by Plehve as counter-revolutionary measure, III 68 f

at Kishinev (April, 1903), III 69 ff; see Kishinev

at Homel (August, 1903), III 87 ff; tried in court and misrepresented by Government, III 101 ff

impending P's. stopped by Government (1904), III 96 f

in Russian South-west (August, 1904), III 99

by mobilized soldiers (September, 1904), III 100

at Moghilev (October, 1904), III 100 f; avenged by Jewish youth, III 107

in government of Vitebsk (October, 1904), III 101

organized by Black Hundred (April, 1905), III 113 ff

INDEX

at Bialystok, III 114 f
at Dusyaty (government of Kovno), III 115
at Melitopol (government of Tavrida), III 115
at Simferopol (government of Tavrida), III 115
at Zhitomir (Volhynia), III 115 f; followed by tragedy at Troyanov, III 116 ff; misrepresented by Government, III 118
intensify revolutionary movement among Jews, III 119
perpetrated by soldiers (summer, 1905), III 119 f
at Minsk, III 119
at Brest-Litovsk, III 119
at Syedletz, III 119
at Lodz, III 119 f
at Bialystok (June, 1905), III 120
at Kerch (Crimea), July, 1905, III 120; prepared by Government, III 120
"October P's." (October 18-25, 1905), III 124 ff; organized by Black Hundred, with help of Tzar and police, III 125 f; vast extent of, III 128; followed by anarchy, III 130 f
at Odessa, III 129; assisted by police, III 129
at Nyezhin (government of Chernigov), III 129
outside Pale (October, 1905), III 130

participation of Government in, denounced by assembled Russian Jews, III 132
Jews threatened with, during elections to First Duma, III 135; to Third Duma, III 153
discussed by First Duma, III 136 ff; and condemned in resolution (1906), III 139
at Bialystok (June, 1906), III 136 f; investigated and reported upon by commission of First Duma, III 137
perpetrators of October P. either untried or pardoned, III 150
planned at Kiev but averted (September, 1911), III 165
List of pogroms according to cities and governments:
Alexandria (Kherson), III 100
Ananyev (Kherson), II 251
Balta (Podolia), II 299 ff
Berdychev (Volhynia), II 256 f
Bialystok, III, 114 f, 120, 136 f
Borispol (Poltava), II 267
Chenstokhov (Poland), III 36 f
Chernigov (city), III 128
Chernigov (government), II 257
Dusyaty (Kovno), III 115
Homel (Moghilev), III 87 ff
Kalarash, III 128

Kamenetz (Podolia), III 128

Kantakuzenka (Kherson), III 33

Karpovich (Chernigov), II 315

Kerch (Tavrida), III 120

Kherson (government), II 304

Kiev (city), I 32, II 251 ff, III 128, 165

Kiev (government), II 256

Kishinev, III 69 ff, 128

Konotop (Chernigov), II 257

Lodz, III 119 f

Melitopol (Tavrida), III 115

Minsk, III 119

Moghilev (city), I 153 f, 245; III 100

Moghilev (government), III 100

Mstislavl (Moghilev), I 248

Nagartava, Jewish agricultural colony, III 35

Nicholayev (Crimea), III 34 f, 128

Nizhni-Novgorod, II 360 f

Novo-Moskvosk (Yekaterinoslav), II 360

Nyezhin (Chernigov), II 267, III 129

Odessa, II 191 ff, 257 f, III 128 f

Orsha (Moghilev), III 128

Pereyaslav (Poltava), II 265

Podolia (government), II 256, 304

Polotzk (Vitebsk), I 243

Romny, III 128

Rostov, II 358

Rovno (Volhynia), III 99

Saratov, III 130

Semyonovka (Chernigov), III 129

Shpola (Kiev), III 33

Simferopol (Tavrida), III 115, 128

Smyela (Kiev), II 256; III 99

Starodub (Chernigov), II 411 ff

Syedletz (Poland), III 119

Troyanov (Volhynia), III 116 ff

Vilna, I 154, 245

Vitebsk (city), I 154, 245

Vitebsk (government), III 101

Volhynia (government), II 256

Voronyezh, III 130

Warsaw, II 280 ff

Yekaterinoslav, II 359 f, III 128

Yelisavetgrad, II 249 ff, III 128

Zhitomir (Volhynia), III 115 ff

See also Self-Defence

Poklonski, Russian colonel, massacres Jews of Moghilev, I 153 f

Pokutye (*Polish*, Pokucie), region in Poland, I 150

Polakov, Lazarus, Jewish financier in Moscow, II 400

Polakov, Samuel, Jewish financier in St. Petersburg, participates in Jewish Conference, II 304

discusses Jewish question with Ignatyev, II 305 f

Poland, first partition of (1772), I 262

condition of Jews in, after first partition, I 263 ff, 270

schemes for improving condition of Jews in, I 271 ff, 284

inner life of Jews in, I 274 ff

Hasidism spreads in, I 231 f

problem of Jews in, discussed in Polish literature, I 280 ff

Polish Diet appoints committee to consider Jewish question, I 287 f; postpones action, I 290

second partition of (1793), and revolution under Kosciuszko, I 292 f

patriotism of Jews in, I 292 ff

third partition of (1795), I 297

reconstituted by Napoleon as Duchy of Warsaw (1807), I 297

equality of all citizens proclaimed in, I 298

Government of, suspends emancipation of Jews (1808), I 299, II 100 f

Government of, passes anti-Jewish restrictions, I 300

assimilated Jews of, apply for equal rights, I 300 ff; and are refused, I 302

Jews of, released from military service (1812), I 304

Jews of, barred from liquor trade (1812), I 304, II 100

French influences among Jews of, I 385 f

growth of Hasidism in, I 384, II 122

Poles side with Napoleon in Franco-Russian War, I 355; and threaten to massacre Jews and Russians, I 357

reconstituted as "Kingdom of Poland," and assigned by Congress of Vienna to Russia [Russian Poland, or Congress Poland] (1815), I 390

granted complete autonomy by Alexander I., II 88

number of Jews in kingdom of, I 390

Government of, appoints Committee on Jewish Question (1815), II 89

David Friedländer of Berlin submits memorandum on Jews of, II 90

Zayonchek, viceroy of, opposed to Jewish emancipation, II 91 f

Polish Diet unfriendly to Jews of, II 93 f, 99 f

Government of, passes anti-Jewish restrictions, II 94 f

condition of Jews in, discussed in Polish literature, II 95 ff

blood accusation in, II 74; forbidden by Russian Government, II 99

assimilationist tendencies among Jews of, II 100 ff

Kahals abolished in, and replaced by *Gminas* (1822), II 102

Government of, appoints Committee to Polonize Jews, II 103

anti-Semitism in, II 104 f, 178

Polish insurrection of 1831, II 33, 105

Jews volunteer in revolutionary army of, II 105 ff

Polish writers express sympathy with Jews, II 108 f

Nicholas I. imposes conscription on Jews of (1843), II 109 f

prohibition of Jewish dress in Russia extended to (1845), II 110

Jews of, continue to wear Jewish dress, II 145

influence of Talmud prevails in, II 51

Hasidism firmly established in, II 122 f

Polish insurrection of 1863, II 178 ff, 182 f

patriotic attitude of Jews in, II 179 ff

Jewish disabilities in, removed by Alexander II. (1862), II 181; and re-established by Alexander III., 367

Jews of, accused of separation, II 195

Poles try to stop pogrom at Warsaw (1881), II 283

Poles perpetrate pogrom on Jews of Chenstokhov (1902), III 36

Jewish labor movement in, III 55

Jews of, active in Russian revolution of 1905, III 107

terrorism in (1905), III 130

Jews in, intimidated during Duma elections, III 134

recrudescence of anti-Semitism in (1905), III 166 ff

Jews of, subjected to economic boycott (1912), III 167 f

Jewish life in, depicted by Perez, III 61; and Ash, III 162

See also Poland (Great), Poland (Little), Polish Language, Polonization, and Warsaw

INDEX

Poland, Great, forms feudal principality, I 41 f

Posen leading city of, **I** 74, 110, 196

part of, conquered by Swedes (1655), I 154 f

part of, annexed by Prussia (1772), I 187; (1793), I 292; (1795), I 297

formed by Napoleon into Duchy of Warsaw (1807), I 297

tribunal of, at Piotrkov, I 96

provincial diet of, I 113

Boleslav, prince of, grants charter to Jews of principality (1264), I 45, 51

Jews of, secure ratification of charter (1548), I 83

Jewish communities of, receive charter of autonomy (1551), I 105 ff

"senior rabbis" of, confirmed by Sigismund I. (1518), I 105

represented on Council of Four Lands, I 110

federated Kahals of, meet periodically, I 196

Jews of, massacred by Polish troops (1656), I 155 f

Poland, Little, forms feudal principality, I 41 f

Cracow, leading city of, I 74

includes Western Galicia, I 53

part of, conquered by Swedes (1655), I 154 f

annexation of, completed by Austria (1795), I 297

added by Napoleon to duchy of Warsaw (1809), I 297

tribunal of, at Lublin, I 96

"senior rabbis" of, confirmed by Sigismund I. (1541), I 105, 109, 122

represented on Council of Four Lands, I 110

federated Kahals of, meet periodically, I 196

Jews of, massacred by Polish troops (1656), I 155 f

Jewish commercial activity held to be injurious to, I 288

Polemics, and Political Literature, between Jews and Christians in Poland, I 136 ff

Police, central department of, in St. Petersburg co-operates with rioters in Kerch, III 120

abets October pogroms (1905), III 125 f

charged by First Duma with complicity in pogroms, II 136

complicity of, in pogroms disclosed by Urussov, III 138

Police, Political, known as "The Third Section," term explained, II 21

chief of, appointed on Committee for Radical Transformation of Jews (1840), II 50

crushes revolutionary endeavors, II 140
calls forth terrorism, II 184
distributes anti-Semitic book among detectives, II 204
reports on revolutionary activities of Jews, II 348

Polish Language used for literary purposes by Nahman and Belzhytz, I 136 f
by rabbi of Khelm, I 283
by anonymous orthodox rabbi, II 98
by Jewish weekly, II 213
See also Language and Polonization

Politz, Universal History by, translated into Hebrew, II 134

Pollak, Jacob, of Prague, introduces *pilpul* method into Poland, I 122

Pollak, of Minsk, offer of, to establish Jewish agricultural colony refused by Government, III 25

Polonization, advocated by David Friedländer and his followers, I 386, II 90
champions of, advocate abolition of Jewish autonomy, II 100
rabbinical seminary at Warsaw established for, II 103
among Jewish *intelligenzia* in Poland, II 182

extreme form of, in Warsaw, II 213

Polonnoye (Volhynia), Khmelnitzki massacre in (1648), I 148 f
Jacob Joseph Cohen, rabbi of, I 227, 230

Polotzk (government of Vitebsk), Jews of, drowned by Russian invaders (1654), I 243
Jewish coachmen of, forbidden to drive beyond Pale, II 70
government of, former name for government of Vitebsk; see Vitebsk (government)
Kahal of, appealed to by Elijah of Vilna against Hasidism, I 373

Polovtzis, succeed Khazars as masters of Crimea, I 29

Poltava (city), Osip Rabinovich, Russian-Jewish writer, native of, II 238

Poltava (region, or government), subject to Poland, I 140
ceded to Russia (1667), I 159
included in Pale (1794), I 317; (1835), II 40
Pavluk, Cossack leader, massacres Jews of (1637), I 144
Jews forbidden residence in (1649), I 151; readmitted (1651), I 152
Jewish communities of, disappear almost entirely (1648), I 157

few Jews survive in (after 1648), I 246

Jews of White Russia settle in, 321

Jews expelled from villages of, II 341

Localities in:

Borispol, II 267

Lokhvitz, I 145

Lubny, I 144, 145

Pereyaslav, I 145; II 265

Piryatin, I 145

Pomerania, annexed by Prussia (1772), I 187, 262

Poniatovski, Stanislav Augustus, king of Poland (1764-1795), reign of, I 180 ff

election of, preceded by change in system of Jewish taxation, I 197

protects Simeon Volfovich, spokesman of Vilna Jewish masses, against Kahal, I 276

receives plan of Jewish reform from Hirshovich, royal broker, I 284

grants solemn audience to Jews, I 290 f

Pontus Euxinus, see Black Sea

Populism (in Russian, *narodnichestvo*), branch of Russian revolutionary movement, II 222 f

anti-Semitic tendency of, II 279 f

influences Jacob Gordin, II 333

Popiel, ancient Polish ruler, I 40

Popov, member of "Jewish Committee" of Russian Government, I 352

Port Arthur, Jews expelled from, III 94; and denied right of residence in, III 157

Posen (*Polish*, Poznan), leading city of Great Poland, I 42, 74, 110, 116

surrendered by Shlakhta to invading Swedes (1655), I 155

refugees from crusades settle in, I 41

Jews of, petition Casimir IV. to renew charter (1447), I 61

Jews of, petition Sigismund I. to ratify election of rabbis (1518), I 104

Jews of, persecuted on charge of host desecration, I 55, 95

riots in, I 64, 75, 90, 95, 161

Jews of, restricted in economic pursuits, I 74, 95

magistracy of, joins other cities in economic fight against Jews, I 75

Jews of, limited to separate quarter, I 75; and forbidden to increase number of houses, I 85

rights of Jews of, enlarged by Stephen Batory, I 89 f

Jews of, accused of ritual murder (1736), I 172, 174 ff

Jewish community of, represented on Council of Four Lands, I 110
exorcism of devils in, I 203
rabbis of:
Naphtali Cohen, I 204
Solomon Edels (*Maharsho*), I 129
Sheftel Horowitz, I 135, 158
Mordecai Jaffe, I 127
Solomon Luria (*Maharshal*), native of, I 120
Arie Leib Calahora, preacher in, I 175

Posen, province of, annexed by Prussia (1772), I 187, 262
Polish troops destroy Jewish communities in (1656), I 156

Posner, Solomon, prominent Jew in Warsaw, II 103

Potemkin, Nota Shklover purveyor to army of, I 338

Pototzki (*Polish*, Potocki), commander of Polish army, I 145

Politzki, voyevoda of Kiev, I 184

Polotzki, Severin, member of "Jewish Committee" of Russian Government (1802), I 335

Politzki, Stanislav, delivers eulogy on Berek Yoselovich, I 303 f

Praga, suburb of Warsaw, attached by Russian Government (1802), I 335
home of Berek Yoselovich, I 294

Prague, capital of Bohemia, visited by Pethahiah of Ratisbon, I 33
Jews attacked by crusaders in, I 41
Mordecai Jaffe, rabbi of, I 127

Pravo ("The Law"), Russian journal, suppressed for protesting against Kishinev massacre, III 77
protests against court verdict in Homel pogrom, III 103 f

Prayer, importance of, emphasized by Besht, I 226
Hasidim adopt Ari's form of, I 231

Press, Russian, used euphemistically to designate Russian Government, II 386
pursues anti-Semitic policy, II 278, 379, III 31 f
makes no reference to expulsion from Moscow, II 407
liberal P. protests against Kishinev massacre, III 76 f
stifled by Plehve, III 77

Press, Jewish, in Russia, II 216 ff
in Hebrew, II 217 f, 372, III 58, 162
in Yiddish, III 58 f, 162
in Russian, II 218 ff, 277 f; yields to press in Hebrew, II 372

Press, Foreign, protest against Jewish disabilities, II 381
reports (together with Russian P.) on anti-Semitic exploits of Russian officials, II 384

denounces expulsion of Jews from Moscow, II 407 f

protests against Kishinev massacre, III 77

See Printing-Presses

Prikahalki, name for minor Kahals, I 108, 193; see Kahals

Priluker, Jacob, founder of Judeo-Christian sect, II 334 f

becomes Christian missionary, II 335

Printing-Press, Hebrew, of Cracow and Lublin, I 131

of Vilna, II 42, 115, 127

of Slavuta, II 42, 123

of Kiev, II 43; transferred to Zhitomir, II 43

establishment of, by Russian Government, suggested by Dyerzhavin, I 333

See Censorship

Professions, restrictions in pursuit of, II 26 f; see Bar, and Physicians; also Education and University

Pro-Gymnazium, term explained, III 29; see Gymnazium

Prokhonvik, Abraham, legendary king of Poland, I 40

Property, Real; see Villages

Propination (*Polish,* Propinacya), right of distilling and selling liquor, term explained, I 67

carried on by Jews in Poland, I 67; and Ukraine, I 141

forced upon Jews by economic factors, I 266 f

from Polish pan by Jewish arendar, I 93, 170, 265

connected with other economic pursuits, I 93, 361 f

elimination of Jews from, advocated by Polish reformers (1782), I 272 f, 280; recommended by Polish Government Committee (1815), II 89; and demanded by Polish Diet (1818), II 100

law barring Jews from, issued by Duchy of Warsaw (1812), I 304 f; but vetoed by Alexander I. (1816), II 94

participation of Jews in, defended by Polish officer, II 98

Jews of annexed White Russia hampered in pursuit of (1784), I 311 ff

Polish nobles of annexed Polish provinces advocate elimination of Jews from, I 323 ff

abuses of, set forth by Russian Government Committee (1804), I 341 f

committee appointed to consider elimination of Jews from (1809), I 352 f; but reports against it(1812), I 353 f

economic mainstay of village Jewry, I 361 f

nobility of White Russia demands elimination of Jews from, I 405; decreed for villages of White Russia (1823), I 406

occupies central place in economic structure of Russian Jewry, II 72

big Jewish capital transferred from, to railroad, II 186

Government Committee recommends elimination of Jews from (1882), II 310

Government monopoly of, urged as means of removing Jews from villages, III 17

effects of Government monopoly of, III 22 f

See Villages

Protestantism, see Reformation

Protoyerey, Russian ecclesiastic title, term explained, II 301

Prussia shares in partition of Poland, I 185 f, 262, 292, 297

participates in siege of Warsaw (1794), I 293

rules over Warsaw (1796-1806), I 385

shattered by Napoleon, I 347

represented at Congress of Aix-la-Chapelle, I 398 f

introduces Jewish reforms in annexed Polish provinces, I 385

Jewish regulations of, serve as model for Russian statemen, I 331, II 46, 49

Jewish socialist expelled from, II 224

See Berlin

Pshemyshl (*Polish*, Pszemysl), see Stupnitza

Pskov, Jews exiled form (1654), I 154

situated outside Pale, II 70

Ptolemies, the Jewish center under rule of, I 14

Pulavy, Poland, Jews of, manifest Polish patriotism, I 292

Pushkin, Russian poet, relation of, to Jews, II 138

Pyetukhov, member of political police, exposes complicity of Government in pogrom, III 140

Quadrennial Diet, see Diet, Quadrennial

Raaben, von, governor of Bessarabia, refuses to stop Kishinev pogrom, III 74 f

sued for damages by Jews, III 92

Rabbanites, in Crimea, I 28, 34

Rabbinical Commission, appointed by Russian Government (1842), II 56

Jews of Western Europe invited to participate in, II 67

Rabbi Mendel of Lubavich member of, II 118

Rabbinical Schools (modern), opened by assimilationist Jews in Warsaw (1826), II 103 f

opening of, decreased by Nicholas I. (1844), II 38

pupils of, promised alleviations in military service, II 58

graduates of, intended to supersede former type of rabbis and teachers, II 58, 176

opened in Vilna and Zhitomir (1847), II 59, 174 f

graduates of, act as Government agents, II 212

graduates of, form revolutionary circle, II 223

Levanda, graduate of, II 239

closed (1873), II 177

Rabbinism opposes Hasidism, I 233 f, 235 ff

opposes enlightenment, I 238 f

firmly entrenched during reign of Alexander I., 380

uncompromising attitude of, II 111 ff

Rabbis (and Rabbinate), officially recognized by Polish king, I 104 ff

clothed with wide powers, I 73, 105 ff

bear title of *Morenu*, I 117

relation of, to Kahal, I 107 f

conferences of, I 108 f

conference of, "tries" demons in Posen, I 203

accused of purchasing offices from pans, I 284

jurisdiction of, limited to religious affairs (1804), I 344

deprived of right of imposing *herem* (1804), I 344

highly respected by Jews of Russia, II 112

exempted from military service, II 20

reform of, recommended by Council of State, II 49; by I. B. Levinsohn, II 128; and by other Maskilim, II 136 f

fanaticism of, attacked by Mapu, II 227 f

See Crown Rabbis

Rabinovich, I., founder of Congregation of New Testament Israelites, II 335

Rabinovich, Osip (Joseph), editor of *Razsvyet*, II 219 f

author of Jewish novels (in Russian), II 238

Rabinovitz, S., see Shalom Aleichem

Radom, see Shidlovitz

Radzieyevski, Polish sub-chancellor, betrays Poland to Swedes, I 155

Radzionovski, Greek-Orthodox priest, admonishes rioters at Balta, I 301 f

Radziwill, Prince, patron of Saul Wahl, I 94

Radziwill, voyevoda of Vilna, settles dispute between rabbis and Kahal, I 276

Railroads, Jews become interested in, II 186

Rakhmistorvka (government of Kiev), hasidic center, II 120

Randar, see Arendar

Rashi, works of, studied in Poland, I 117

Ratisbon, see Pethahiah of Ratisbon

Ratner, M., counsel for victims of Homel pogrom, III 102 member of Central Committee of League for Equal Rights, III 112

Rav (or *Rov*), name for rabbi, II 120

Ravski, M., prominent Jew in Warsaw, II 103

Razryaden, "Assortment" of Jews; see Assortment

Razsvyet ("The Dawn"), Jewish periodical in Russian, II 218, 219 f, 238

champions "Love of Zion," II 332

discontinued (1883), II 372

appears again in St. Petersburg, III 162

resumes publication, after interruption, in St. Petersburg, II 221, 277

publishes statement of Ignatyev inviting Jews to emigrate, II 285

favors organization of emigration movement, II 298

Razumovksi, president of Russian academy, deplores anti-Jewish prejudice, I 258

Real Estate, see Villages

Rebbe, popular name for Tzaddik, or hasidic leader, II 120; see Tzaddik

Recanati, Menahem, Italian Cabalist, work of, studied in Poland, I 134

Recruits (and Recruiting), recruiting ukase of 1827, II 18 ff

minor recruits, see Cantonists

Jewish committee, or Kahals, held responsible for quota of, II 19 f

oath of allegiance of, marked by great solemnity, II 20

kept apart from non-Jewish recruits, II 21

recruiting (or conscription) trustees of Kahals, II 19 f; turned into police agents, II 22 f; retained after abolition of Kahal, II 60; made personally responsible for completion of quota, II 147

sent to recruiting jails, II 24

divorce wives before leaving home, II 28

drafting of "penal" recruits decreed (1850), II 147 f community of Mstislavl punished by drafting penal recruits, II 96 individual Jews permitted to capture recruits as substitutes (1853), II 148 f See Military Service and Soldiers

Red Russia, see Russia, Red

Reforms, religious, in Judaism, advocated by Lilienblum, II 236 preached by Jacob Gordin (and others), II 333 ff reform Judaism attacked by Smolenskin, II 234

Reformation affects unfavorably position of Jews in Poland, I 79 f, 85 ff stimulates literary polemics, I 135 ff Polish adherents of, welcome invading Swedes, I 155 fear of, responsible for Jewish tragedy in Cracow, I 164 f Russian sect of Stundists traceable to influence of, II 333

Reisin, Yiddish writer, III 162

Renan protests against Jewish persecutions, II 326

Repnin, governor-general of Lithuania, promises to respect Jewish autonomy, I 320

"**Republic**" (*Polish*, Rzecz Pospolita), title applied to Poland (after 1572), I 88, 262

Residence, Right of, denied to Jews in towns of ancient Poland; see "*De non Tolerandis Judais";* particularly in Warsaw, I 85, 268, 300; II 94 f tax paid by Jews for, in Warsaw, II 95 all restrictions in, abolished in Poland (1862), II 181; reintroduced by Alexander III. (1891), II 367 withdrawn from Jews of Ukraina (1649), I 151; and returned to them (1651), II 152 withdrawn from Jews of Little Russia (1727), I 250 in ancient Russia, see Moscow, principality of in modern Russia, see Interior, Pale of Settlement, and Expulsions outside of cities and towns, see Villages non-Jews plead before Government for grant of, to Jews, I 256, II 319 denied to Jews in health and summer resorts, III 18 ff, 154, 157 See also Capitals, and under Kiev and Moscow

Resolution, term explained, I 253
by Empress Anna, sentencing Borukhov and Voznitzin to death (1738), I 253
by Empress Elizabeth, excluding Jews from Russia (1741), I 257; referred to by Empress Catherine II., I 259, 261
by Paul I., approving of anti-Jewish restrictions (1797), I 323
by Nicholas I., postponing expulsion of Jews from villages, opposing admission of Jewish merchants to Interior, II 36; expelling Jews form 50-vert zone, II 62; limiting Jewish coachmen to Pale, II 70; closing synagogues in Velizh, II 78; expressing doubt about existence of ritual murder, II 80; punishing Jews of Mstislavl, II 86
R's. of Alexander III. assume power of laws, II 339
by Nicholas II., opposing abrogation of Pale, III 11
Resorts, see Residence, Right of
Restrictions, against Jews, enormous extent of, admitted by Pahlen Commission, II 364
Guildhall meeting in London protests against, II 391
Russian governors favor repeal of, III 93

regarded by Council of Ministers as cause of revolutionary movement among Jews, III 141
new R's. decreed by Third Duma, III 156 f
in army, II 319 f, 354 ff
in commerce, see Commerce
in dress, see Dress
in keeping domestics, see Domestics
in education, II 348 ff, III 27 ff; see Educational Restriction
in language, see Language
in professions, II 352 f, III 26 f
in trades, see Artisans
in rights of residence, see Residence, Right of, also Interior and Pale
Revolutionary Movement, in Russia, unfriendly attitude of, towards Jews, I 409 ff
anti-Semitic tendency of, II 279 f
early pogroms ascribed to influence of, II 259 f, 269, 279
Jews participate in, II 198, 221 ff, 243 f, III 67 ff, 105 ff
Jewish college men join ranks of, II 348; particularly graduates of foreign universities, III 31
Jews held responsible for, III 70

spread of, among Jews, admitted by Russian officials as due to restrictive laws, II 364 f, III 93, 141

participation of Jews in, blamed for pogroms, II 305, III 89 152; intensifies anti-Semitism, III 16; prompts anti-Jewish restrictions at universities, III 28

pogroms engineered for suppression of, III 66 ff, 137

pogroms intensify spread of, among Jews, III 90

Zionism prohibited as contributory to, III 82

intensified after death of Plehve, III 98

combated by Black Hundred, III 124 ff

Jewish participants in, executed, III 140; see Bund and Socialism

Rhescupondes, Dynasty of, rulers of Jewish colonies in Crimea, I 14 f

Rhine, the, Jewish immigration into Poland from, I 41

Richelieu, Duke, governor of Kherson, interested in Jewish agriculture, I 363 f

Richter, De, aide-de-camp of Alexander III., receives pro-Jewish petition from Mayor of London, II 393

Riesser, Gabriel, German-Jewish publicist, II 219

compared with Osip Rabinovich, II 238

Riga, magistracy of, protests against contemplated expulsion of Jews (1743), I 256

Jews of White Russia forbidden to settle in, I 313

Max Lilienthal resides in, II 52

Lilienthal's school in, pointed to as model, II 137

Jewish community of, protests against denial of Jewish franchise (1905), III 121

See also Livonia

Rindfleisch, persecution of, in Germany, drives Jews into Poland, I 50

Riots, see Pogroms

Ripon, Bishop of, addresses Guildhall meeting in favor of Russian Jews, II 391

Rishon-le-Zion, Jewish colony in Palestine, II 322, 375

Ritual Murder Libel (blood accusation), forbidden by Boleslav of Kalish (1264), I 47; by Sigismund II. (1564 and 1566), I 88; by Stephen Batory (1575), I 89

frequency of, in Poland, I 95, 172 ff, II 74, 99

General of Dominican Order in Rome warns Poles against (1664), I 165

Polish Jews appeal to pope against (1758), I 179

prohibition of, confirmed by Augustus III. (1763), I 180
supported by sect of Frankists, I 216 f
forbidden in kingdom of Poland by Russian Government (1817), II 99
repeated by Abbé Chiarini in Warsaw, II 104
prejudices Peter the Great against Jews, I 247 f
assumes malign aspect under Nicholas I., II 73
believed by Nicholas I., I 79, 83
affects Jewish legislation in Russia, II 79
refuted by Isaac Baer Levinsohn, II 131
commission for investigation of, appointed by Nicholas I. (1854), II 151
defended by Lutostanski, II 203 f, 244
Alexander III. gives credence to, II 203, 244
championed by *Novoye Vremya*, II 205
preached by Krushevan, III 70
cases of (in Poland):
Bielsk, I 87
Cracow, I 56 f
Lenchitza, I 100 f
Lublin, I 96, 100
Posen, I 172
Ruzhany, I 162 ff
Sandomir, I 172 ff

Zaslav, I 172
Zhitomir, I 178
minor places, I 178
cases of (in Russia):
Dubossary, III 71
Gordonya, II 247 f
Grodno, II 73
Kiev (Beilis trial), see Beilis
Kishinev, III 71
Kutais (Caucasus), II 204
Nizhni-Novgorod, II 360 f
Saratov, II 150 ff
Velizh, II 75 ff
Vilna (Blondes trial), III 37
Rivkes, Moses, of Vilna, Hebrew author, I 200
Rodichev, Duma deputy, denounces Bialystok pogrom, II 137, 139
defends Jews, III 156
Rodkinson, publishes *ha-Kol*, II 223
Rogov, Anton, propagates "Judaizing heresy," I 402
Roman Empire, immigration into Western Europe proceeds from, I 13
sovereignty of, acknowledged by rulers of Crimea, I 14 f
menaced by Khazars, I 20
Rome, nuncio Lippomano dispatched from, to Poland, I 86
general of Dominican Order in, defends Polish Jews, I 165
Ambassador of Muscovy at, I 242

INDEX

Romny, pogrom at (October 1905), III 128

Ronne and Simon, quoted, I 331

Rosenthal, Leon, founder of Society for Diffusion of Enlightenment, II 214

Rosenthal, N., leader of Vilna Maskilim, II 136

Rosh-Pinah, Jewish colony in Palestine, II 375

Rosh-Yeshibah, head of Talmudic academy, recognized by Polish Government, I 115 f position of in Jewish community, I 116 ff

Rossie, mythical philosopher, quoted in support of blood accusation, II 73

Rostov (on the Don), placed outside Pale and closed to Jews, II 346 pogrom at, II 358

Rothschild, Alphonse de, of Paris, refuses to participate in Russian loan, II 408 attacked by *Novoye Vremya,* II 410 refusal of, infuriates Russian Government, II 417

Rothschild, Edmond de, of Paris, supports Jewish colonization of Palestine, II 375 f, 422

Rothschild, Nathaniel de, of London, member of Committee for Pogrom Victims, II 291

Rothschilds, the, of Paris, offer to pay transportation of Russian Jews to Algiers, II 69 expected to participate in Russian loan, II 407 f

Roumania compelled by Congress of Berlin to emancipate Jews, II 202 Jews of, establish colonies in Palestine, II 375

Rovno (Volhynia), pogrom at, III 99

Rum, name for Byzantium, I 24

Russ, old name for Russia, I 33; Red Russia, I 115

Russ, anti-Semitic newspaper in Moscow, II 278, 325

Russia, ancient, see Moscow, principality of, and Kiev, principality of exercises protectorate over Poland, I 181 Jews expelled from (1741), I 255 shares in partition of Poland, I 186 f, 262, 292, 297, 314 joins Prussia in besieging Warsaw (1794), I 293 represented at Congress of Aix-la-Chapelle, I 398 Jews of Poland transferred to, I 241 Jews of White Russia brought under dominion of (1792), I 306 ff

attitude of, towards Jews, I 242 ff

admission of Jews to, favored by Senate and refused by Catherine II., I 259 f

follows traditional Muscovite policy in excluding Jews, I 246 f, 341, II 35 f

institutes Pale of Settlement, I 314

adopts policy of exceptional laws, I 314 ff

Jews loyal to, in Franco-Russian War (1812), I 355 ff

Zionists of, assemble at Minsk Convention, III 45

importance of Zionism for Jews of, II 146 ff

Russia, Great, laborers from, active in pogroms, II 248, 256, 359

Russia, Little, population of, I 53 ceded to Russia (1654), I 94, 153

annexed by Russia (1667), I 159, 244

Jews barred from, I 246

ritual murder in, I 247 f

Jews expelled from (1727), I 249 f

Cossacks of, protest against exclusion of Jews, I 250

Jews admitted to fairs of, I 250 f

Jews penetrate into, and settle in, I 253, 255

expelled again from (1740), I 254

inhabitants of, protest against exclusion of Jews, I 256

admission of Jews into, favored by Senate, I 257

Empress Elizabeth insists on expulsion of Jews from (1844), I 257

representatives of, plead for admission of Jews, I 260

Catherine II. refuses to admit Jews into, I 261

included in Pale (1794), I 317; (1804), 342; (1835), II 40

Jews of White Russia settle in, I 321 f

Great Russians, or *Katzaps*, prepare pogroms in, II 248, 256, 359

Russia, New (South Russia), steppes of, inhabited by Cossacks, I 142 f

Jews permitted to settle in (1791), I 316

Karaites of, granted special privileges (1795), I 318

included in Pale (1804), I 342; (1835), II 40

expelled village Jews beg to be transferred to, I 352

Jews of White Russia settle as farmers in, I 363 f

agricultural immigration into, temporarily stopped (1810), I 365

Government attempts to settle "Israelitish Christians" in, I 400

Jewish agricultural colonies in, II 70 f, 197

Max Lilienthal makes educational tour, through, II 56

represented on Rabbinical Commission of Bezalel Stern, II 57

Odessa, capital of, center of Haskalah, II 132

Vorontzov, governor-general of, defends Jews, II 64 ff

Stroganov, governor-general of, advocates emancipation of Jews, II 168 f

pogroms in, II 249 ff

See Odessa

Russia, Red, occasionally called Russia (or Russ), I 75, 115

corresponds to Eastern Galicia, I 53

forms independent principality, I 53

annexed by Casimir the Great, I 42, 53

Lemberg, leading city of, I 74

invaded by Khmelnitzki, I 150 f

Jews forbidden to sell cloth in, I 75

Jews of, represented on Council of Four Lands, I 110

federated Kahals of, I 196

Solomon of Lemberg, chosen spiritual head of, I 115

voyevoda of, grants constitution to Lemberg Jews, I 191

See Lemberg

Russia, White, Ukrainian bands penetrate into (1648), I 149

invaded by Russian troops (1654), I 153 f, 244 f

annexed by Russia (1772), I 186, 262, 306

divided into two governments (Moghilev and Vitebsk), I 307

becomes Jewish intellectual center, I 159 f

federated Kahals of, I 196

traces of Sabbatian propaganda in, I 205

differs intellectually from South-west, I 221

Hasidism spreads in, I 230, 238, 372; but excelled by Rabbinism, I 274

distinct character of Hasidism in, I 233 ff

Kahals of, appealed to by Elijah Gaon against Hasidism, I 373

Hasidism in, founded by Shneor Zalman, I 234, 356, II 57; and represented by his dynasty, II 117

Jews of, penetrate into Moscow, I 245; and Smolensk, I 249

Russian Government promises Jews of, preservation of ancient liberties (1772), I 306 f, 366

Jews of, numbered and taxed, I 307

internal organization of Jews in, I 308 ff

Kahals of, recognized by Government, I 309; but restricted to spiritual affairs and collection of taxes, I 313

Jews of, oppressed by Passek, governor-general, I 310 ff

Jews of, appeal to Catherine II., I 311

Jews of, refused permission to settle in Riga, I 313; and outside of White Russia in general, 315 f

included in Pale (1794), I 317; (1804), I 342; (1835, except villages), II 40

Jews of, immigrate to New Russia, I 364, II 70

famine in (1821), I 329

Dyerzhavin sent as investigator to, I 328 f, 386

Jews of, emigrate to New Russia, I 364; II 70

Jews in, elected to municipal offices, I 368

Jews of, marked by public spirit, I 379

traces of "Enlightenment" in, I 386

new famine in (1821), suggests expulsion of Jews from villages, I 405 f

expulsion of Jews from villages of, decreed (1823), I 406; and carried out, I 407; denounced as useless by Council of State (1835), I 407, II 34 f

expelled village Jews of, settle in New Russia, II 70

Jewish agricultural settlements in, II 72

Khovanski, governor-general of, active in ritual murder trial, II 76 ff; see Velizh

pogroms checked by authorities of (1881), II 267

pogroms spread in, III 87 ff, 100 f; see Moghilev, Vitebsk, and Villages

Russian Language, the, Jewish literature in, II 238 ff

Jewish writers in, hail from South, II 238

declared native language of Jews by sect "New Israel," II 334

Jewish press in, III 59, 162

Frug, Jewish poet, writes in, III 63

Jewish science in, III 65

See also Language

Russian Poland, see Poland

Russians, the, tribe, in land of Khazars, I 22

relation of, to Khazars, I 26, 28
converted to Greek-Orthodoxy, I 31
See Russia

Russification of Jews, under Alexander II., II 174 ff, 206 ff, 215
advocated by Orshanski, II 239; and Levanda, II 239 f
discarded by Jewish *intelligentzia*, II 326 ff, III 163

Russkaya Zhizn ("Russian Life"), newspaper in St. Petersburg, pictures sufferings of Moscow Jews, II 397

Russki Vyestnik ("Russian Herald"), Russian magazine, defends Jews, II 207 f

Russki Yevrey ("The Russian Jew"), Jewish weekly in Russian, in St. Petersburg, II 221, 277
pursues moderate policy, II 332
discontinued (1884), II 372

Russo-Japanese War interrupts labor of Government Commission on Jewish Question, III 93
participation of Jews in, III 94 ff
Jewish veterans of, granted universal right of residence, III 98 f
Jewish surgeons in, accused of revolutionary propaganda, III 156

Jewish soldiers in, denied residence in Port Arthur, III 157

Ruthenians, or Little Russians, the, I 53
belong to Uniat Church, I 141; see Russia, Little

Ruzhany (province of Grodno), ritual murder case of, I 162

Ruzhin, Israel of, hasidic leader, II 120 f

Rybalenko, alleged victim of ritual murder, III 71

Sabbatai Zevi, name of, left out by Halperin, contemporary Polish-Jewish chronicler, I 201
Hayyun, emissary of, I 204
Polish Jews respond to claims of, I 204; and send deputation to, I 206 f
betrayed by Nehemiah Cohen, I 207
Polish Jews loyal to, I 207
Jacob Frank considered reincarnation of, I 212 f, 214; and follows example of, I 216
See Sabbatians

Sabbatarians, the, "Sabbath observers," "Judaizing" sect in Russia, I 401 ff

Sabbatians, the, adherents of Sabbatai Zevi, movement of, in Poland, I 204 ff

Council of Four Lands objects to, I 196
join adherents of Judah Hasid, I 209
pose as Mohammedans, I 210
continue secretly in Podolia and Galicia, I 210 f
Jacob Frank associates with, I 212 ff
Hasidim accused of continuing work of, I 376

Sack, St. Petersburg banker, member of Jewish deputation to Alexander III., II 261

"**Sacred League**," The, organization of high Russian officials, suspected of assisting pogroms, II 248

Sadogora (Bukovina), Israel of Ruzhin settles in, II 121
hasidic dynasty of, II 121

Safed (Palestine), *Ari* and Vital. Cabalists, in, I 134, 134

Salant (government of Kovno), M. A. Ginzburg, Hebrew writer, native of, II 133

Salisbury, Lord, English premier, answers interpellation concerning Jewish persecutions in Russia, II 382

Saloniki, center of Sabbatian movement, I 207
Jacob Frank resides in, I 212

Samkers, Jewish city on Taman Peninsula, I 23.

Samkrtz (Samkers), locality in Crimea, I 26

Samogitia (Zhmud), Russian province, name explained, I 293, II 133

Samson, of Ostropol, cabalist and martyr, I 148 f

Samoyeds, tribe in government of Archangel, II 367

Samuel Ben Ali, Gaon of Bagdad, corresponds with Moses of Kiev, I 33

San, river, provinces on, invaded by Swedes, I 154

Sanchez, Antonio, Jewish court physician in Russia, I 258

Sandomir (Galicia), ritual murder of, I 172 ff
Jews expelled from, I 173

Saratov (city), ritual murder of, II 150 ff
pogrom at, III 130

Saratov (government), "Judaizing" movement in, I 401 f

Sardis, city in Asia Minor, Jewish community in, I 14

Sarkel, city in Crimea, I 26

Sarmatians, tribe, I 14

Sassanido, dynasty of, in Persia, I 19

Satanov (Podolia), rabbis assemble at, I 213
Mendel Lewin, Hebrew writer, native of, I 388

Savitzki, convert, accuses Jews of ritual murder, II 73

Savory, Sir Jospeh, Lord Mayor of London, presides at Guildhall meeting, II 390 ff signs and forwards to Tzar petition on behalf of Russian Jews, II 392

Savranski, Moses, hasidic leader, II 121

Saym (*Polish,* Sejm), see Diet

Saymists, the, name of Jewish Socialistic Labor Party, III 145

Sazónov, Russian terrorist, kills Plehve, III 97

Schechter, Solomon, quoted, I 27

Schiller, impressed by autobiography of Solomon Maimon, I 240

works of, translated into Hebrew, II 226

Schiltberber, German traveller, refers to Jews in Crimea, I 34

Schluesselburg, near St. Petersburg, prison at, II 97

Schneider, warden of Moscow synagogue, exiled, II 424

School, traditional Jewish, see Heder and Yeshibah

modern Jewish S's. in Odessa (1826), II 133; and in Riga and Kishinev, II 52

S. of Handicrafts (in Zhitomir) closed by Alexander III. (1884), II 347

large S. fund offered to Russian Government by Baron Hirsch, II 415; transferred to S's. in Galicia, II 416

Jewish trade S. in Moscow, III 13

Talmud Torah S. in Moscow, III 13

sending of Jews to Russian Government S's. urged by Friesel, governor of Vilna, I 327, and Dyerzhavin, I 333

Statute of 1804 permits Jews to attend Government S's., or to open secular S's. of their own, I 344 f

Jews shun secular S's., I 350, 380

graduates of Government S's. exempted from military service (1827), II 20

Council of State criticises traditional Jewish S. (1840), II 48; and suggests special Government (or Crown) S's. for Jews, II 49

opening of network of Jewish Crown S's. urged by Uvarov, II 51

S. of Lilienthal in Riga serves as model, II 52

Lilienthal commissioned to organize Crown S's., II 56

opening of Crown S's. decreed by Nicholas I. (1844), II 58

attendance at Crown S's. made compulsory, II 58

attendance at Crown S's. stimulated by alleviation in military service, II 58, 164, 174 graduation from Crown S's. made obligatory for rabbis and teachers, II 58

Crown S's. expected to weaken influence of Talmud, II 51, 58

Crown S's. opened (1847), II 59, 174

attendance at Crown S's. insignificant, II 175

Crown S's. closed (1873), II 177

J. L. Gordon and Levanda active as teachers in Crown S's., II 228, 239

Russian Government abandons fight against traditional Jewish S. (1879), II 177

attendance at general Government S's. urged by Russian officials, II 163 ff

Jews begin to flock to Russian S's., II 209

Russian S's. as assimilationist factor, II 209

governors-general of Odessa and Kharkov suggest restrictive percentage for Jews at gymnazia (school norm), II 339

question of S. norm submitted by Pahlen Commission, II 339; and disapproved by majority thereof, II 348

Dyelanov, Minister of Public Instruction, directed by Alexander III. to frame enactment embodying S. norm, II 339, 349

S. norm decreed by ministerial circular (1887), II 350 f; without preliminary submission to Council of State, II 349

S. norm results in large number of Jewish "externs," II 351, III 31

attendance at commercial S's. and gymnazia further restricted (1901), III 29 f

Jewish girls free to attend secondary S's. (gymnazia), but restricted in higher S's., III 30 f

Pahlen, governor of Vilna, advocates separate S's. for Jews (1903), III 152

S. norm abolished in institutions of higher learning (1905), III 124; but restored (1907), III 152

S. norm placed on Statute books (1909), III 158

many higher S's. barred to Jews, III 158

S. norm applied to private S's., III 158 f; and extended to "externs" (1911), III 159

one hundred Jewish students excluded from Kiev Polytechnicum (1907), III 152

INDEX

Jews barred from Military Academy of Medicine (1910), III 156

See Education, Enlightenment, and University

Schorr, Solomon, follower of Jacob Frank, I 217

Schülergelauf, see Pogroms (in Poland)

Schussberg, Gabriel, describes Cossack massacres of 1648, I 158

Schwartz, informer against Jews, II 48

Schwartz, Russian Minister of Public Instruction, opposed to Jews, III 157 f

Scythians, the, tribe, I 14

Sejm, see Saym

Selek, see Jacob Zelig

Seleucids, dynasty of, I 14

Self-Defence, organized by Jews, in riot at Lemberg (1664), I 161 f

in Posen (1687), I 166

in massacre at Uman (1768), I 184 f

averts pogrom at Berdychev (1881), I 256 f

intensifies pogrom at Konotop (Chernigov, 1881), II 257

checked by police in Odessa (1881), II 258; and punished in court, II 264

active in pogrom at Warsaw (1881), II 281

forbidden by authorities (during Balta pogrom, 1882), II 300

organized after Kishinev massacre, III 80

forbidden by Plehve, III 80, 90

active in pogrom at Homel (1903), III 87 ff; attacked by police, III 88; arraigned in court, III 102

Jews of Odessa organize (1904), III 96

pogroms checked by, at Melitopol and Simferopol (government of Tavrida, 1905), III 115

displays heroism during pogrom at Zhitomir (1905), III 116 ff

movement for, intensified during revolution of 1905, III 119

attacked by soldiers during pogrom at Kerch (1905), III 120

police and soldiers ordered to drive off, III 129

displays heroism in Odessa pogrom (October, 1905), III 129; court-martialed, III 150

Self-Government, Jewish, see Autonomy

local and rural, see Zemstvos

urban, see Municipalities

Selim II., Sultan of Turkey, attended by Jewish body-physician, I 132

Semender (Tarku), city in Caucasus, I 26

Semipalatinsk (territory), in Central Asia, uncivilized tribes of, placed on level with Jews, II 367

Semiryechensk (territory), in Central Asia, semi-civilized tribes of, placed on level with Jews, II 367

Semyonovka (government of Chernigov), pogrom at, III 129

Senate, the, in Poland, forms upper Chamber, I 167
- censures King Sobieski for favoring Jews, I 167
- re-established by Napoleon in duchy of Warsaw, I 298
- refuses petition of Jews for equal rights, I 301 f

Senate, the, in Russia, recommends death penalty for conversion to Judaism (1738), I 253
- decrees expulsion of Jews from Little Russia (1739), I 254
- recommends admission of Jews to Little Russia and Livonia (1743), I 257
- favors admission of Jews into Russian empire (1763), I 259
- sanctions Kahals in White Russia (1778), I 309; but suddenly questions their legality (1782), I 310; and restricts them to spiritual affairs and collection of taxes (1786), I 313
- restricts Jews of White Russia in liquor trade (1786), I 312
- refuses permission to White Russian Jews to settle in Riga, thus laying foundation for Pale (1786), I 313 f
- reaffirms Catherine's ukase ordering transfer of village Jews to towns (1797), I 323 f
- Friesel, governor of Vilna, forwards suggestions of Jewish reforms to, I 326 f
- declares Jews not subject to serfdom, I 328
- Dyerzhavin's memorandum on Jews laid before (1800), I 334
- loses executive power with creation of Council of State (1801), I 335
- case against Shneor Zalman transferred to, I 378
- Jewish communal affairs transferred from, to Minister of Ecclesiastic Affairs (1817), I 392
- prohibits keeping of Christian domestics (1820), I 404

puts harsh interpretation on decree of Nicholas I. expelling Jews from Fifty-Verst Zone (1843), II 62 f

takes over ritual murder case of Velizh (1830), II 81

sends ukase to governors warning against pogroms (1882), II 313

sets aside misconstruction of Temporary Rules (1884), II 341

sustains law of 1874 denying universal right of residence to discharged Jewish soldiers (1885), II 355

passes upon complaints against misapplication of Temporary Rules, III 17; and reverses decisions of lower courts, III 18

sustains expulsion of consumptive Jewish student from health resort, III 19

sustains practice of confining Jews of Siberia to their places of registration (1897), III 22

orders second trial of Blondes, III 37

sustains sentence against Dashevski, assailant of Krushevan, II 82

dismisses complaint of victims of Kishinev massacres, III 92

receives ukase from Nicholas II. permitting submission of suggestions to Government (1905), III 110

declares Zionism illegal (1907), III 152

prohibits Jewish soldiers from residing in Port Arthur, III 157

"Senior," the, title for elder in Poland, I 72 f, 94

title for chief rabbi in Poland, I 105

Separatism, of Jews, ascribed by Russian Government to their inferior "moral status," II 158

combated by Russian Government, II 190 ff

commented upon unfavorably by Ignatyev, II 273; by Gubernatorial Commissions, II 275; and by Pahlen Commission, II 365

Serafinovich, Jewish convert, upholds blood accusation, I 173 f

Serfs, or Khlops, form separate estate in Poland, I 442

S's. of Ukraina, resent Polish rule, I 140

Jews in Ukraina mediators between pans and, I 142

S's. of Ukraina rise against Poles and Jews, I 182

conversion of Jews into, rejected by Polish Diet, I 170
subjection of Jews to serfdom not recognized by Russian Senate, I 328

Sergius, grand duke, appointed governor-general of Moscow, II 400 f
entrance into Moscow of, preceded by expulsion of Jews, II
closes Moscow synagogue, II 423 f
refuses petition of Jews to reopen it, III 12 f
assassinated, III 110

Serra, papal nuncio, skeptical towards Frankists, I 216

Servia instructed by Berlin Congress to grant equality to Jews, II 202

Service, Military, see Military service

Sevastopol (Crimea), ancient Jewish Community in neighborhood of, I 17
Jews expelled from (1829), II 32
barred to Jews (1835), II 40
reopened to Jews by Alexander II., II 172
thousands of Jewish soldiers fall at (in Crimean War), II 149
consumptive Jewish student marched through streets of, III 19

Sever, Slav tribe, subject to Khazars, I 26

Sforza, see Bona Sforza

Shaftsbury, Earl of, addresses Mansion House meeting in London on behalf of Russian Jews, II 288

Shakhna, see Shalom Shakhna

Shaizari, Ash-, Arabic writer, quoted, I 23

Shak, see Cohen, Sabbatai

Shalom Aleichem (S. Rabinovitz), editor of *Jüdische Volksbibliothek*, III 59
Yiddish writer, III 62

Shalom Shakhna, rabbi of Lublin and Little Poland, I 105, 109
pioneer of Talmud study in Poland, I 122 f
rabbinical conferences initiated by, I 123
responsa of, I 123

Shamir-Khan-Shur, city in Caucasus, I 26

Shantung Peninsula, see Kuantung

Shapiro, Samuel Abba and Phinehas, Russian-Jewish printers, II 123 f

Shargorod (Volhynia), Jacob Joseph Cohen, rabbi of, I 227, 230

"**Shabsitzvinnikes**," nickname for adherents of Sabbatai Zevi, I 210

INDEX

Shaving of heads by Jewish women forbidden by Nicholas I. (1852), II 144

Shchebreshin (*Polish*, Szczebrzeszyn), Meir, Hebrew author, native of, I 158

Shchedrin-Saïtykov, Russian satirist, protests against persecution of Jews, II 325 f denounces *Novoye Vremya*, I 380

Shcheglovitov, anti-Semitic Minister of Justice, secures pardon for pogrom makers, III 150 engineers Beilis case, III 165 St. Petersburg Bar Association protests against, III 166

"Shebsen," nickname for adherents of Sabbatai Zevi, I 211

Shedletz (*Polish*, Siedlce), Judah Hasid, native of, I 208 Lukov, in province of, I 287

Sheitel, Jewish name for wig, II 144

Shekel, societies of Sh. prayers organized by Zionists, III 45

Shidlovitz (*Polish*, Szydlowiec), near Radom, Poland, home of Judah Hasid, I 208

Shishkov, Minister of Public Instruction, advocates abolition of institution of Jewish deputies, I 395 I. B. Levinsohn applies for subsidy to, II 129

Shklov, rabbis assembled at, condemn Shneor Zalman, I 238 Dyerzhavin sent to, in response to complaints of Jews, I 328

Shklover, Borukh, see Borukh Shklover

Shklover, Nota, of St. Petersburg (family name Notkin), I 333 purveyor to Potemkin's army, I 330 proposes establishment of Jewish colonies near Black Sea, I 331 participates in work of Jewish Government Commission, I 338

Shlakhovski, Baruch, killed in pogrom, II 303

Shlakhta (*Polish*, Szlachta: Polish nobility), term explained, I 58 forms separate estate, I 44 growing influence of, I 58 favors Jews on account of financial advantages, I 69 controls diets, I 77 attitude of, towards Jews, I 77 granted jurisdiction over Jews of its estates, I 84 elects kings, I 89 usurps power, I 91 ff resorts to services of Jews, I 93 represented among sect of Socinians, I 91 acts contemptuously towards serfs in Ukraina, I 141 f surrenders cities to Swedes, I 155

diets, controlled by clergy and S., impose restrictions on, I 160

oppresses Jewish arendars, I 170

tries to turn Jews into serfs, I 170

forces kings to impose restrictions on Jews, I 181 f

exterminated in Ukraina, I 183 ff

Kahals warn Jews against acting as stewards of, I 188

controls Quadrennial Diet, I 278

bars Jews from buying crown lands, I 296

Jews forbidden to acquire estates of (1808), I 300

proposes anti-Jewish restrictions to Russian Government, I 322 ff, 324 ff

hypocrisy of, exposed by Polish writer, II 98

Shleshkovski, Polish physician, attacks Jewish physicians in Poland in anti-Semitic pamphlet, I 96

Shlieferman, Jewish soldier in Saratov, accused of ritual murder, II 151

sentenced to penal servitude, II 152

Shmakov, anti-Semitic lawyer, defends Krushevan, III 82

appears in Beilis case, III 82

acts as counsel for Kishinev rioters, III 91 f

Shmerling, of Moghilev, dies while attending Jewish Conference in St. Petersburg, II 304

Shneor Zalman, founder of "rational Hasidism," or *Habad*, I 234

resides at Ladi (government of Moghilev), I 234, II 117

moves to Lozno (government of Moghilev), I 234, II 117, 330

favors Russian arms in Franco-Russian War, I 356 f

establishes hasidic center in White Russia, I 372

arouses ire of Vilna Gaon, I 374

denounced to Russian Government, I 376

dispatched as prisoner to St. Petersburg and liberated by Paul I., I 376

dispatched again to St. Petersburg and liberated by Alexander I., I 378

author of philosophic work entitled *Tanyo*, I 374

philosophy of, I 381 f

rejects *Tzaddik* cult, I 382

Mendel, grandson of, II 57

successors of, II 117 f

See Shneorsohn

Shneor, Hebrew poet, III 162

INDEX

Shneorsohn, Mendel, leader of White Russian Hasidim, II 57

establishes residence at Lubavichi, II 117

member of Rabbinical Commission, II 118

forced to approve Mendelssohn's Bible translation, II 118

rejects innovations in Jewish education, II 118 f

Shpola (government of Kiev), pogrom at, III 33

Shtadlan, representative of Jews before Government, term explained, I 111

officially designated in Poland as "general syndic," I 111, 160

appointed by Council of Four Lands, I 111, 193

secures ratification of Jewish privileges, I 160

presents applications of Polish Jews to King Sobieski, I 167

Shtar Isko, rabbinical form of promissory note, term explained, I 350

Shtiblach, name for hasidic houses of prayer, II 124

Shulhan Arukh, rabbinical code of law, composed by Joseph Caro, I 123

arrangement of, I 128

supplemented by Isserles, I 124

criticised by Solomon Luria, I 125

rivalled by code of Mordecai Jaffe, I 127 f

Polish rabbis write commentaries on, I 128, 130, 200

firmly established in Poland, I 130

amplified by Gaon in Vilna, I 236

Siberia, Jewish prisoners in Russo-Polish War deported to (1654), I 245

"Judaizing" sectarians deported to, I 402 ff

Jewish juvenile recruits, or cantonists, sent to, II 24

failure of Courland Jews to leave province punished by deportation to, II 34

colonization of Jews in, started by Government (1836); and stopped (1837), II 71

swamps of, considered for Jewish settlement (1882), II 285

accusers of Jews, in ritual murder trial of Velizh, deported to (1835), II 82

accused Jews of Novoya Ushitza (Podolia) deported to (1836), II 85

Jewish printers of Slavuta (Volhynia) deported to, II 123

revolutionaries exiled to, II 243

Jewish revolutionaries exiled to, II 224

governors granted right of deportation to, II 246

criminals sentenced to deportation to, placed in transportation prisons, II 403

"aliens" (semi-savage tribes) in, placed on level with Jews, II 367

Jews of, denied right of movement, III 21 f

Jewish recruits dispatched to, III 94

Sicilist, vulgar pronunciation for Socialist, III 116

Sigismund (*Polish*, Zygmynt), **I.**, king of Poland and duke of Lithuania (1606-1548), favorable to Jews, I 71 f

appoints Jewish tax-farmers in Lithuania, I 72

warns authorities of Posen to respect Jewish privileges, I 74

forbids Jews of Posen to keep stores on market-place, I 74; and restricts Jews of Posen to separate quarters, I 75

restricts Jews of Lemberg in pursuit of commerce, I 75

prevents anti-Jewish riot in Cracow, I 76

wife of, accepts bribes from Jews, I 76

appoints commission to investigate charges against Jews of Lithuania, I 80

exonerates Lithuanian Jews, I 81

places Jews on estates under jurisdiction of nobles, I 84

appoints Michael Yosefovich "senior," or chief rabbi of Lithuanian Jews, I 72 f, 104

confirms election of other chief rabbis, I 104 f, 122

confers large powers on rabbis, I 73, 104 f

rabbinical conferences meet during reign of, I 109 f

kindness of, to Jews commented upon by Polish writer, II 98

Sigismund (*Polish*, Zygmunt) **II.** Augustus, king of Poland (1548-1572), ratifies Jewish privileges, I 83

enlarges and establishes Jewish autonomy, I 83

places Jews on estates under jurisdiction of nobles, I 84

endeavors to stop execution of Jews accused of host desecration, I 86 f

forbids ritual murder and host trials, I 88

bestows on Jews of Great Poland charter of autonomy (1551), I 105 ff confers on Jews right of establishing *yeshibahs*, and bestows large powers on presidents of *yeshibahs*, I 115

grants Jews of Cracow monopoly of importing Hebrew books, I 131

attended by Jewish body physician, I 132

writes to Ivan the Terrible demanding admission of Jews to Russia, I 243

last king of Yaguello dynasty, I 88

Sigismund (*Polish*, Zygmunt) **III.**, king of Poland (1588-1632), I 91

ratifies Jewish privileges, I 93

protects Jews against magistracies, I 94

reaction against "Arian" heresy during reign of, I 91

requires consent of clergy for erection of synagogues, I 98

attended by Jewish court physician, I 136

Silesia, Jews fleeing from Crusades seek shelter in, I 41

Jews own estates in, I 42

John Casimir, king of Poland, flees to, I 155

Solomon Maimon ends days in, I 240

Simferopol (government of Tavrida), pogrom at, checked (April, 1905), III 115

pogrom at (October, 1905), III 128

Simeon Volfovich, see Volfovich

Simon, of Trent, alleged victim of ritual murder, I 179

Simon, Sir John, interpellates Gladstone concerning Russian Jews, II 291

Simon, Leon, quoted, III 51, 60

Sion ("Zion"), Jewish periodical in Russian, II 218, 220

Sipyaghin, Russian Minister of Interior, pursues reactionary policy, III 16

assassinated, III 66

Sirkis, Joel, called *Bah*, Polish rabbi and Talmudist, I 130, 206

opposed to philosophy, I 133

Sittenfeld, manager of secular Jewish school in Odessa, II 133

Skarga, Peter, leading Jesuit in Poland, I 90

Skharia (Zechariah) converts Russian priests to Judaism, I 36

Skvir (government of Kiev), hasidic center, II 120

Slaves, manumission of, among Jews of ancient Crimea, I 15 f

Slavium, Slav tribe, tributary to Khazars, I 26

Slavs, the, tributary to Khazars, I 26

treated tolerantly by Khazars, I 22

throw off Khazar yoke, I 28

German Jews visit lands of, I 33, 39

Slavuta (Volhynia), Jewish printing-press in, II 42 f, 123

Sliosberg, G., counsel for Jewish victims of Homel pogrom, III 102

members of Central Committee of League for Equal Rights, III 112

Sloboda, older name for government of Kharkov, I 251

Slutzk, Jewish community of, represented on Lithuanian *Waad*, I 112

Smith, Charles Emory, United States Minister at St. Petersburg, II 395 f

Smolensk, Polish king appoints Jewish convert *starosta* of, I 73

visited by Jewish merchants of Poland and Lithuania, I 242

colony of White Russian Jews in, I 249

Borukh Leibov, resident of, converts captain of navy to Judaism, I 249, 251

visited by Jewish merchants of White Russia, I 315 f; but Jews barred from settling in, I 316

anti-Semitic play produced in, III 38

Smolenskin, Perez, editor of *ha-Shahar*, II 218, 234

Hebrew writer, II 234 ff

theory of Judaism by, II 235 f

joins "Love of Zion" movement, II 232

Smorgoni or **Smorgon** (government of Vilna), home of Menashe Ilyer, II 114

Jewish labor movement in, III 55

Smyela (government of Kiev), pogrom at (1881), II 256; (1904), III 99

Smyrna, Asia Minor, Sabbatai Zevi appears in, I 205

center of Sabbatian movement, I 206

Sobieski, king of Poland (1674-1696), protects Jews, I 165 f

enlarges autonomy of Jews, I 166

rebuked by Polish diet for protection of Jews, I 167

protects Jewish tax-farmer Bezalel, I 167

upholds authority of *Waads*, I 194

Socialism (and Socialists), in Russia, propaganda of, in Hebrew, II 223 f

rise of, among Jews, III 55 ff

championed by "League of Jewish Workingmen" ("*Bund*"), III 56

combined with Zionism by *Poale Zion*, III 57, 145

represented in Russia by Social-Democrats and Social Revolutionaries, III 66, 119

Jews active in both wings of, III 67

extreme wing of, resorts to terrorism, III 66, 109 f

INDEX

Socialists and Zionists organize self-defence at Homel, II 87

spread of, among Jews blamed for pogroms, III 89

gains in Second Duma, III 142

loses in Third Duma, III 153

Jewish socialists refuse co-operation with other Jewish parties, III 144

socialistic factions among Jews, III 145

socialistic candidate elected in Warsaw with help of Jews, III 167

See Bund and Revolutionary Movement

Society of Israelitish Christians, designed for conversion of Jews, I 396, II 74

Alexander I. looked to, for solution of Jewish problem, I 399

endeavors of, futile, I 400

disbandment of, recommended by Golitzin (1824), I 400

disbanded (1833), I 400

Society for Diffusion of Enlightenment established in St. Petersburg (1867), II 214 f

branch of, established in Odessa, II 215 f

accused by Brafman of forming part of World Kahal, II 316

employs J. L. Gordon as secretary, II 229

adopts resolution demanding constitution for Russia, III 111

creates new type of Jewish school, III 160

Society for Granting Assistance to Jewish Colonists and Artisans in Syria and Palestine legalized by Russian Government (1891), II 421 f

Socinians, the, Christian rationalistic sect in Poland, I 91, 136

Socinus, Faustus, founder of Socinian sect, I 91

Sokhachev, host trial in, I 86 f

Jews of, display Polish patriotism, I 292

Sokolov, Russian lawyer, acts as council for Jewish victims of Kishinev pogrom, III 91; and of Homel pogrom, III 102

Sokolow, Nahum, editor of *ha-Tzefirah,* III 60

joins political Zionism, III 60

Soldiers, Jewish, refused right of universal residence by Alexander II., II 171

permitted to remain in St. Petersburg, II 172

forbidden to return to native villages, II 384

forbidden to remain in Moscow, II 404

forbidden to spend furlough outside of Pale, III 21

stationed in Siberia, III 94 families of, expelled, III 95 forbidden to reside in Port Arthur, III 157 Russian S's. make pogroms, III 100 f See Conscription, Military Service, "Nicholas Soldiers," and Recruiting

Solkhat (now Eski Krym, Crimea), ancient capital of Tatar Khans, Jewish communities in, I 34 f

Solomon (Shelomo), of Karlin, hasidic leader, I 372

Solomon, of Lemberg, recognized by Polish king as *Rosh-Yeshibah*, I 115

Solomon Ephraim, of Lenchytaa, criticises system of Jewish education in Poland, I 119 f

Solovaychik, editor of *Sion*, II 220

Solovyov, Vladimir, Russian historian, quoted, I 247 collects signatures for public protest against persecution of Jews, II 386 ff appeals to Alexander III. on behalf of Jews, II 388

Sonnenberg, Sundel, of Grodno, represents Jews at Russian army headquarters, I 358 acts as deputy of Russian Jews in St. Petersburg, I 392 ff

deprived of office, I 395 active against ritual murder libel, II 74, 99

South (and South-west), of Russia, forms part of Pale (1835), II 342 Max Lilienthal tours through, II 56 represented on Rabbinical Commission, II 57 Tzaddiks in, II 119 ff Jewish writers in Russian language hail from, II 238 pogroms in, II 267 f, 209, 258 f, III 99 ff emigration from, II 297 f agricultural colonies in, III 24; see Agriculture; see also North-west and Russia, White

Spain, Caliphate of Cordova in, I 24 epistle of king of Khazars arrives in, I 27 Jewish physicians in Poland natives of, I 131 offers shelter to Russian Jews, II 268

Spector, Isaac Elhanan, rabbi of Kovno, attends Jewish Conference in St. Petersburg, II 304

Spektor, editor of Yiddish magazine, III 59

Spencer, Herbert, influences Russian-Jewish *intelligenzia*, II 209

INDEX

Speranski, Russian statesman, recommends liberal policy towards Jews, I 399 ff

Statute of 1804 contravenes policy of, I 345

Spiessruten (running the gauntlet), term explained, II 85 applied as punishment, II 85, 123

abolished in 1863, II 85

Spira, Nathan, Cabalist, I 135

Spiritual Biblical Brotherhood, Jewish reform sect in Yelisavetgrad, II 333 f

St. Bartholomew Night, I 89

St. Petersburg, capital of Russia, Jewish financial agents admitted by Peter the Great to, I 248

Borukh and Vornitzin tried at, and burned, I 252 f

delegates of Gubernatorial Kahals assembled at (1803), I 337, 386

beginnings of Jewish community in, I 337 f

Committee for Jewish Affairs appointed in (1809), I 352

Finkelstein, delegate of Moghilev Jews, proceeds to, I 363

Shneor Zalman arrested and dispatched to, I 376, 378

Deputies of Jewish People reside in, I 393 f; II 74

temporary residence in, permitted to Jewish merchants (1835), II 40

Jews illegally residing in, severely punished, II 42

"harmful" Hebrew books ordered sent to, II 43

Max Lilienthal invited to, II 53

Rabbinical Commission summoned to, II 56, 118

influential Jews of Western Europe invited to, II 67

visited by Moses Montefiore, II 68

visited by Altaras of Marseilles, II 69

Congregation Board of Warsaw sends deputation to, II 110

Baron Joseph Günzburg presides over Jewish community of, II 152

influential Jews of, apply for equal rights, II 159 f

Jewish physicians barred from. II 167

Jewish soldiers in body-guard of, permitted to remain in, II 172

Lutostanski, accuser of Jews, welcomed in, II 203

Illustratzia, Russian magazine in, attacks Jews, II 207 f

Jewish intellectuals in, II 214

Society for Diffusion of Enlightenment established in, II 214 f

Russian-Jewish press in St. Petersburg, II 221, 332 f, 59, III 77, 162

Yiddish press in, III 59, 162
Hebrew press in, see *ha-Melitz*
Alexander II. assassinated in, III 243
governor of, granted wide discretionary powers, II 246
emissaries from, prepare pogroms in South, II 248
Jewish community of, presided over by Baron Horace Günzburg, II 260
English Jew expelled from, II 262
Jews of, forbidden to collect pogrom fund, II 263
Conference of Jewish Notables in (1881), II 277; (1882), II 299, 304 ff
Jewish demonstration against pogroms in, II 286
Dr. Drabkin, rabbi of, interviews Ignatyev, II 305
Jews of Balta, send deputation to, II 316 f
Jews expelled from, II 319
Jews of, persecuted by Gresser, city-governor, II 343 ff, 397 f
admission of Jews to educational institutions of, limited to 3%, II 350, III 158
Jews prominent at bar of, II 352
Jewish notables of, consulted by Pahlen Commission, II 369 f

British ambassador at, assured of discontinuation of Jewish persecutions, II 382
Jews of, harassed anew, II 385
Solovyov collects signatures for public protest against Jewish persecutions in, II 387
petition of Guildhall meeting in London sent to, II 392
American Minister at, instructed to exert influence on behalf of Jews, II 395
Russkaya Zhizn ("Russian Life"), paper in, depicts Jewish sufferings, II 397
Novosti ("The News"), paper in, confiscated for defending Jews, II 407
expulsion of all Jews from, contemplated, II 410 f
visited by White, representative of Baron Hirsch, II 416 f, 419
Central Committee of Jewish Colonization Association established in, II 420
Jewish Colonization Association sends deputation to, III 10
Jews of, submit memorandum to Government, III 11
Jews of, ask permission to acquire land for agriculture, III 24

new educational restrictions in, III 30

"Smugglers," anti-Semitic play, produced in, III 38

Znamya ("The Banner"), anti-Semitic paper, appears in, III 70

Levendahl, Government agent dispatched from, to arrange pogroms, III 71

visited by Dr. Herzl, III 89

American ambassadors in, reported to have protested against persecution, III 96

Plehve assassinated in, III 97

Conference of Zemstvo workers in, opposes autocracy (1904), III 105

"Bloody Sunday" in, III 106

Jewish community of, signs petition for equal rights, III 108

Society for Diffusion of Enlightenment in, demands constitution for Russia, III 111

League for Equal Rights establishes central bureau in, III 112

Jewish community of, protests against denial of Jewish franchise, III 121

Bogdanovich, general in, assists October pogroms, III 125

League for Equal Rights holds convention in, III 131

Jewish parties form permanent council in, III 148

Jewish Literary Society founded in, III 160 f

Bar Association of, protests against Beilis trial, III 166

Natives and residents of:

J. L. Gordon, Hebrew poet, II 229

Nyevakhovich, convert, Russian poet, I 386 f

Abraham Peretz, Jewish merchant (convert), I 338, 386, 412

Antonio Sanchez, court physician, I 258

Nota Shklover, Jewish merchant, I 330

St. Petersburg (government), Jews expelled from villages of, I 409

Localities in:

Luga, I 409

Schlüsselburg, II 97

Stage, Russian, anti-Semitism on, III 38 f

Stanislav Augustus Poniatovski, see Poniatovski

Staro-Constantinov, see Constantinov

Starodub (government of Chernigov), Cossack massacre at (1648), I 149

pogrom at (1891), II 411 f

Starosta, high Polish office, name explained, I 60

encroaches on duties of voyevoda, I 46

Lithuanian Jews subject to jurisdiction of, I 60, 94, 104

S. of Sokhachev ordered by king to stop execution of Jews, I 86

S. of Brest supports Kahal, I 190

S. of Kaniev makes sport of Jews, I 169 f

S's. administer Ukraina, I 142

S's. begin to oppress Jews, I 169

determines extent of Jewish autonomy, I 191

Stashitz (*Polish*, Stashyc), Polish priest and statesman, anti-Semitic author, I 281 f, II 95 f

opposes plan of reform favorable to Jews, II 93

Statistics, of Jews, in Poland, I 66, 187, 263 f, 390

in Russia, II 341, 415

in White Russia, I 307

in Pale, II 168

of Jewish first-guild merchants in Pale, II 162

of Jewish artisans in Pale, II 168

of Jewish economic activity in Russian South-west, II 194

of Jews in agrarian pursuits, III 24

of Jewish recruits, II 355 f

of Jewish physicians in Russian army, III 95

of Jewish pauperism, III 23 f

of Jews expelled from Russia, I 254, 258

of Jewish emigration to United States, II 373, 421, III 148

of Jewish emigration to Argentina, II 419

Statute, "Lithuanian S." (1566), I 87

"S. concerning the Organization of the Jews" (1804), I 342 ff; criticized by Jewish representatives, I 349 ff

"S. of Conscription and Military Service" (1827), II 18 ff, 29; extended to Poland (1843), II 109; leaves inner life of Jews unchanged, II 48

Military S. (1874), II 199 ff, 355

"S. on the Jews" (1835), II 28, 33, 34 ff, 39 ff; fixes age of marriage, II 112; fails to assimilate Jews, II 47

"S. concerning Zemstvos Organizations" (1864), admits Jews to local self-government, II 173

"S. concerning Zemstvos Organizations" (1890) bars Jews from local self-government, II 385 f

INDEX

Municipal S. (1870) limits, admission of Jews to one-third and bars Jews from office of burgomaster, II 198 f

" S. concerning Enforced Public Safety" (1881), II 246 See Charter

Stavropol (government), nomads of, placed on level with Jews, II 367

Stephen Batory, see Batory

Stern, Abraham, Jewish scholar and mathematician in Warsaw, II 103

Stern, Bezalel, principal of modern Jewish school in Odessa, II 57, 133

Stillman, Jewish workingman, fires at Odessa Chief of Police, III 107

Stolypin, Russian Minister of Interior, answers interpellation concerning pogroms, III 136, 138

appointed Prime Minister, III 138, 140

attacked by terrorist, III 140

promises mitigation of Jewish disabilities, III 141

controlled by League of Russian People, III 151

excludes Jewish students from Kiev Polytechnicum, III 152

stops expulsion of Jews from Interior, III 154

becomes more reactionary, III 156 f

determines to uproot alien cultures in Russia, III 159 f

assassinated at Kiev, III 164

Strakhov, Russian official entrusted with conduct of Velizh ritual murder case, II 76 ff

Strashun, Mattathiah, Talmudist and Maskil in Vilna, II 136

Strelnikov, Russian public prosecutor, calls upon Jews to leave Russia, II 264 f

Strigolnik, Carp, founder of Strigolniki sect, I 36

Strikes adopted as revolutionary weapon, III 125 f

arranged by "Bund," III 130

Stroganov, Russian Minister of Interior, advocates liberal attitude towards Jews, II 47

Stroganov, Count, governor-general of New Russia, advocates emancipation of Jews, II 168 f

Studzienski, alleged victim of ritual murder, I 178 f

Stundists, the, rationalistic Christian sect in Russia, II 333

Jacob Gordin influenced by, II 333

Stupnitza, near Pshemysl (Galicia), ritual murder libel at, I 178

Sub-Starosta, Polish official, Jews subject to jurisdiction of, I 60; see Starosta

Subbotin, Russian economist, points out pauperism in Pale, III 23

Sudak, locality in Crimea, subject to Khazars, I 26

Sugdas, locality in Crimea, subject to Khazars, I 26

Summer Resorts, Jews barred from, III 18 f

bill admitting Jews to, rejected, III 154

Jews expelled from, III 157

See Residence, Right of

Superstition rampant in Poland, I 203 f

Supreme Secret Council, official body in Russia (18th century), I 249 f

Surgeons, see Physicians

Suvar, Slav tribe, subject to Khazars, I 26

Suvarov, Russian general, attacks Praga, suburb of Warsaw, I 296

Suvorin, editor of *Novoye Vremya*, II 380

produces anti-Semitic play, III 38

Svyatopolk II., prince of Kiev (1093-1113), favors Jews, I 32

Svyatopolk-Mirski, governor-general of Vilna and later Russian Minister of Interior, pursues liberal policy, III 99, 105

dismissed, III 107

Svyatoslav, prince of Kiev, defeats Khazars, I 23

Swedes, the, invade Poland, I 154 ff

Switzerland, Zionist Congresses held in, III 44

Syech, name of Cossack Republic, I 143

Syedletz (*Polish*, Siedlce), pogroms at (1905), III 119, 140 f

Syn Otyechestva ("Son of the Fatherland"), Russian magazine, protests against pogroms, III 35

Synagogue, in Bosporus, I 15 f

erection of, in Poland, requires royal permission, I 98

building of new S's., in Poland, forbidden (1720), I 171

erection of, near church in Russia, forbidden (1835), II 41

S's. in Moscow closed, II 397

Great S. of Moscow closed, II 423 ff, III 12

Jews fight for preservation of Moscow S., III 12 ff

Synhedrion, convoked by Napoleon, I 298, 351

convocation of, viewed with suspicion by Austria and Russia, I 346 ff

represented by Russian Government both as anti-Jewish and anti-Christian, I 348
influences Jews of Warsaw, I 386
fatal error of, in denying Jewish nationality, III 53
creation of, in Russia, advocated by Dyerzhavin, I 333
convocation of, in Russia suggested by Pestel, Russian revolutionary, I 412
Synod, the, see Church Council
Synod, Holy, in Russia, issues circular against Napoleon, I 348
deals severely with "Judaizers," I 402 f
appoints Brafman, Jewish informer, instructor of Hebrew, II 187
presided over by Pobyedonostzev, II 245; III 9 f
Syria, emigration of Jews from, to Tauris, I 16

Taganrog (government of Yekaterinoslav), excluded from Pale, II 346
Talmud, the, studied by Khazars, I 21
study of, pursued by early Russian Jews in Germany, I 33
predominant factor in Jewish education, I 114 ff

study of, stimulated by Jewish autonomy, I 121 ff
reigns supreme in Russia and Poland, I 195, 221, 264, 198 ff, 380, II 51
rejected by Frankists, I 214 f
burned at Kamenetz-Podolsk, I 215
importance of study of, minimized by Besht, founder of Hasidism, I 224 ff
arrogance of students of, attacked by Besht's disciple, I 230
neglected by Hasidim, I 235
burning of, recommended by Polish reformers, I 282
opposed by Frank of Kreslavka, Jewish Mendelssohnian, I 331
regarded by Russian Council of State as source of Jewish suffering, II 47
accused by Uvarov of demoralizing Jews, II 51
weakening and uprooting of, aimed at by Nicholas I., II 58, 66
criticised by David Friedländer, II 90
assailed by Abbé Chiarini in Warsaw, II 104
defended by I. B. Levinsohn, II 131
injuriousness of, emphasized by Russian Commission, II 195

attacked by Lutostanski, II 204
conceived by Lilienblum as factor in Jewish reform, II 236
attacked by Gubernatorial Commissions, II 275
rejected by New Israel Sect, II 334

Talmud Torah, Jewish public school in Poland, I 114, 118
maintained by Waads, I 195
in Moscow, placed in Synagogue, III 13

Talno (government of Kiev), hasidic center, II 120

Taman Peninsula, Greek city-republic on, I 14
Samkers, Jewish city on, I 23
owned by Guizolfi, Italian Jew, I 36

Tannaim, names of, collected by Polish rabbi, I 200

Tanyo, philosophic work by Shneor Zalman, I 372, II 117

Tarashkevich, anti-Semitic priest in Velizh, II 77

Targovitza (*Polish*, Targowica), confederacy of, between Russians and Poles (1792), I 292

Tarku (Semender), Caucasian city, subject to Khazars, I 26

Tarnopol (Galicia), Meir of, Hebrew author, I 201

Tarsus (Asia Minor), Jewish community in, I 14

Tatars, the, Russia under dominion of, I 29

conquer Crimea, I 33
Jews of Crimea under rule of, I 34 ff
T. of Lemberg granted autonomy by Casimir the Great, I 53
barred from office and from keeping Christian domestics in Lithuania, I 87
invade Polish border provinces and combated by Cossacks, I 142 f
form alliance with Cossacks under Khmelnitzki, I 144 ff, 150
spare Jewish prisoners, I 145, 157, 205
take Jews of Polonnoye captive, I 148
cause spread of Mohammedanism, I 254

Tauri, or Taurians, tribe, I 13 ff

Taurian Bosporus, see Kerch

Taurian Chersonesus, see Bosporus

Tauris, northern shores of Black Sea, I 13
immigration of Jews into, I 13 ff
Khazars move towards, I 19
bishops of, try to proselytize Khazars, I 20
remnant of Khazar kingdom in, I 28
ruled by Pechenegs and Polovtzis, I 29
retains name Khazaria, I 29
in relations with Kiev, I 33 ff

INDEX

Tavrida (region, or government), extent of, I 13
Jews permitted to settle in (1791), I 316 f
Karaites settled in, I 318
included in Pale (1835), II 40, 428
pogroms in, III 115, 120, 128
Cities in:
Kerch, III 115, 120
Melitopol, III 115
Simferopol, III 115, 128
Mylta, II 428 f

Tax, under Polish régime, paid by Jews to Church, I 57 f
paid by Jews to Catholic academies (called Kozubales), I 161, 166
Polish king conditions protection to Jews on payment of, I 84
collected by Jews on estates of Shlakhta, I 93
apportioned by Waads and collected by Kahals, I 107, 181, 189 f, 197 f
Council of Four Lands declines responsibility for collection of, I 194
increased (1717), I 169
changed into individual T. of two gulden per head (1764), I 197
raised to three gulden per head (1775), I 267

disproportionately assessed by Kahals, I 275
Jews of Minsk complain about abuses in collection of, I 275
paid on taking possession of real estate, I 190
paid for right of sojourn in Warsaw, I 269, II 95
imposed on Jews in lieu of conscription (1817), I 95; (1831), I 107

Tax, under Russian régime, per capita T. of one rubel imposed on Jews of White Russia (1772), I 307
Kahals of White Russia charged with collection of, I 309
Jews of annexed Polish provinces required to pay double T. (1794), I 318
payment of double T. confirmed by Paul I., I 321
Karaites relieved from payment of double T., I 318
payment of double T. by Jews commented upon by "Jewish Committee" (1804), I 341
manufacturers and artisans relieved from payment of double T. (1804), I 344
Jewish deputies plead for abolition of double T., I 349
Kahals in Courland organized for collection of, I 321

estates, subject to payment of (so-called taxable estates), hindered in right of transit, I 322

alleviations in payment of, promised to converts, I 397

in lieu of conscription, I 318; II 15, 20

irregularity in payment of, punished by conscription, II 19

modification in payment of, suggested by Council of State, II 49

Kahals limited to conscription and collection of (1844), I 60

revenue from meat or basket T., called *Korobka*, placed under control of Russian authorities (1844), I 61

"auxiliary basket T." (on immovable property, etc.), instituted, II 61

levied on Sabbath candles for maintenance of Crown schools, I 61 f

levied on traditional Jewish dress in Russia (1843), II 110; extended to Poland, I 110, 144

T. on passports waived in case of Jewish immigrants, I 418, 420

basket T. represented as Jewish system of finance, II 194

abuses of basket T. depicted by Mendele Mokher Sforim, II 232

Pahlen Commission inquires about purposes of basket T., II 370

use of basket T. for defraying emigration suggested by Russian official, II 420

basket and candle T. for non-Jewish purposes, II 426 f

basket T. used to defray night raids upon Jews, III 20

Tax Farming (and **Tax Farmers**), Jews engage in, in Poland, I 44, 67, 69, 71

in Lithuania, I 60, 65

forbidden by Church Councils, I 49

opposed by petty Shlakhta, I 77

forbidden by Piotrkov Diet of 1538, I 77 f

Shlakhta forces king to bar Jews from, I 182

law barring Jews from, upheld by rabbis, I 110

Kahals call upon Jews to refrain from, I 188

Jews from White Russia engage in, in Smolensk, I 249

class of Jewish tax farmers in Russia, II 72

Individual tax farmers:

Bezalel, I 167

Borukh Leibov, I 249

Abraham and Michael Yosefovich, I 73
Yosko, I 71
Saul Yudich, I 94

Teachers, Jewish, see Heder and School

"Temporary Rules" of May 3, 1882, known as May Laws, genesis of, II 309 ff
contents of, II 312
effect of, II 318 f
old settlers permitted to stay in villages under, II 16
misconstrued to apply to old settlers, II 340 ff
check agriculture among Jews, III 24 f

Tennyson, English poet, expresses sympathy with Russian Jews, II 258

Teplitz, T., prominent Jew of Warsaw, II 103

Terentyeva, Mary, accuses Jews of ritual murder, II 75 ff
exiled to Siberia for false accusation, II 82

Territorialism accepts idea of Pinsker's *Autoemancipation*, II 332
rise of, III 41
born out of Zionist organization, III 185
secedes from Zionist organization, III 144

Terrorism, rampant under Alexander II., II 243

favored by Social-Revolutionary party, III 66, 109 f
Jews take small part in, III 67
acts of, committed by Jews, III 107
rampant in Poland and Baltic provinces (1905), III 130
used as pretext for pogroms, III 136
intensified after dissolution of First Duma, III 140

Tetyev (government of Kiev), massacre at, I 184

Teutonic Order, the, name explained, I 63
engages in war with Poland, I 63

Theodosia, see Kaffa

Theodosius II., emperor of Byzantium, persecutes Jews, I 18

Theodosius, Abbot of Kiev monastery, persecutes Jews, I 31

Theophanes, Byzantine writer, quoted, I 18

"Third Section," the, see Police, Political

Thorn (*Polish*, Torun), annexed by Prussia (1793), I 292

Tiberias (Palestine), visited by Nahman of Bratzlav, I 383

Tiflis (Caucasia), anti-Semitic play produced at, III 38

Tikhanovich, chief of political police in Syedletz, engineers pogrom, III 140
thanked by governor-general of Warsaw, III 141

Tilsit, Peace of (1807), leads to establishment of duchy of Warsaw, I 297

affects policy of Alexander I. towards Jews, I 350

Tlusta (Galicia), Besht settles in, I 223

Tobias, of Ruzhany, martyr, I 162 f

Tobolsk (government), lands in, set aside for colonization of Jews, II 71

Toledo (Spain), Jacob ben Asher rabbi of, I 118

Tolstoi, Demetrius, Minister of Interior, II 314

adopts energetic measures against pogroms, II 315

anti-pogrom circular of, quoted by United States Minister, II 293

destroys plans of Pahlen Commission, II 370

takes into consideration economic importance of Jews, II 428

Tolstoi, Leo, preaches "Going to the People," II 222

keeps silent on Jewish persecutions, II 325

preaches doctrine of non-resistance, II 371

protests against Jewish persecutions in Russia, II 387 f

condemns Kishinev massacre, III 76

protests against atrocities of Russian Government, III 149

Tomsk (Siberia), pogrom against intellectuals at, III 128

Tosafists, the, name explained, I 117

Rabbi Eliezer, of school of, quoted, I 43

work of, studied in Poland, I 117

method of, followed by Solomon Luria, I 125

Totleben, Russian governor-general of Vilna, opposes settling of Jews in villages, II 276

checks pogroms, II 276

Tovyanski (*Polish*, Towianski), Polish mystic, preaches union of Jews and Poles peoples, II 108

Trades, see Artisans

Trade-Unions, or Trade-Guilds, in Poland, hostile to Jews, I 70, 74

Trans-Caspian Region, Akhal-Tekke, oasis in, suggested for settlement of Jews, II 306

alien tribes of, placed on level with Jews, II 367

Transportation Prisons, term explained, II 403

exiled Moscow Jews placed in, II 403, 405 f

INDEX

Trepov, Assistant-Minister of Interior, favors Jewish franchise, III 122

Trepov, Chief of Police, orders suppression of revolution, III 126

Tribunal, Crown T. in Poland, name explained, I 96

tries ritual murder cases, I 96, 100, 172 f

Troitza Monastery, near Moscow, II 203

Troki (province of Vilna), Crimean Jews settle in, I 35 Jewish community in, I 59 Karaites settle in, I 60 Jews expelled from (1495), I 65

Troki, Isaac, author of anti-Christian treatise, I 137 f

Tromba, Nicholas, archbishop of Gnesen, attends Synod of Constance and presides over Synod of Kalish, I 57

Troyanov (Volhynia), tragic fate of Jewish self-defence at, III 116 ff

Trubetzkoy, Russian commissioner, exonerates Jews of Mstislavl, II 87

Trubetzkoy, professor, head of delegation to Nicholas II., III 122

Trudoviki ("Laborites"), Bramson, Jewish member of, III 134

lose in Third Duma, III 153

Tsushima, Russian fleet destroyed by Japanese in vicinity of, III 119

Tudela (Spain), Benjamin of, Jewish traveller, I 32

Tugendhold, Jacob, Jewish assimilationist in Warsaw, II 98 f

refutes Abbé Chiarini, II 104

Tugendhold, Wolf, brother of former, censor in Vilna, II 136

Tula (government), "Judaizers" in, I 401 f

Tulchinski, Borukh, see Borukh of Tulchin

Tulchyn (Podolia), Khmelnitzki massacre at, 146 f

residence of Pestel, Russian revolutionary, II 411

Turgay, Territory of (Central Asia), semi-civilized tribes of, placed on level with Jews, II 367

Turgenieff (Turgeniev), Russian writer, II 210

influences S. J. Abramovich, II 231

keeps silent on Jewish persecutions, II 325

Turish, hasidic center, II 120

Turkey, takes over colony in Kaffa, I 34

Jewish center in, I 66

Polish Jews export goods to, I 68

Jews of Lithuania suspected of preparing to flee to, I 51 raided by Cossacks, I 143 Jewish prisoners of war carried by Tatars to, I 145, 157, 205 lays claim to Ukraina, I 159 Sabbatai Zevi carries on propaganda in, I 205, 210 influence of, on Polish Jewry, I 207 f annexes part of Podolia (1672), I 208; returns it to Poland (1699), I 208 Jacob Frank travels about in, I 212; sent back from Poland to, I 213; returns to Poland from, I 216 engages in war with Russia (1739), I 253 f establishment of Jewish State in, suggested by Russian revolutionary, I 412 Moses Montefiore pays visit to, II 68 *Bilu* pioneers enter into negotiations with, II 322 hampers Palestinian colonization, II 375, 422, III 42 Dr. Herzl enters into negotiations with, III 45 f Russian Government promises to exert influence over, in favor of Zionism, II 83

Twenty-One-Verst Zone, see Border Zone

Twer (Central Russia), pogrom against intellectuals at, III 128

Typography, see Printing-Press

Tzaddik ("The **Righteous Man**"), title of hasidic leader, rival of rabbi, I 235 revered by Jewish masses, I 274; II 112 controls rabbinate in Russian South-west, I 371 gains foothold in Lithuania, I 372 type of, in Poland, resembles that of *Habad*, II 123 miraculous stories about, circulate among Hasidim, II 124 firmly entrenched, II 116 ff forbidden by Russian Government to travel about, II 212 See Tzaddikism and Hasidism

Tzaddikism (cult of *Tzaddik*), as conceived by Besht, I 227 developed by Baer of Mezherich, I 230 practical consequences of, I 231 f extreme formulation of, I 232 f viewed with apprehension by Elijah of Vilna, I 374 triumphant in South-west, I 381 vulgar form of, rejected by Shneor Zalman, I 382 degeneration of, I 382 f

extermination of, advocated by Kalmansohn, I 385
criticised by Pestel, Russian revolutionary, I 411
attacked by Maskilim, II 210; see Tzaddik and Hasidism
Tzarmis, Slav tribe, subject to Khazars, I 26

Uganda (British East Africa), offered as Jewish settlement to Zionists, III 84 f
Ukase, term explained, I 249; spelling of word, I 6
Ukraina (Ukraine), name explained, I 140
part of, called Little Russia, invaded and annexed by Russia (1654), I 153, 244 f
divided between Poland and Russia (1667), I 159
Jewish massacres in (1648), I 139 ff
part of, barred to Jews (1649), I 151; reopened to Jews (1651), I 152
Jews decimated in, I 157
uprisings against Poles and Jews in (18th century), I 182 ff
Jewish massacres in, stimulate propaganda of Sabbatai Zevi, I 205
talmudic culture deteriorates in, I 199
intellectual development of Jews in, differs from that in North-west, I 221

character of Hasidism in, I 232, II 119 ff
type of Tzaddik in, I 233; differs from that in Poland, II 123
Tzaddik dynasty of Chernobyl widely ramified in, I 382
Jews expelled from (1727), I 249
transfer of Polish Jews to, suggested, I 284
included in Pale (1794), I 317
Galatovski, Ukrainian writer, refers to Sabbatai Zevi, I 205
Russian revolutionaries appeal to Ukrainian people, II 274
Ukrainian cultural institutions suppressed by Russian Government, III 160
See Russia, Little
Ulrich Von Hutten, epistles of, imitated in Hebrew, II 126
Uman (*Polish,* Human, province of Kiev), massacre at, I 184
Nahman of Bratzlav dies at, I 383
place of pilgrimage for Bratzlav Hasidim, I 383, II 122
Uniat Church, the, I 141
Union of American Hebrew Congregations appeals to United States Government on behalf of Russian Jews, II 293
"Union of Lublin" (1569), I 88
Unitarians, the, Christian rationalistic sect in Poland, I 136

United States of America, Max Lilienthal emigrates to, II 59

Marcus Jastrow emigrates to, II 179

emigration of Russian Jews to, II 268 f, 297 f, 321, 327 f, 373 ff, 421, III 104

stirred by Warsaw pogrom, II 283

Government of, protests against Jewish persecutions in Russia, II 292 ff, 394 ff, 408 ff

Congress of, protests against Jewish persecutions in Russia, II 294 ff, 394

Jewish center in, suggested as alternative by Pinsker, II 331

Jacob Gordin settles in, II 335

Jewish agricultural colonies in, II 374

economic condition of Jews in, II 374

Jewish emigrants in, said to wish for return to Russia, II 393

Government of, sends two Commissioners to Russia, II 407

exiled Moscow Jews emigrate to, II 413, 416

emigration to, embodied in Jewish pogrom of Dubnow, III 54

agitated over Kishinev massacre, III 78

Kishinev massacre stimulates emigration to, III 85 f

fear of new Kishinev pogrom intensifies emigration to, III 96

ambassador of, in St. Petersburg, reported to have protested against Jewish persecutions, III 96

emigration to, embodied in pogrom of Jewish National Party in Russia, III 147 f

statistics of Jewish emigration to, III 148

Hebrew writers in, III 163

University, Polish Jews study at U. of Padua, I 132

"Statute of 1804" admits Jews to Russian U's., I 345

Jewish U. graduates admitted into Russian Interior and to civil service (1861), II 166; required to possess learned degree, II 165, 167; requirement dropped (1879), II 167

Jewish U. graduates permitted to keep two Jewish servants in Russian Interior, II 166; fictitious servants of, II 344 ff

Jews with U. education permitted to live in villages and own property (1904), III 98; privilege extended to wives and children, III 99

INDEX

Jewish U. students suspected of revolutionary leanings, II 348, III 28

admission of Jews to, restricted (1887), II 350; placed on Statute books (1908), III 157 f

restricted admission drives Jews into foreign U's, II 351, III 31, 158; and makes them antagonistic to Government, III 31

restricted admission to, abolished by professional councils (1905), III 124; restored (1907), III 152; placed on Statute books (1908), III 157 f

See Education and School

Ural, territory of, semi-civilized tribes of placed on level with Jews, II 367

Urussov, governor of Bessarabia, and later Assistant-Minister of Interior, favors mitigation of Jewish disabilities, III 93

discloses personal animosity of Nicholas II. against Jews, III 93

issues warning against pogroms, III 97

reveals in *Memoirs* Plehve's share in pogroms, III 97

discloses in Duma share of Russian Government in October pogroms, III 126, 138

Ushitza, see Novaya Ushitza

Ussishkin, Russian Zionist leader, III 47

Ustrugov, deputy-governor of Bessarabia, persecutes Jews, III 70

assists in arranging Kishinev massacre, VIII 71

sued by Jews, III 92

Uvarov, Sergius, Minister of Public Instruction, endeavors to spread enlightenment among Russian Jews, II 46 ff

lays plans before "Jewish Committee," II 50 ff

visits Lilienthal's school in Riga, II 52

negotiates with Lilienthal, II 53

instructs Lilienthal to enter into correspondence with Jewish leaders in Western Europe, II 67

petitioned by Moses Montefiore on behalf of Russian Jews, II 68

plans of, received favorably by Jews of Vilna, II 136 f

See Lilienthal

Valnyev, Minister of Interior, favors admission of Jewish artisans and mechanics into Russian Interior, II 169 f

Vannovski, Minister of War, restricts number of Jewish surgeons in Russian army, II 319 f accepts post of Minister of Public Instruction and curtails admission of Jews to universities, III 29

Varta (*Polish*, Warta), Diet of (1423), restricts commercial operations of Jews, I 58

Varta (*Polish*, Warta), river, lands on banks of, attract Jews, I 39

Vasa Dynasty, of Swedish origin, rules in Poland, I 91

Vasilchikov, Count, governor-general of Kiev, favors admission of Jewish artisans into Russian Interior, II 168

Veitelson, Marcus, Jewish deputy in St. Petersburg, I 393

Velizh (government of Vitebsk), ritual murder trial at, II 75 ff

Alexander I. passes through, and orders opening of case, II 76

Jews of, acquitted, II 83

Venentit, Slav tribe, subject to Khazars, I 26

Venice, Jewish Palestine pilgrims from Poland pass through, I 209

Master Leon, Russian court physician, invited from, I 37

Victoria, Queen of England, recommends Moses Montefiore to Nicholas I., II 68

Vienna, Jewish bankers in, petition Polish king on behalf of Posen Jews, I 176

Jews of, assist Jewish Palestine pilgrims from Poland to reach Constantinople, I 209

Congress of, inaugurates European reaction, I 359

Congress of, transfers duchy of Warsaw to Russia, I 390, II 88

Lieberman, Russian-Jewish socialist, publishes *ha-Emet* in, II 223

Smolenskin resides in, II 234; and publishes *ha-Shahar* in, II 218

secret circular of Plehve made known in, II 381

Dr. Herzl resides in, III 42

Vigdorovich, Samuel, rabbi of Vilna, engages in litigation with Kahal, I 275 f

Vilenski Vyestnik ("The Vilna Herald"), publishes Brafman's articles against Kahal, II 189

Vilkomir (government of Kovno), home of M. L. Lilienblum, II 236

Villages, transfer of Jews from, to towns ordered by Catherine II. (1795), I 319

Jews retained in, by landowners, I 323

INDEX

Russian officials given wide powers in dislodging Jews from (1797), I 323 f

expulsion of Jews from, decreed in Statute of 1804, I 343

projected expulsion from, affects half million Jews, I 346

expulsion checked by fear of Napoleon's invasion (1807), I 347 f

Jewish deputies plead for repeal, or postponement of expulsion from, I 349

expulsion of Jews from, reaffirmed (1808), I 351

expulsion from, started, I 351

Alexander I. admits impossibility of removing Jews from (1809), I 352

"Jewish Committee" advises against expulsion of Jews from (1812), I 353 f

economic importance of Jews in, I 361 f

evil effects of endeavors to dislodge Jews from, I 362 f

renewal of effort to remove Jews from, I 405

Jews expelled from, in White Russia (1823), I 406 f

uselessness of expulsion from, in White Russia pointed out by Council of State (1835), I 407 f, II 34 f

Jews expelled from, in government of Grodno (1827), II 30 f

expulsion of Jews from, in government of Kiev, decreed (1830), II 33; delayed, II 33; objected to by Council of State and indefinitely postponed, II 35

barred to Jews in government of Kiev and Little Russia in Statute of 1835, II 40

barred to Jews in Fifty-Verst-Zone under same law, II 40

Jews of Poland permitted to live in (1862), II 181, 367; permission invalidated by restriction of property rights (1891), 367

Jews of Poland permitted to acquire land in (1862), II 172, 181; permission withdrawn as result of Polish insurrection (1864), II 173

exclusion of Jews from, recommended by Totleben, governor-general of Vilna, II 276

complete elimination of Jews from, recommended by "Jewish Committee" (1882), II 310

expulsion of old settlers objected to by Committee of Ministers, II 311

Jews forbidden to settle anew in, and to acquire property in ("Temporary Rules" of May 3, 1882), II 312

remain closed to Jews, II 318

old Jewish settlers expelled from, by peasant communes, II 318 f

peasants encouraged to expel old Jewish settlers from, II 319, 340

Jews in, harassed by Russian officials, II 340 ff

thousands of Jews expelled from, in governments of Chernigov and Poltava, II 341

disabilities of Jews in, commented upon by Pahlen Commission, II 366

discharged Jewish soldiers, being regarded as "new settlers," barred from returning to, II 384

towns transferred into, and barred to Jews (1890), II 385; reopened to Jews (1903), III 80 f

policy of eliminating Jews from, continued under Nicholas II., III 16 ff

Jews dislodged from, by introduction of liquor monopoly (1894) III 23

privileged Jews, though admitted into Interior, prohibited from acquiring property in (1903), III 81; exception made for Jews with higher education (1904), III 98

wholesale expulsions of Jews from (1910), III 157

See Expulsion, and Residence, Right of

Villani, Matteo, Italian chronicler, quoted, I 52

Vilna (*Polish*, Wilna, city), superseded by Warsaw as capital, I 85

conquered by Russians (1654), I 154, 245

surrendered by Poles, I 155

Lithuanian Hetman resides in, I 192

anti-Jewish riots in (under Polish Régime), I 94, 99, 161, 166; by invading Russian troops, I 245

Jews of, permitted to engage in petty trade, I 99

Jews of, restricted to "Jewish Street" and placed under jurisdiction of Municipal Courts (1633), I 99

Jewish community of, represented on Lithuanian Waad, I 112

Kahal of, engaged in litigation with rabbi of, I 275 f

Jews of, support Polish troops fighting against Russians (1792), I 292

INDEX

Christian burghers of, protest to Alexander I., against admission of Jews to city-government (1805), I 370

Jews of, barred from city-government in (1805), I 370

exclusion of Jews from city-government of, confirmed in Statute of 1835, II 41

hasidic societies secretly organized in, I 237

visited by Shneor Zalman to request interview with Gaon, I 238

Kahal of, excommunicates Hasidim (1772), I 237, 371; (1796), II 371, 373

Hasidim reside "illegally" in, I 372

Kahal of, sends out messengers to stir up anti-hasidic agitation, I 373

Hasidim of, rejoice over death of Gaon, I 375

Kahal elders of, vow to avenge insult to Gaon, I 375; and denounce Hasidism to Government, I 375 f

Hasidim arrested in, I 376

Hasidim of, depose Kahal elders, I 377

conference of Jewish deputies at (1815), I 393 f

Kahal of, pleads for abolition of cantonists, II 36

Kahal of, complains to Council of State about Jewish disabilities, II 38; and begs permission to send spokesmen to St. Petersburg, II 39

printing-press in, II 42, 127

censorship committee in, II 44

visited by Max Lilienthal, II 54

Maskilim of, promise support to Lilienthal, II 55; and form his mainstay, II 136

Rabbinical Institute opened in (1847), II 59, 174; closed (1873), II 177; gradutes of, un-Jewish, II 212

Teachers' Institute in, II 177

pupils of both Institutes form revolutionary circle in, II 223

visited by Moses Montefiore, II 68

center of Haskalah, II 132 ff

Maskilim circle in, II 136 ff

residential restrictions in, abolished by Alexander II., II 172

Brafman carries on anti-Jewish agitation in, II 187 ff, 240

pauperism among Jews of, III 24

Blondes, Jewish barber in, accused of ritual murder, II 37

Jewish labor movement in, III 55

"Bund" holds convention in (1897), III 56

Lekkert, Jewish workingman in, assails governor of Vilna, III 66 f

Dr. Herzl enthusiastically received by Jews of, III 84

Jews of, assured by Svyatopolk-Mirski of just treatment, III 99

Jewish community of, signs petition for equal rights, III 108; and demands self-determination, III 109

league for Attainment of Equal Rights formed in (1905), III 111

Jewish community of, protests against denial of Jewish franchise, III 121 f

place of publication, II 115, 126, 131, 134, 136, 226

ha-Karmel, published in, II 217

ha-Zeman, Hebrew daily, published in, III 162

Sabbatai Cohen (*Shak*), famous Talmudist, native of, I 130, 157 f

Budny, Christian theologian, of, I 136

Moses Rivkes, Talmudist, of, I 200

Elijah of; see Elijah of Vilna

Masalski, bishop of, employs Berek Yoselovich, I 294

Saul Katzenellenbogen, rabbi of, II 115

M. A. Ginzberg, Hebrew writer, resident of, II 133 f

Abraham Baer Lebensohn, Hebrew poet, resident of, II 134 f

Micah Joseph Lebensohn, Hebrew poet, native of, II 226

Levanda, Russian-Jewish writer, resident of, II 239

S. M. Dubnow, author of present work, resident of, III 112

See Vilna (government)

Vilna (province or government), annexed by Russia (1795), I 297

included in Pale (1794), I 317; (1835), I 39

includes later government of Kovno, I 317

Jews of, invited to elect deputies (1807), I 349

Poles threaten to massacres Russians and Jews in, I 357

Samuel Epstein elected Jewish deputy from, I 393

Poles and Jews forbidden to acquire estate in (1864), II 173

placed under jurisdiction of Muravyov, II 188

Friesel, governor of, suggests Jewish reforms, I 325 ff

governor of, testifies to loyalty of Jews to Russia (1812), I 357

governor-general of, opposes admission of Jewish artisans into Russian Interior, II 168

INDEX

Muravyov, governor-general of, pursues policy of Russification, II 183, 239

Totleben, governor-general of, favors forbidding Jews to settle in villages, II 276

Kakhanov, governor-general of, insults Jewish deputation of welcome, II 383

governor of, favors abrogation of Pale (1895), III 11

Pahlen, governor of, favors mitigation of restrictive laws, III 93

Svyatopolk-Mirski, governor-general, promises Jewish deputation favorable treatment of Jews, III 99

Localities in:

Ilya, II 114

Mikhailishok, II 134

Troki, see Troki

Volozhin, I 380, II 57, 113

Vinaver, M., Russian-Jewish lawyer, acts as counsel for Jewish victims of Kishinev pogrom, III 92; and Homel pogrom, III 102

member of Central Bureau of League for Equal Rights, III 112

elected president of League for Equal Rights, III 134

deputy to First Duma, III 134

leader of Constitutional Democratic party, III 134

denounces in Duma oppression of Jews, III 136; and pogroms, III 139

head of Jewish People's Group, III 146

Vinchevski, M., publishes Hebrew periodical *Asefat Hakamim*, II 223

Vinnitza, Kahal of, appealed to by Vilna Gaon against Hasidim, I 373

Virgil, Aeneid of, translated into Hebrew, II 226

Visconti, papal nuncio at Warsaw, ordered to report on ritual murder trial in Poland, I 179

Vishniovetzki (*Polish*, Wisnio-wiecki), **Count Jeremiah**, Polish commander, protects Jews against Cossacks, I 149, 161

Vishniovetzki (*Polish*, Wisnio-wiecki), **Michael**, Polish king (1669-1673), son of former, ratifies Jewish privileges, I 160

Vistula, river, lands on banks of, attract Jews, I 39

provinces on banks of, invaded by Swedes, I 154

Plotzk, on banks of, I 243

Poles perish in, defending Warsaw against Russians, I 296

Hasidism established on banks of, I 384

Gher, or Goora Kalvarya, on left bank of, II 122

Poles admit only "one nation on banks of," III 168

Vital, Hayyim, Cabalist, I 134

Vitebsk (city), Jews of, defend city against invading Russians, I 154

Jews of, robbed by Cossacks and maltreated or exiled, I 154

Jews of, made prisoners of war by Russians, I 245

Mendel of, hasidic leader, I 234, II 117

Dyerzhavin writes "Opinion" on Jews in, I 330

pogrom at, III 101

Jewish community of, protests against denial of Jewish franchise, III 121

See Vitebsk (government)

Vitebsk (government), annexed by Russia (1772), I 186, 262

Jews from, made prisoners of war by Russia, I 245

formerly called government of Polotzk, 1 307, 315, 317

forms part of White Russia, I 307, 315

included in Pale (1794), I 317; (1835), II 40

Jews of, visit Smolensk and Moscow, I 315

Jews of, invited to elect deputies, I 349

Jewish deputies from, I 393

expulsion of Jews from villages of, begun (1808), I 351

Jews, expelled from villages of, economically ruined, I 364

Jews elected to municipal offices in, I 368

expulsion of Jews from villages of, decreed (1823), I 406

Supreme Court acquits Velizh Jews accused of ritual murder, II 76

placed under jurisdiction of Muravyov, II 188

Cities in:

Kreslavka, I 331

Polotzk, I 243

Velizh, II 75

See Vitebsk (city), and Russia, White

Vitovt (also Vitold, or Witold; *Polish,* Witowt), grand duke of Lithuania (1388-1430), protects Jews of Lithuania, I 35

grants Jews charter (1388), and additional privileges (1389), I 59

Vladimir (*Polish,* Wlodzimierz; Volhynia), early Jewish community in, I 59

Vladimir, prince of Kiev, receives Khazar Jews (986), I 30

Vladimir, Monomakh, prince of Kiev, stops anti-Jewish riots, I 32

INDEX

Vladimir, grand duke, brother of Alexander III., holds Russian revolutionaries responsible for pogroms, II 260

Vladimir, archbishop (Mitropolit) of St. Petersburg, encourages pogroms, III 125

Vladislav (also Wladislaus and Leidislaus; *Polish*, Wladyslaw), **Lokietek**, Polish ruler, unites Great Poland and Little Poland, and assumes royal title (1319), I 42, 50

Vladislav (*Polish*, Wladyslaw) IV., Polish king (1632-1648), I 91 tolerant to other creeds, I 97 confirms Jewish privileges, I 98 makes erection of synagogues and establishment of cemeteries dependent on royal permission, I 98 restricts Jews in response to anti-Jewish petitions, I 98 f uprising of Khmelnitzki during reign of, I 144 dies during uprising, I 145 offered, as crown prince, Russian throne (1610), I 244

Voislovitza, near Lublin, Jews of, accused of ritual murder, I 178 f

Volfovich, Simeon, denounces abuses of Vilna Kahal, I 276

persecuted and imprisoned, I 276 advocates abolition of Kahal, I 276

Volga, river, Khazars move towards banks of, I 19 Khazar capital situated at mouth of, I 23, 26, 28 called Ityl by Khazars, I 26, 28 bodies of alleged ritual murder victims found in, II 150

Volhynia (*Polish*, Volyn), forms part of Lithuania, I 59 ceded to Poland (1569), I 110 controlled economically by Polish magnates, I 140 uprising against Poles in (1648), I 145 returned to Poland (1667), I 159 annexed by Russia (1793), I 292 included in Pale (1794), I 317, (1804), I 342; (1835), II 39 called formerly government of Izyaslav, I 317 Cossack massacres in (1648), I 148 f Jews decimated in, I 157 Jews of, slain by haidamacks (18th century), I 182 f Jewish *arendar* of, oppressed by Polish squire, I 266 Jews of, suffer from Polish civil war (1792), I 292

Polish nobility of, advocates anti-Jewish restrictions, I 324

Jews of, hold conference and decide to appeal to Tzar (1798), I 324 f

Jews of, invited by Alexander I. to elect deputies, I 349

woolen mills established by Jews in, I 363

Jews of, indifferent towards Polish revolution (1831), I 107

statistics of Jews in, II 194

pogroms in, II 256

represented on Council of Four Lands, I 110

Jewish Provincial Assembly (or Dietine) of, I 113; called "Volhynia Synagogue," I 196

Talmudism deteriorates in, I 199

intellectual development of Jews of, differs from that in North-west, I 221

Besht travels about in, I 224

Baer of Mezherich, hasidic preacher in, I 227

Hasidism spreads in, I 229, 274

becomes hasidic headquarters, I 229 f

Hasidism triumphant in, I 371, II 119 f

Gubernatorial Kahal of, appealed to by Vilna Gaon, against Hasidism, I 373

Isaiah Horowitz (*Shelo*), Cabalist, rabbi in, I 135

Levi Itzhok of Berdychev, leader of Hasidim in, I 382

Menashe Ilyer, Talmudist and writer, resides in, II 115

Isaac Baer Levinsohn, native of, II 125 ff

rabbis of, request Levinsohn to refute blood accusation, II 131

Localities in:

Chudnov, III 117

Kremenetz, II 125 *

Old (Staro-)-Constantinov, II 21 f

Ostrog, I 125

Rovno, III 99

Slavuta, II 42, 123

Troyanov, III 116

Zaslav, I 116, 177

Zhitomir, see Zhitomir

Volkspartei, see Jewish National Party

Volozhin (government of Vilna), yeshibah of, established by Hayyim Volozhiner, pupil of Vilna Gaon (1803), I 380 f

sends forth large number of pupils, II 113

* Page 125, line 3 from bottom, read Volhynia, instead of Podolia. The mistake is due to a confusion with Kamenetz.

INDEX

Itzhok Itzhaki, president of, member of Rabbinical Commission, II 57

Volozhiner, Hayyim; see Volozhin

Voltaire, praises polemical treatise of Isaac Troki, I 138

Vorontzov, governor-general of New Russia, protests against proposed "assortment" of Jews by Nicholas I., II 64 ff, 142

Voronyezh (city and government), "Judaizers" spread in, I 401

archbishop of, reports to Government on "Judaizers," I 401 f

Senate refers to "Judaizers" in, I 404

pogrom in city of (1905), III 130

Voskhod ("The Sunrise"), Jewish weekly and monthly, in Russian, published in St. Petersburg, II 221, 277, 332, 372, III 162

opposes organizing of emigration, as subversive of emancipation, II 298 f

protests against anti-Semitic speech of governor-general of Kiev, II 317

opposes "Love of Zion" movement, II 332

suppressed by censor, II 407

publishes Dubnow's "Letters on Old and New Judaism," III 52

leaning towards nationalism, III 59

suppressed for protesting against Kishinev massacre, III 77

appeals to patriotism of Jews in Russio-Japanese War, III 94

warns against impending pogroms, III 96

confiscated by censor, III 98

points out rightlessness of Jews, III 124

Voyevodas (*Polish*, Wojewoda), high Polish officials, name and functions of, explained, I 46

correspond to *Starostas* in Lithuania, I 60

exercise, as representatives of sovereign, special jurisdiction over Jews, I 46, 94

V. courts, see Courts

Jewish Dietines assemble by order of, I 196 f

instructed by Stephen Batory to protect Jews, I 8 9

accept bribes, I 76

begin to oppress Jews, I 169

V. of Cracow accepts bribes from Jews and their opponents, I 76

V. of Kiev owns city of Uman, I 184

V. of Lemberg, or Red Russia, upholds prestige of Kahal, I 190; grants constitution to Kahal of Lemberg (1692), I 191

V. of Vilna sides with Kahal against rabbi, I 276; imprisons Simeon Volfovich, opponent of Kahal, I 276

Voyevodstvo (*Polish*, Wojewodstwo), name for Polish province, term explained, I 46, 76

Voznitzin, Alexander, captain in Russian navy, converted by Borukh Leibov to Judaism, I 251 f

burned at stake in St. Petersburg (1738), I 253

Vperyod ("Forward"), Russian revolutionary periodical in London, II 223

Vratislav, prince of Bohemia, robs Jews fleeing to Poland, I 41

Vyatka (government) cantonists carried to, II 24

Vyberg (Finland), V. Manifesto, protesting against dissolution of First Duma, signed by Jewish deputies, III 139 signatories to, prosecuted, III 142

Vyelepolski, Marquis, Polish statesman, secures assent of Alexander II. to Act of Emancipation of Polish Jews (1862), II 181, 195

Vyestnik Russkikh Yevreyev ("Herald of Russian Jews"), Russian Jewish periodical, II 221

Waad Arba Aratzoth ("Council of Four Lands"), central organization of Polish Jewry, pronunciation of word *Waad*, I 108

grows out of conferences of rabbis and Kahal leaders, l 108 f; which meet at fair of Lublin, I 109; at initiative of Shalom Shakhna, rabbi of Lublin, I 123; exercising judicial as well as administrative and legislative functions, I 109 f

presided over by Mordecai Jaffe, I 127

presided over by Joshua Falk Cohen, I 128

meets periodically at Lublin and Yaroslav, I 110, 194

composition of, I 110

provincial *Waads* represented on, I 113, 196 f

oligarchic character of, I 195

acts as court of appeals, I 111

decides litigations between Kahals, I 193

INDEX

activities of, stimulate rabbinical learning, I 126 f

regulates inner life of Jews, I 111 f, 152, 188 f

concerned about maintenance of Talmud Torahs and yeshibahs, I 195

exercises censorship over Hebrew books, I 195 f

issues *herem* against Frankists, I 214

appoints *Shtadlans* to represent Jews before Government, I 111, 193

apportions head-tax among Kahals, I 181, 189 f, 194

authority of, in apportioning head-tax upheld by King Sobieski (1687), I 194

authority of, undermined by withdrawing right of apportioning head-tax (1764), I 181, 197

meetings of, forbidden by diet of 1764, I 198

Waad Kehilloth Rashioth Di-Medinath Lita ("Council of the Principal Communities of the Province of Lithuania"), central organization of Lithuanian Jews, formed in 1623, I 112

provincial Waads represented on, I 113, 196

meets periodically, I 194

functions of, I 112 f

cultivates Jewish education, I 195

appoints *Shtadlans* to represent Jews before Government, I 193

apportions head-tax among Jews, I 181

Waddington, English representative at Berlin Congress, favors emancipation of Jews, I 202

Wagenseil, German professor, publishes Isaac Troki's *Hizzuk Emuna*, I 138

Wahl, Saul, legendary king of Poland, I 94

Wahl, Von, governor of Vilna, flogs Jewish workingmen, I 67

Wallachia, Jacob Frank settles in, I 212

Besht born on border of, I 222; see Moldavo-Wallachia

Warsaw (*Polish*, Warszawa), capital of Poland, I 85, 111

capital of duchy of Warsaw, I 298

meeting-place of Polish diet, I 76, 98, 99, 111, 160, 165, 169, 171, 181, 278, II 96; see Diet

Khmelnitzki moves towards, I 151

conquered by Swedes (1655), I 154

Russia maintains Resident at, I 279
besieged by Russo-Russian troops (1794), I 293
stormed by Suvarov, I 296
annexed by Prussia (1795), I 296; held by it (1796-1806), I 385
granted right of excluding Jews, I 85, 268
Jews permitted temporary visits to, I 111, 268
Serafinovich, converted Jew, invited to disputation in, to prove blood accusation, I 173 f
Jews of, appeal to Polish king on behalf of Posen Jews, I 176
Visconti, papal nuncio at, instructed to report on ritual murder cases, I 177
Jacob Frank, baptized at, I 217 f; arrested at, and exiled to Chenstokhov, I 218; returns to, I 219
Jews permitted to stay in, during sessions of diet (1768), I 268
procedure in admitting Jews to, I 269
Jews pay tax for sojourn in, I 269, II 95
Polish dignitaries rent houses to Jews in outskirts of, I 269
"New Jerusalem," district in, I 269

Jews expelled from (1775), I 269
Jews return surreptitiously to, I 269 f, 285
burghers of, demand expulsion of Jews, I 285 f
anti-Jewish riot at (1790), I 286 f
Jews expelled from (1790), I 287
Jews volunteer in defence of, I 293
siege of, arouses patriotism of Berek Yoselovich, I 294; appeal for special Jewish regiment, II 295
Jews display heroism in defence of, I 296
Jews barred from principal streets of, (1809), I 300, II 94; exception made for widow of Berek Yoselovich, I 304
assimilated Jews of, plead for special privileges, I 300
representatives of Jewish community of, complain about disabilities, I 301 f
"Enlightenment" among Jews of, I 385
visited by Moses Montefiore, II 68
visited by Altaras of Marseilles, II 69
Tugendhold, Jewish assimilator in, II 98
Jewish assimilators in, II 100 ff

INDEX

Congregational Board of, objects to special Jewish regiment, II 106

Jewish militia participates in defence of (1831), II 106

Congregational Board of, sends deputation to St. Petersburg to plead for equal rights, II 110

adherents of hasidic dynasty of Gher numerous in, II 122

assimilation in, II 177 f; assumes menacing proportions, II 213

Jews of, display Polish patriotism in uprising against Russia (1861-1863), II 179 ff

pogrom at (1881), II 280 ff

archbishop of, endeavors to check pogrom, II 283

prominent Poles of, offer to organize civil guard for protection of Jews, II 283; offer refused by governor-general of, II 283

number of writers arrested at, II 291

effect of pogrom in, upon Western Europe and America, II 283, 287

governor-general of, reports to Tzar on pogroms in, II 284

pogrom in, welcomed by Central Jewish Committee, II 310

center of "Love of Zion" movement, II 376

Jewish labor movement in, III 55

economic progress of Jews in, III 166

Jews of, instrumental in election of socialistic deputy to Duma, III 167

Hebrew papers and periodicals published in, II 333, 372, III 58, 60, 162

Yiddish papers and periodicals published in, III 59, 162

Goora Kalvarya (Gher), in vicinity of, II 122

Kotzk, in vicinity of, I 303, II 122

Praga, suburb of, I 294

Way, Lewis, representative of London Bible Society, I 397

submits memorandum to Alexander I. pleading for Jewish emancipation, I 398

memorandum of, laid before Congress of Aix-la-Chapelle, I 398

Weber, United States Commissioner to Russia, II 407

Wertheimer, banking house of, in Vienna, exerts influence over Polish king, I 176

Wessely, Naphtali Hirz, Hebrew poet, compared with A. B. Lebensohn, II 135

Western Euorpe, Jewish diaspora in, I 13

emigration from, into Poland, I 39 ff

leading Jews of, invited by Russian Government to participate in work of enlightenment, II 67

Jews of, intercede on behalf of Russian Jews, II 67 ff

public opinion of, influences Russia, II 262

effect of Warsaw pogrom on, II 283, 287

emigration from Russia to, II 321, 408, 413

Political Zionism originates in, III 42, 46

Jews of, deny Jewish nationalism, III 53

public opinion of, agitated over Kishinev massacre, III 78

"**Western Region,**" term explained, II 16

number of Jews in, II 168

Jews form majority of population in cities of, III 11

Westminster, duke of, addresses Guildhall meeting in London against oppression of Russian Jews, II 390 f

White, Arnold, member of English parliament, sent by Baron Hirsch to Russia, II 417

discusses Jewish question with Russian dignitaries, II 417

visits Pale and is favorably impressed by Jews, II 418

recommends regulation of emigration, II 418

dispatched to Russia a second time, II 419

White Russia, see Russia, White

Wine grown by Jews in Palestine, II 376; see Liquor

Witsen, burgomaster of Amsterdam, petitions Peter the Great to admit Jews into Russia, I 246

Witte, Russian Minister of Finance, advocates liquor monopoly as means of dislodging Jews from villages, III 17; and eliminating Jewish "exploitation," III 22

favors mitigation of Jewish disabilities, III 107 f

Jews address petitions for equal rights to, III 108 f

receives, as president of Council of State, memorandum on pogroms, III 125

appointed Prime Minister, author of manifesto of October 17, 1905, III 127

adopts policy of oppression, III 131

League for Equal Rights votes down proposal to send delegation to, III 131

Wolff, Sir H. D., member of English parliament, interpellates Government concerning pogroms, II 262

INDEX

Worms, Baron Henry De, member of English parliament, interpellates Government concerning pogroms, II 262 Gladstone replies to interpellation of, II 292

Yadviga (*Polish*, Jadwiga), Polish queen, marries Yaguello, grand duke of Lithuania (1386), I 54

Yaguello, Vladislav II. (*Polish*, Wladyslaw Jagiello), king of Poland and grand duke of Lithuania (1386-1434), I 54 converted from paganism to Catholicism, I 55 restricts commercial operations of Jews, I 58 Lithuania ruled by Vitovt, as representative of, I 59 extinction of Y. dynasty, I 88 f, 91

Yalta, health resort in Crimea, Jews expelled from, II 428 f, III 18 f

Yampol (Volhynia), ritual murder trial at, I 178

Yaroshevski, Russian-Jewish novelist and physician, protests against affront to Jewish army surgeons, II 320

Yaroslav (*Polish*, Jaroslaw; Galicia), meeting-place of Council of Four Lands, I 110, 194

Yekaterinoslav (city), Orshanski, Russian-Jewish writer, native of, II 238 pogrom at (1883), II 358 ff; (October, 1905), III 128

Yekaterinoslav (government), territory of, raided by Turks and defended by Cossacks, I 143 territory of, opened to Jews (1791), I 316 tract of land in, set aside for Jewish converts (1820), I 400 included in Pale (1794), I 317; (1835), II 403 Jewish agricultural colonies in, II 72 Rostov and Taganrog transferred from, to territory of Don army and barred to Jews (1887), II 346 pogroms in (1883), II 360

Yelisavetgrad (government of Kherson), Government agents appear in, to prepare pogroms, II 248 pogroms at (1881), II 249 ff, 333; (October, 1905), III 128 "Spiritual Biblical Brotherhood," heterodox Jewish sect, founded by Jacob Gordin in (1881), II 333 f

Yellow Waters (*Polish*, Zolte Wody), Polish army defeated by Cossacks near, I 145

Yemetyanov, Theodore, alleged victim of ritual murder, II 75 f

Yeremyeyeva, Russian woman, accuses Jews of Velizh of ritual murder, II 75 convicted by Council of State, II 82

Yeshibah, or Talmudic Academy, imparts higher rabbinical education, I 114 f secular studies excluded from, I 120, 277 maintained by Council of Four Lands, I 195 sanctioned by Sigismund II. under name of *gymnasium*, I 115 head of, or *rosh-yeshibah*, granted wide powers by Polish kings, I 115 f; enjoys great distinction, I 119 Y's spread all over Poland and Lithuania, I 115 f Y's of Lithuania adopt method of Talmud study of Vilna Gaon, I 380 f important Y's in Lithuania, II 113 f negative effect of, II 113 f placed under Government supervision (1842), II 56 Joshua Falk Cohen, head of, in Lemberg, I 128 Moses Isserles, head of, in Cracow, I 123

Nathan Spira, head of, in Cracow, I 135 Isaiah Horowitz (*Shelo*), studies in, of Lemberg and Cracow, I 135 Eliezer, head of, in Homel, I 150 Abel Gumbiner, head of, in Kalish, I 200 Hayyim Volozhiner, head of, in Volozhin, I 381 Itzhok Itzhaki, head of, in Volozhin, II 57

Yesod Hama'Alah, Jewish colony in Galilee, II 375

Yevrey, Russian term for Jew, officially introduced, I 320

Yevreyskaya Bibliotyeka ("Jewish Library"), Jewish periodical in Russian, II 221 Orshanski contributes to, II 238

Yeveryskaya Starina ("Jewish Antiquity"), Jewish periodical in Russian, III 160

Yevreyski Mir ("Jewish World"), Jewish weekly in Russian, III 162

Yezierski, Polish statesman, chairman of Jewish Commission of Polish Diet, l 287 recognizes economic importance of Polish Jews, I 287 f defends Jews in Diet, I 289

INDEX

Yiddish, brought by Jews from Germany, I 43, 114

translations of prayers in, used by women, I 121

read by women and lower classes, I 202

Mendel Lewin translates Bible into, I 388; attacked by Tobias Feder, I 388

Y. press, II 217 f, III 58 f, 162

Y. literature, III 61 ff, 162

Mendele Mokher Sforim turns to, II 232

Gordin writes plays in, II 335

Frug, Russian-Jewish poet, writes in, III 63, 78

used as propaganda means by Jewish Labor movement, III 56 f

position of, hotly discussed, III 161

adherents of (Yiddishists), III 161

Yosefovich, Hirsh, rabbi of Khelm, author of Polish pamphlet defending Jews, I 283

Yosefovich, Abraham, Jewish tax-farmer in Poland, I 73

converted to Christianity and appointed Chancellor of Lithuanian Exchequer, I 73

Yosefovich, Michael, brother of former, Jewish tax-farmer in Poland, 172 f

appointed by Sigismund I. "senior" of Lithuanian Jews, I 72 f, 104

Yoselovich (*Polish*, Joselowicz) **Berek**, Polish-Jewish patriot, I 293 ff

accompanies Bishop Masalski to Paris, I 294

offers to form special Jewish regiment, I 294 f

regiment of, displays heroism, I 296

flees to France, I 296 f

returns to Poland and dies heroic death, I 303

eulogized by Pototzki, I 303 f

widow of, granted special permission to sell liquor, I 304

Yosko, Jewish tax-farmer in Poland, I 71

Yudich, Saul, Jewish tax-farmer in Lithuania, I 94

possibly identical with Saul Wahl, legendary king of Poland, I 94

Yurkevich, Peter, accused of stealing host for Jews, 1 101 f

Yurkovski, Moscow police commissioner, makes raid on Jews, II 403

Yushkevicher, Yankel, of Saratov, accused of ritual murder, II 151

sentenced, with son, to penal servitude, II 152

pardoned by Alexander II. through intercession of Crémieux, II 153

Zadok, Messianic propagandist in Lithuania, I 208

Zaleshkovska, Catherine, suspected of leanings towards Judaism and burned at stake, I 79 f

Zalman Shneorsohn, or **Zalman Borukhovich;** see Shneor Zalman

Zamyatin, Minister of Justice, defends Jews of Saratov accused of ritual murder, II 152

Zamoiski, Andreas, Polish chancellor, suggests reforms for Jews of Poland, I 271 ff

Zamoshch (*Polish*, Zamosc), Joel Baal-Shem of, I 203

Zangwill, Israel, founder of Territorialism, III 144

Zaporozhians, the, or **Zaporozhian Cossacks,** name explained, I 143

raid Turks and fight Tatars, I 143

cultivate relations with Ukrainian Cossacks, I 143

form alliance with Tatars, I 144

exterminate Jews and Poles, I 145 f

plunder Jews of Vitebsk, I 154

form bands attacking Poles and Jews, I 182 f

petition Russian Government to admit Jews to fairs of Little Russia, I 250

See Cossacks

Zarudny, Counsel of Jewish victims of Homel pogrom, III 102

Zaryadye, part of Moscow illegally inhabited by Jews, II 403

Zaslav (*Polish*, Zaslaw; Volhynia), Cossack massacre at (1648), I 149

ritual murder case in (1747), I 172, 177 f

Nathan Hannover of, see Hannover, Nathan

Zayonchek, Polish general, flees from Poland, I 296

appointed viceroy of Poland, II 91

opposes measures in favor of Jews, II 93

makes insulting remark about Jews, II 94

Zborov, Treaty of, between Poles and Cossacks (1649), I 151

not kept by Polish Government, I 152

Zebulun, king of Khazars, I 26

INDEX

Zederbaum, Alexander, editor of *ha-Melitz* in St. Petersburg, II 217

refutes charge of ritual murder, I 204

publishes *Vyestnik Russkikh Yevreyev*, I 221

Zelenoy, city-governor of, warns Jews to use polite manners, II 383

Zelig, see Jacob Selig

Zelikin, Isaac, called Rabbi Itzele, secures acquittal of Mstislavl Jews, II 86 f

Zelva (province of Grodno), rabbis issue *herem* against Hasidim at fair of, I 237

Zemstvos (local self-governments in Russia), term explained, II 173

Jews admitted to (1864), II 173

rights of, curtailed by Alexander III., II 379, 386

Jews barred from (1890), II 385 f

liberal Z. voice desire for constitution, III 7 f

refuse to appoint Jewish physicians, III 27

conference of, in St. Petersburg protests against autocracy (1904), III 105

combined deputation to Nicholas II. of municipalities and Z. express desire for abolition of restrictions (1905), III 122

Zetlin, Yevzik, of Velizh, arrested on charge of ritual murder, II 75, 77

Zetlin, Hannah, wife of former, arrested on same charge, II 77

Zeno, emperor of Byzantium, persecutes Jews, I 18

Zhelezniak, Cossack leader, massacres Jews (1768), I 183 f

Zhitomir, see Zhytomir

Zhmud (Samogitia) region in North-west Russia, I 293, II 133

Zhukhovski, Stephen, Polish priest, accuses Jews of ritual murder, I 172 f

Zhyd (and Zhydovski), Russian derogatory appellation for Jew, I 184, 320, 403, II 14, 78, III 155

officially abolished by Catherine II., I 320

Zhytomir (*Polish*, Zytomir; Volhynia), ritual murder trial at (1753), I 178

Kahal of, appealed to by Vilna Gaon against Hasidism, I 373

printing-press of, II 43

Rabbinical Institute opened in (1847), II 59, 174; closed (1873), II 177; graduates of, un-Jewish, II 212

Teachers Institute in, closed (1873), II 177

old privilege of, excluding Jews from parts of town, abolished by Alexander II., II 172

Mendele Mokher Sforim removes to, II 232

School of Handicrafts in, closed by Alexander III., II 347

pogrom in (1905), III 115 ff

Jews of Chudnov attempt to defend Jews of Zhytomir and are massacred, III 116 f

Jewish community of, protests against denial of Jewish franchise, III 121

Zikhron Jacob, Jewish colony in Galilee, II 375

Zionism, before Herzl, called in Hebrew *Hibbat Zion* (in Russian, *Palestinophilstvo*) "Love of Zion," preached by Lilienblum, II 237, 328 ff

expounded by Pinsker, II 220, 330 ff

adopted by Lilienblum, II 237

engages in colonization of Palestine, II 375 f, 422 f

adherents of, assemble in Kattowitz (1884), II 376; and Druskeniki (1887), II 377

legalized by Russian Government (1890), II 377

center of, in Odessa and Warsaw, II 376

wins over orthodoxy, II 376 f

failure of, III 42

leaders of, join political Zionism, III 47

modified by Ahad Ha'am, II 423, III 49 f

rise of political Z., III 41 ff

proclaimed by Herzl, III 42 f

First Zionist Congress (1897), III 44

political and cultural tendency within, III 44 f

effects of, III 46 f

Spiritual Z., or Ahad Ha'amism, III 41, 48 ff

Russian Zionists Convention at Minsk, III 51

inadequacy of, III 51 f

combined with Socialism by *Poale-Zion*, III 57 f, 145

Nahum Sokolow declares allegiance to, III 60

reflected in poems of Frug, III 63

indifference to, denounced by Bialik, III 63

forbidden in Russia by Plehve, III 82 f

Plehve promises support of, as result of Dr. Herzl's visit, III 83

Vilna Zionists give ovation to Dr. Herzl, III 84

crisis of, at Sixth Congress, III 84 f

Schism between Palestinianism and Territorialism, III 85

INDEX

organize self-defence at Homel, III 87

Shmaryahu Levin, representative of, deputy to First Duma, III 134

forms contrast to Social Democracy, III 143

Seventh Zionist Congress reaffirms allegiance to Palestine, III 144

Russian Zionist Convention at Helsingfors (1906) recognizes rights of diaspora, III 144 f

adherents of, secede from League for Equal Rights, III 146

declared illegal by Senate, III 152

Znamya ("The Banner") anti-Semitic paper in St. Petersburg, III 70

demands execution of Dashevski, assailant of Krushevan, III 81 f

Zohar, the, cabalistic standard work, study of, not permitted before the age of thirty, I 214

Frankists recognize authority of, I 214; call themselves Zoharists, 214

used by Besht to foretell the future, I 224

Zonch, Russian general, maltreats Jews on his estates, I 328

Zubov, Count, governor-general of New Russia, secures equal rights for Karaites, I 318

member of "Jewish Commission" appointed by Alexander I., I 335

Zunz, refutes charges of Abbé Chiarini, II 104

Zverovich, synagogue built in, by Borukh Leibov of Smolensk, I 249, 252

The Lord Baltimore Press
BALTIMORE, MD., U. S. A.